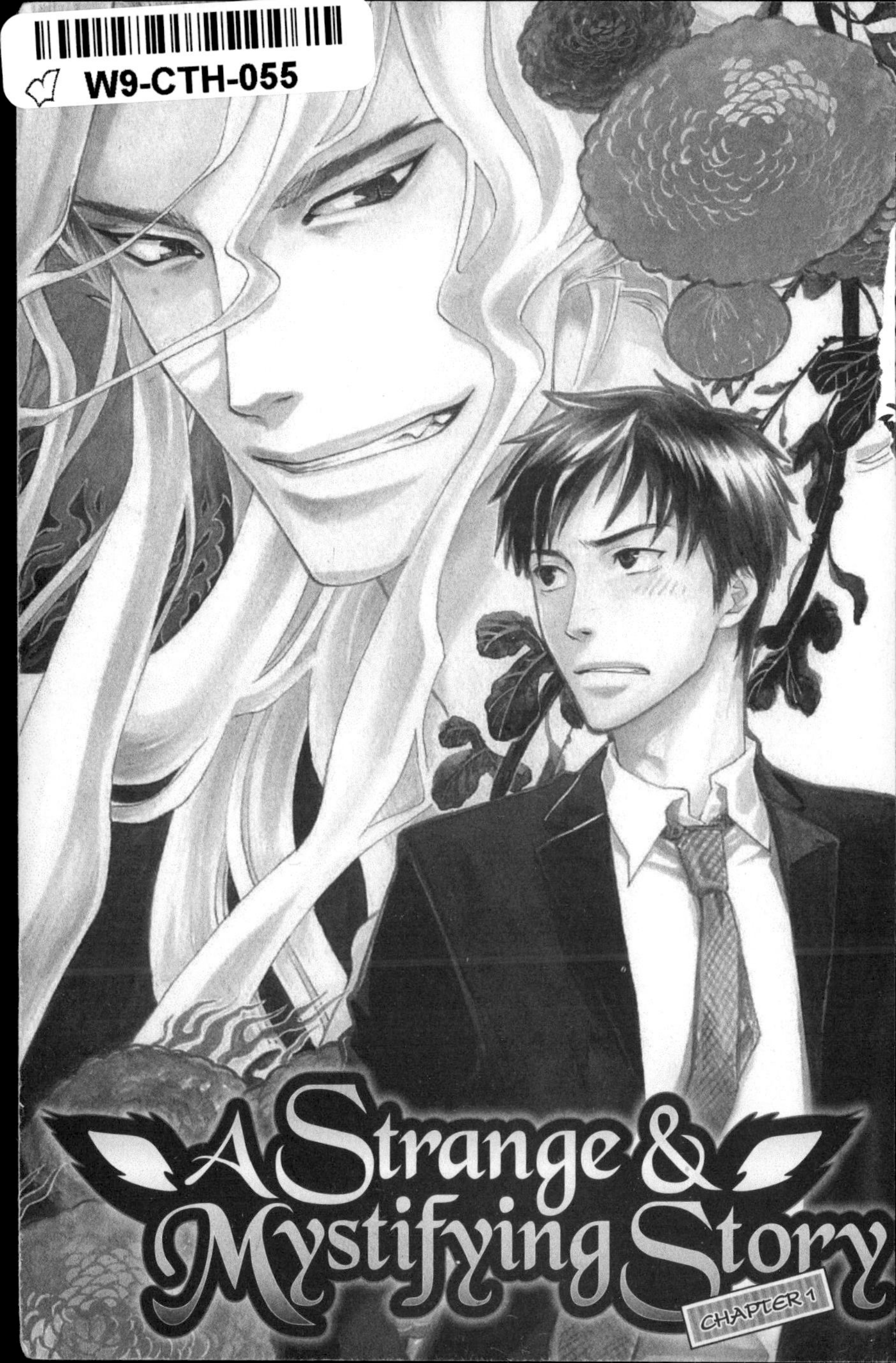
A Strange &
Mystifying Story
CHAPTER 1

A Strange & Mystifying Story

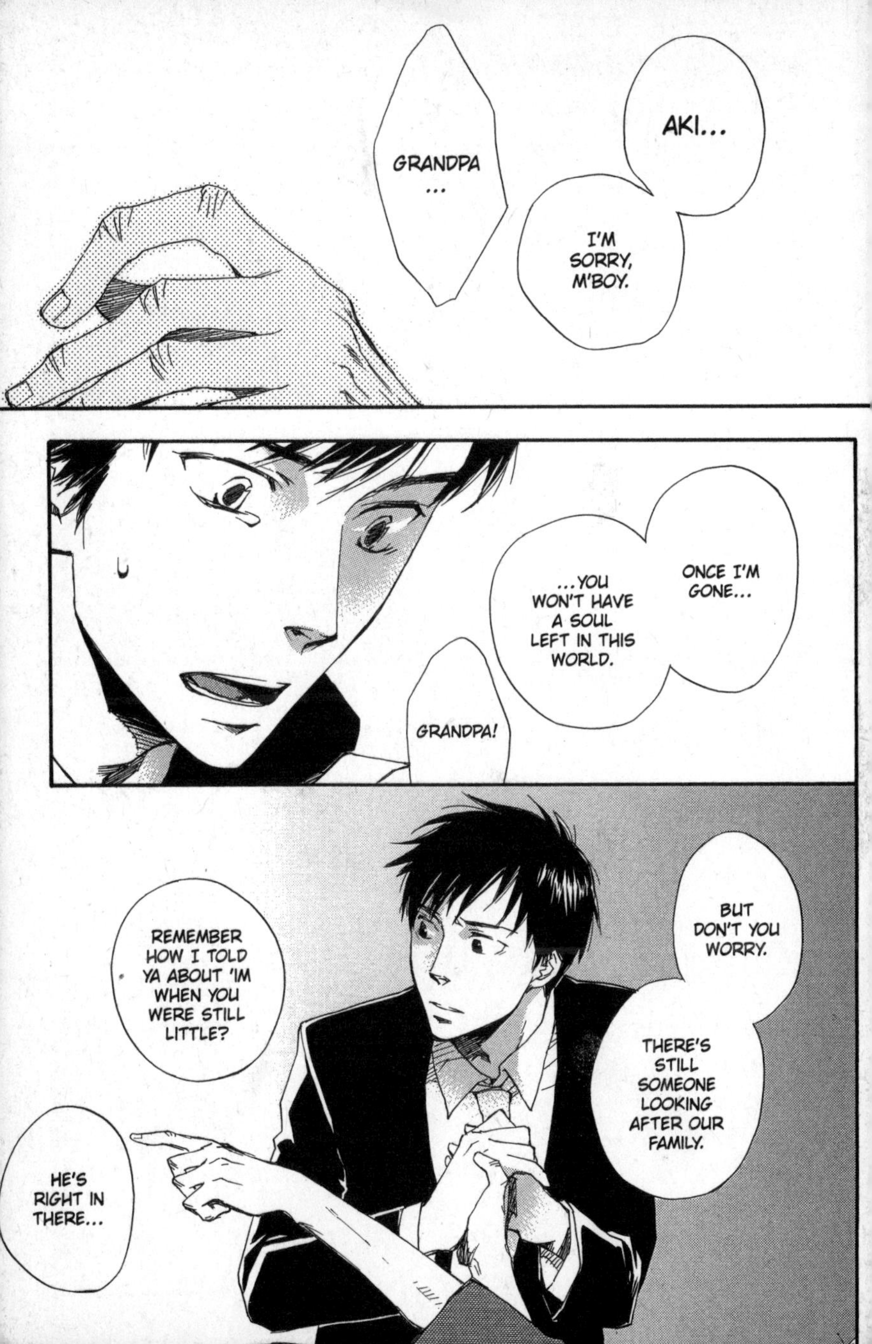
AKI...
I'M SORRY, M'BOY.
GRANDPA ...
ONCE I'M GONE...
...YOU WON'T HAVE A SOUL LEFT IN THIS WORLD.
GRANDPA!
BUT DON'T YOU WORRY.
THERE'S STILL SOMEONE LOOKING AFTER OUR FAMILY.
REMEMBER HOW I TOLD YA ABOUT 'IM WHEN YOU WERE STILL LITTLE?
HE'S RIGHT IN THERE...

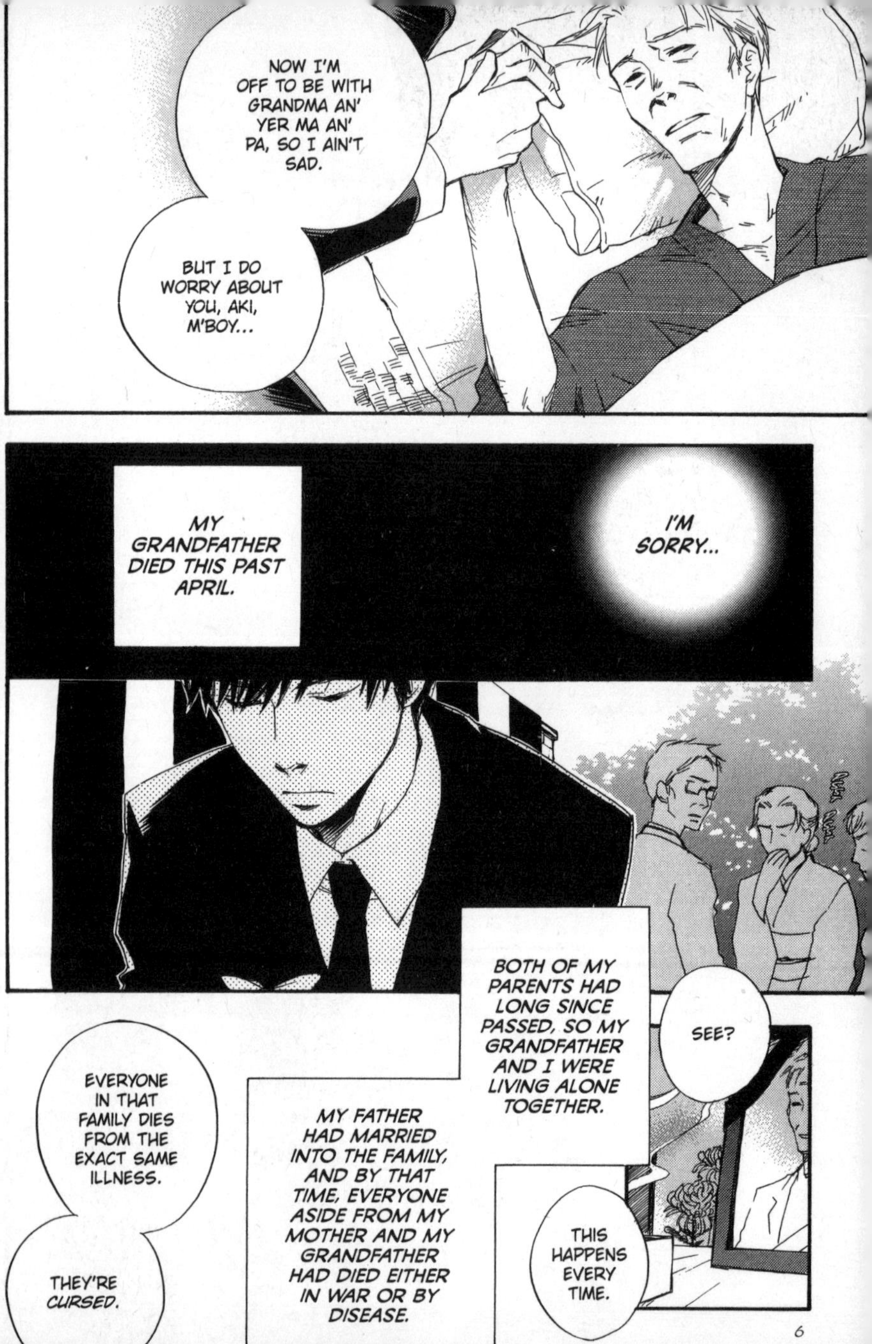
NOW I'M OFF TO BE WITH GRANDMA AN' YER MA AN' PA, SO I AIN'T SAD.
BUT I DO WORRY ABOUT YOU, AKI, M'BOY...
I'M SORRY...
MY GRANDFATHER DIED THIS PAST APRIL.
BOTH OF MY PARENTS HAD LONG SINCE PASSED, SO MY GRANDFATHER AND I WERE LIVING ALONE TOGETHER.
SEE?
THIS HAPPENS EVERY TIME.
MY FATHER HAD MARRIED INTO THE FAMILY, AND BY THAT TIME, EVERYONE ASIDE FROM MY MOTHER AND MY GRANDFATHER HAD DIED EITHER IN WAR OR BY DISEASE.
EVERYONE IN THAT FAMILY DIES FROM THE EXACT SAME ILLNESS.
THEY'RE CURSED.

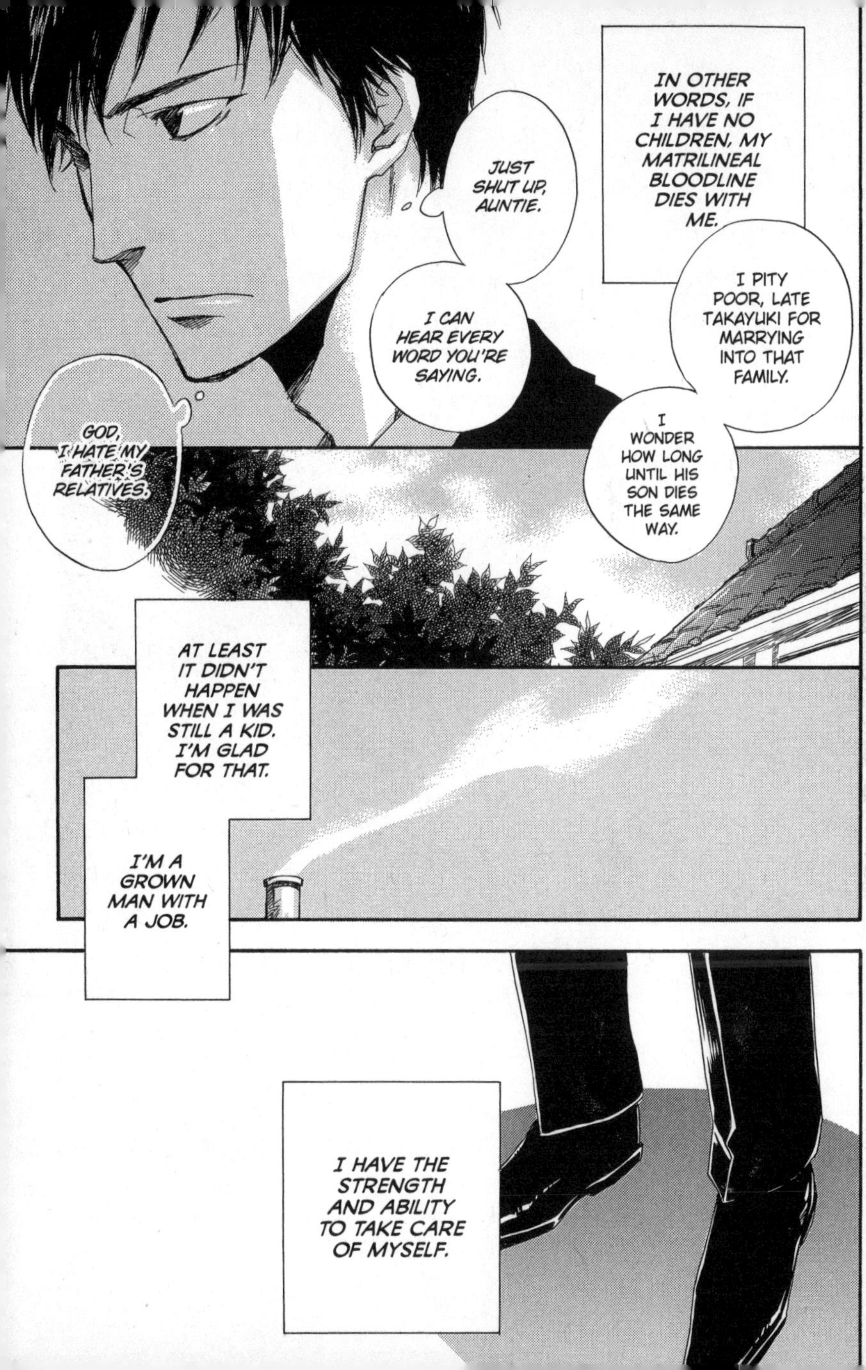
IN OTHER WORDS, IF I HAVE NO CHILDREN, MY MATRILINEAL BLOODLINE DIES WITH ME.
I PITY POOR, LATE TAKAYUKI FOR MARRYING INTO THAT FAMILY.
I WONDER HOW LONG UNTIL HIS SON DIES THE SAME WAY.
JUST SHUT UP, AUNTIE.
I CAN HEAR EVERY WORD YOU'RE SAYING.
GOD, I HATE MY FATHER'S RELATIVES.
AT LEAST IT DIDN'T HAPPEN WHEN I WAS STILL A KID. I'M GLAD FOR THAT.
I'M A GROWN MAN WITH A JOB.
I HAVE THE STRENGTH AND ABILITY TO TAKE CARE OF MYSELF.

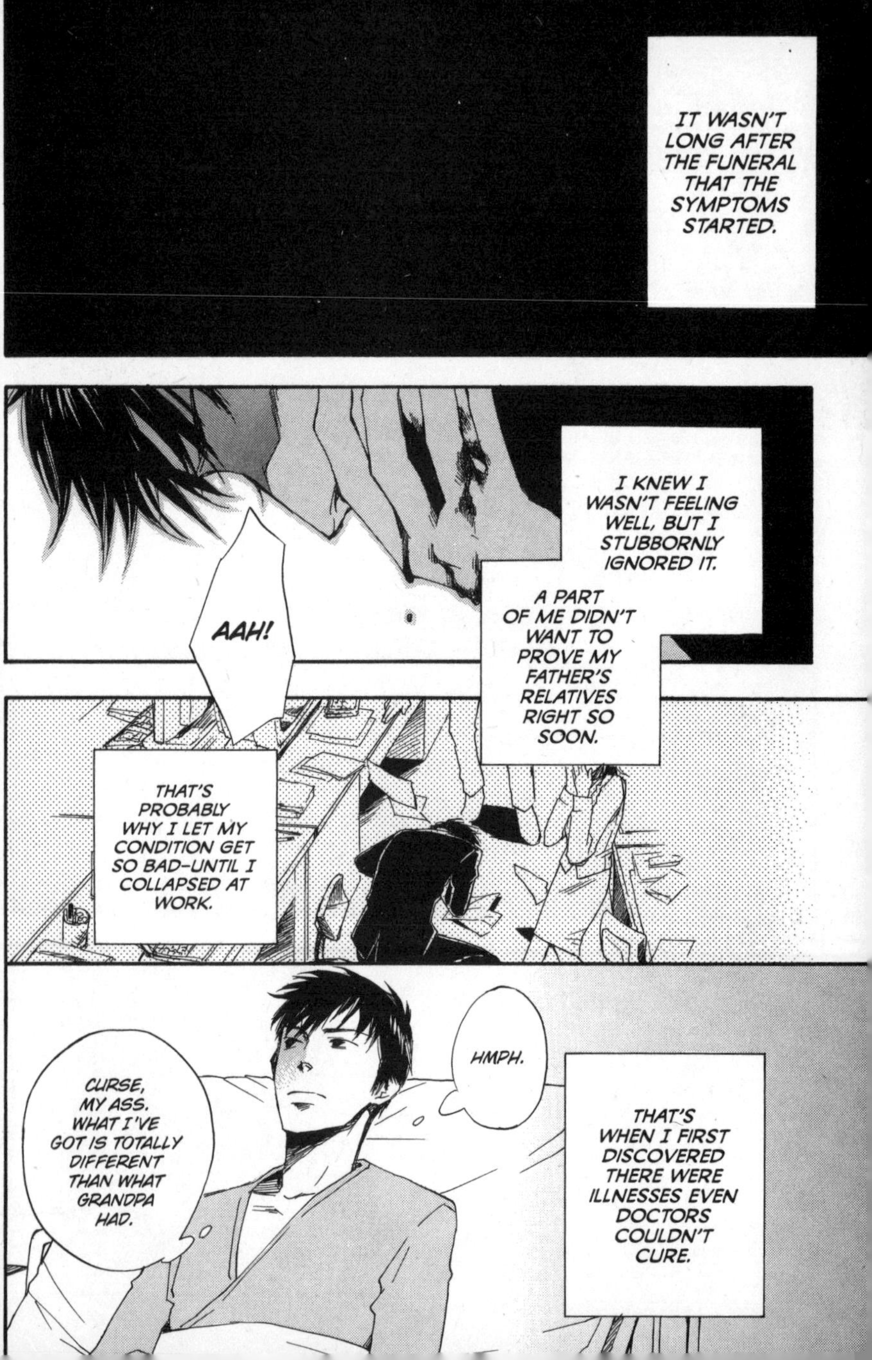
IT WASN'T LONG AFTER THE FUNERAL THAT THE SYMPTOMS STARTED.
I KNEW I WASN'T FEELING WELL, BUT I STUBBORNLY IGNORED IT.
AAH!
A PART OF ME DIDN'T WANT TO PROVE MY FATHER'S RELATIVES RIGHT SO SOON.
THAT'S PROBABLY WHY I LET MY CONDITION GET SO BAD–UNTIL I COLLAPSED AT WORK.
THAT'S WHEN I FIRST DISCOVERED THERE WERE ILLNESSES EVEN DOCTORS COULDN'T CURE.
HMPH.
CURSE, MY ASS. WHAT I'VE GOT IS TOTALLY DIFFERENT THAN WHAT GRANDPA HAD.

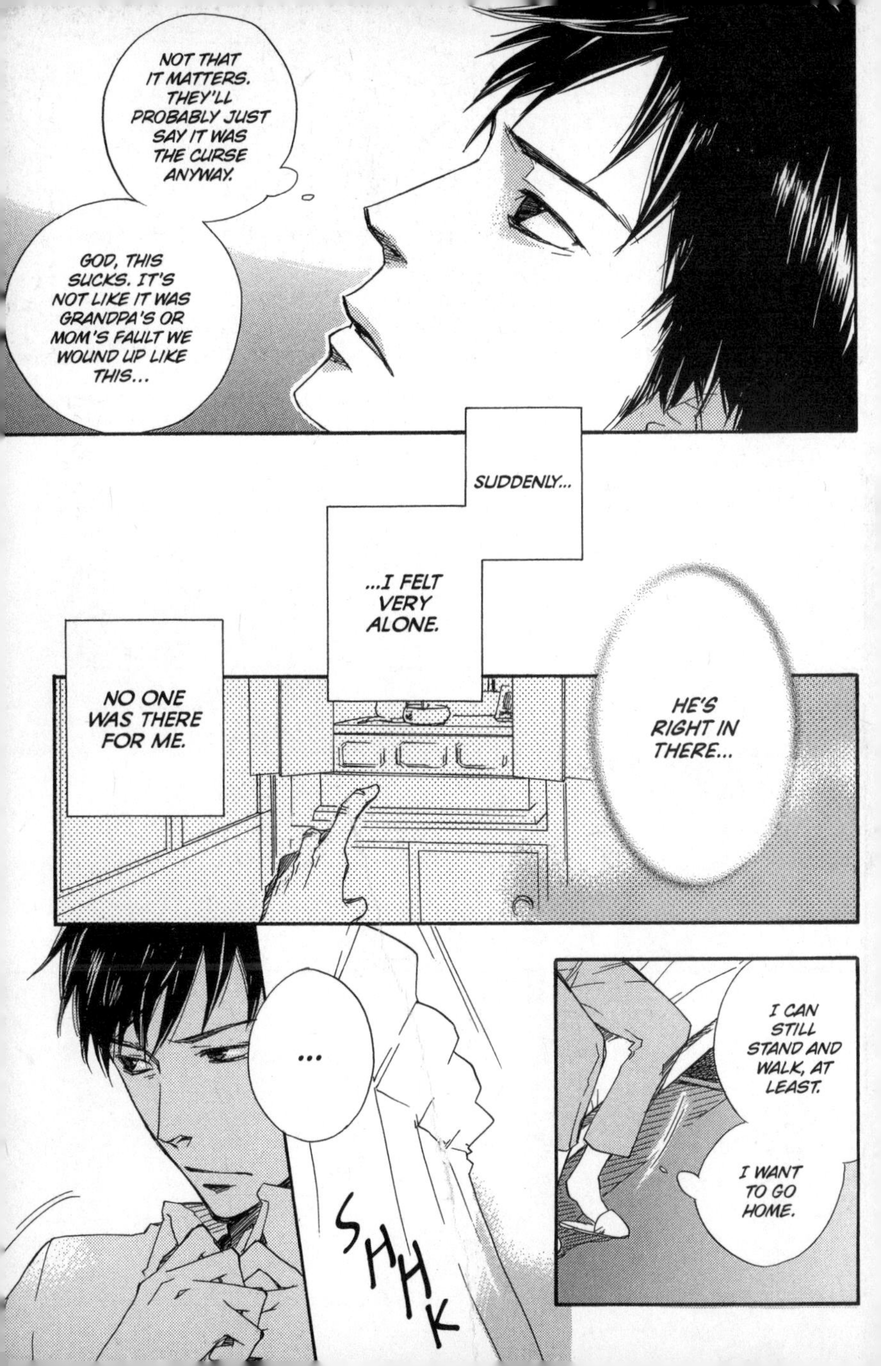
NOT THAT IT MATTERS. THEY'LL PROBABLY JUST SAY IT WAS THE CURSE ANYWAY.
GOD, THIS SUCKS. IT'S NOT LIKE IT WAS GRANDPA'S OR MOM'S FAULT WE WOUND UP LIKE THIS...
SUDDENLY...
...I FELT VERY ALONE.
NO ONE WAS THERE FOR ME.
HE'S RIGHT IN THERE...
I CAN STILL STAND AND WALK, AT LEAST.
I WANT TO GO HOME.
...
SHHK

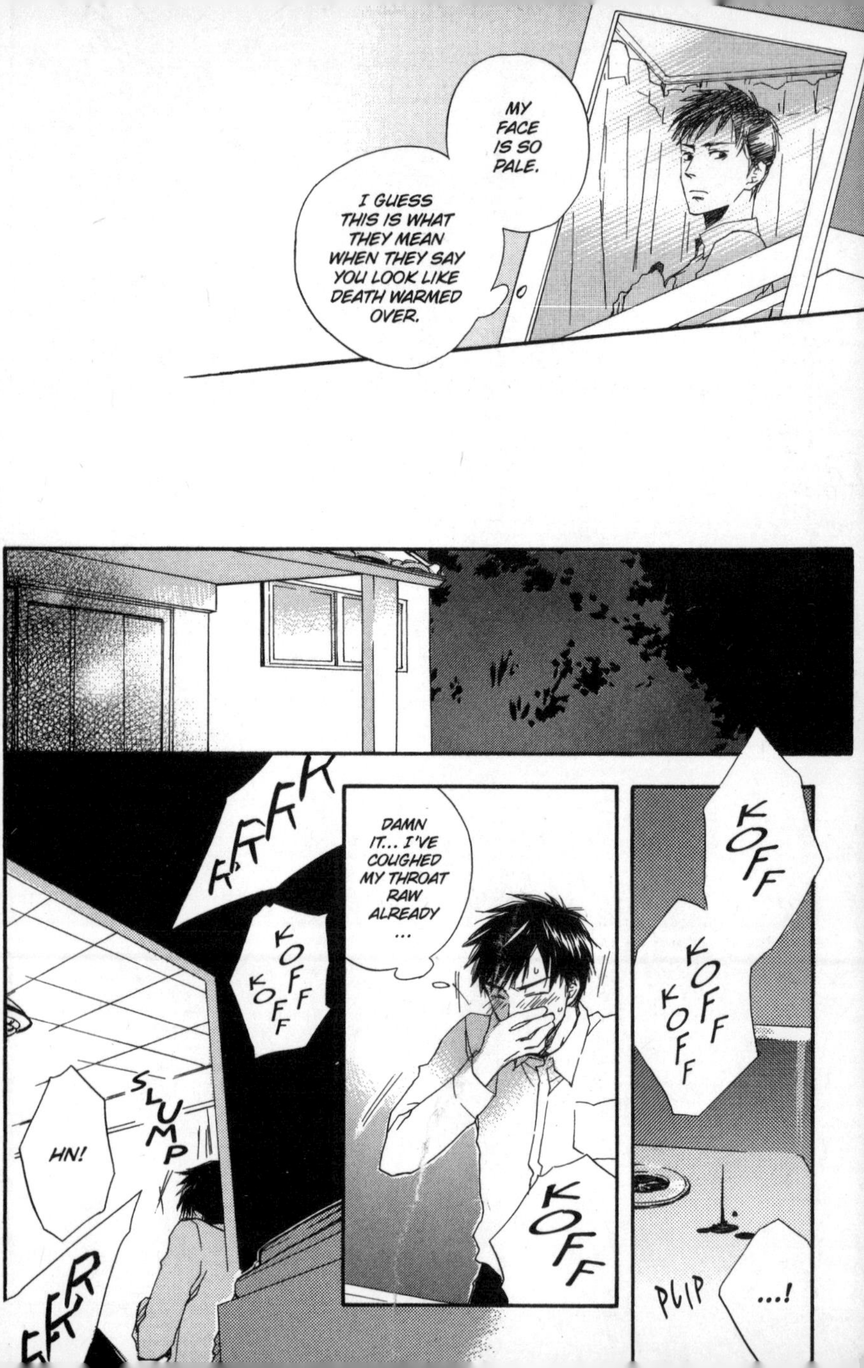
MY FACE IS SO PALE.
I GUESS THIS IS WHAT THEY MEAN WHEN THEY SAY YOU LOOK LIKE DEATH WARMED OVER.
KOFF
KOFF KOFF
PLIP
...!
DAMN IT... I'VE COUGHED MY THROAT RAW ALREADY...
KOFF
RRRR
KOFF KOFF
SLUMP
HN!

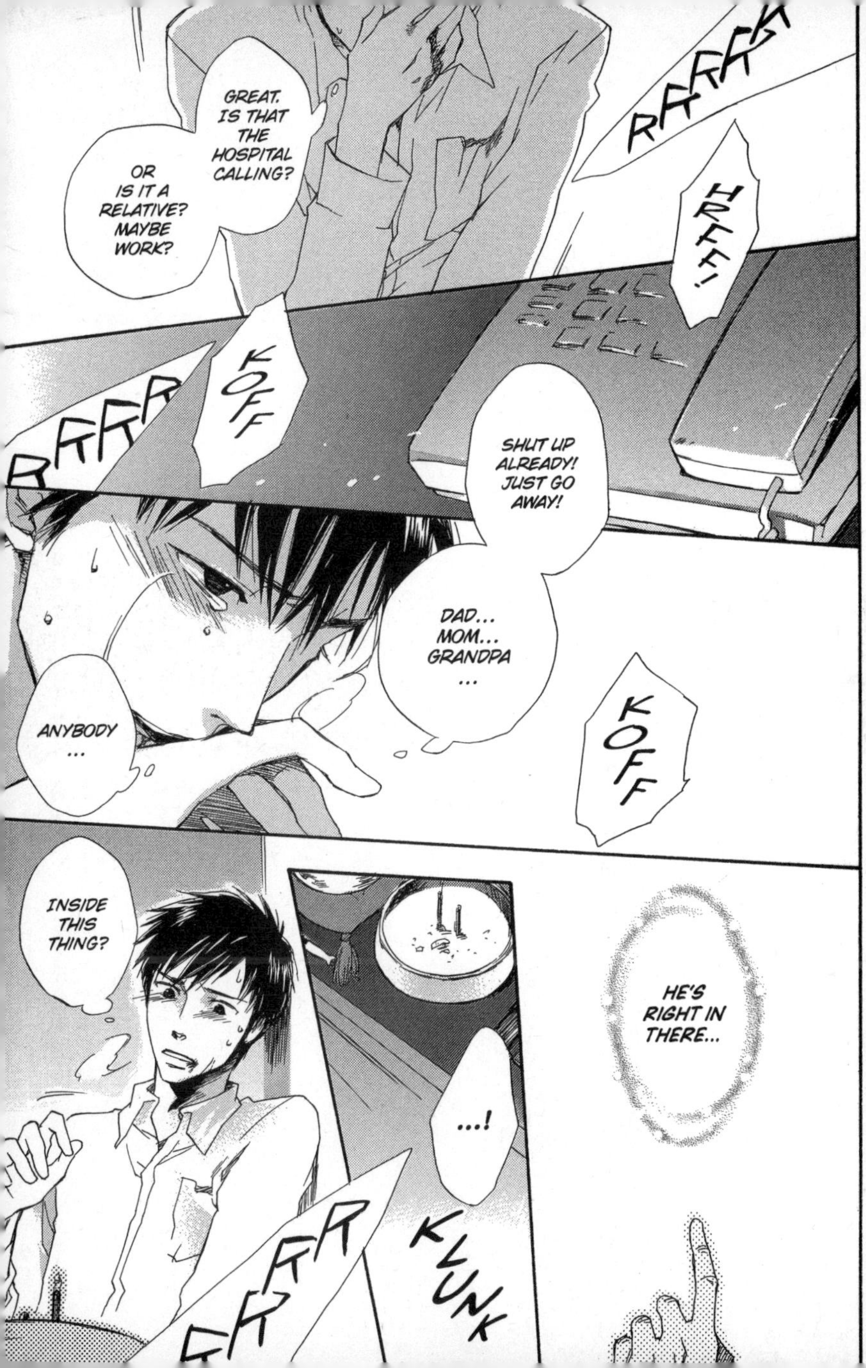
RRRRRK
HRKKK!
GREAT. IS THAT THE HOSPITAL CALLING?
OR IS IT A RELATIVE? MAYBE WORK?
KOFF
RRRRR
SHUT UP ALREADY! JUST GO AWAY!
DAD... MOM... GRANDPA ...
KOFF
ANYBODY ...
HE'S RIGHT IN THERE...
...!
KLUNK
RRRR
INSIDE THIS THING?

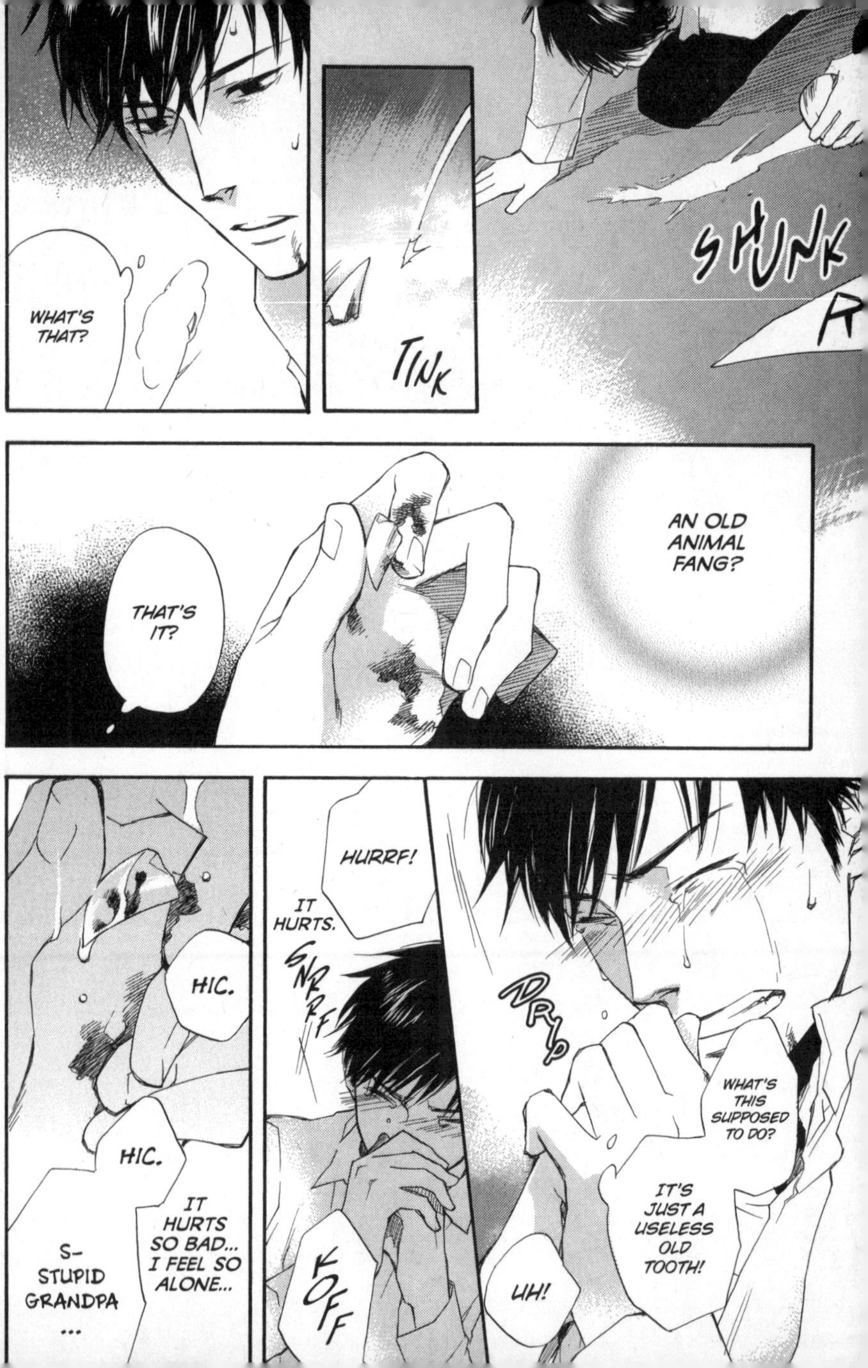
SHUNK
R
TINK
WHAT'S THAT?
AN OLD ANIMAL FANG?
THAT'S IT?
HURRF!
IT HURTS.
SNRRF
DRIP
WHAT'S THIS SUPPOSED TO DO?
IT'S JUST A USELESS OLD TOOTH!
UH!
KOFF
HIC.
HIC.
IT HURTS SO BAD... I FEEL SO ALONE...
S-STUPID GRANDPA
...

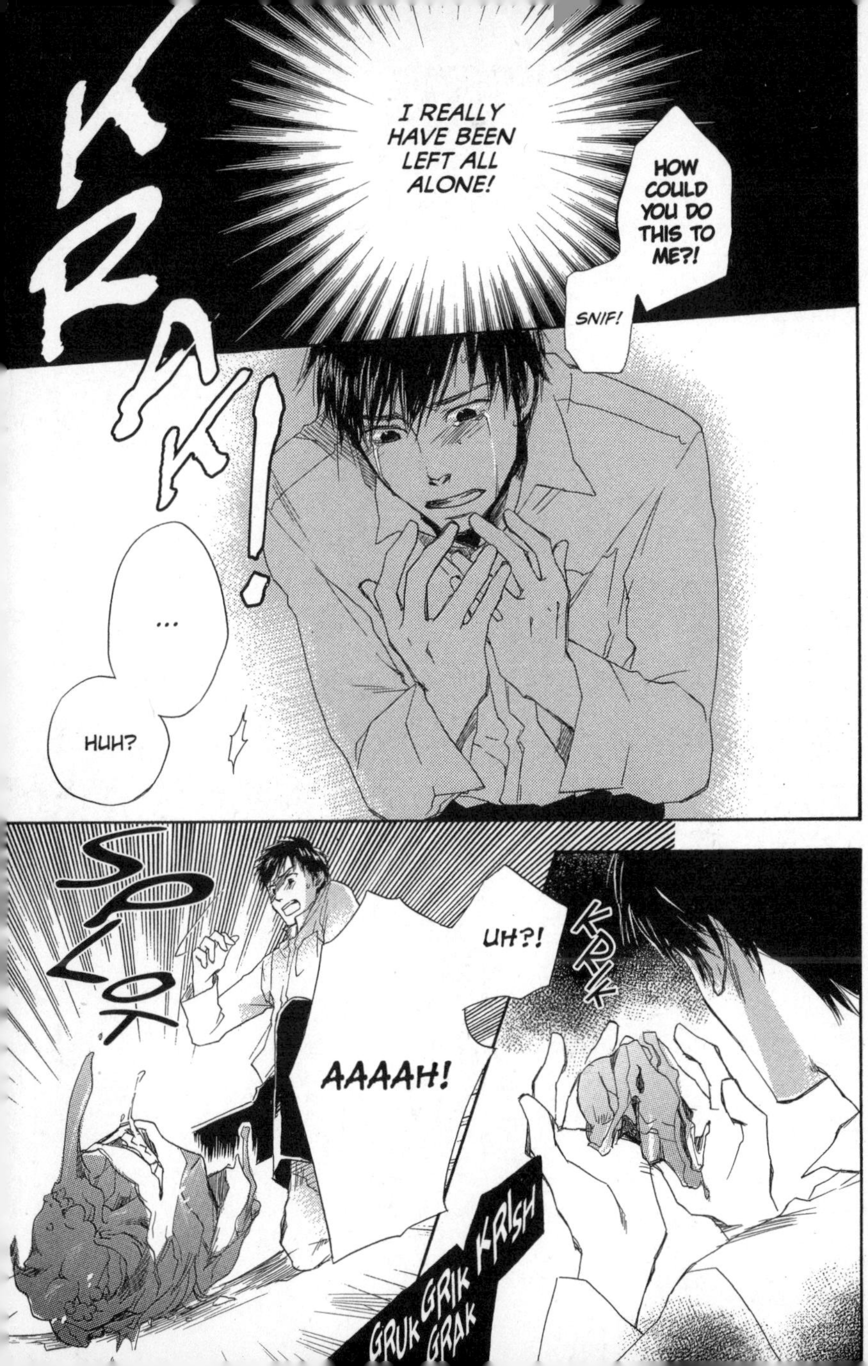
HOW COULD YOU DO THIS TO ME?!
I REALLY HAVE BEEN LEFT ALL ALONE!
SNIF!
KRAK!
...
HUH?
KRIK
UH?!
AAAAH!
KRISH
GRIK
GRUK
GRAK
SPLOK

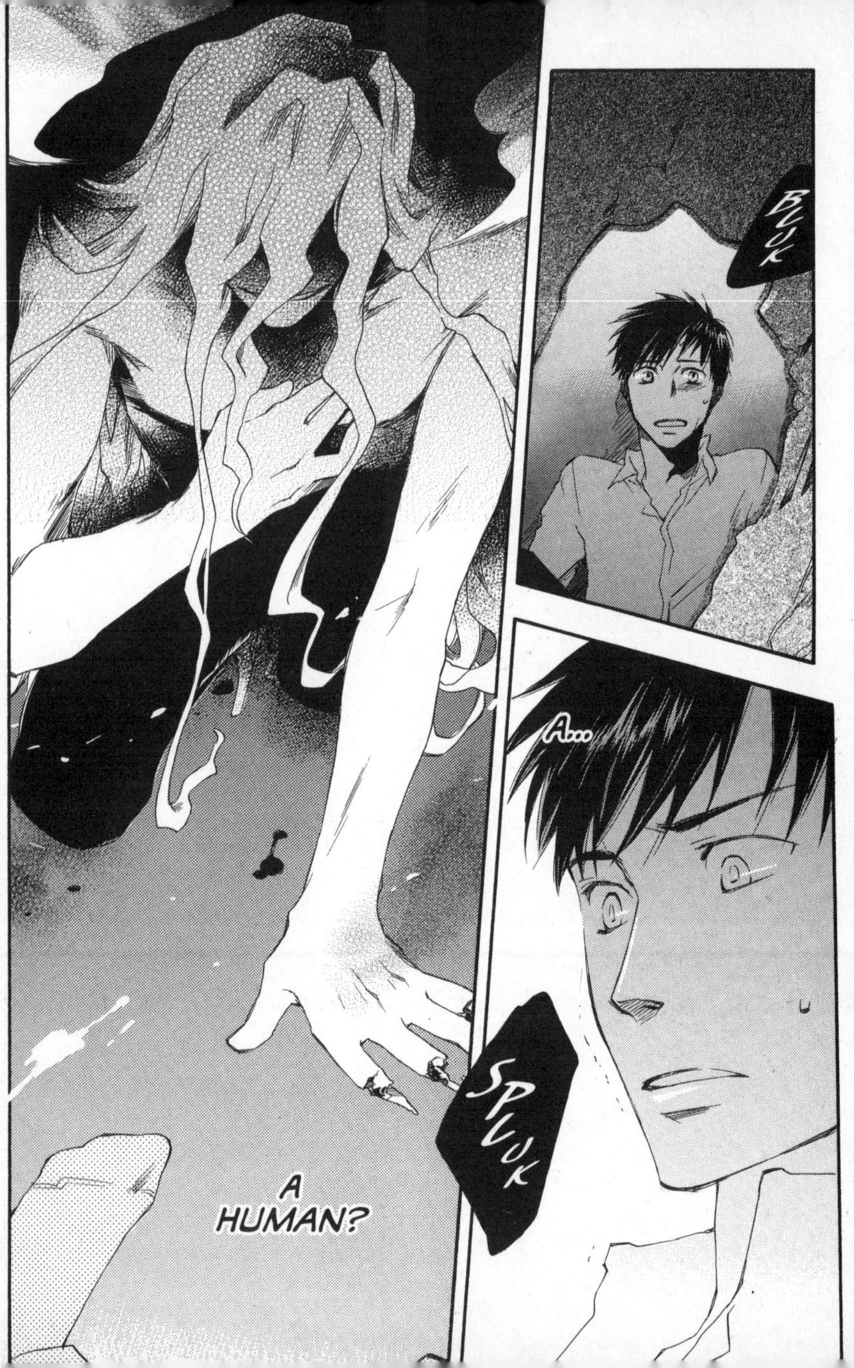
BLUK
A...
SPLUK
A HUMAN?

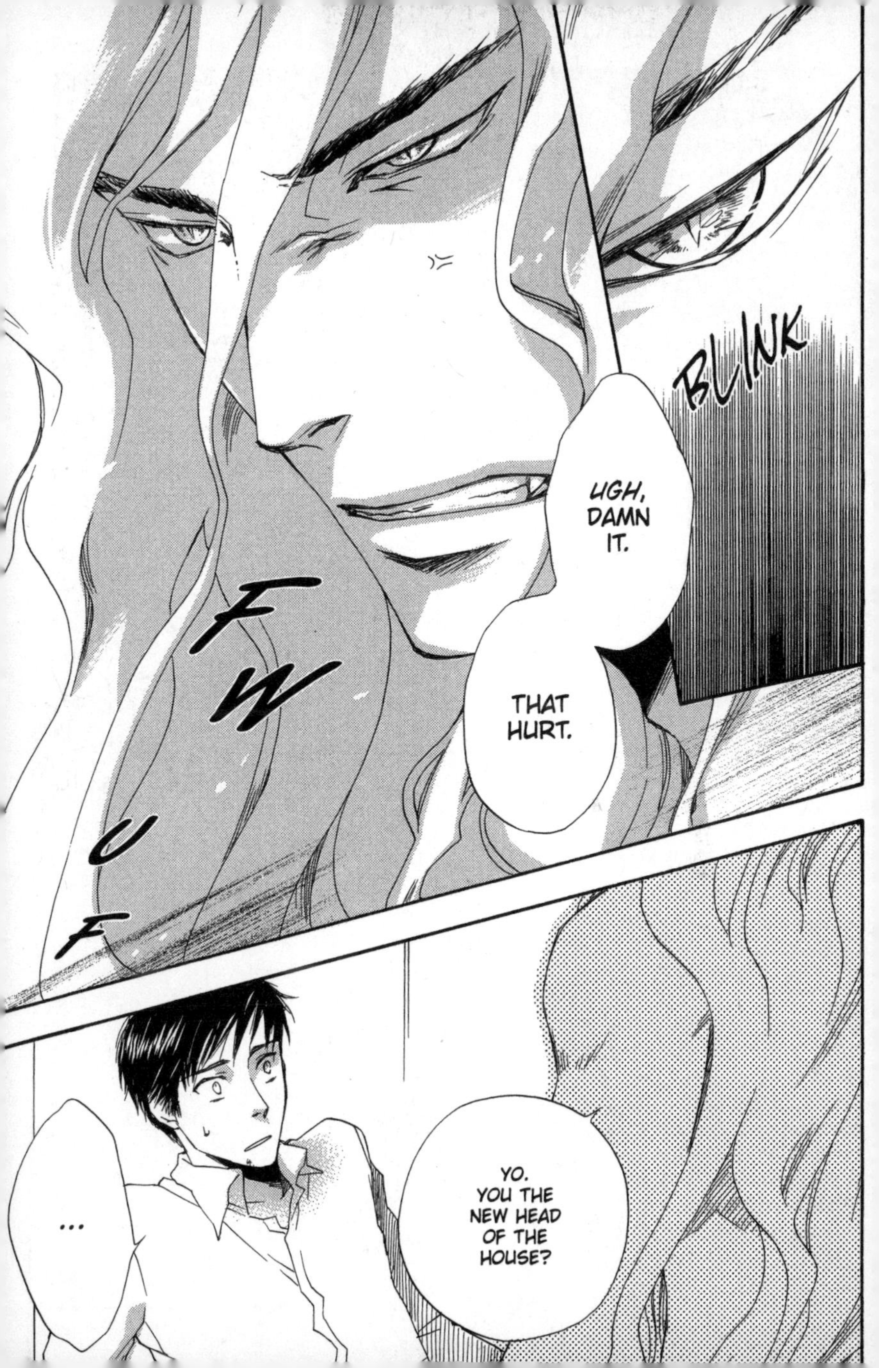
BLINK
UGH, DAMN IT.
THAT HURT.
FWUF
YO. YOU THE NEW HEAD OF THE HOUSE?
...

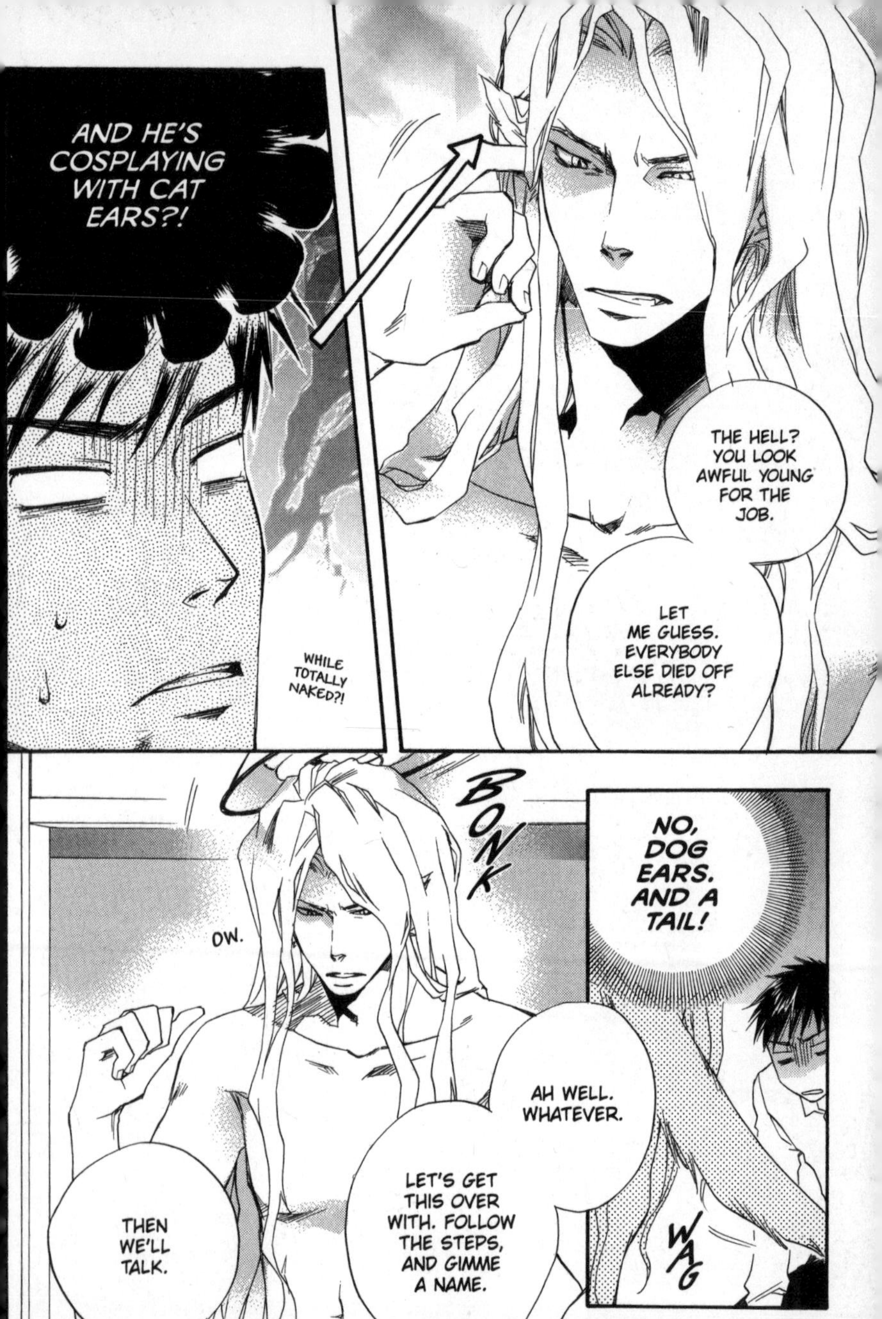
THE HELL? YOU LOOK AWFUL YOUNG FOR THE JOB.
LET ME GUESS. EVERYBODY ELSE DIED OFF ALREADY?
AND HE'S COSPLAYING WITH CAT EARS?!
WHILE TOTALLY NAKED?!
NO, DOG EARS. AND A TAIL!
WAG
BONK
OW.
AH WELL. WHATEVER.
LET'S GET THIS OVER WITH. FOLLOW THE STEPS, AND GIMME A NAME.
THEN WE'LL TALK.

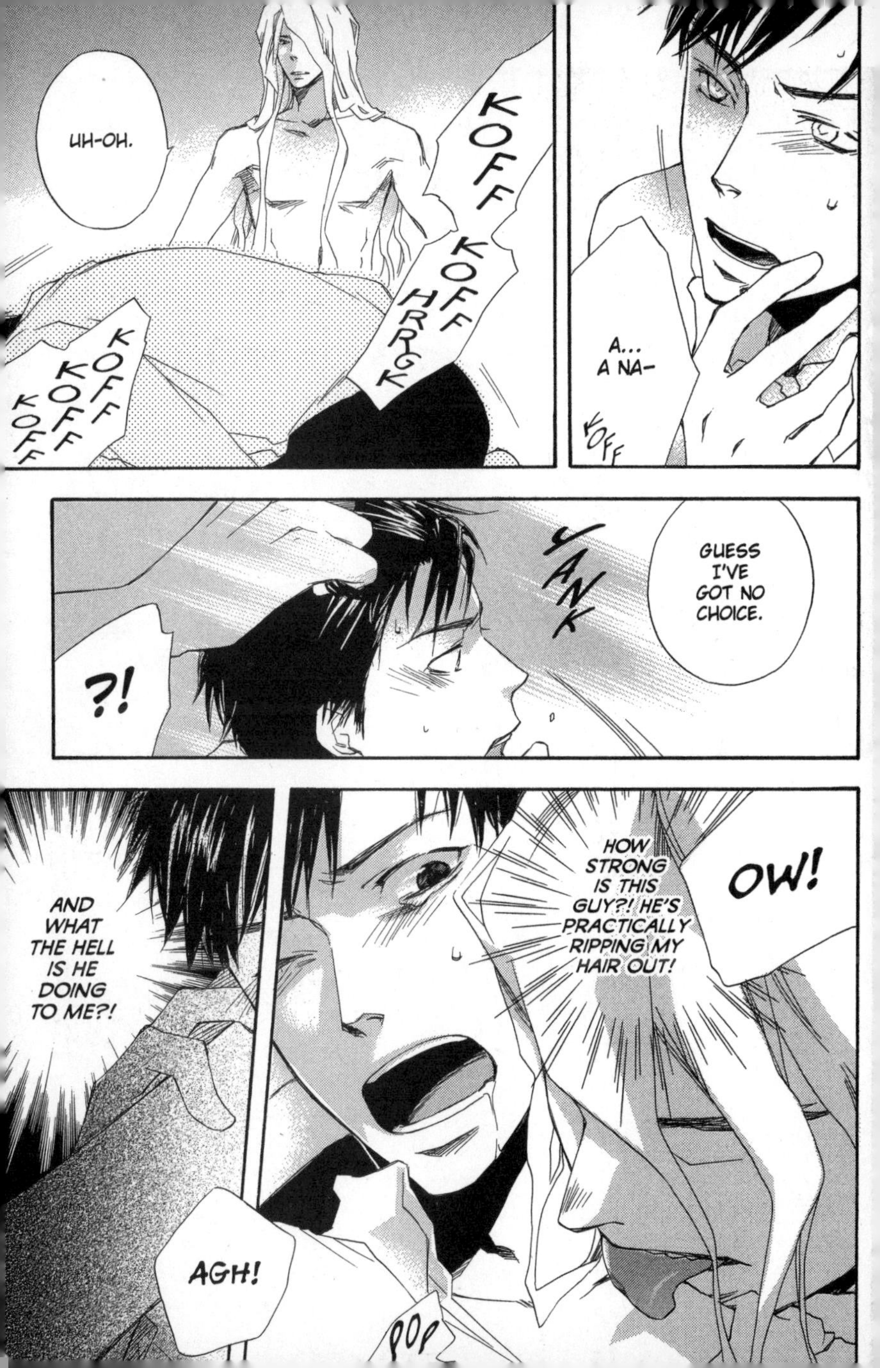
A...
A NA-
KOFF
KOFF KOFF HRRGK
UH-OH.
KOFF KOFF KOFF
GUESS I'VE GOT NO CHOICE.
YANK
?!
OW!
HOW STRONG IS THIS GUY?! HE'S PRACTICALLY RIPPING MY HAIR OUT!
AGH!
POP
AND WHAT THE HELL IS HE DOING TO ME?!

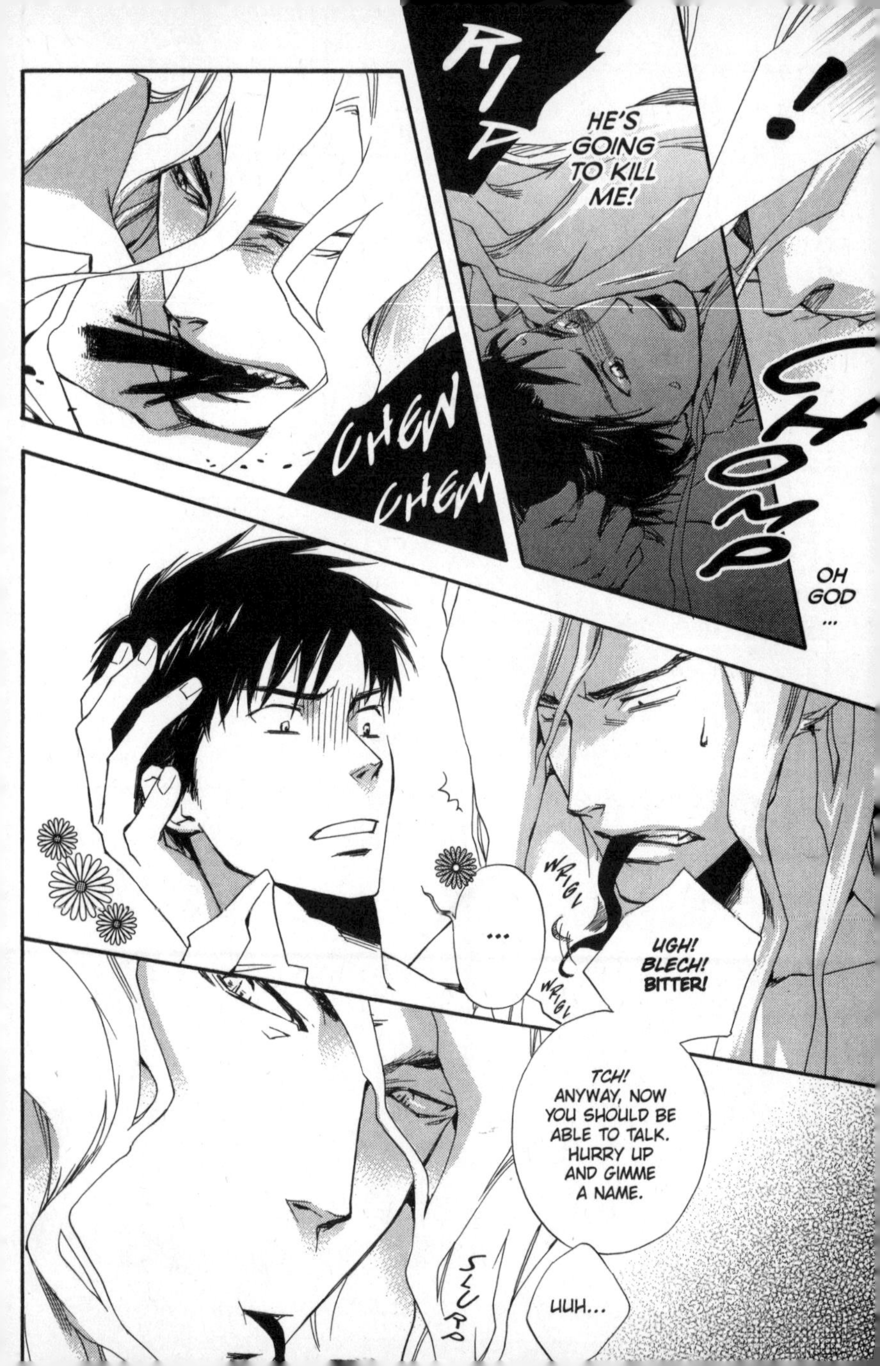
!
CHOMP
OH GOD ...
RIP
HE'S GOING TO KILL ME!
CHEW CHEW
WRIGL WRIGL
UGH! BLECH! BITTER!
...
TCH! ANYWAY, NOW YOU SHOULD BE ABLE TO TALK. HURRY UP AND GIMME A NAME.
SLURP
UUH...

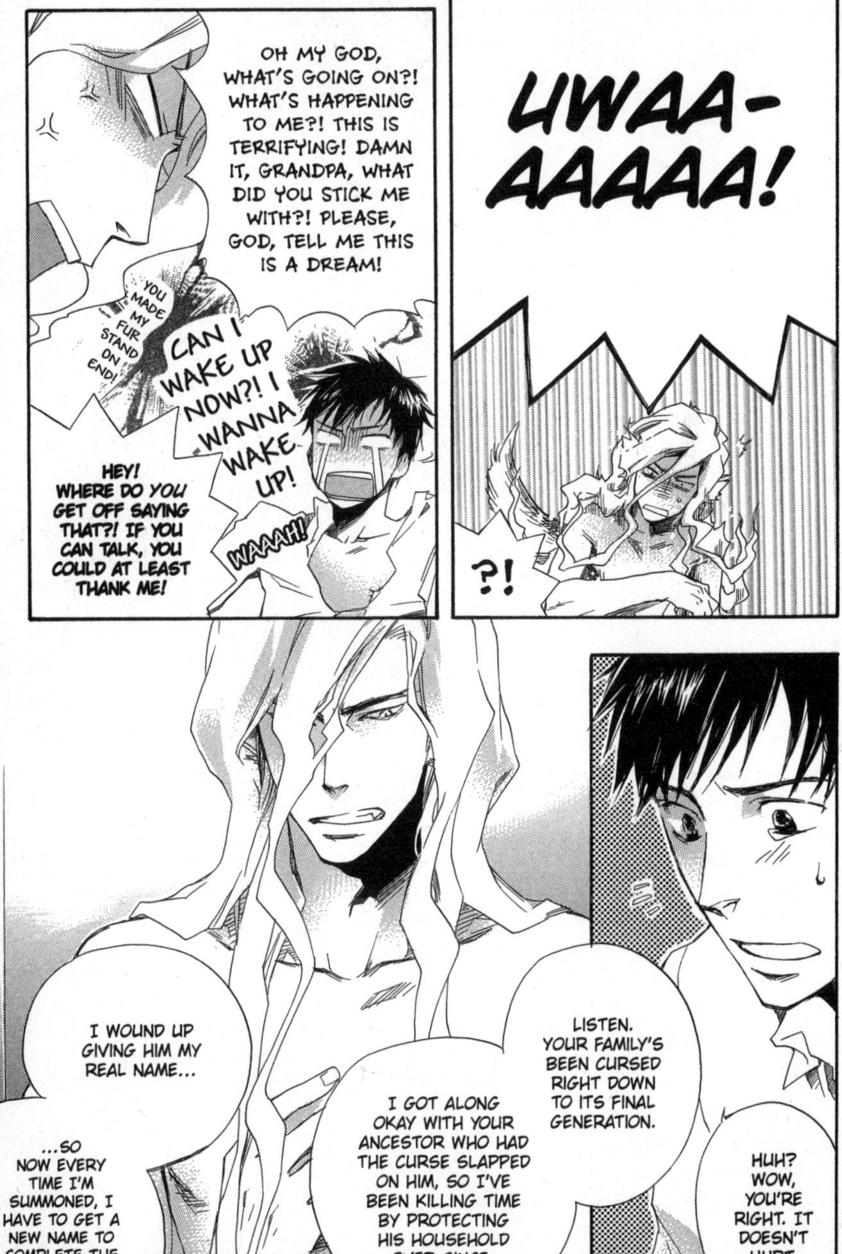
UWAA-AAAAA!
?!
OH MY GOD, WHAT'S GOING ON?! WHAT'S HAPPENING TO ME?! THIS IS TERRIFYING! DAMN IT, GRANDPA, WHAT DID YOU STICK ME WITH?! PLEASE, GOD, TELL ME THIS IS A DREAM!
CAN I WAKE UP NOW?! I WANNA WAKE UP!
YOU MADE MY FUR STAND ON END!
WAAAH!
HEY! WHERE DO *YOU* GET OFF SAYING THAT?! IF YOU CAN TALK, YOU COULD AT LEAST THANK ME!
HUH? WOW, YOU'RE RIGHT. IT DOESN'T HURT.
LISTEN. YOUR FAMILY'S BEEN CURSED RIGHT DOWN TO ITS FINAL GENERATION.
I GOT ALONG OKAY WITH YOUR ANCESTOR WHO HAD THE CURSE SLAPPED ON HIM, SO I'VE BEEN KILLING TIME BY PROTECTING HIS HOUSEHOLD EVER SINCE.
I WOUND UP GIVING HIM MY REAL NAME...
...SO NOW EVERY TIME I'M SUMMONED, I HAVE TO GET A NEW NAME TO COMPLETE THE SPELL.

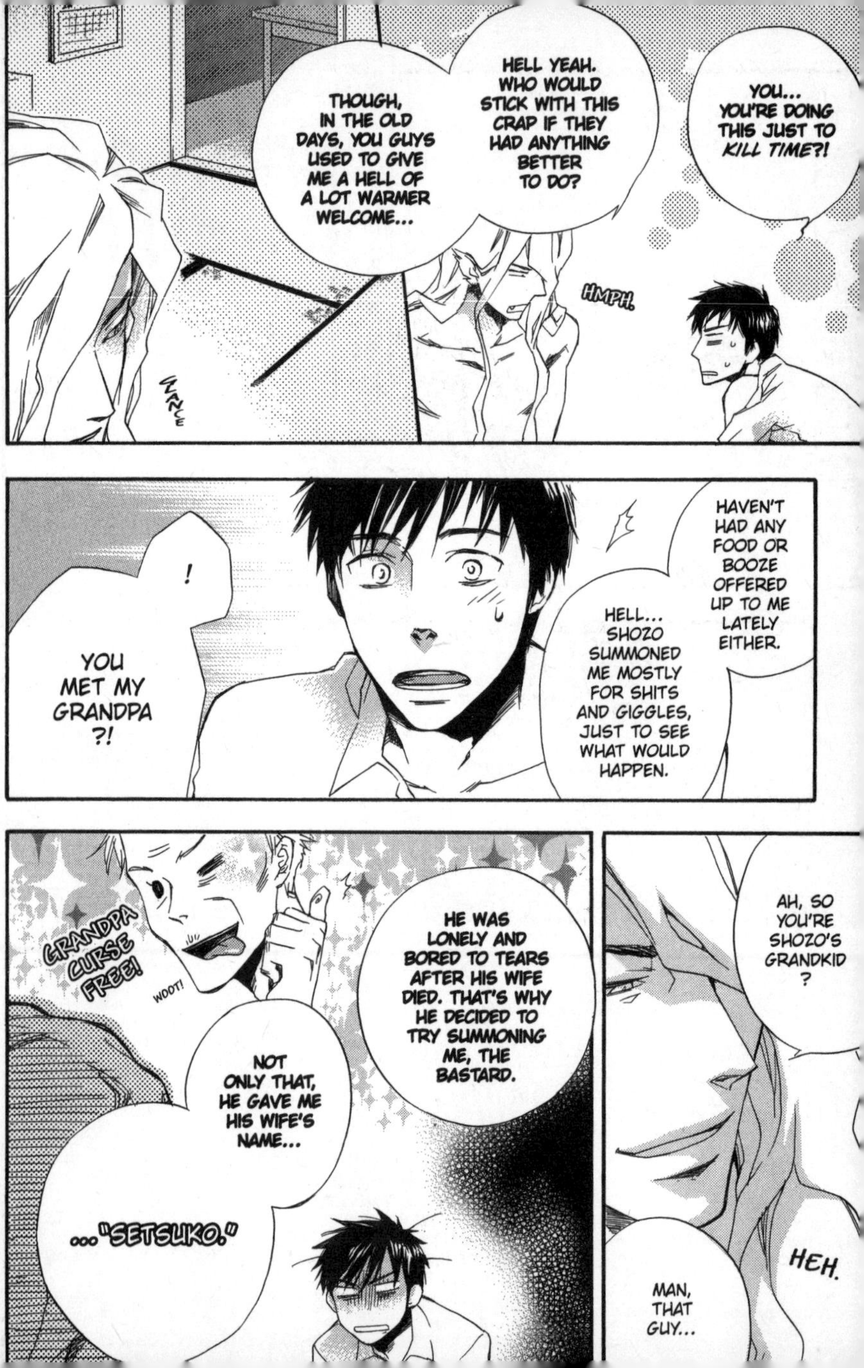
YOU... YOU'RE DOING THIS JUST TO KILL TIME?!
HELL YEAH. WHO WOULD STICK WITH THIS CRAP IF THEY HAD ANYTHING BETTER TO DO?
HMPH.
THOUGH, IN THE OLD DAYS, YOU GUYS USED TO GIVE ME A HELL OF A LOT WARMER WELCOME...
GLANCE
HAVEN'T HAD ANY FOOD OR BOOZE OFFERED UP TO ME LATELY EITHER.
HELL... SHOZO SUMMONED ME MOSTLY FOR SHITS AND GIGGLES, JUST TO SEE WHAT WOULD HAPPEN.
!
YOU MET MY GRANDPA ?!
AH, SO YOU'RE SHOZO'S GRANDKID ?
HEH.
MAN, THAT GUY...
HE WAS LONELY AND BORED TO TEARS AFTER HIS WIFE DIED. THAT'S WHY HE DECIDED TO TRY SUMMONING ME, THE BASTARD.
GRANDPA CURSE FREE!
WOOT!
NOT ONLY THAT, HE GAVE ME HIS WIFE'S NAME...
..."SETSUKO."

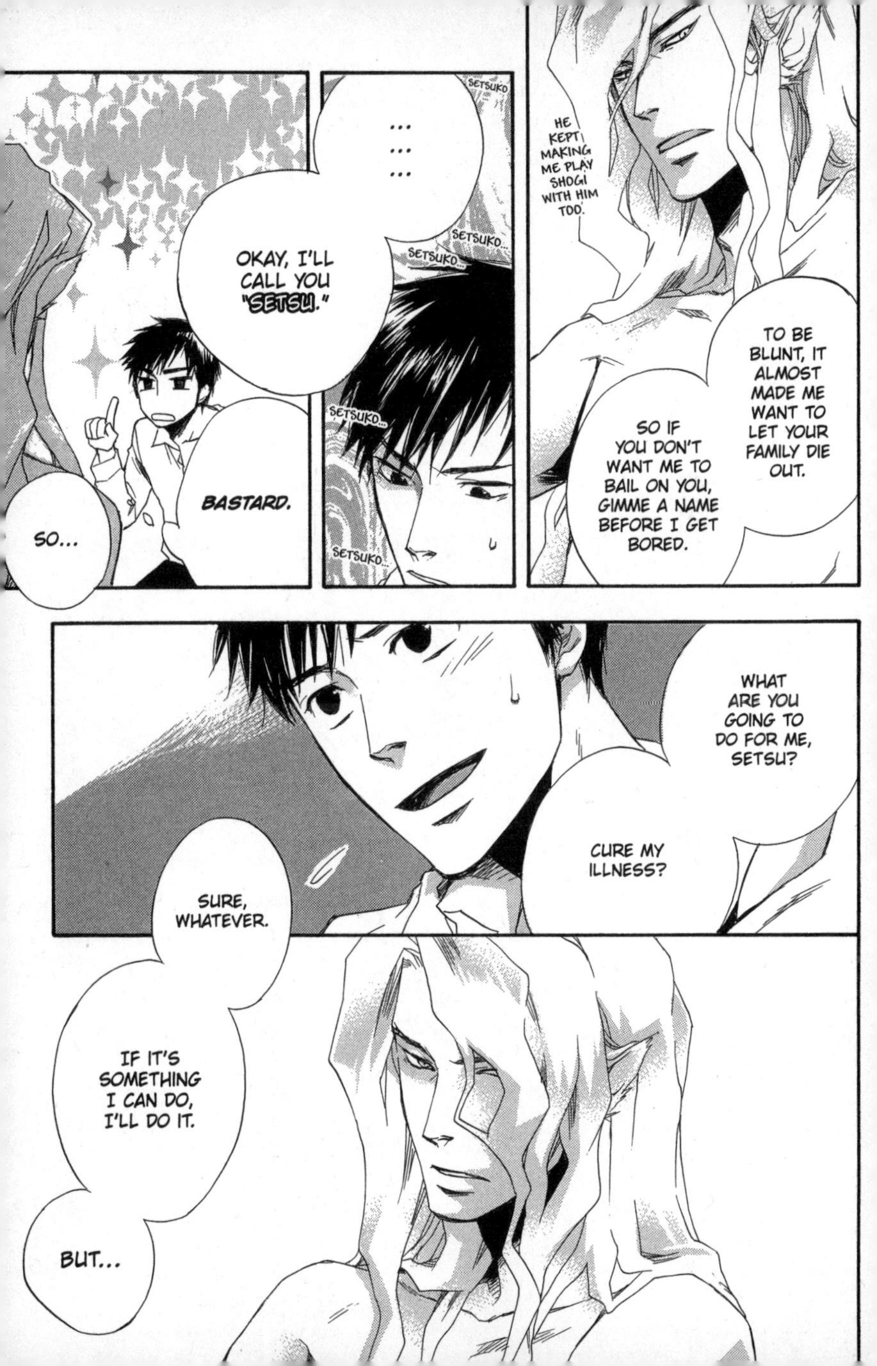
HE KEPT MAKING ME PLAY SHOGI WITH HIM TOO.
TO BE BLUNT, IT ALMOST MADE ME WANT TO LET YOUR FAMILY DIE OUT.
SO IF YOU DON'T WANT ME TO BAIL ON YOU, GIMME A NAME BEFORE I GET BORED.
SETSUKO
...
...
...
SETSUKO...
SETSUKO...
SETSUKO...
SETSUKO...
OKAY, I'LL CALL YOU "SETSU."
BASTARD.
SO...
WHAT ARE YOU GOING TO DO FOR ME, SETSU?
CURE MY ILLNESS?
SURE, WHATEVER.
IF IT'S SOMETHING I CAN DO, I'LL DO IT.
BUT...

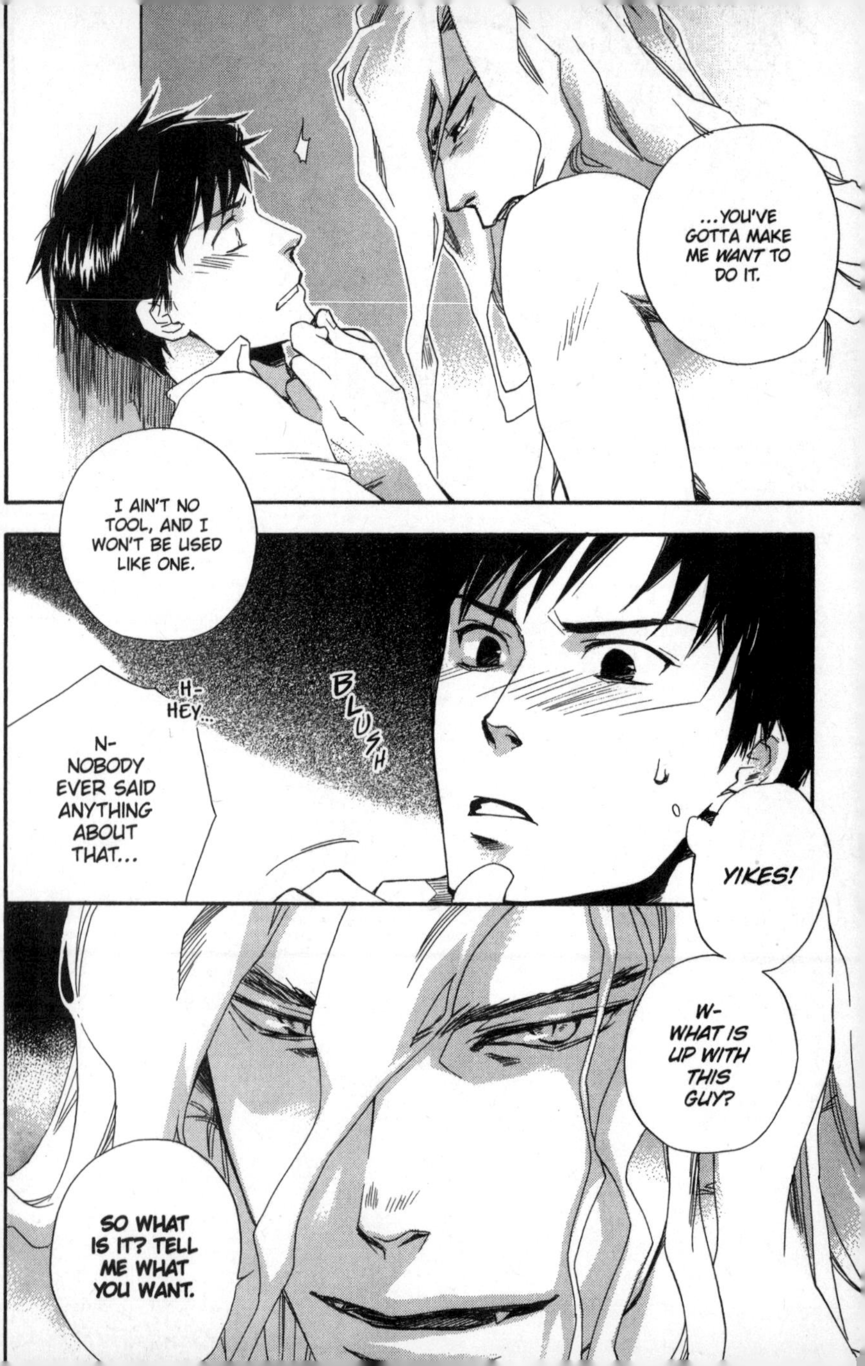
...YOU'VE GOTTA MAKE ME *WANT* TO DO IT.
I AIN'T NO TOOL, AND I WON'T BE USED LIKE ONE.
YIKES!
BLUSH
H-HEY...
N-NOBODY EVER SAID ANYTHING ABOUT THAT...
W-WHAT IS UP WITH THIS GUY?
SO WHAT IS IT? TELL ME WHAT YOU WANT.

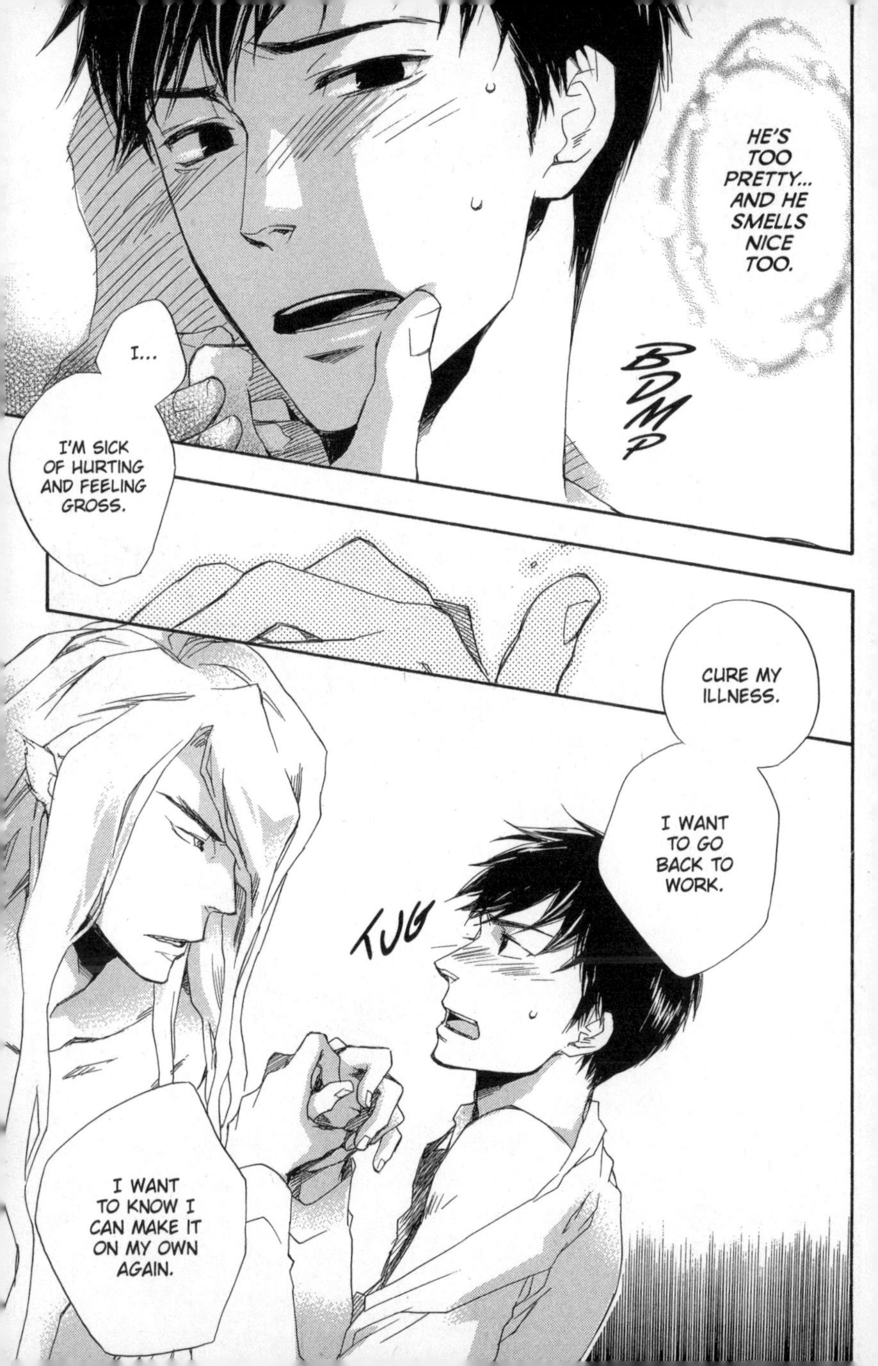
HE'S TOO PRETTY... AND HE SMELLS NICE TOO.
BDMP
I...
I'M SICK OF HURTING AND FEELING GROSS.
CURE MY ILLNESS.
I WANT TO GO BACK TO WORK.
TUG
I WANT TO KNOW I CAN MAKE IT ON MY OWN AGAIN.

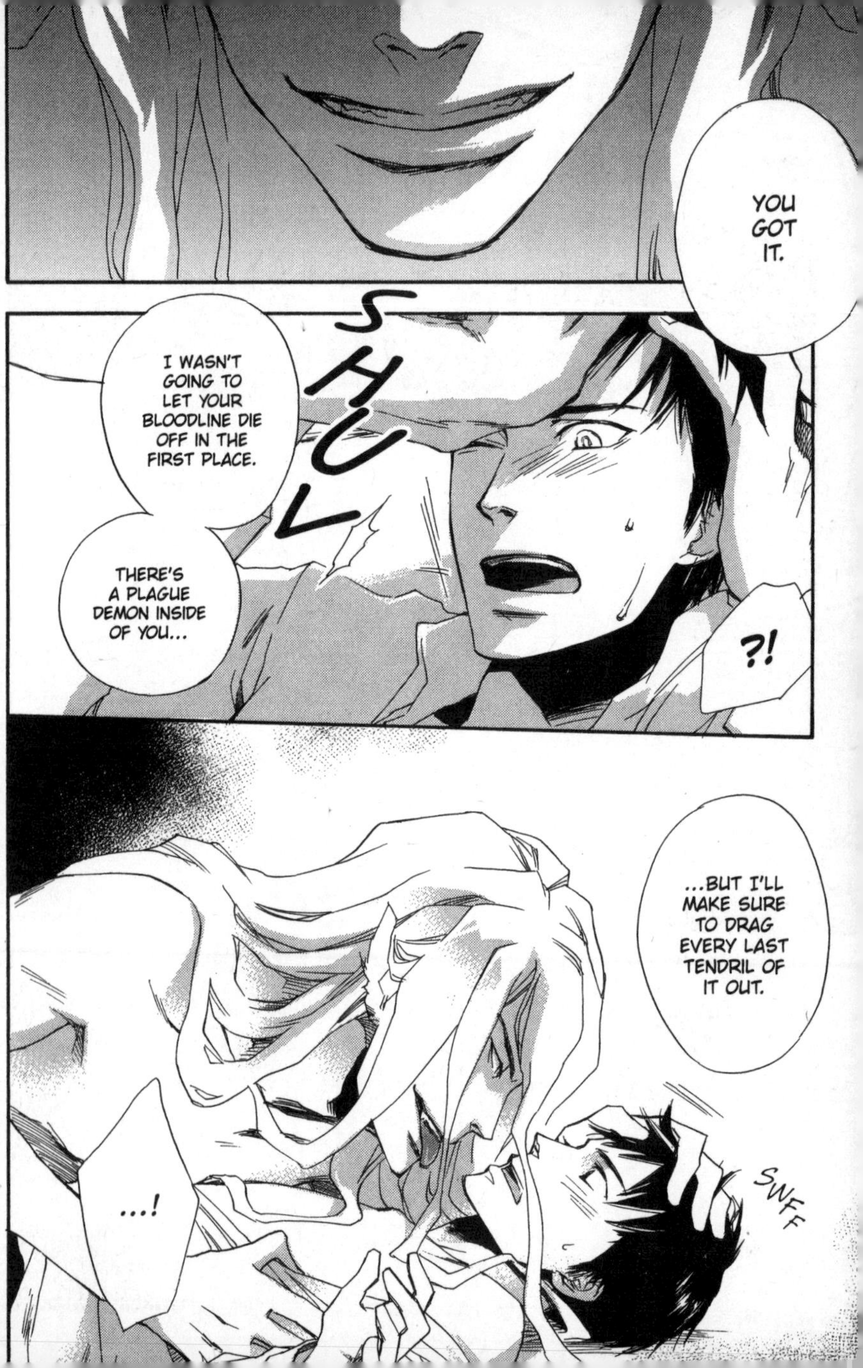
YOU GOT IT.
SHUV
?!
I WASN'T GOING TO LET YOUR BLOODLINE DIE OFF IN THE FIRST PLACE.
THERE'S A PLAGUE DEMON INSIDE OF YOU...
...BUT I'LL MAKE SURE TO DRAG EVERY LAST TENDRIL OF IT OUT.
SNFF
...!

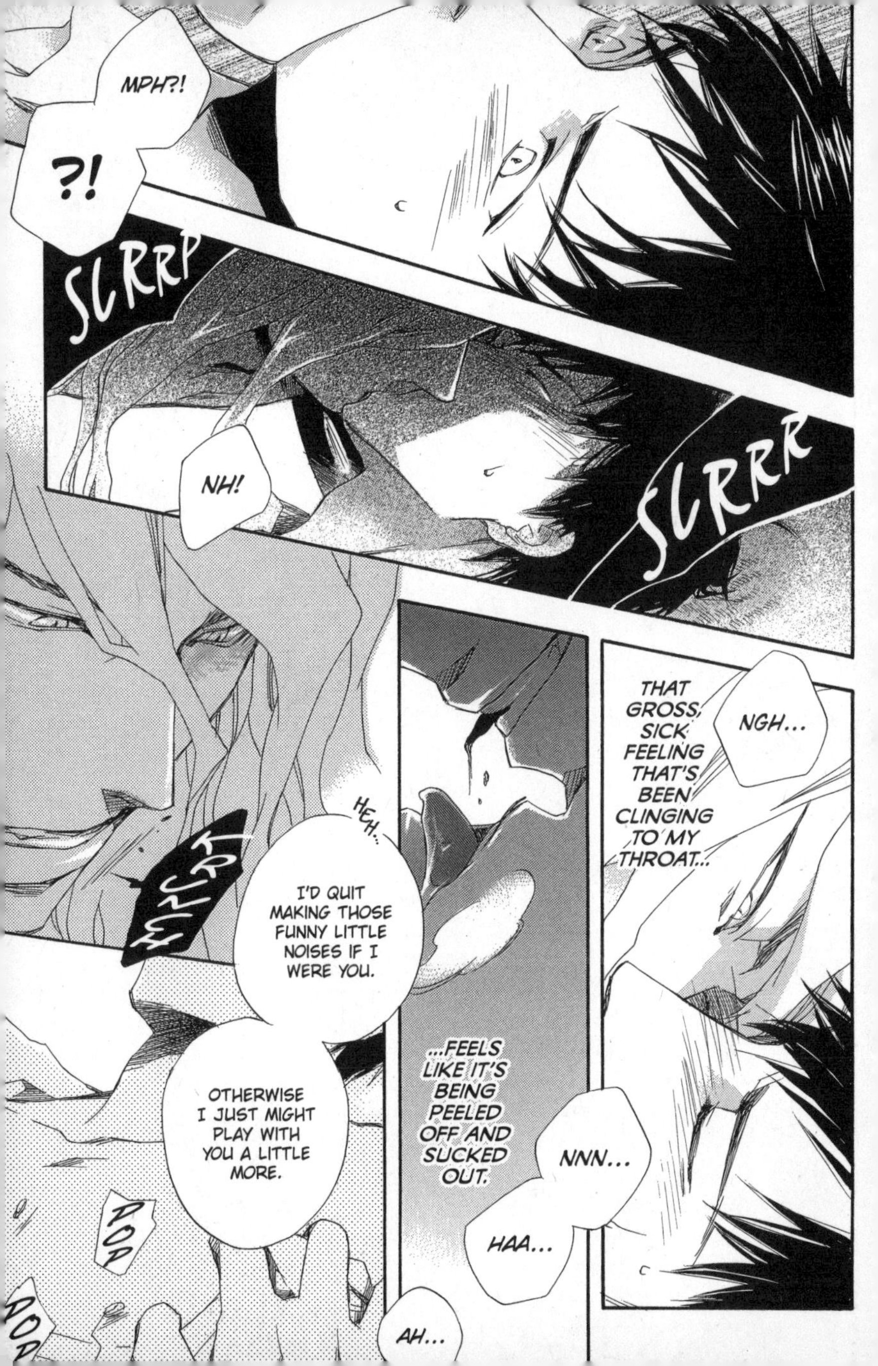
MPH?!
?!
SLRRP
NH!
SLRRR
THAT GROSS, SICK FEELING THAT'S BEEN CLINGING TO MY THROAT...
NGH...
NNN...
HAA...
...FEELS LIKE IT'S BEING PEELED OFF AND SUCKED OUT.
AH...
HEH...
I'D QUIT MAKING THOSE FUNNY LITTLE NOISES IF I WERE YOU.
KRUNCH
OTHERWISE I JUST MIGHT PLAY WITH YOU A LITTLE MORE.
POP
POP

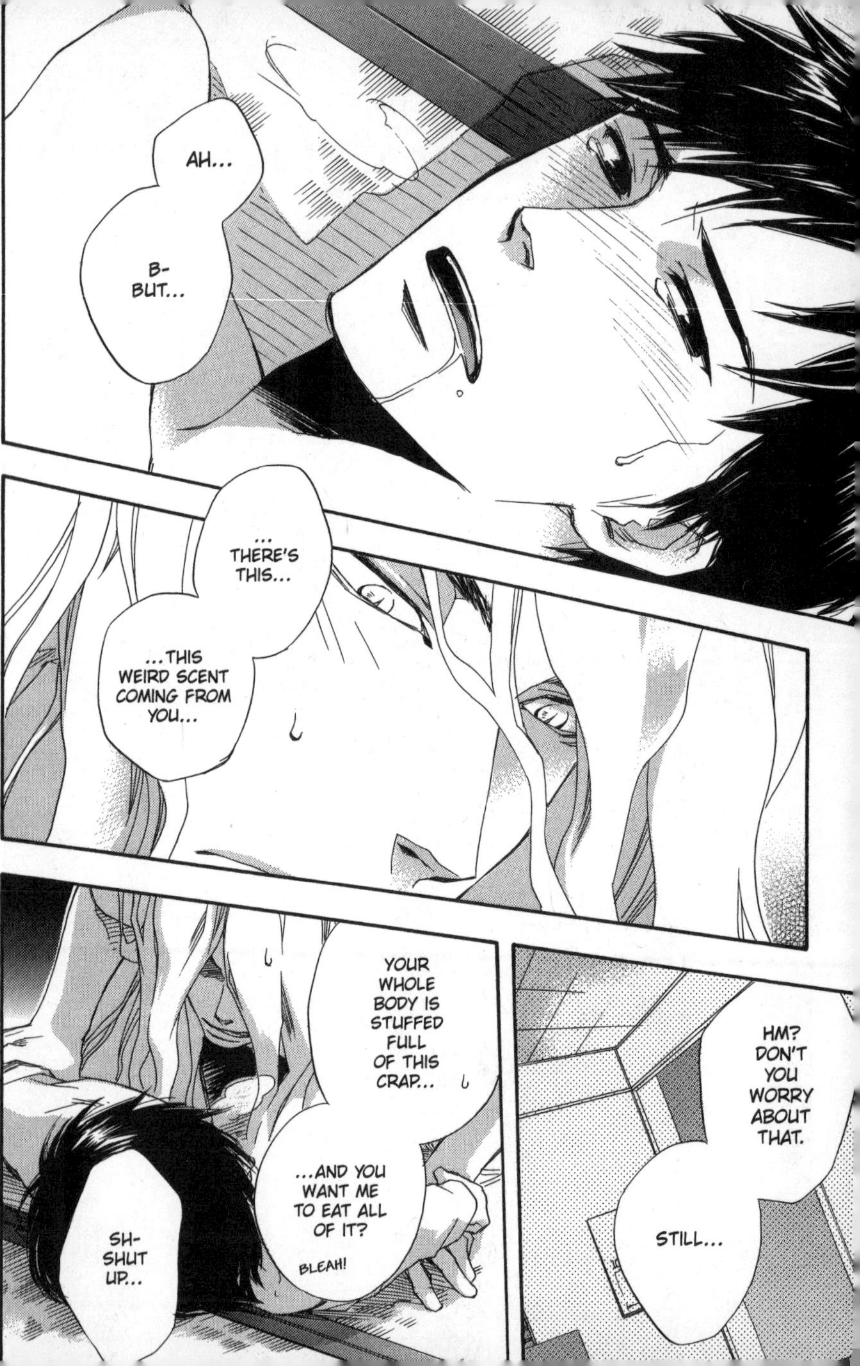
AH...
B- BUT...
... THERE'S THIS...
...THIS WEIRD SCENT COMING FROM YOU...
HM? DON'T YOU WORRY ABOUT THAT.
STILL...
YOUR WHOLE BODY IS STUFFED FULL OF THIS CRAP...
...AND YOU WANT ME TO EAT ALL OF IT?
BLEAH!
SH- SHUT UP...

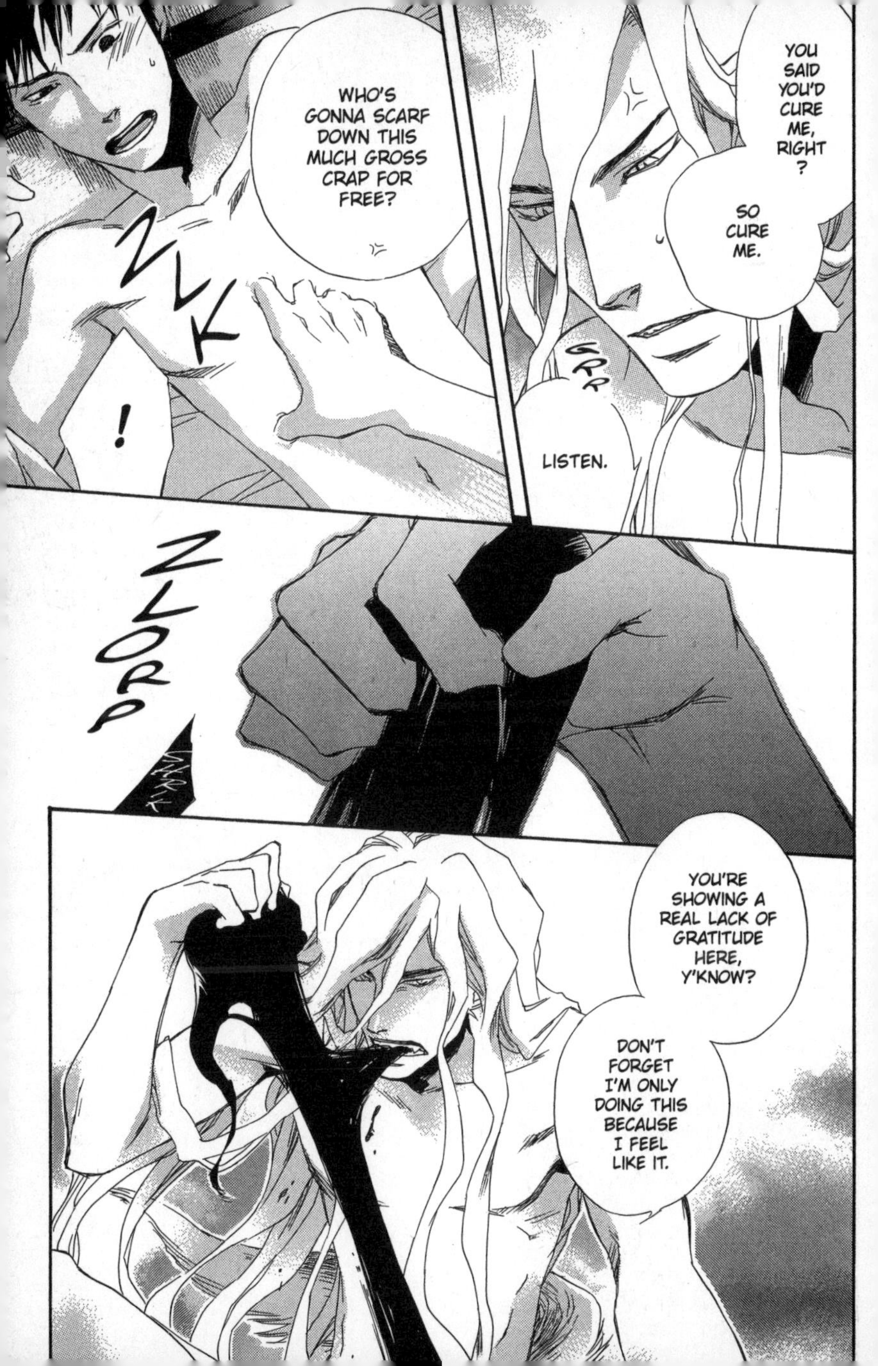
YOU SAID YOU'D CURE ME, RIGHT?
SO CURE ME.
GRR
LISTEN.
WHO'S GONNA SCARF DOWN THIS MUCH GROSS CRAP FOR FREE?
ZLLK
!
ZLORP
YOU'RE SHOWING A REAL LACK OF GRATITUDE HERE, Y'KNOW?
DON'T FORGET I'M ONLY DOING THIS BECAUSE I FEEL LIKE IT.

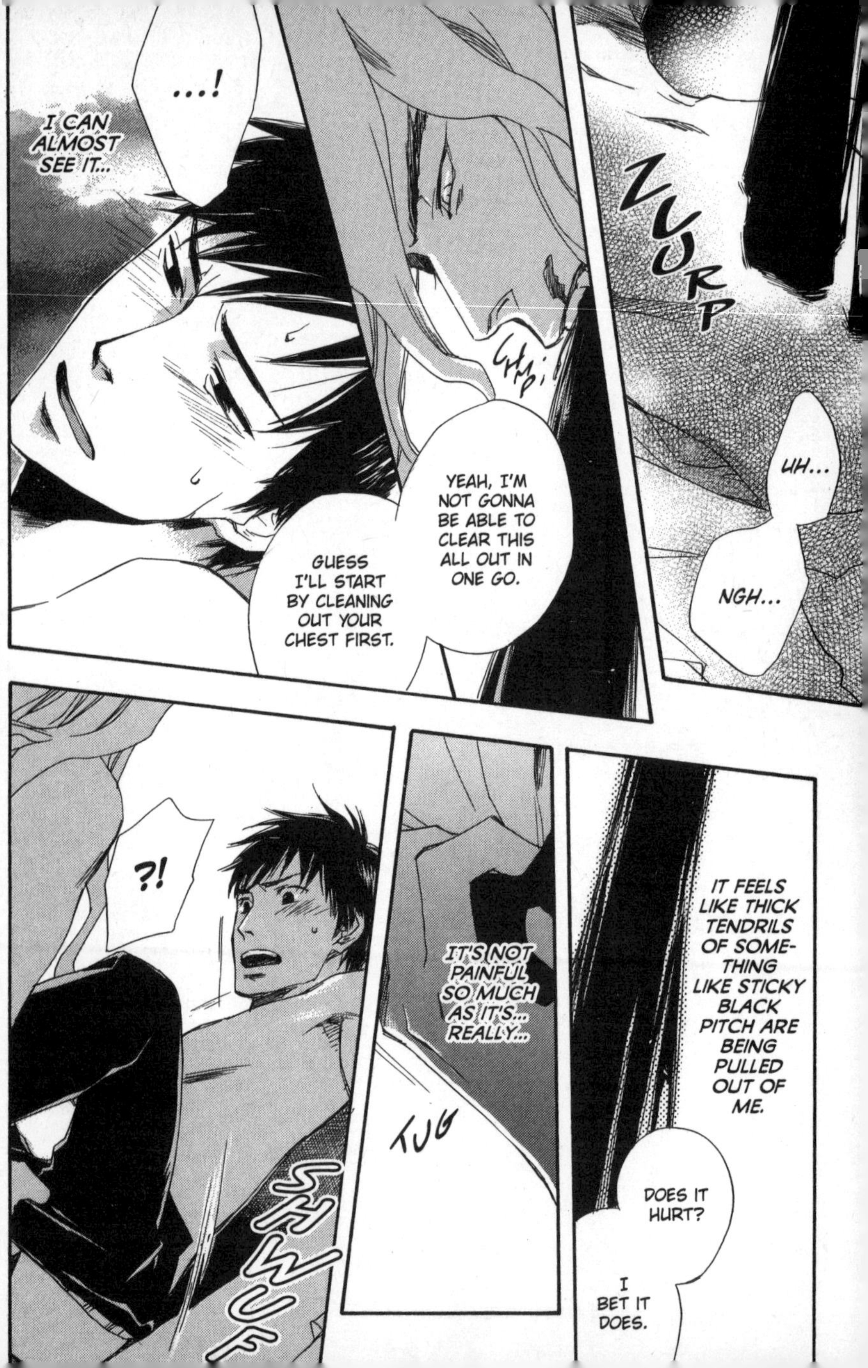
ZUURP
UH...
NGH...
YEAH, I'M NOT GONNA BE ABLE TO CLEAR THIS ALL OUT IN ONE GO.
GUESS I'LL START BY CLEANING OUT YOUR CHEST FIRST.
...!
I CAN ALMOST SEE IT...
IT FEELS LIKE THICK TENDRILS OF SOME-THING LIKE STICKY BLACK PITCH ARE BEING PULLED OUT OF ME.
DOES IT HURT?
I BET IT DOES.
IT'S NOT PAINFUL SO MUCH AS IT'S... REALLY...
TUG
?!
SHWUF

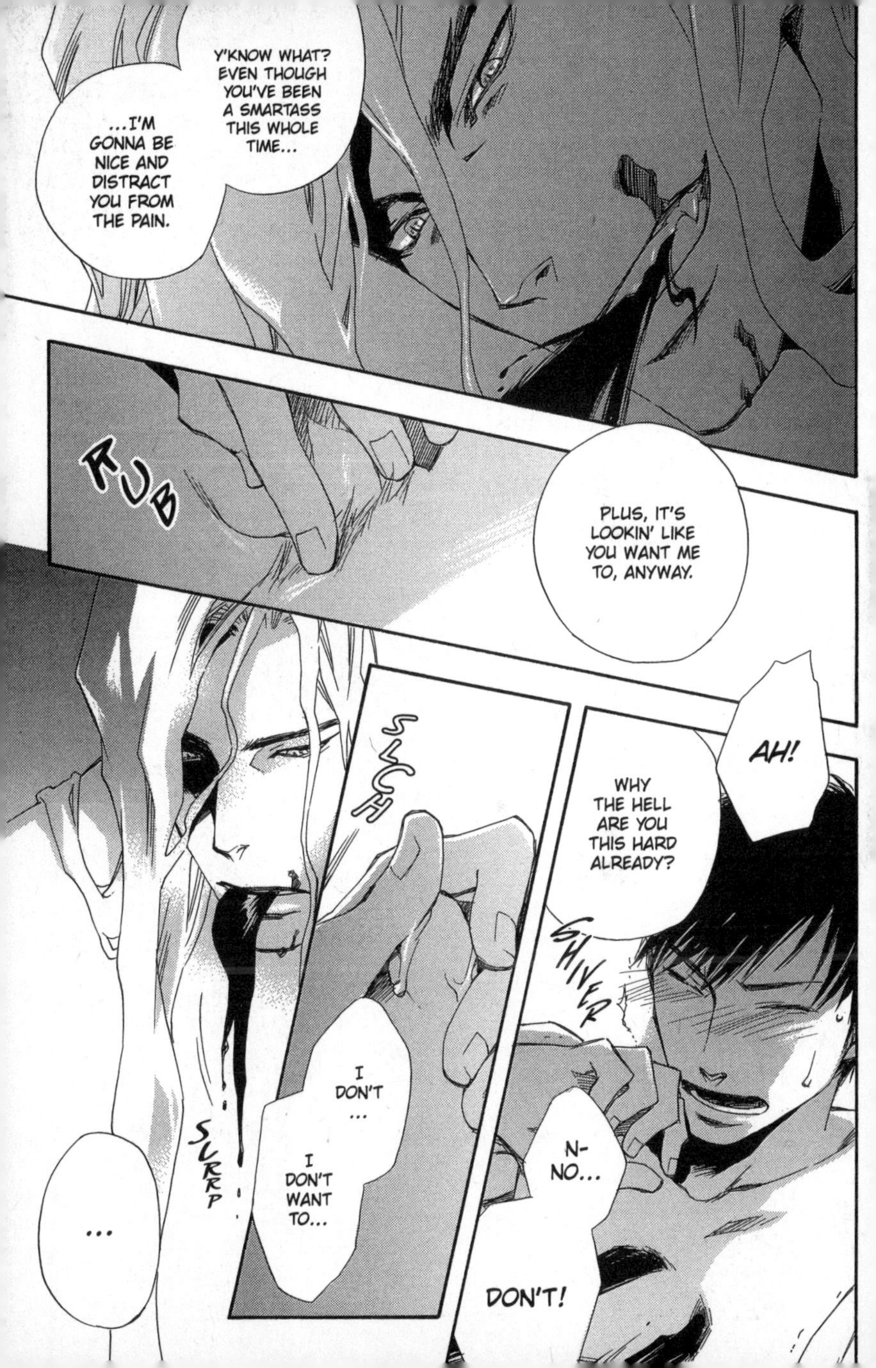
Y'KNOW WHAT? EVEN THOUGH YOU'VE BEEN A SMARTASS THIS WHOLE TIME...
...I'M GONNA BE NICE AND DISTRACT YOU FROM THE PAIN.
PLUS, IT'S LOOKIN' LIKE YOU WANT ME TO, ANYWAY.
RUB
AH!
WHY THE HELL ARE YOU THIS HARD ALREADY?
SHIVER
N-NO...
DON'T!
SLCH
I DON'T...
I DON'T WANT TO...
SURRP
...

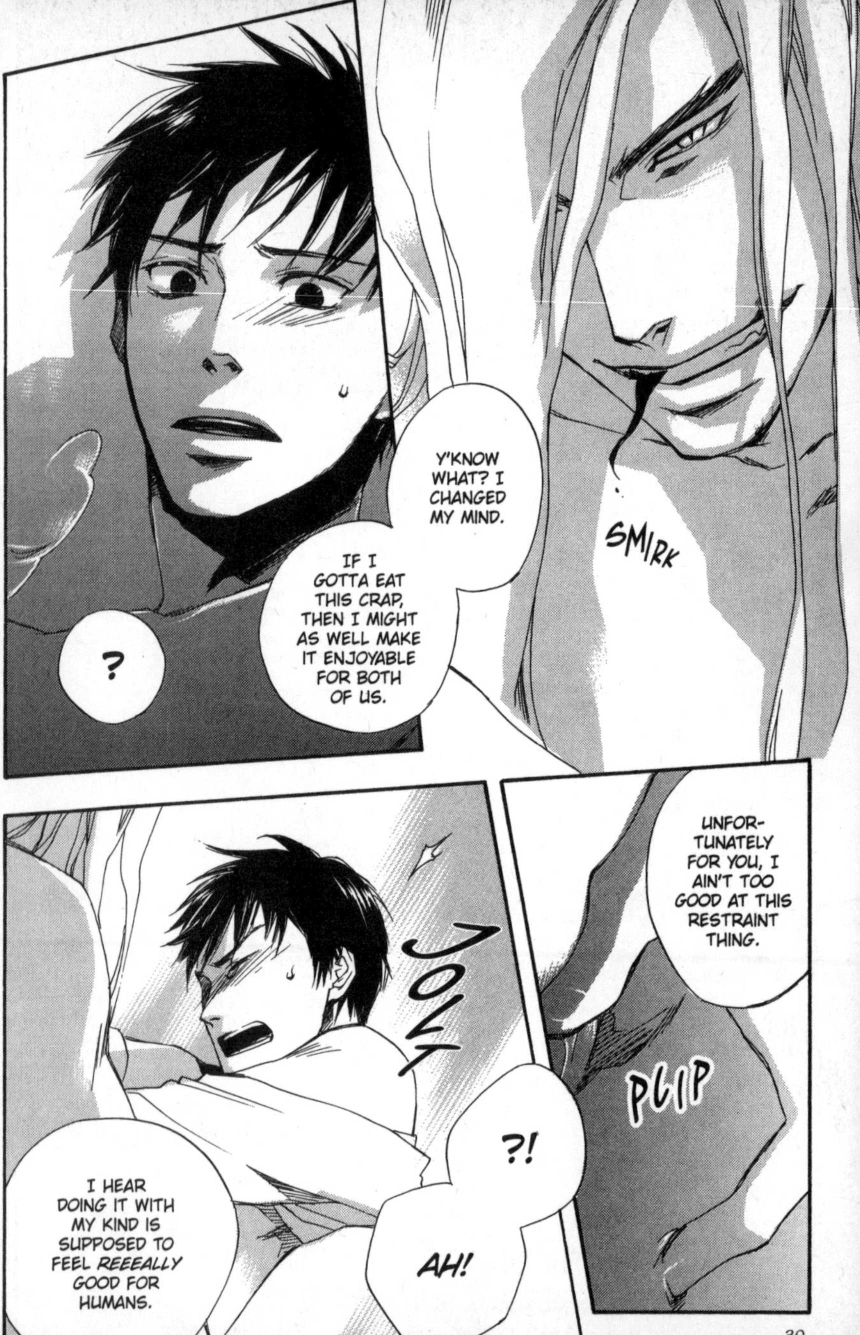
Y'KNOW WHAT? I CHANGED MY MIND.
SMIRK
IF I GOTTA EAT THIS CRAP, THEN I MIGHT AS WELL MAKE IT ENJOYABLE FOR BOTH OF US.
?
UNFORTUNATELY FOR YOU, I AIN'T TOO GOOD AT THIS RESTRAINT THING.
PLIP
JOLT
?!
AH!
I HEAR DOING IT WITH MY KIND IS SUPPOSED TO FEEL *REEEALLY* GOOD FOR HUMANS.

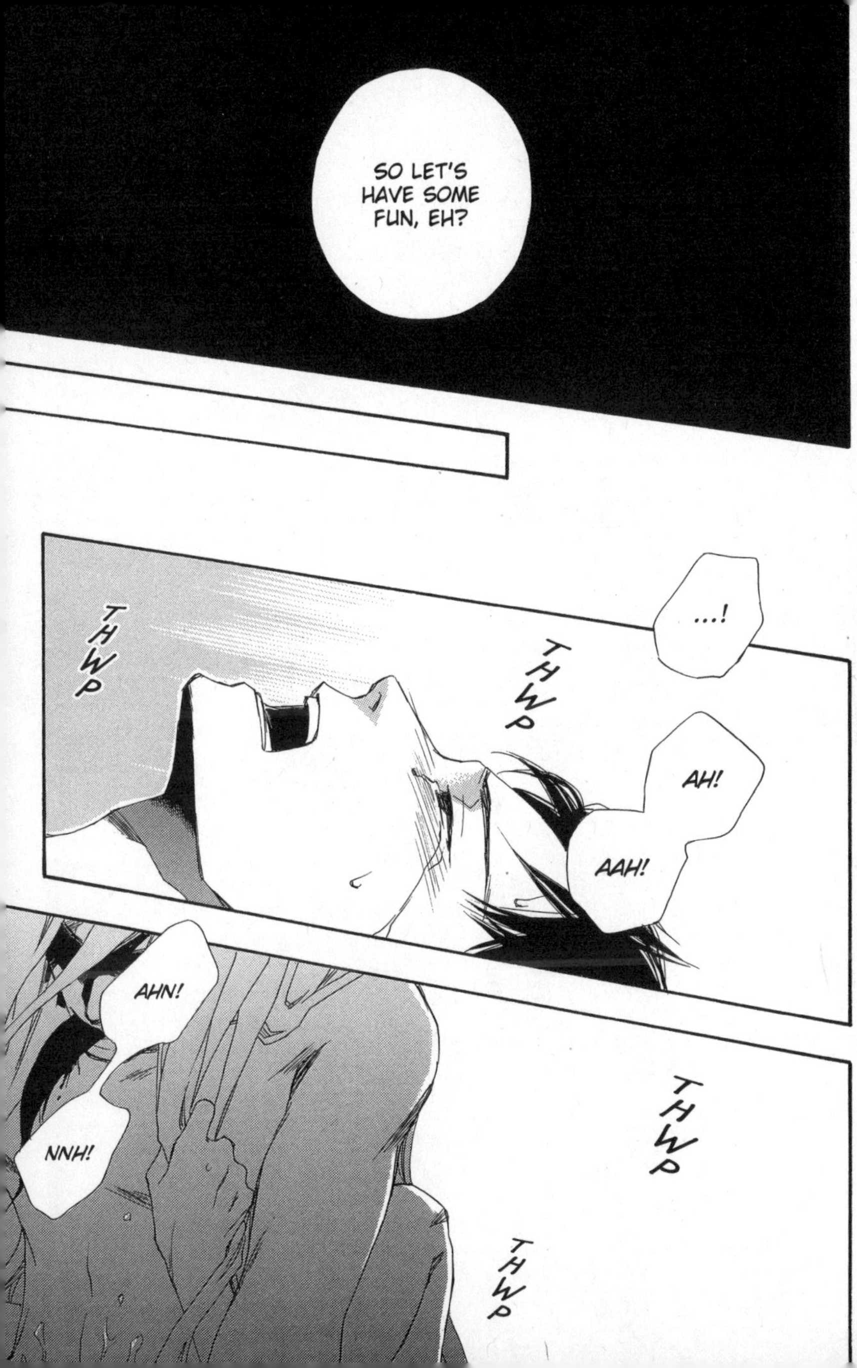
SO LET'S HAVE SOME FUN, EH?
...!
THWP
AH!
AAH!
THWP
THWP
THWP
AHN!
NNH!

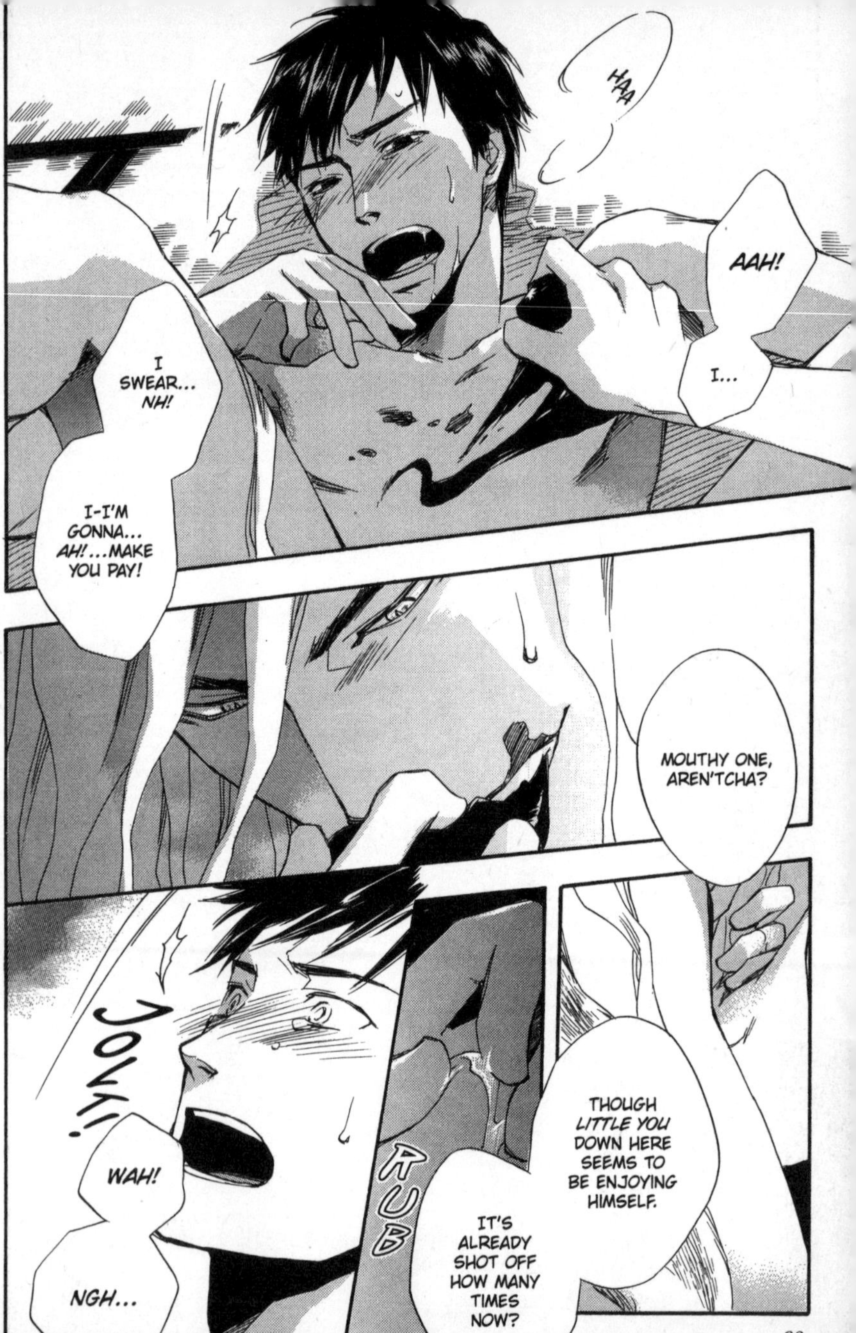
HAA
AAH!
I...
I SWEAR... NH!
I-I'M GONNA... AH!...MAKE YOU PAY!
MOUTHY ONE, AREN'TCHA?
THOUGH LITTLE YOU DOWN HERE SEEMS TO BE ENJOYING HIMSELF.
RUB
IT'S ALREADY SHOT OFF HOW MANY TIMES NOW?
JOLT!!
WAH!
NGH...

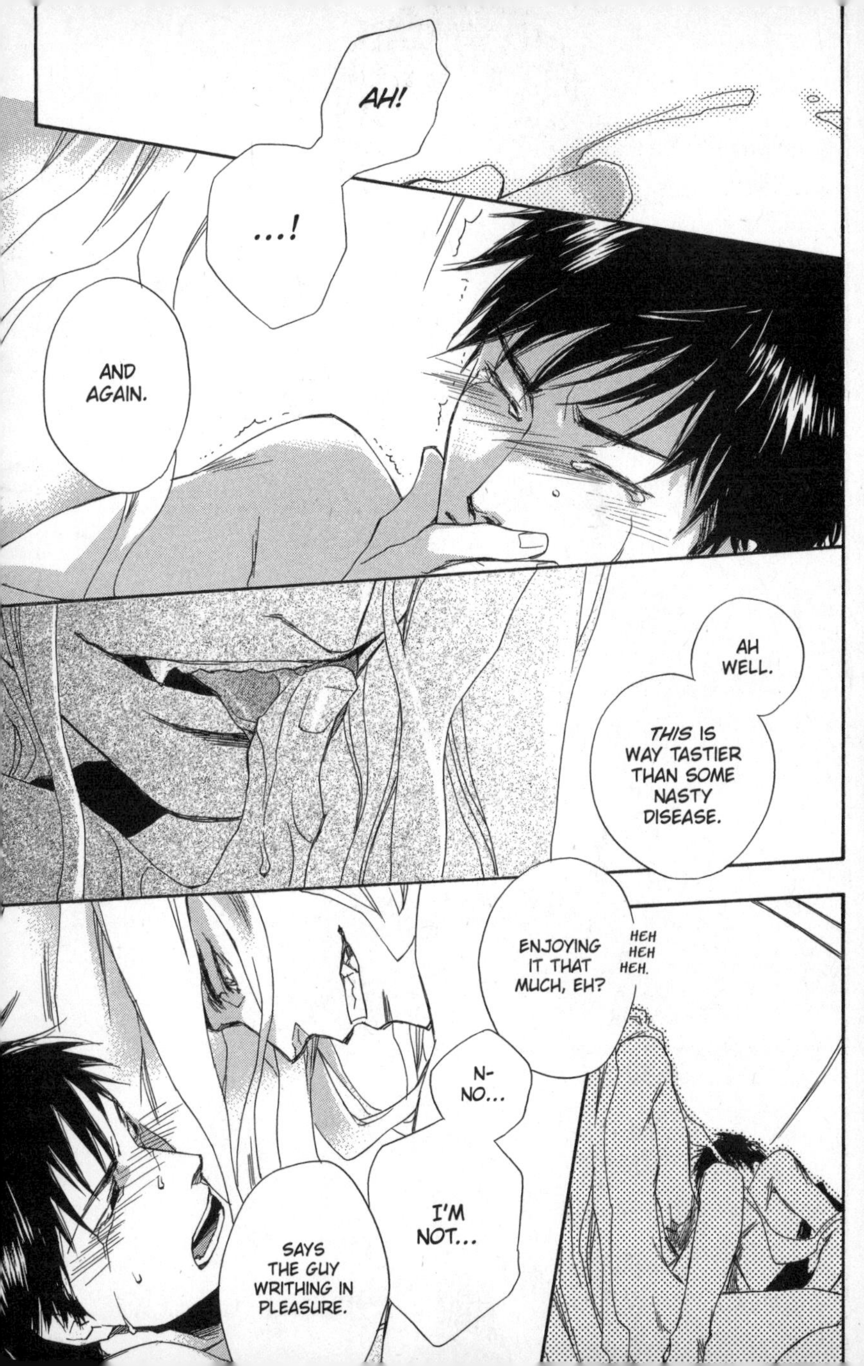
AH!
...!
AND AGAIN.
AH WELL.
THIS IS WAY TASTIER THAN SOME NASTY DISEASE.
HEH HEH HEH.
ENJOYING IT THAT MUCH, EH?
N- NO...
I'M NOT...
SAYS THE GUY WRITHING IN PLEASURE.

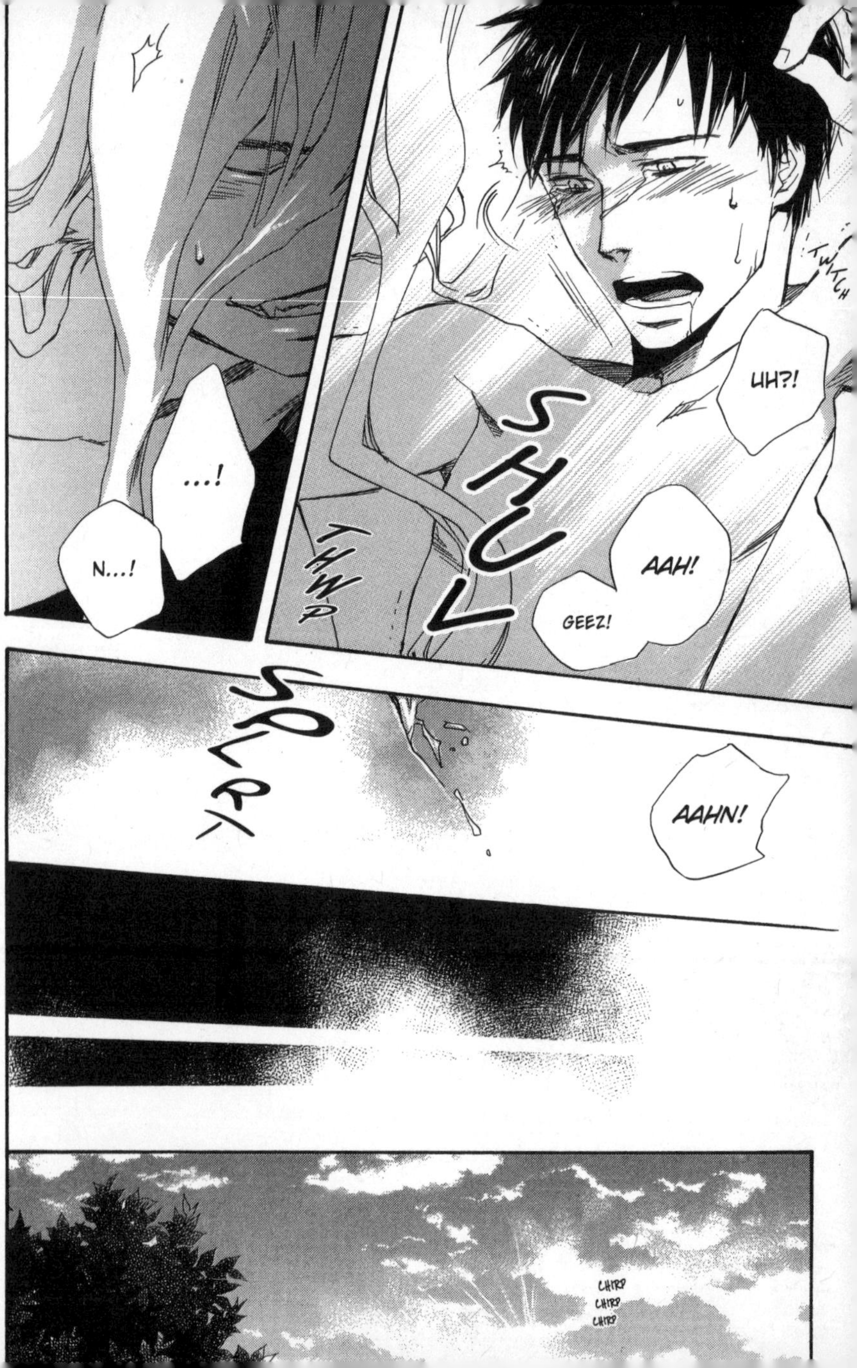
TWITCH
UH?!
SHUV
AAH!
GEEZ!
THWP
...!
N...!
SPLRT
AAHN!
CHIRP
CHIRP
CHIRP

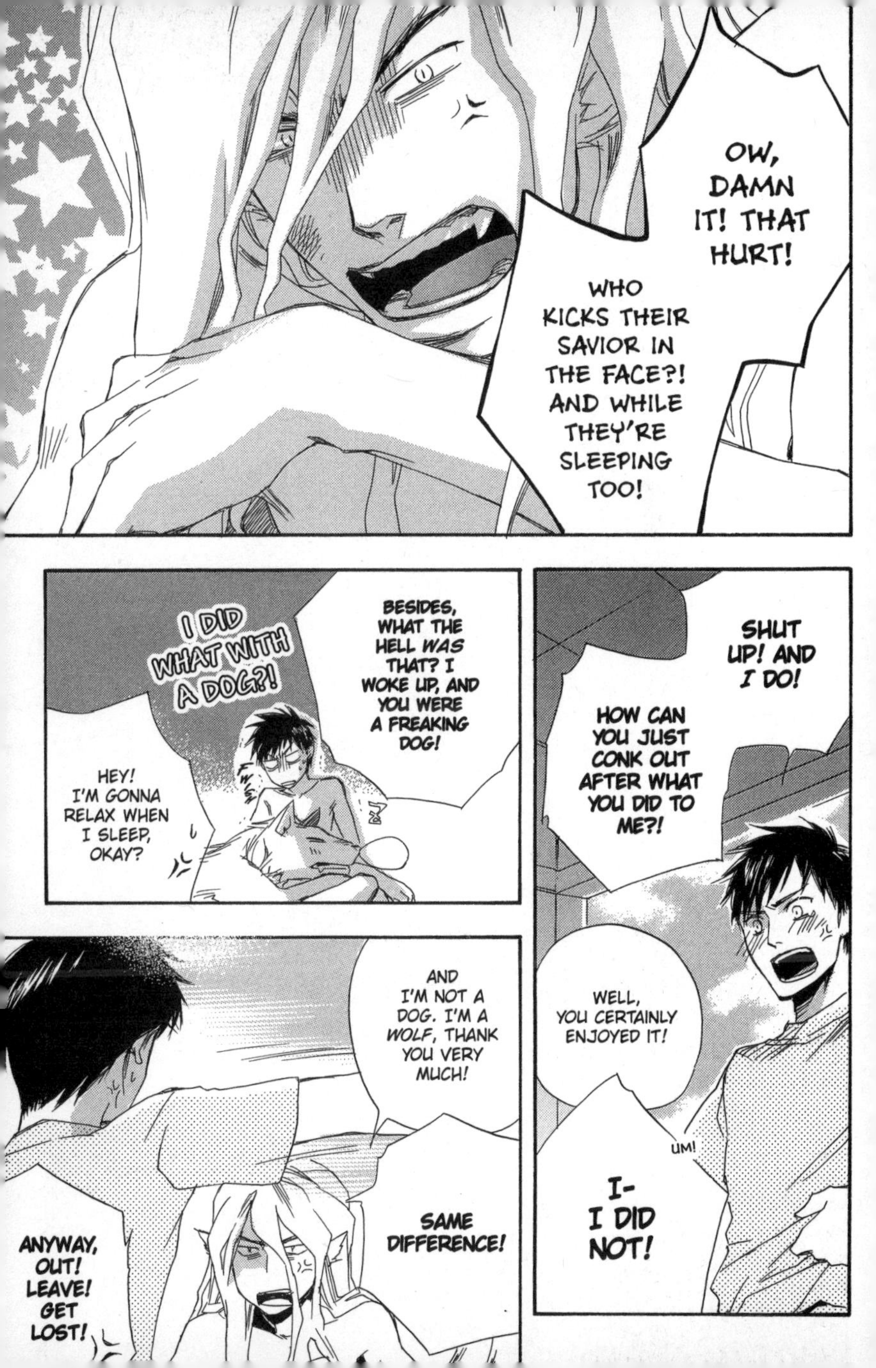
OW, DAMN IT! THAT HURT!
WHO KICKS THEIR SAVIOR IN THE FACE?! AND WHILE THEY'RE SLEEPING TOO!
SHUT UP! AND *I DO!*
HOW CAN YOU JUST CONK OUT AFTER WHAT YOU DID TO ME?!
WELL, YOU CERTAINLY ENJOYED IT!
UM!
I- I DID NOT!
BESIDES, WHAT THE HELL *WAS* THAT? I WOKE UP, AND YOU WERE A FREAKING DOG!
I DID WHAT WITH A DOG?!
HEY! I'M GONNA RELAX WHEN I SLEEP, OKAY?
AND I'M NOT A DOG. I'M A *WOLF*, THANK YOU VERY MUCH!
SAME DIFFERENCE!
ANYWAY, OUT! LEAVE! GET LOST!

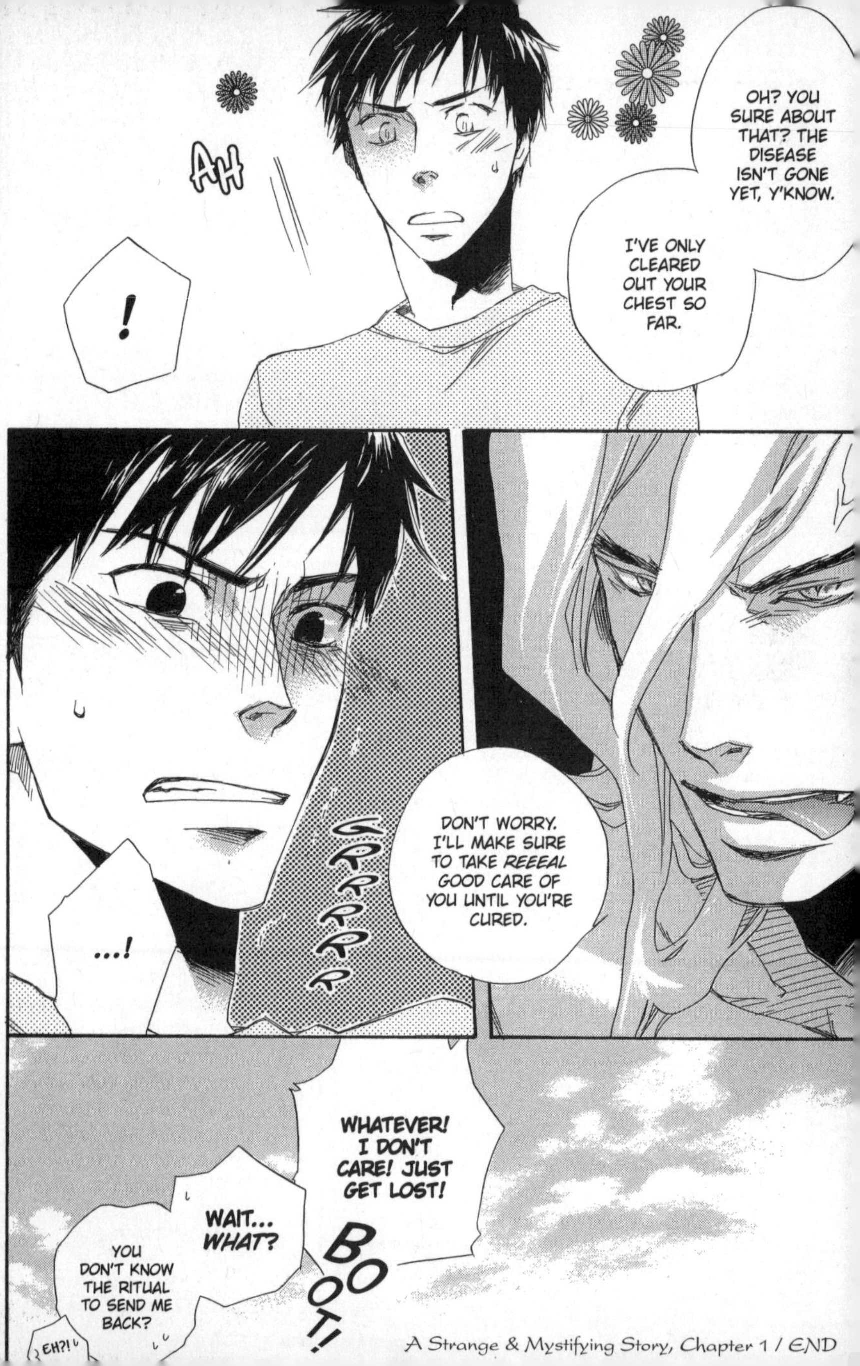
OH? YOU SURE ABOUT THAT? THE DISEASE ISN'T GONE YET, Y'KNOW.
I'VE ONLY CLEARED OUT YOUR CHEST SO FAR.
AH
!
DON'T WORRY. I'LL MAKE SURE TO TAKE *REEEAL* GOOD CARE OF YOU UNTIL YOU'RE CURED.
GRRRRRR
...!
WHATEVER! I DON'T CARE! JUST GET LOST!
BOOT!
WAIT... WHAT?
YOU DON'T KNOW THE RITUAL TO SEND ME BACK?
EH?!

A Strange & Mystifying Story, Chapter 1 / END

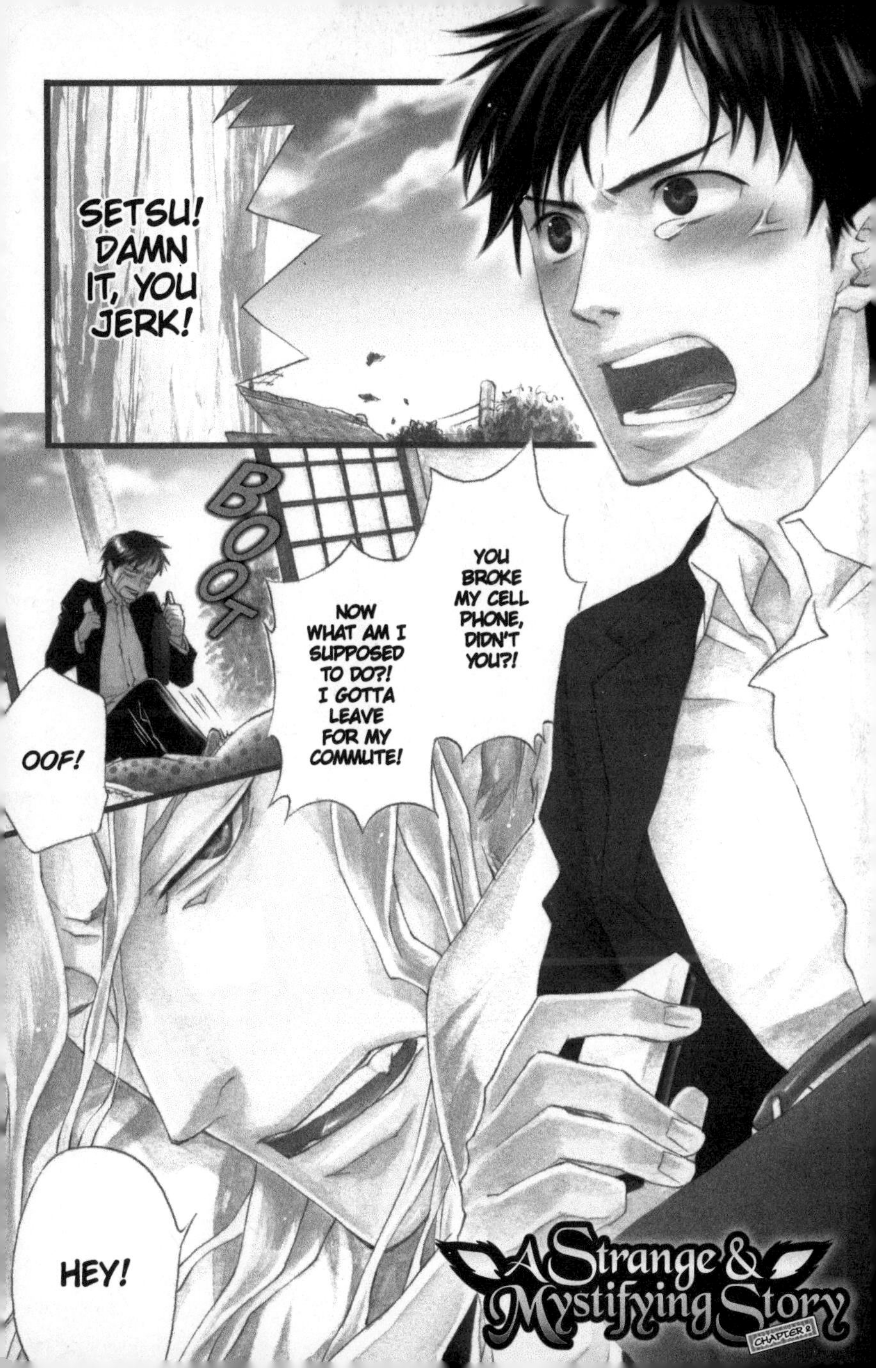
SETSU! DAMN IT, YOU JERK!
YOU BROKE MY CELL PHONE, DIDN'T YOU?!
NOW WHAT AM I SUPPOSED TO DO?! I GOTTA LEAVE FOR MY COMMUTE!
BOOT
OOF!
HEY!
A Strange & Mystifying Story
CHAPTER 2

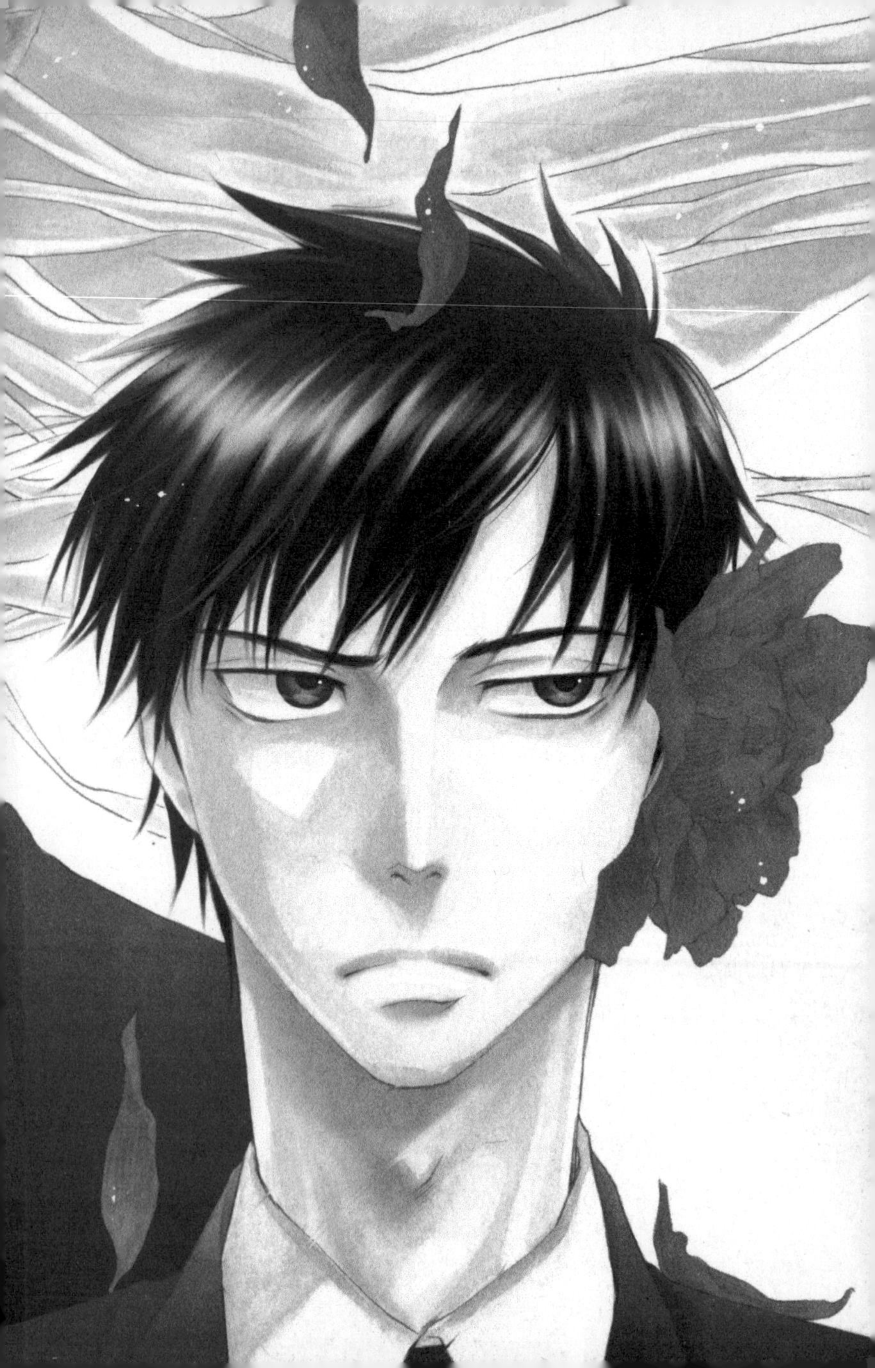

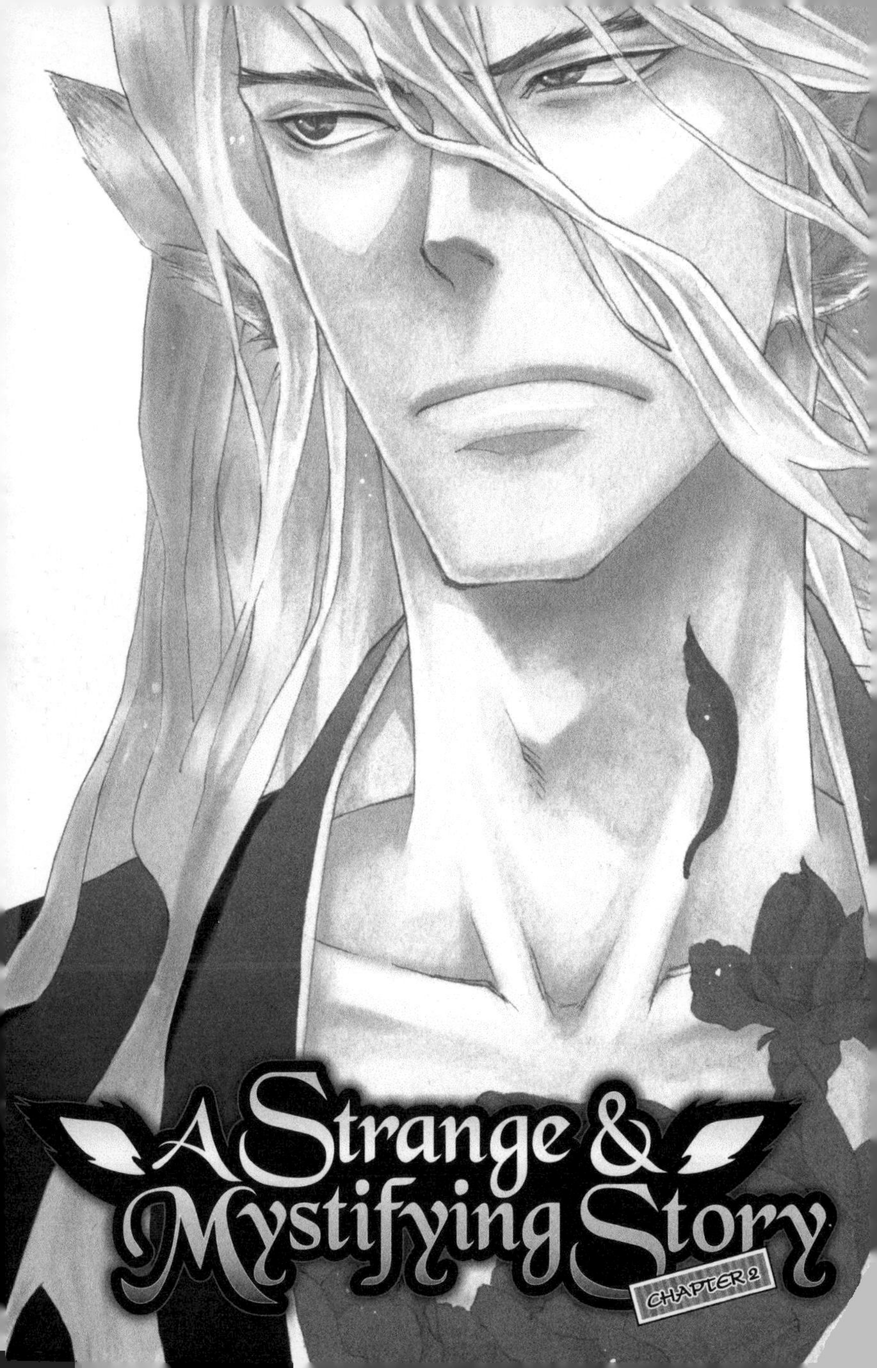
A Strange & Mystifying Story
CHAPTER 2

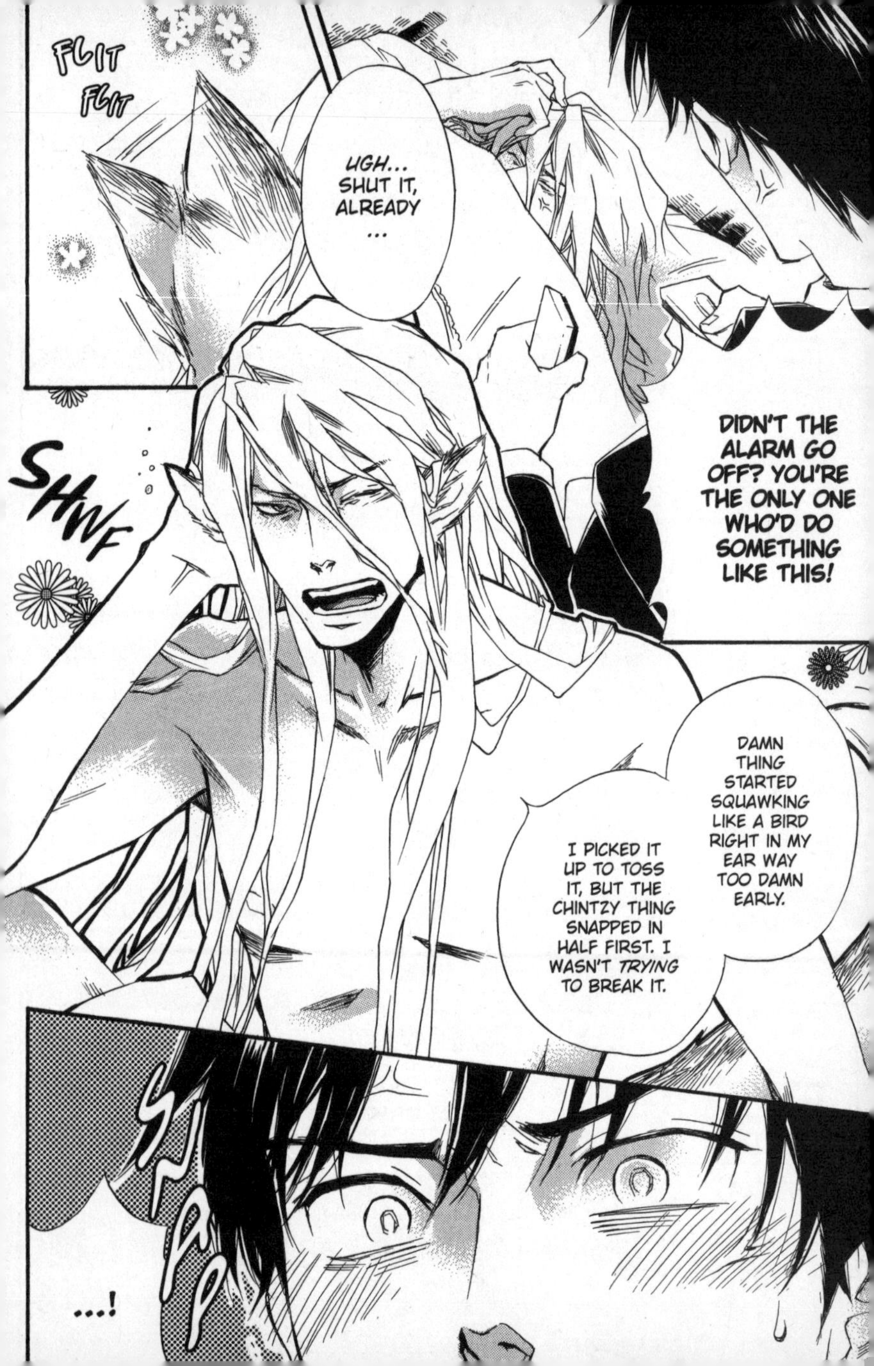

UGH... SHUT IT, ALREADY ...
FLIT FLIT
DIDN'T THE ALARM GO OFF? YOU'RE THE ONLY ONE WHO'D DO SOMETHING LIKE THIS!
SHWF
DAMN THING STARTED SQUAWKING LIKE A BIRD RIGHT IN MY EAR WAY TOO DAMN EARLY.
I PICKED IT UP TO TOSS IT, BUT THE CHINTZY THING SNAPPED IN HALF FIRST. I WASN'T *TRYING* TO BREAK IT.
...!

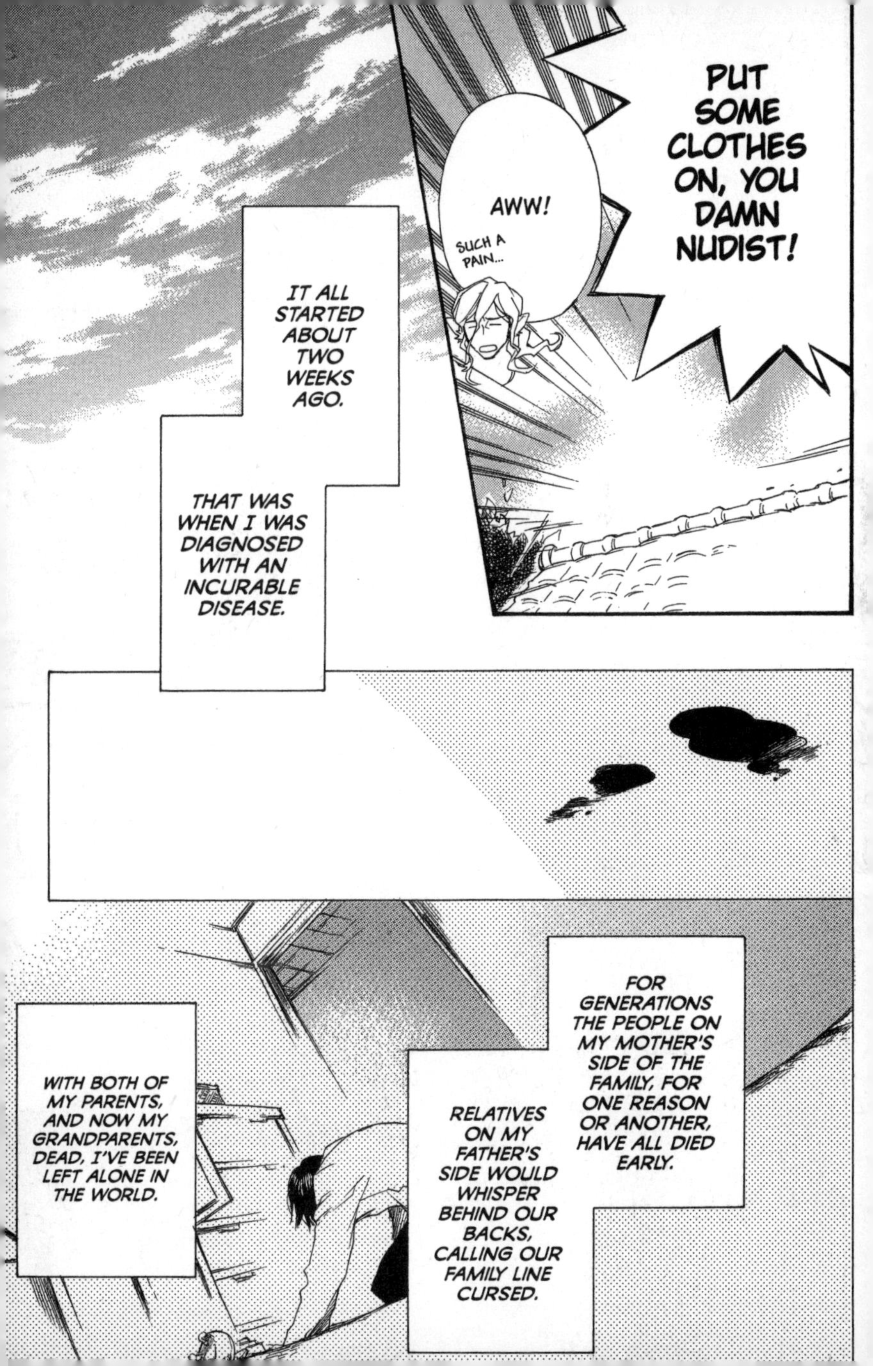
PUT SOME CLOTHES ON, YOU DAMN NUDIST!
AWW!
SUCH A PAIN...
IT ALL STARTED ABOUT TWO WEEKS AGO.
THAT WAS WHEN I WAS DIAGNOSED WITH AN INCURABLE DISEASE.
FOR GENERATIONS THE PEOPLE ON MY MOTHER'S SIDE OF THE FAMILY, FOR ONE REASON OR ANOTHER, HAVE ALL DIED EARLY.
RELATIVES ON MY FATHER'S SIDE WOULD WHISPER BEHIND OUR BACKS, CALLING OUR FAMILY LINE CURSED.
WITH BOTH OF MY PARENTS, AND NOW MY GRANDPARENTS, DEAD, I'VE BEEN LEFT ALONE IN THE WORLD.

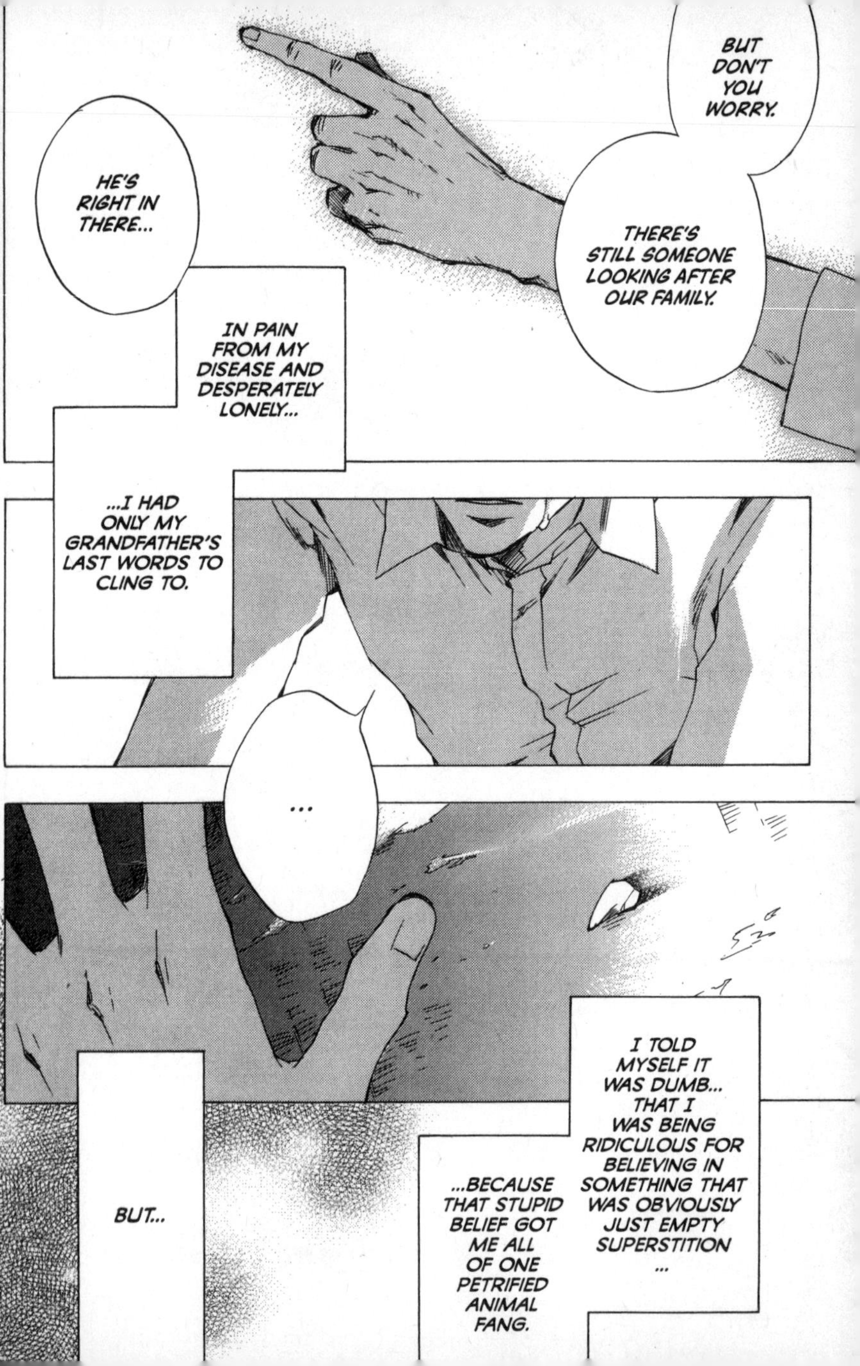
BUT DON'T YOU WORRY.
THERE'S STILL SOMEONE LOOKING AFTER OUR FAMILY.
HE'S RIGHT IN THERE...
IN PAIN FROM MY DISEASE AND DESPERATELY LONELY...
...I HAD ONLY MY GRANDFATHER'S LAST WORDS TO CLING TO.
...
I TOLD MYSELF IT WAS DUMB... THAT I WAS BEING RIDICULOUS FOR BELIEVING IN SOMETHING THAT WAS OBVIOUSLY JUST EMPTY SUPERSTITION ...
...BECAUSE THAT STUPID BELIEF GOT ME ALL OF ONE PETRIFIED ANIMAL FANG.
BUT...

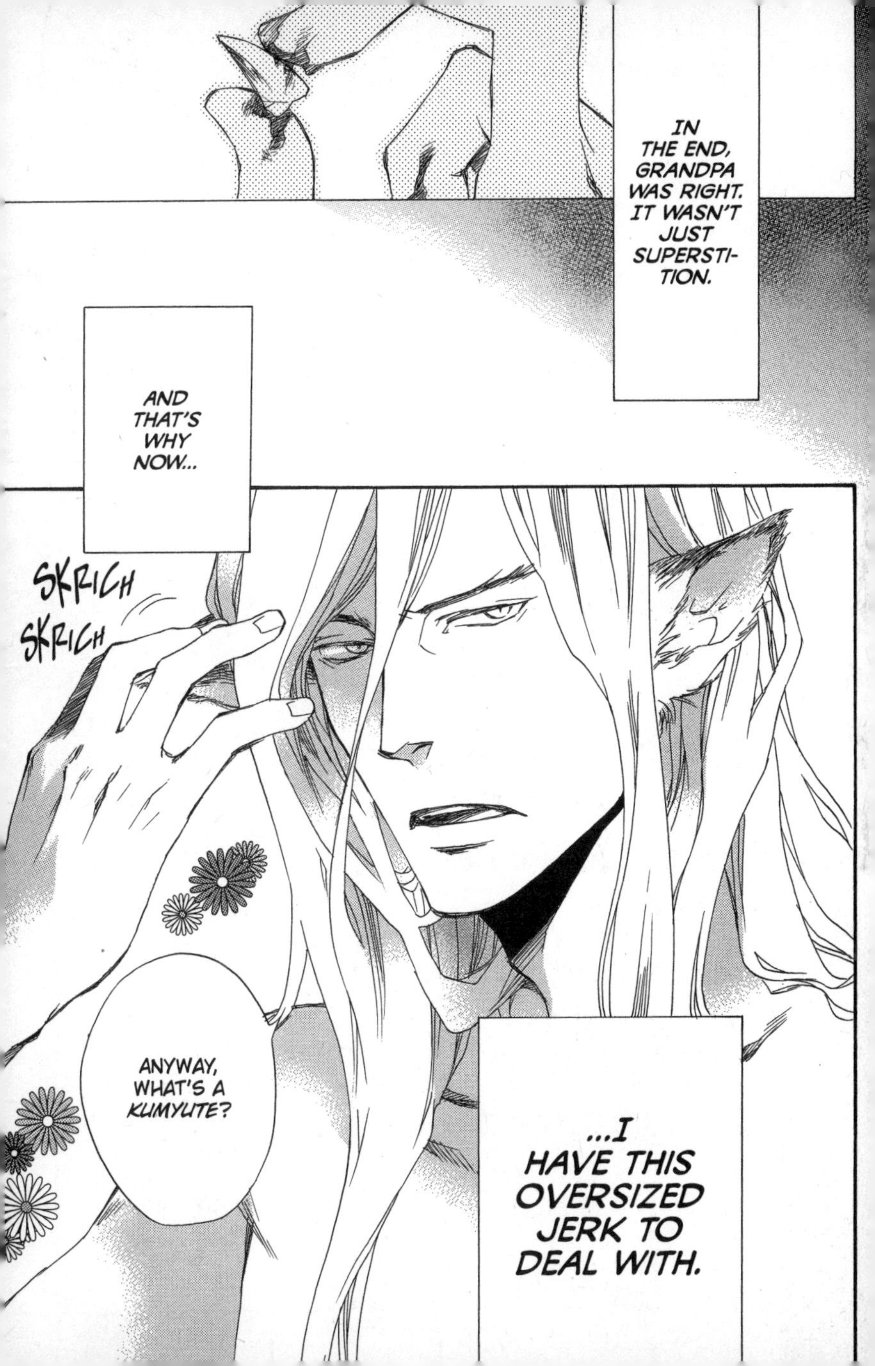
IN THE END, GRANDPA WAS RIGHT. IT WASN'T JUST SUPERSTITION.
AND THAT'S WHY NOW...
SKRICH SKRICH
...I HAVE THIS OVERSIZED JERK TO DEAL WITH.
ANYWAY, WHAT'S A KUMYUTE?

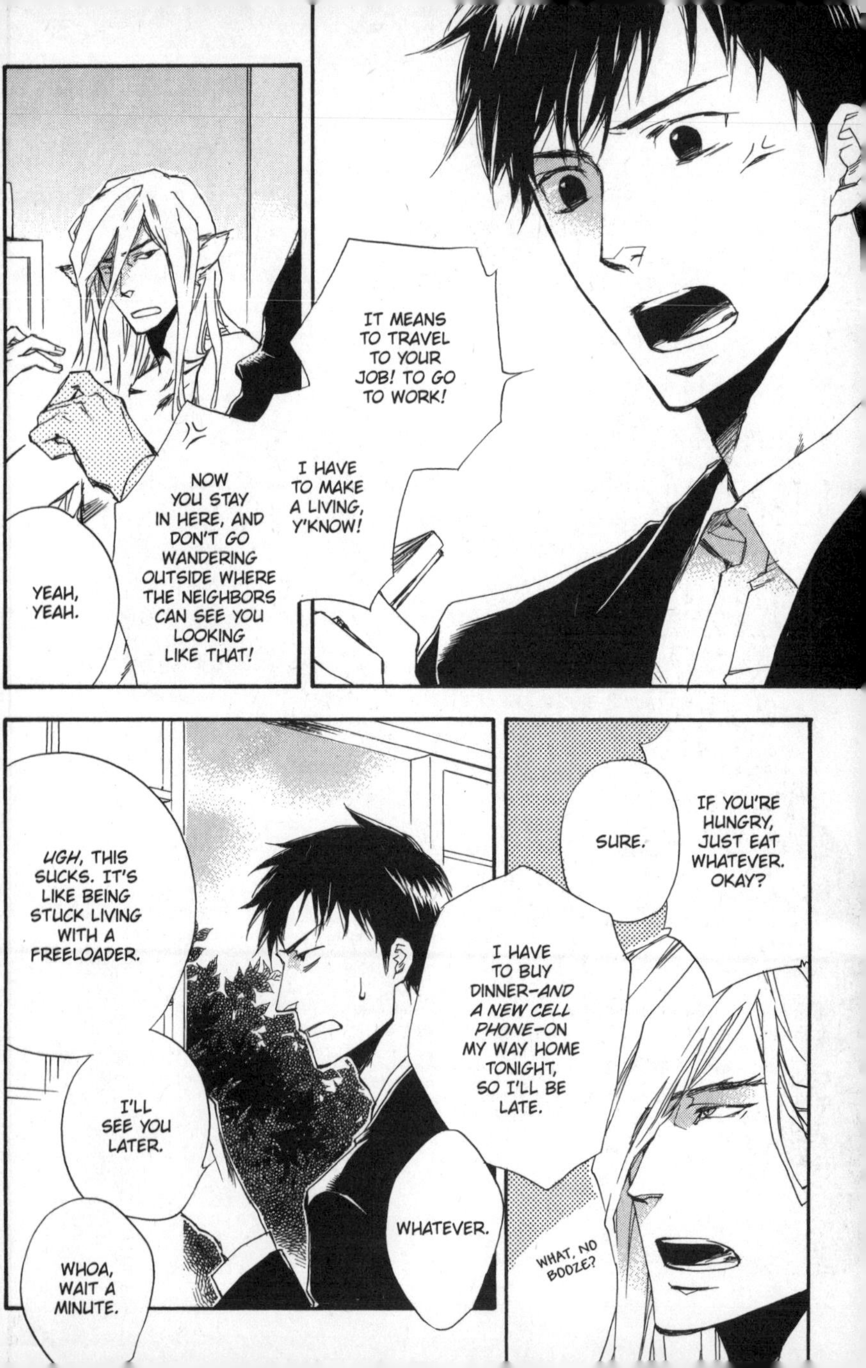
IT MEANS TO TRAVEL TO YOUR JOB! TO GO TO WORK!
I HAVE TO MAKE A LIVING, Y'KNOW!
NOW YOU STAY IN HERE, AND DON'T GO WANDERING OUTSIDE WHERE THE NEIGHBORS CAN SEE YOU LOOKING LIKE THAT!
YEAH, YEAH.
IF YOU'RE HUNGRY, JUST EAT WHATEVER. OKAY?
SURE.
I HAVE TO BUY DINNER–*AND A NEW CELL PHONE*–ON MY WAY HOME TONIGHT, SO I'LL BE LATE.
WHAT, NO BOOZE?
WHATEVER.
UGH, THIS SUCKS. IT'S LIKE BEING STUCK LIVING WITH A FREELOADER.
I'LL SEE YOU LATER.
WHOA, WAIT A MINUTE.

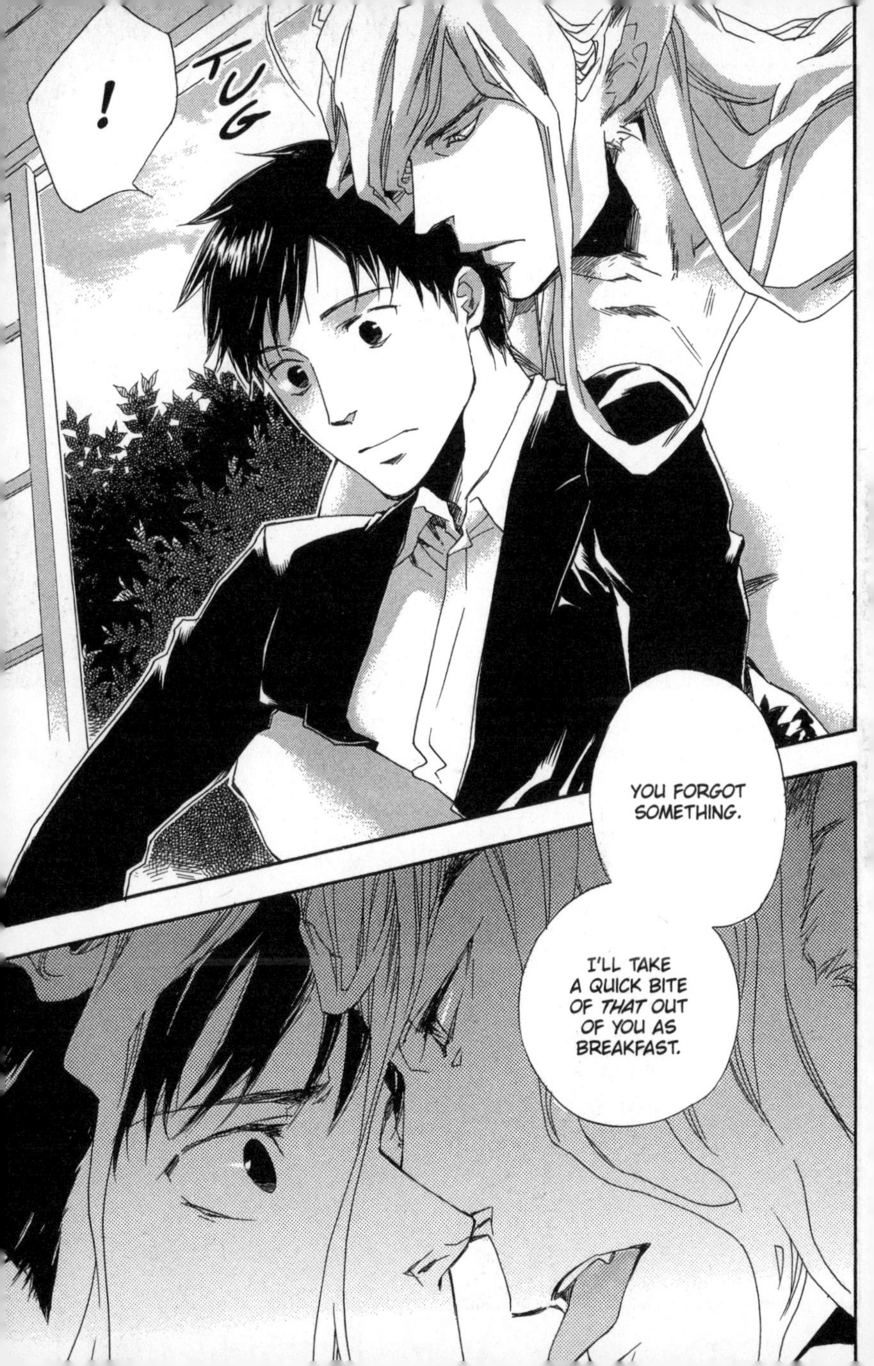
!
TUG
YOU FORGOT SOMETHING.
I'LL TAKE A QUICK BITE OF *THAT* OUT OF YOU AS BREAKFAST.

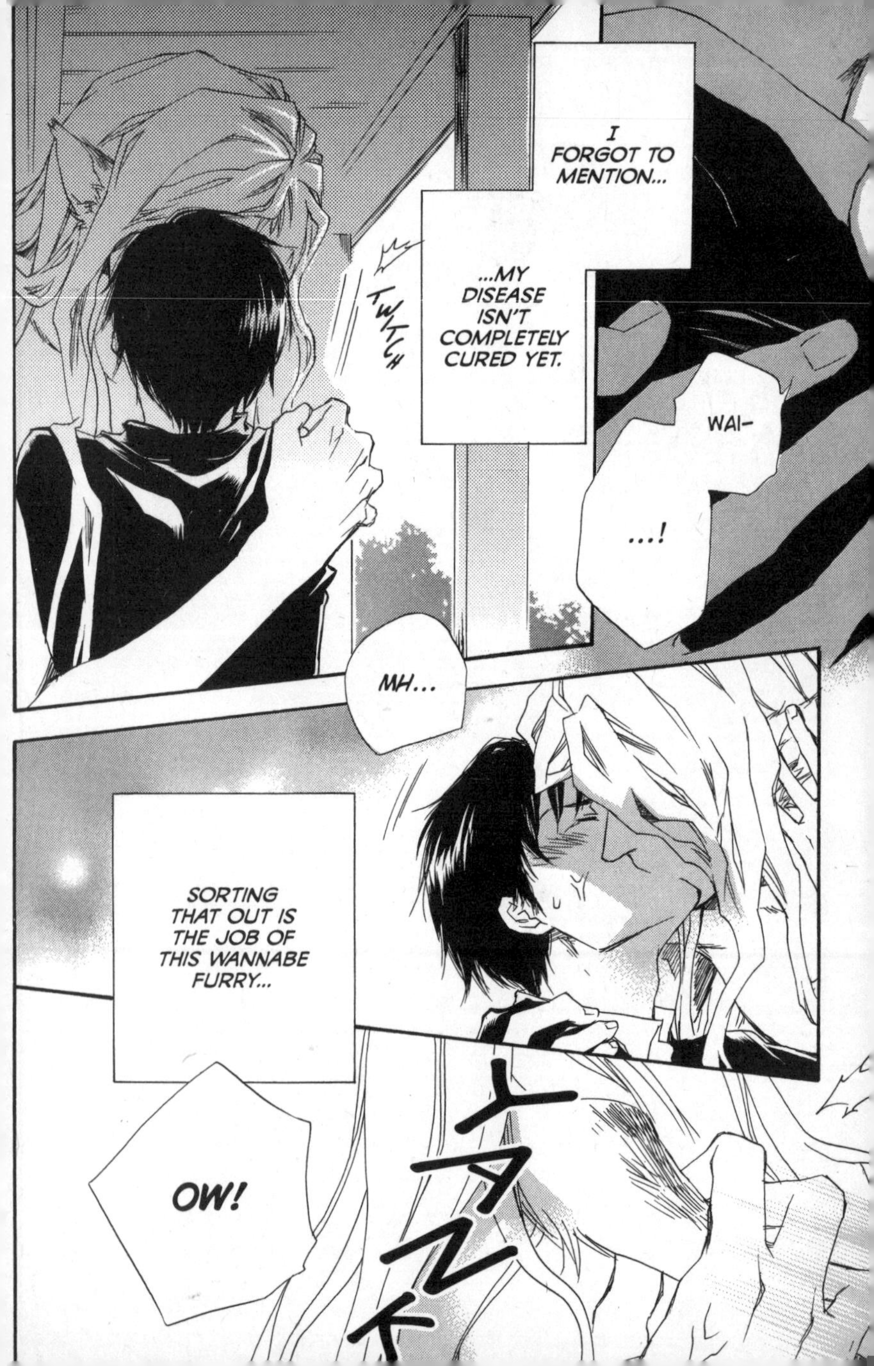
I FORGOT TO MENTION...
...MY DISEASE ISN'T COMPLETELY CURED YET.
WAI-
...!
TWITCH
MH...
SORTING THAT OUT IS THE JOB OF THIS WANNABE FURRY...
OW!
YANK

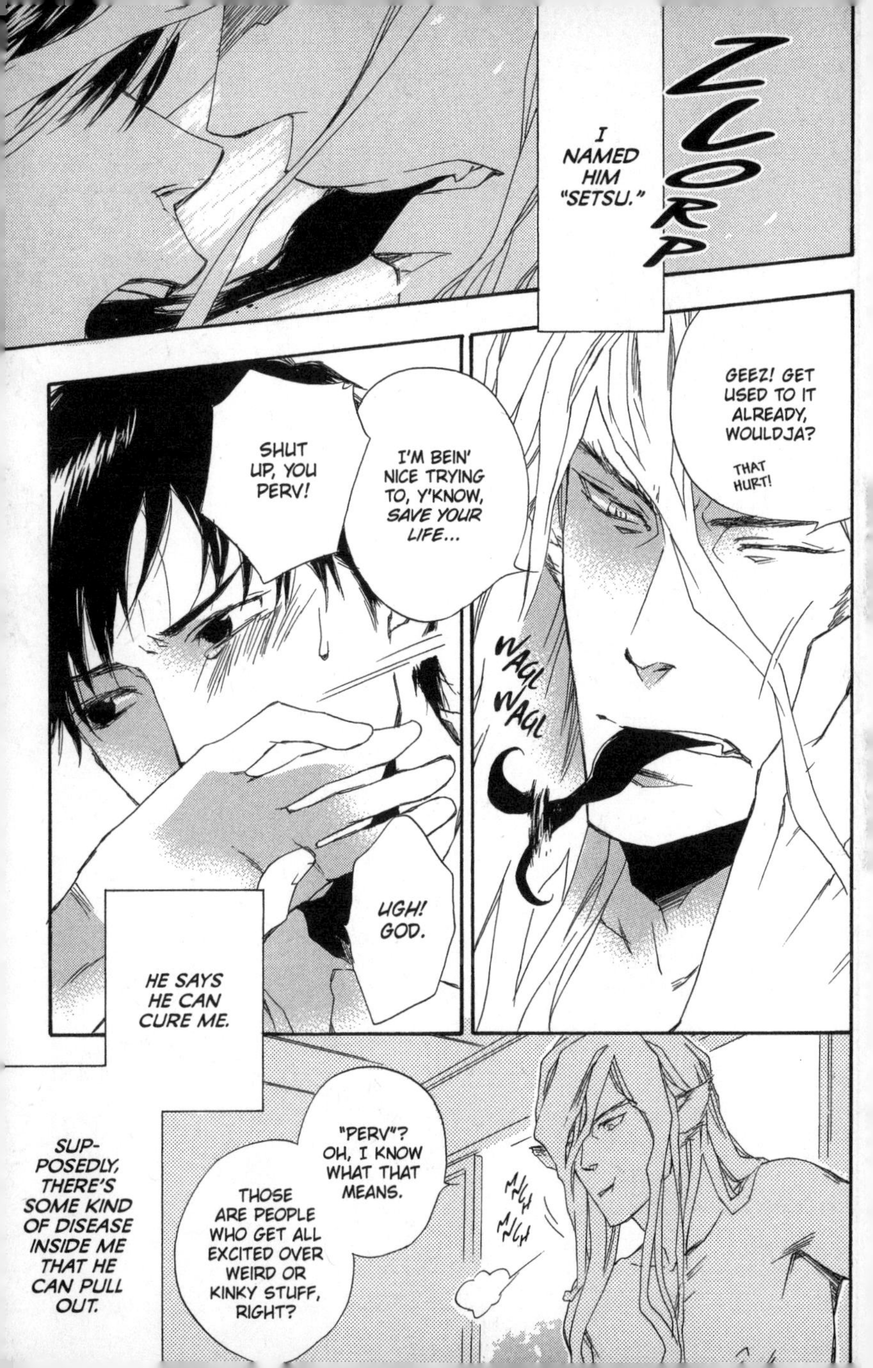
ZLORP
I NAMED HIM "SETSU."
GEEZ! GET USED TO IT ALREADY, WOULDJA?
THAT HURT!
WAGL WAGL
I'M BEIN' NICE TRYING TO, Y'KNOW, SAVE YOUR LIFE...
SHUT UP, YOU PERV!
UGH! GOD.
HE SAYS HE CAN CURE ME.
MGH MGH
"PERV"? OH, I KNOW WHAT THAT MEANS.
THOSE ARE PEOPLE WHO GET ALL EXCITED OVER WEIRD OR KINKY STUFF, RIGHT?
SUP-POSEDLY, THERE'S SOME KIND OF DISEASE INSIDE ME THAT HE CAN PULL OUT.

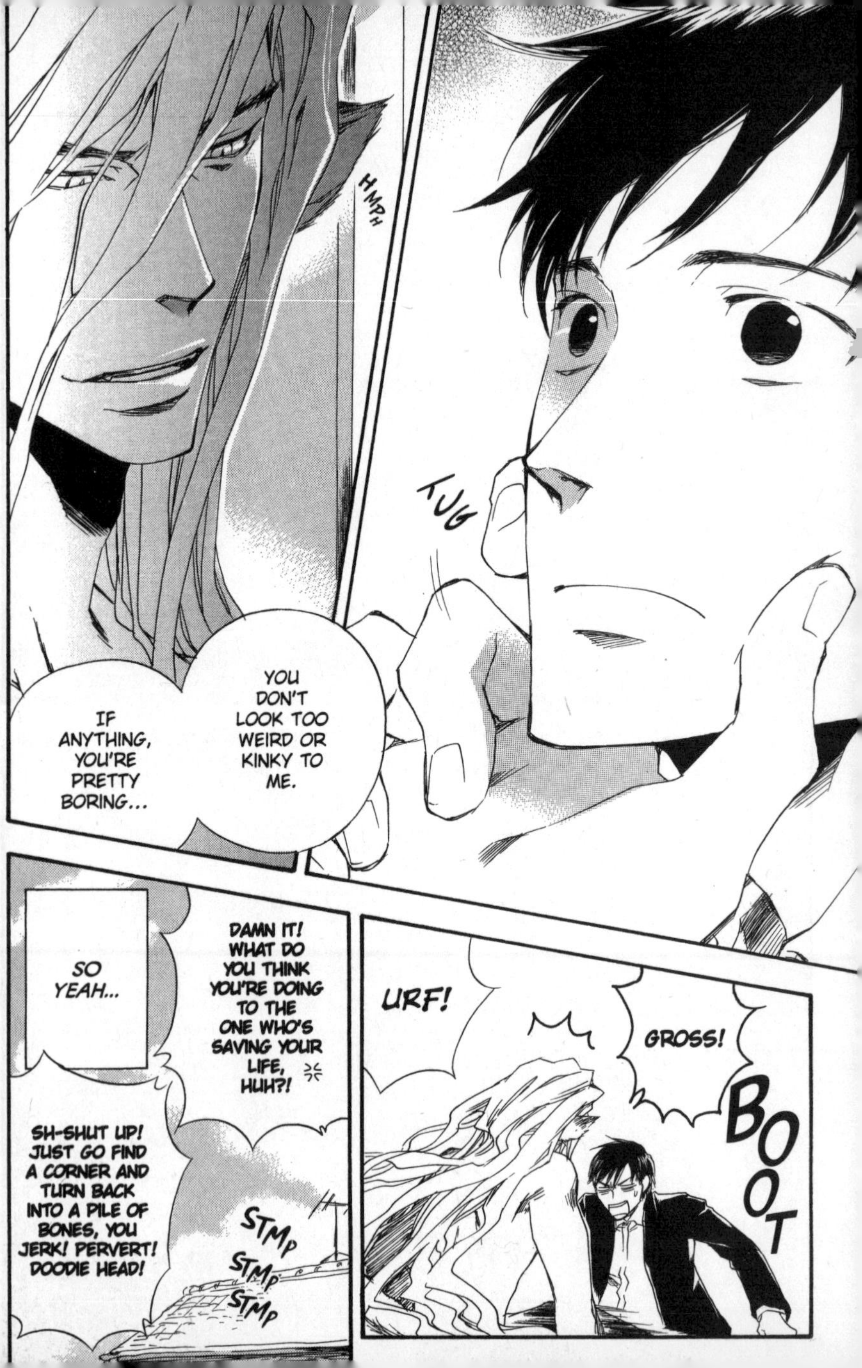
TUG
HMPH
YOU DON'T LOOK TOO WEIRD OR KINKY TO ME.
IF ANYTHING, YOU'RE PRETTY BORING...
GROSS!
BOOT
URF!
DAMN IT! WHAT DO YOU THINK YOU'RE DOING TO THE ONE WHO'S SAVING YOUR LIFE, HUH?!
SO YEAH...
SH-SHUT UP! JUST GO FIND A CORNER AND TURN BACK INTO A PILE OF BONES, YOU JERK! PERVERT! DOODIE HEAD!
STMP
STMP
STMP

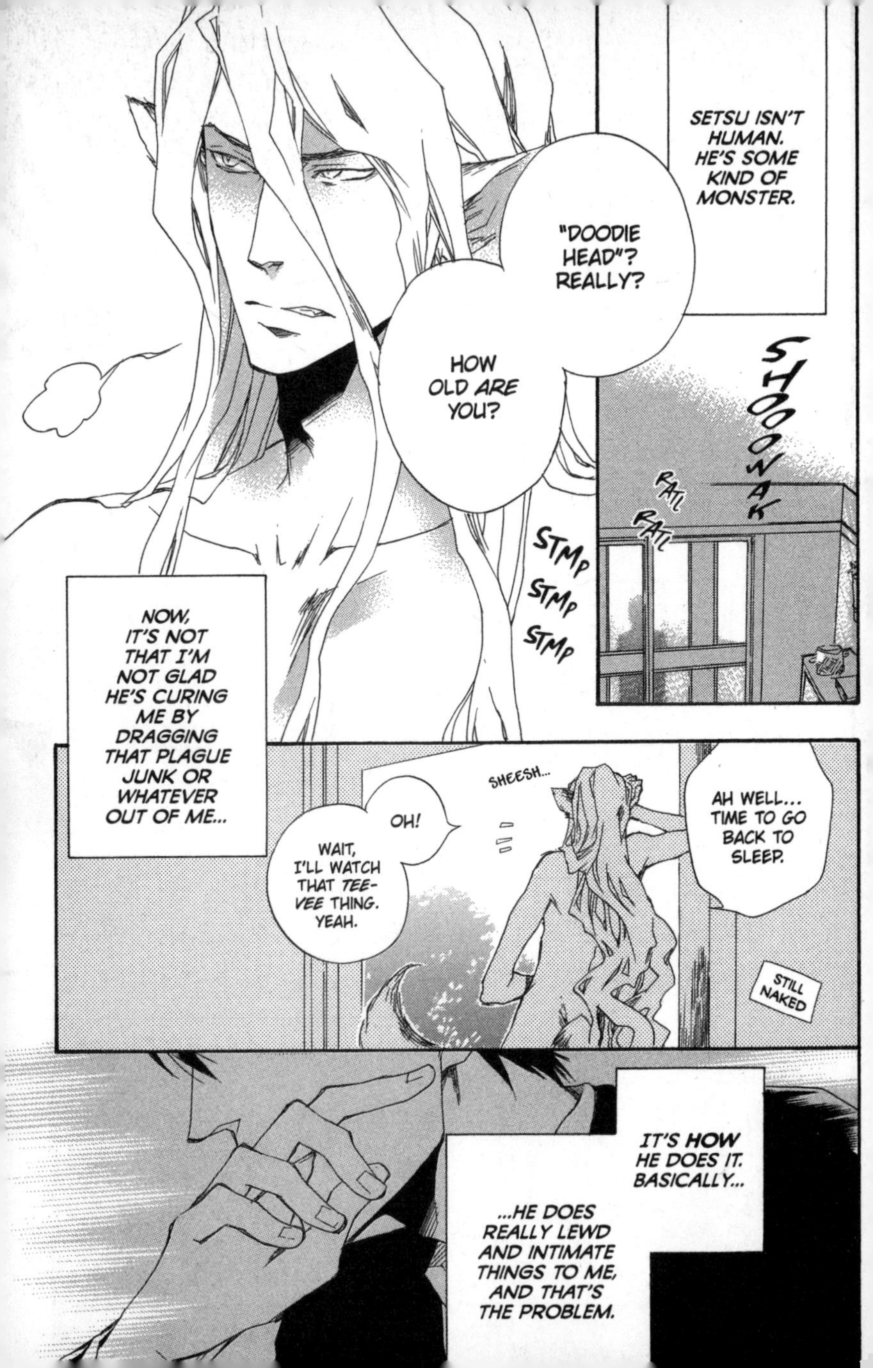
SETSU ISN'T HUMAN. HE'S SOME KIND OF MONSTER.
SHOOOOWAK
RATL
RATL
"DOODIE HEAD"? REALLY?
HOW OLD ARE YOU?
STMP
STMP
STMP
NOW, IT'S NOT THAT I'M NOT GLAD HE'S CURING ME BY DRAGGING THAT PLAGUE JUNK OR WHATEVER OUT OF ME...
AH WELL... TIME TO GO BACK TO SLEEP.
SHEESH...
OH!
WAIT, I'LL WATCH THAT TEE-VEE THING. YEAH.
STILL NAKED
IT'S HOW HE DOES IT. BASICALLY...
...HE DOES REALLY LEWD AND INTIMATE THINGS TO ME, AND THAT'S THE PROBLEM.

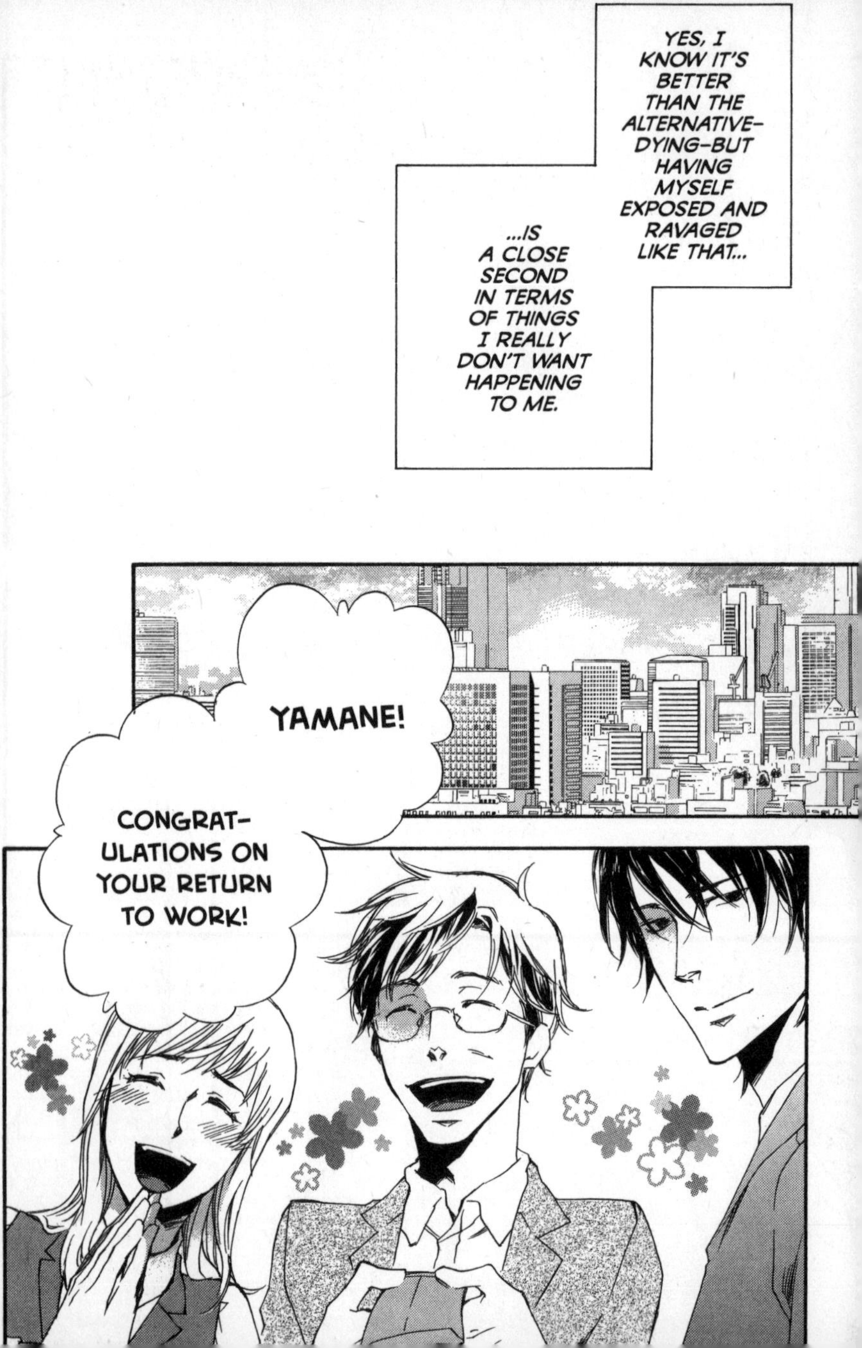
YES, I KNOW IT'S BETTER THAN THE ALTERNATIVE-DYING-BUT HAVING MYSELF EXPOSED AND RAVAGED LIKE THAT...
...IS A CLOSE SECOND IN TERMS OF THINGS I REALLY DON'T WANT HAPPENING TO ME.
YAMANE!
CONGRAT-ULATIONS ON YOUR RETURN TO WORK!

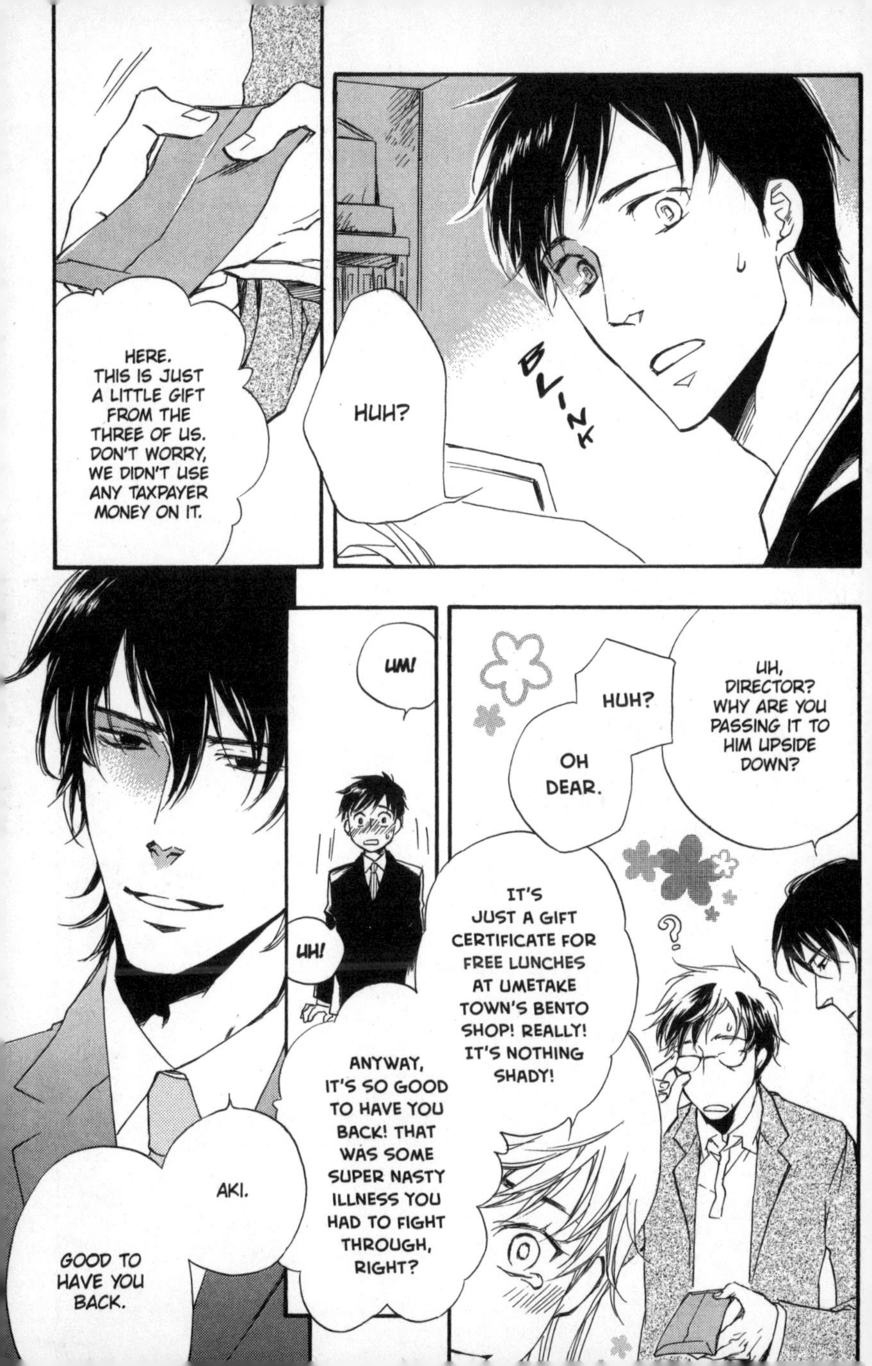
HUH?
BLINK
HERE. THIS IS JUST A LITTLE GIFT FROM THE THREE OF US. DON'T WORRY, WE DIDN'T USE ANY TAXPAYER MONEY ON IT.
UH, DIRECTOR? WHY ARE YOU PASSING IT TO HIM UPSIDE DOWN?
HUH?
OH DEAR.
IT'S JUST A GIFT CERTIFICATE FOR FREE LUNCHES AT UMETAKE TOWN'S BENTO SHOP! REALLY! IT'S NOTHING SHADY!
UM!
UH!
ANYWAY, IT'S SO GOOD TO HAVE YOU BACK! THAT WAS SOME SUPER NASTY ILLNESS YOU HAD TO FIGHT THROUGH, RIGHT?
AKI.
GOOD TO HAVE YOU BACK.

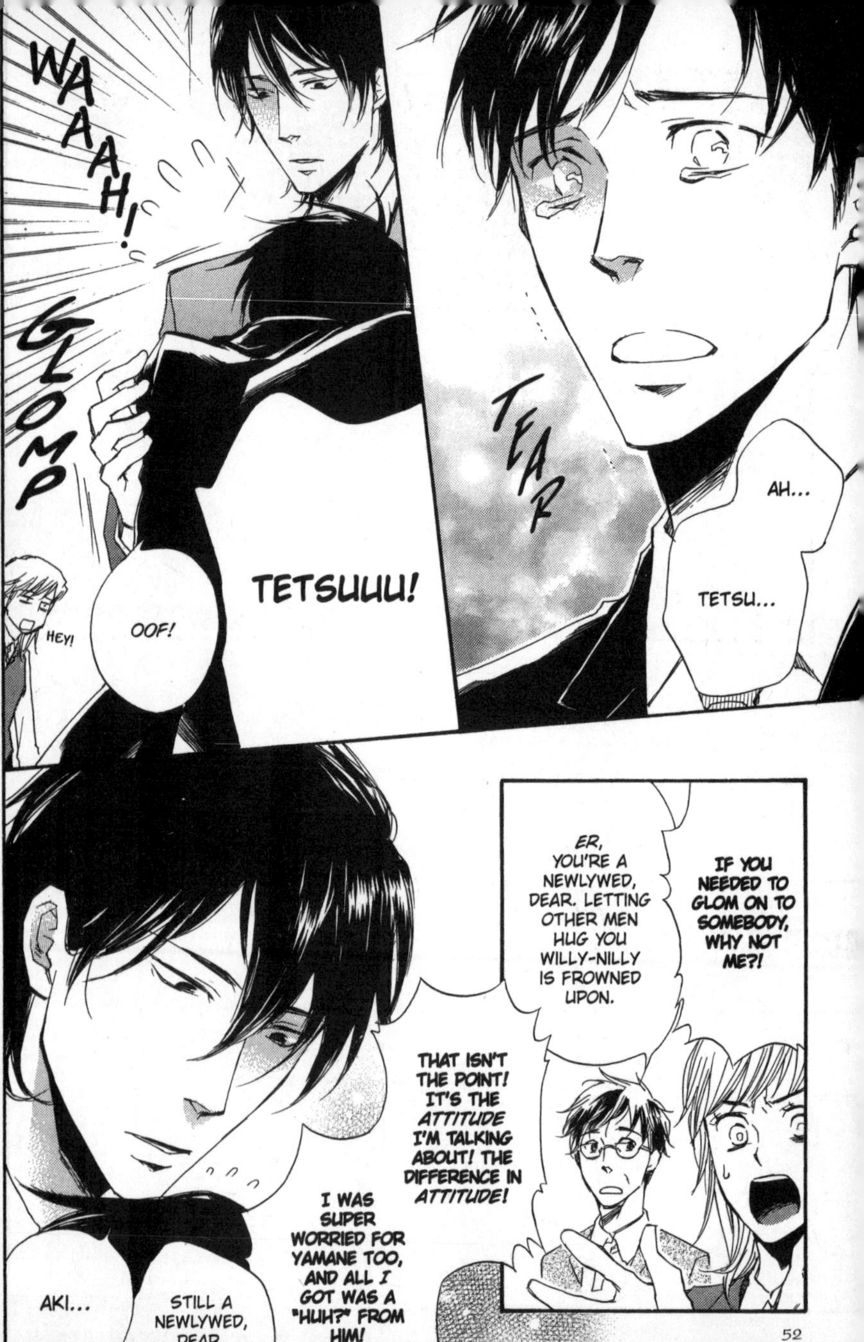
TEAR
AH...
TETSU...
WAAAH!
GLOMP
TETSUUU!
OOF!
HEY!
IF YOU NEEDED TO GLOM ON TO SOMEBODY, WHY NOT ME?!
ER, YOU'RE A NEWLYWED, DEAR. LETTING OTHER MEN HUG YOU WILLY-NILLY IS FROWNED UPON.
THAT ISN'T THE POINT! IT'S THE *ATTITUDE* I'M TALKING ABOUT! THE DIFFERENCE IN *ATTITUDE*!
I WAS SUPER WORRIED FOR YAMANE TOO, AND ALL *I* GOT WAS A "HUH?" FROM HIM!
STILL A NEWLYWED, DEAR.
AKI...

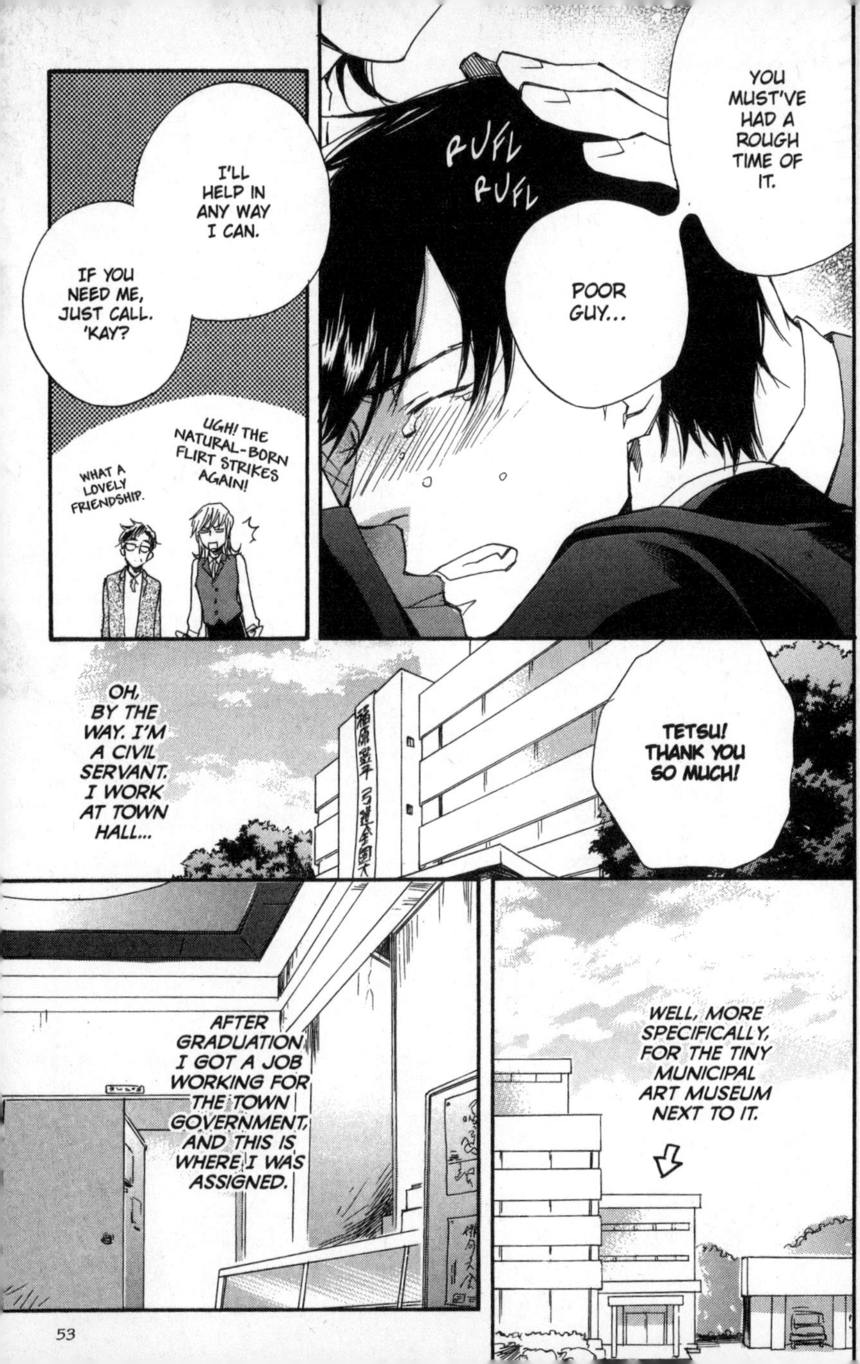
YOU MUST'VE HAD A ROUGH TIME OF IT.
RUFL RUFL
POOR GUY...
I'LL HELP IN ANY WAY I CAN.
IF YOU NEED ME, JUST CALL. 'KAY?
UGH! THE NATURAL-BORN FLIRT STRIKES AGAIN!
WHAT A LOVELY FRIENDSHIP.
TETSU! THANK YOU SO MUCH!
OH, BY THE WAY. I'M A CIVIL SERVANT. I WORK AT TOWN HALL...
WELL, MORE SPECIFICALLY, FOR THE TINY MUNICIPAL ART MUSEUM NEXT TO IT.
AFTER GRADUATION I GOT A JOB WORKING FOR THE TOWN GOVERNMENT, AND THIS IS WHERE I WAS ASSIGNED.

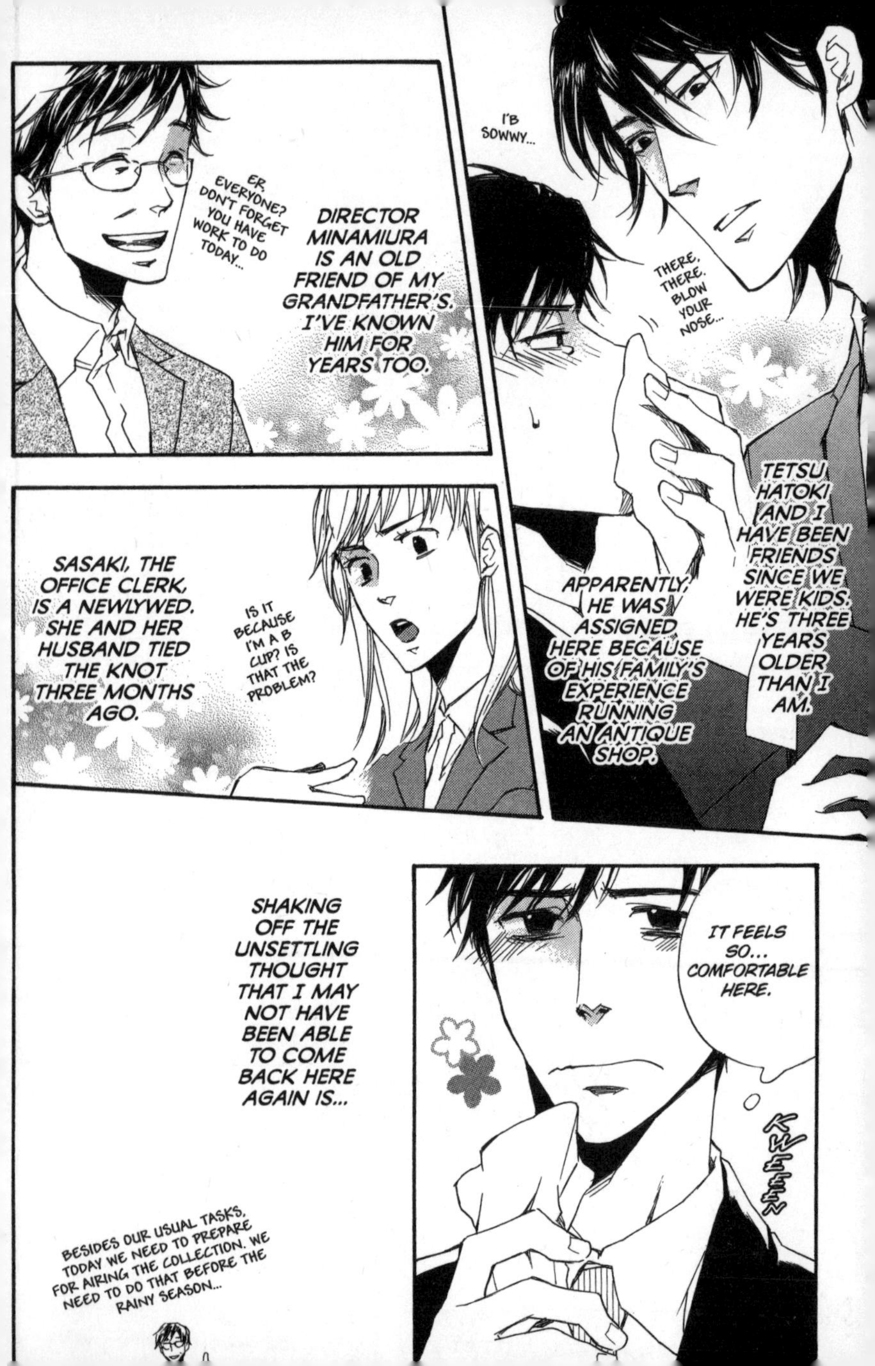
I'B SOWWY...
THERE, THERE. BLOW YOUR NOSE...
TETSU HATOKI AND I HAVE BEEN FRIENDS SINCE WE WERE KIDS. HE'S THREE YEARS OLDER THAN I AM.
APPARENTLY, HE WAS ASSIGNED HERE BECAUSE OF HIS FAMILY'S EXPERIENCE RUNNING AN ANTIQUE SHOP.
DIRECTOR MINAMIURA IS AN OLD FRIEND OF MY GRANDFATHER'S. I'VE KNOWN HIM FOR YEARS TOO.
ER, EVERYONE? DON'T FORGET YOU HAVE WORK TO DO TODAY...
IS IT BECAUSE I'M A B CUP? IS THAT THE PROBLEM?
SASAKI, THE OFFICE CLERK, IS A NEWLYWED. SHE AND HER HUSBAND TIED THE KNOT THREE MONTHS AGO.
IT FEELS SO... COMFORTABLE HERE.
KWEEN
SHAKING OFF THE UNSETTLING THOUGHT THAT I MAY NOT HAVE BEEN ABLE TO COME BACK HERE AGAIN IS...
BESIDES OUR USUAL TASKS, TODAY WE NEED TO PREPARE FOR AIRING THE COLLECTION. WE NEED TO DO THAT BEFORE THE RAINY SEASON...

I SETTLED IN TO WORK FEELING AS THOUGH I HAD FINALLY RETURNED TO NORMAL LIFE.

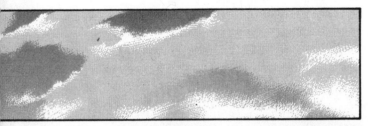

AKI.

LET'S THROW A PARTY TO CELEBRATE YOUR RECOVERY.

HUH?

REALLY?!

YEAH. FORGET ABOUT WORK FOR TODAY. WE DON'T NEED TO AIR THE COLLECTION UNTIL TOMORROW, RIGHT?

IS THERE ANYTHING YOU WANT TO EAT? WE'LL TREAT YOU TO WHATEVER YOU WANT.

OOH! HMM... I THINK I WANT TO HAVE SOME GOOD S—

AH

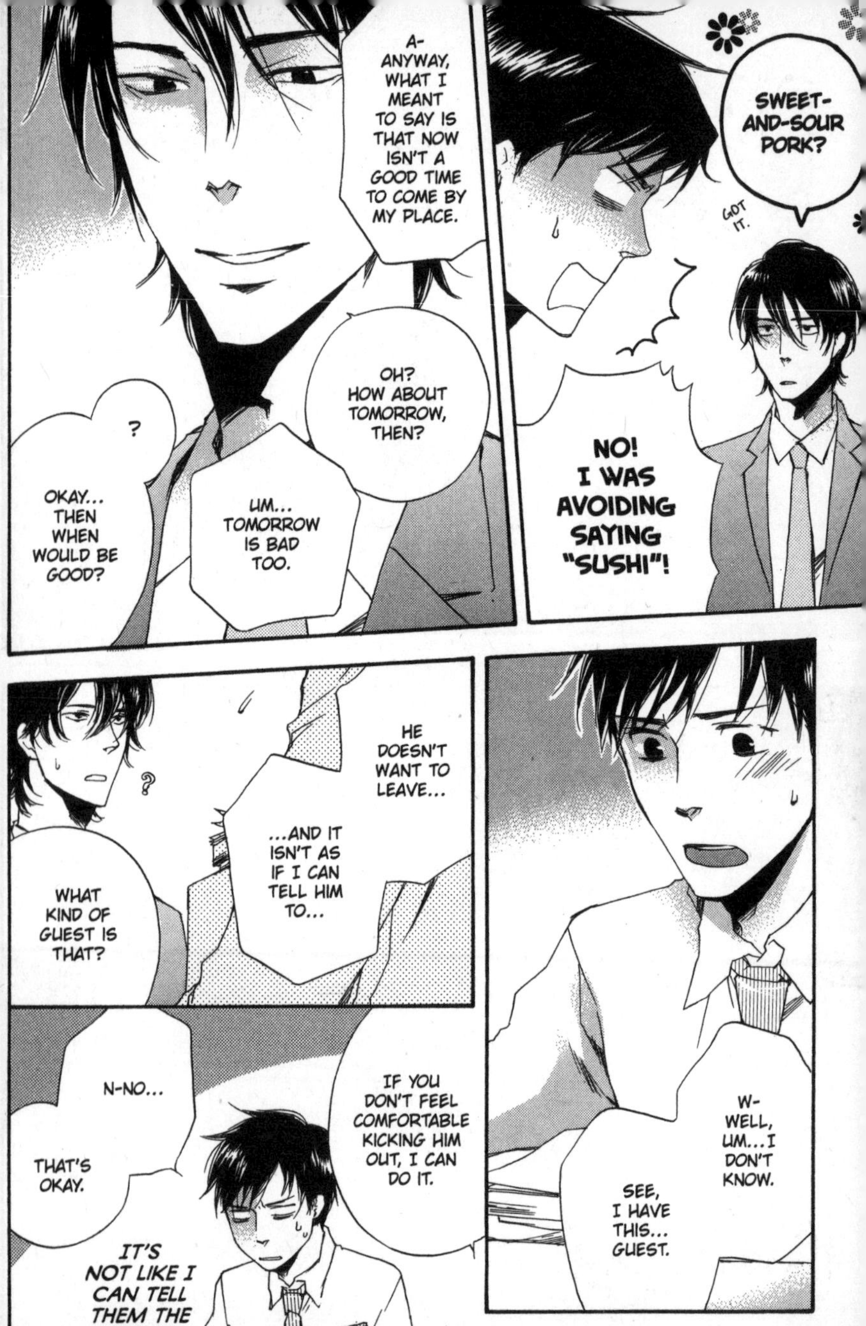
SWEET-AND-SOUR PORK?
GOT IT.
NO! I WAS AVOIDING SAYING "SUSHI"!
A- ANYWAY, WHAT I MEANT TO SAY IS THAT NOW ISN'T A GOOD TIME TO COME BY MY PLACE.
OH? HOW ABOUT TOMORROW, THEN?
UM... TOMORROW IS BAD TOO.
?
OKAY... THEN WHEN WOULD BE GOOD?
W-WELL, UM...I DON'T KNOW.
SEE, I HAVE THIS... GUEST.
HE DOESN'T WANT TO LEAVE...
...AND IT ISN'T AS IF I CAN TELL HIM TO...
?
WHAT KIND OF GUEST IS THAT?
IF YOU DON'T FEEL COMFORTABLE KICKING HIM OUT, I CAN DO IT.
N-NO...
THAT'S OKAY.
IT'S NOT LIKE I CAN TELL THEM THE TRUTH.

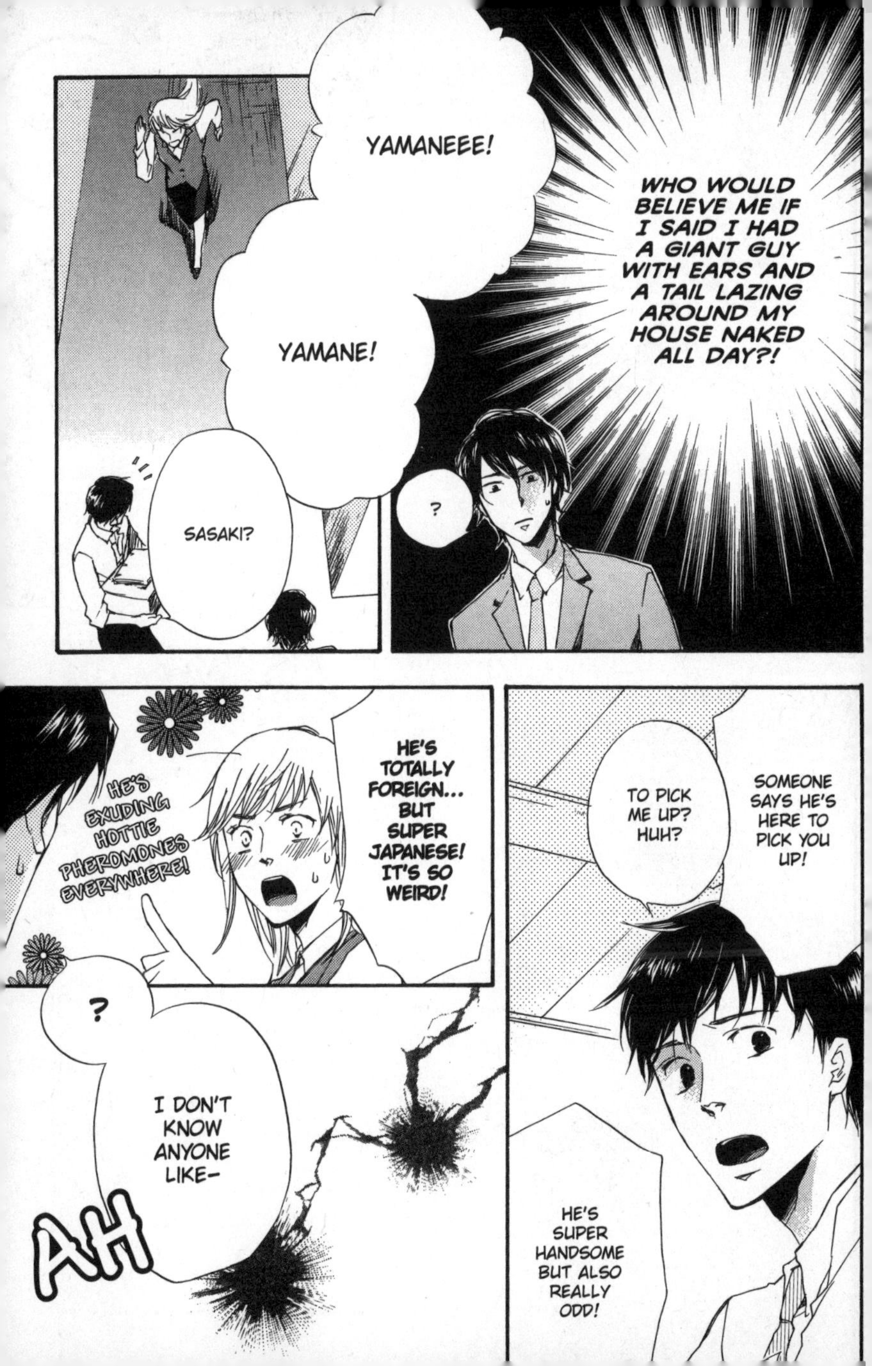
WHO WOULD BELIEVE ME IF I SAID I HAD A GIANT GUY WITH EARS AND A TAIL LAZING AROUND MY HOUSE NAKED ALL DAY?!
?
YAMANEEE!
YAMANE!
SASAKI?
SOMEONE SAYS HE'S HERE TO PICK YOU UP!
TO PICK ME UP? HUH?
HE'S SUPER HANDSOME BUT ALSO REALLY ODD!
HE'S TOTALLY FOREIGN... BUT SUPER JAPANESE! IT'S SO WEIRD!
HE'S EXUDING HOTTIE PHEROMONES EVERYWHERE!
?
I DON'T KNOW ANYONE LIKE-
AH

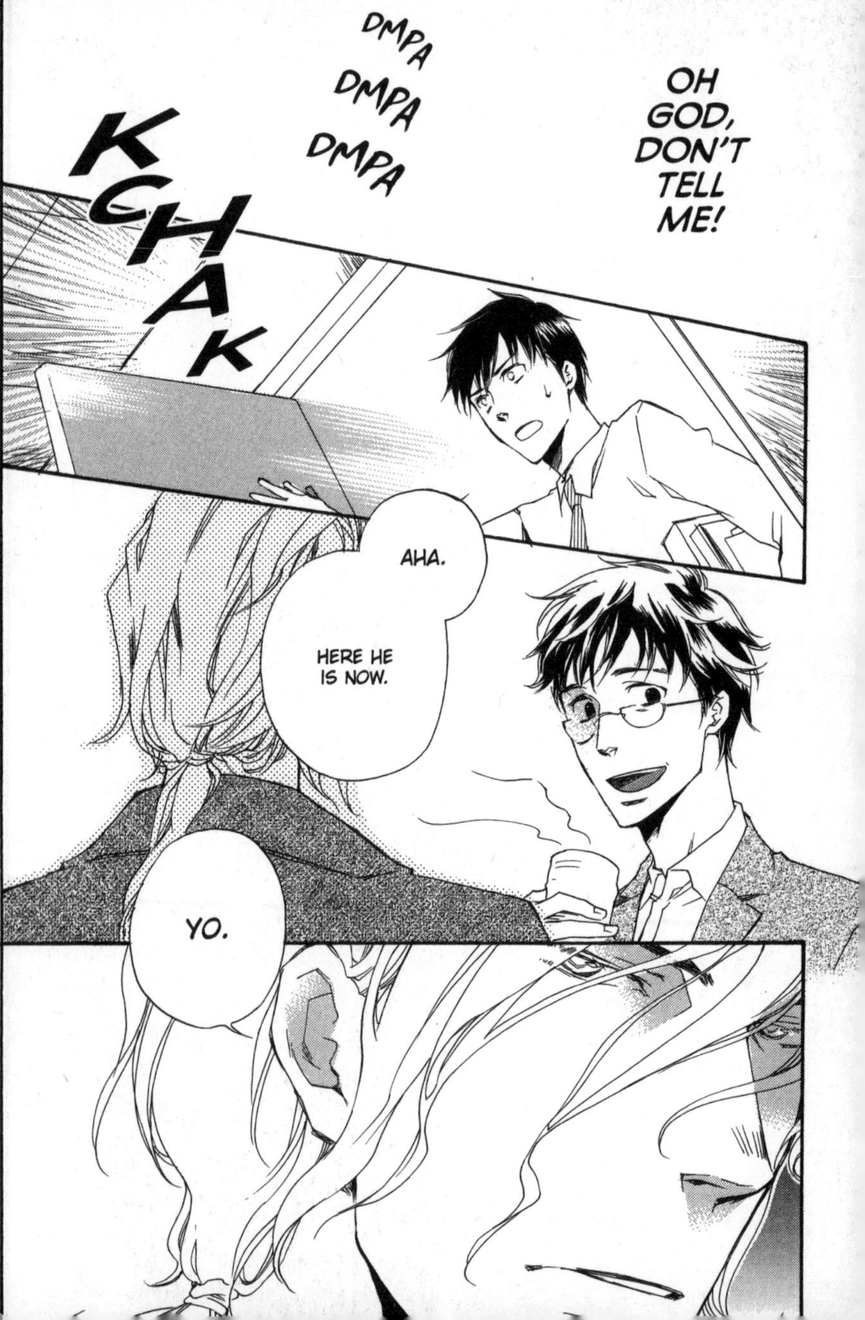
OH GOD, DON'T TELL ME!
DMPA
DMPA
DMPA
KCHAK
AHA.
HERE HE IS NOW.
YO.

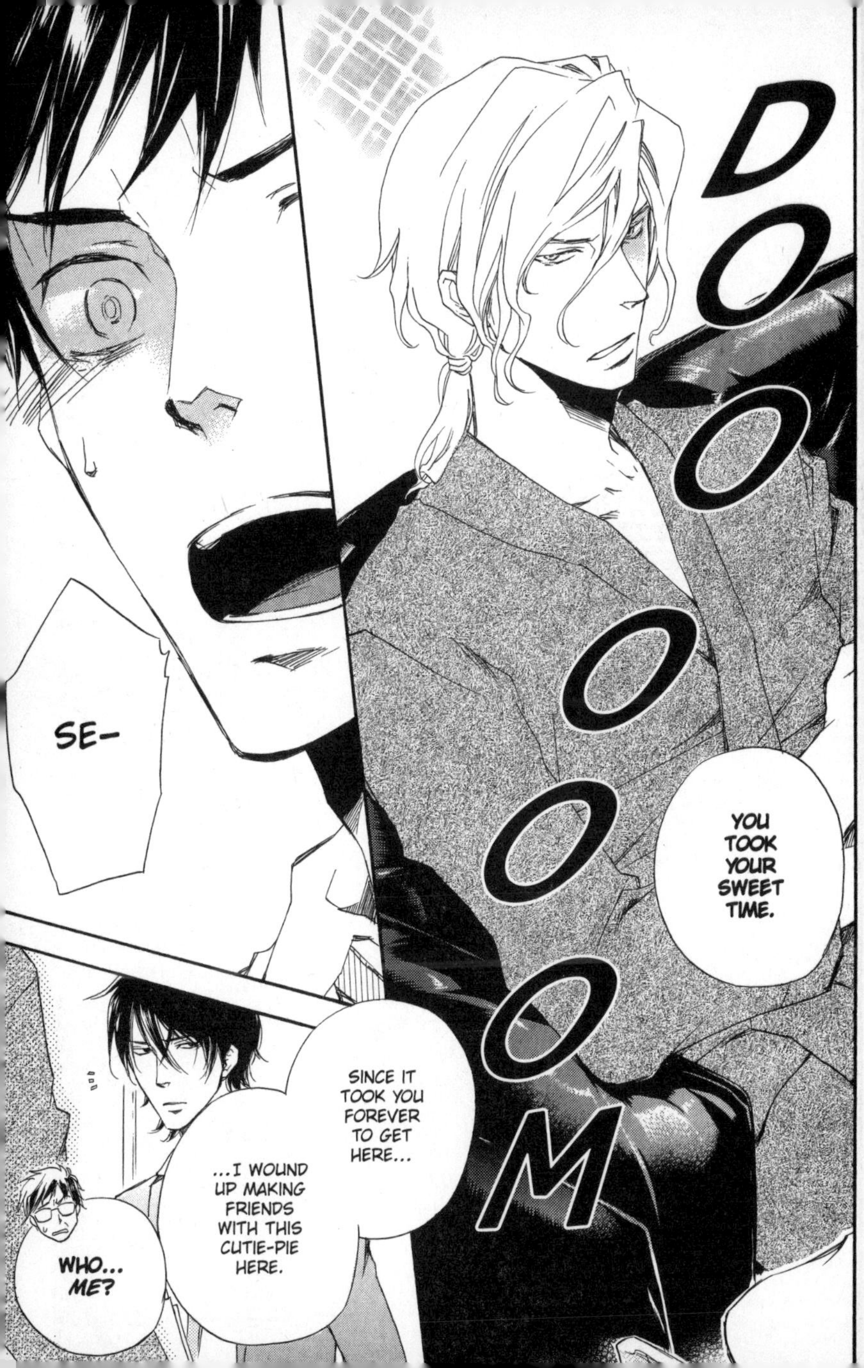
DOOOOOM
YOU TOOK YOUR SWEET TIME.
SE-
SINCE IT TOOK YOU FOREVER TO GET HERE...
...I WOUND UP MAKING FRIENDS WITH THIS CUTIE-PIE HERE.
WHO... ME?

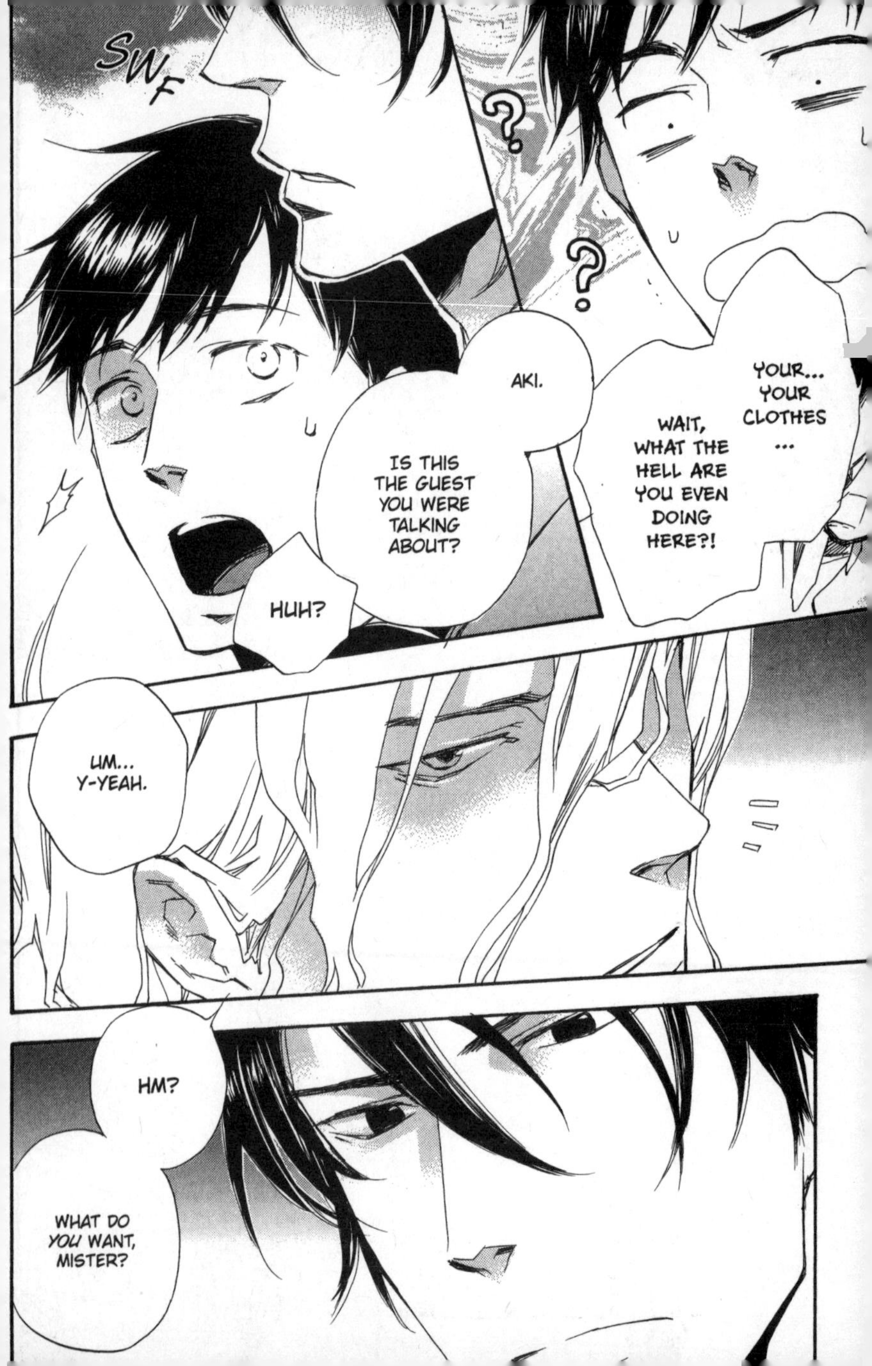
YOUR... YOUR CLOTHES ...
WAIT, WHAT THE HELL ARE YOU EVEN DOING HERE?!
AKI.
IS THIS THE GUEST YOU WERE TALKING ABOUT?
SWF
HUH?
UM... Y-YEAH.
HM?
WHAT DO *YOU* WANT, MISTER?

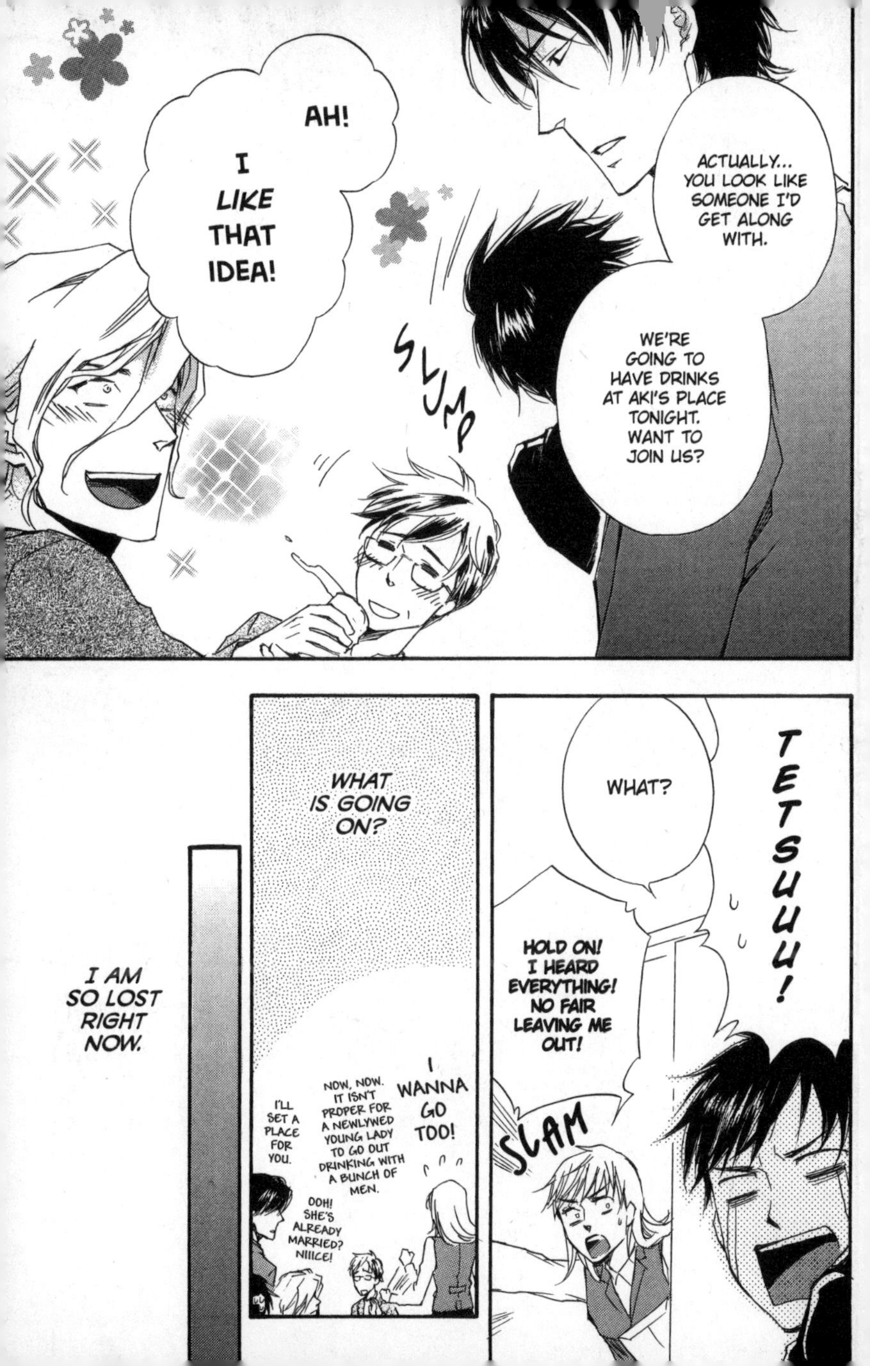
ACTUALLY... YOU LOOK LIKE SOMEONE I'D GET ALONG WITH.
WE'RE GOING TO HAVE DRINKS AT AKI'S PLACE TONIGHT. WANT TO JOIN US?
SLUMP
AH!
I LIKE THAT IDEA!
TETSUUU!
WHAT?
HOLD ON! I HEARD EVERYTHING! NO FAIR LEAVING ME OUT!
SLAM
WHAT IS GOING ON?
I WANNA GO TOO!
NOW, NOW. IT ISN'T PROPER FOR A NEWLYWED YOUNG LADY TO GO OUT DRINKING WITH A BUNCH OF MEN.
I'LL SET A PLACE FOR YOU.
OOH! SHE'S ALREADY MARRIED? NIIICE!
I AM SO LOST RIGHT NOW.

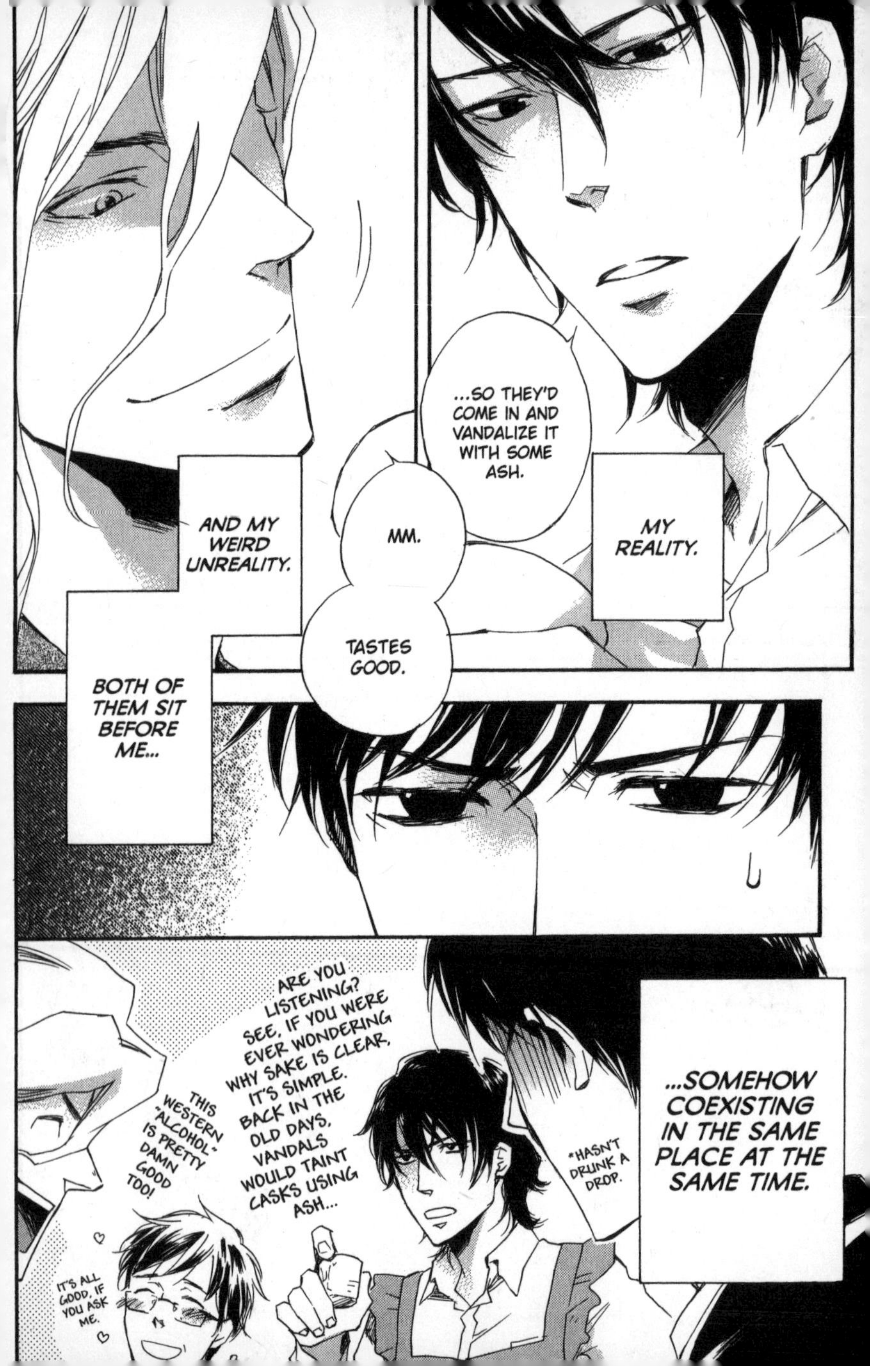
...SO THEY'D COME IN AND VANDALIZE IT WITH SOME ASH.
MY REALITY.
MM.
TASTES GOOD.
AND MY WEIRD UNREALITY.
BOTH OF THEM SIT BEFORE ME...
...SOMEHOW COEXISTING IN THE SAME PLACE AT THE SAME TIME.
*HASN'T DRUNK A DROP.
ARE YOU LISTENING? SEE, IF YOU WERE EVER WONDERING WHY SAKE IS CLEAR, IT'S SIMPLE. BACK IN THE OLD DAYS, VANDALS WOULD TAINT CASKS USING ASH...
THIS WESTERN "ALCOHOL" IS PRETTY DAMN GOOD TOO!
IT'S ALL GOOD, IF YOU ASK ME.

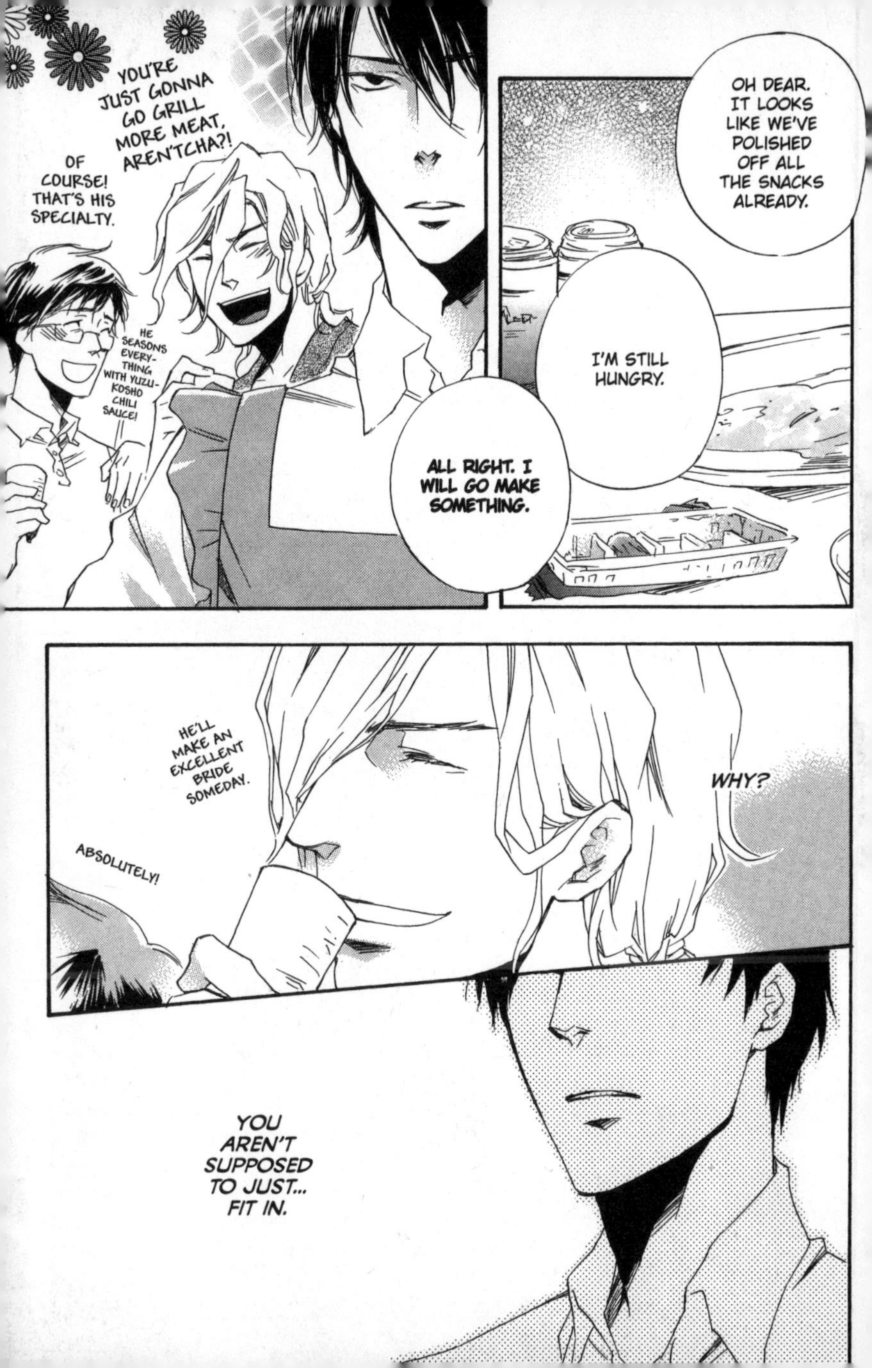
OH DEAR. IT LOOKS LIKE WE'VE POLISHED OFF ALL THE SNACKS ALREADY.
I'M STILL HUNGRY.
ALL RIGHT. I WILL GO MAKE SOMETHING.
YOU'RE JUST GONNA GO GRILL MORE MEAT, AREN'TCHA?!
OF COURSE! THAT'S HIS SPECIALTY.
HE SEASONS EVERY-THING WITH YUZU-KOSHO CHILI SAUCE!
WHY?
HE'LL MAKE AN EXCELLENT BRIDE SOMEDAY.
ABSOLUTELY!
YOU AREN'T SUPPOSED TO JUST... FIT IN.

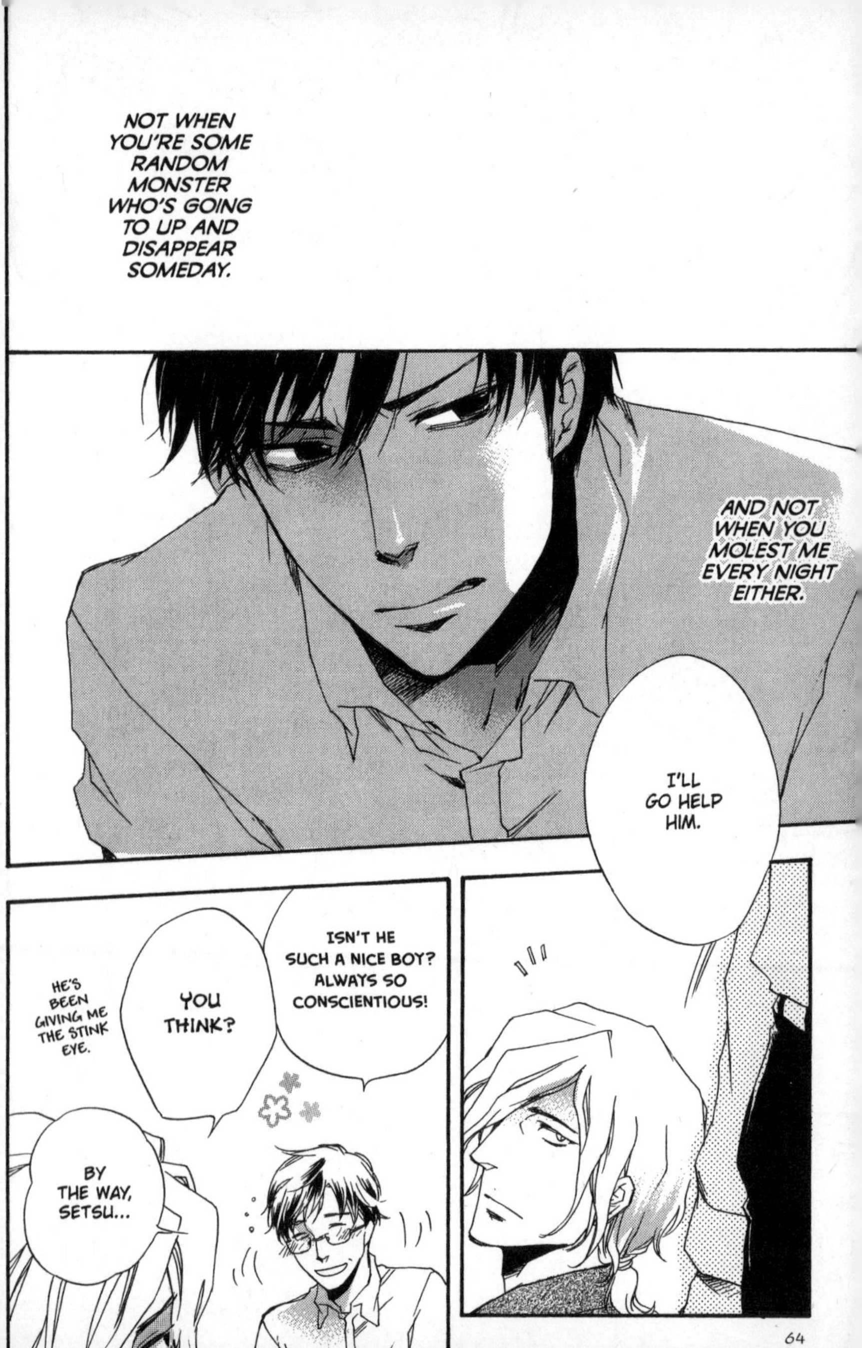
NOT WHEN YOU'RE SOME RANDOM MONSTER WHO'S GOING TO UP AND DISAPPEAR SOMEDAY.
AND NOT WHEN YOU MOLEST ME EVERY NIGHT EITHER.
I'LL GO HELP HIM.
ISN'T HE SUCH A NICE BOY? ALWAYS SO CONSCIENTIOUS!
YOU THINK?
HE'S BEEN GIVING ME THE STINK EYE.
BY THE WAY, SETSU...

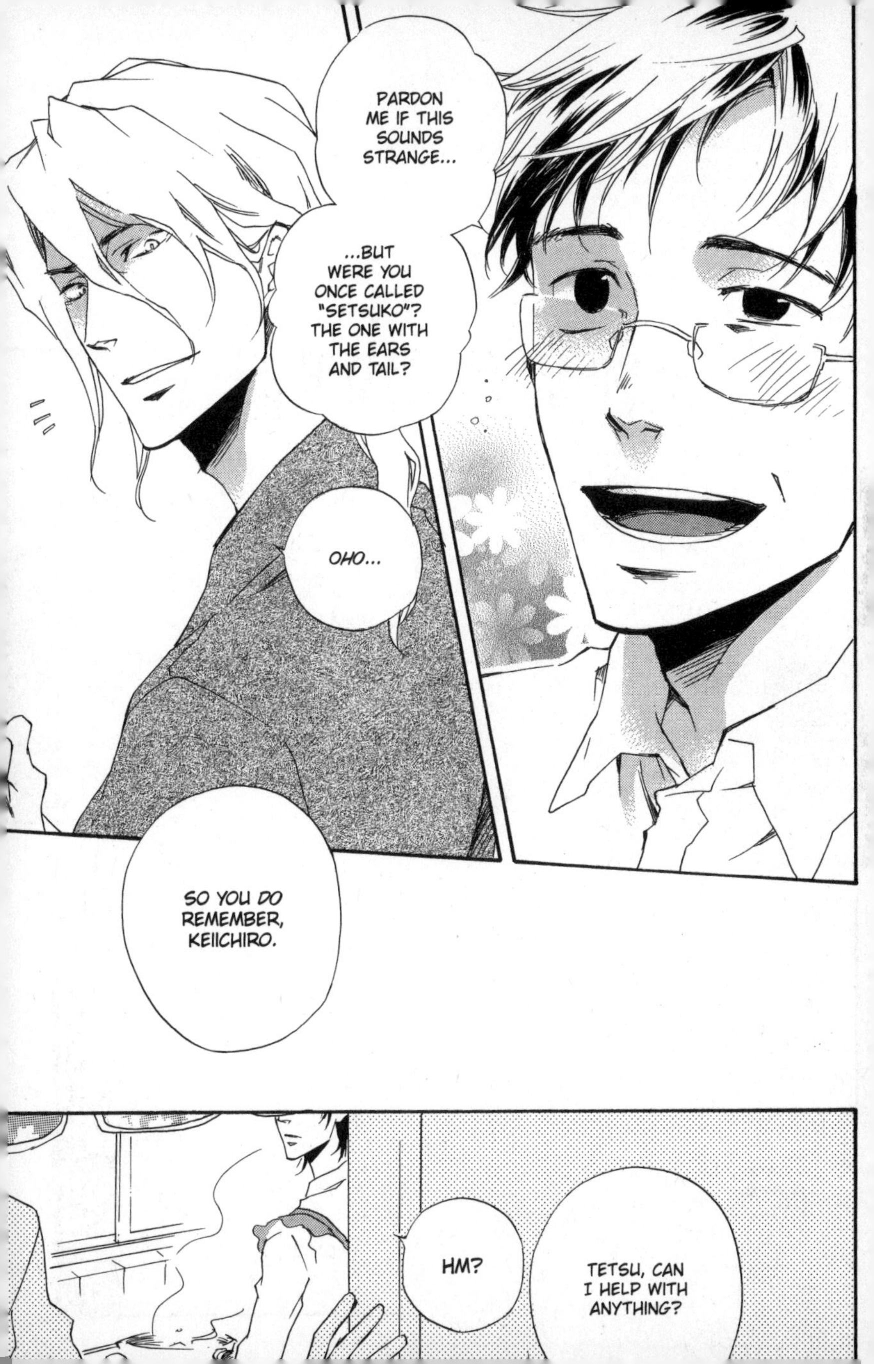
PARDON ME IF THIS SOUNDS STRANGE...
...BUT WERE YOU ONCE CALLED "SETSUKO"? THE ONE WITH THE EARS AND TAIL?
OHO...
SO YOU DO REMEMBER, KEIICHIRO.
TETSU, CAN I HELP WITH ANYTHING?
HM?

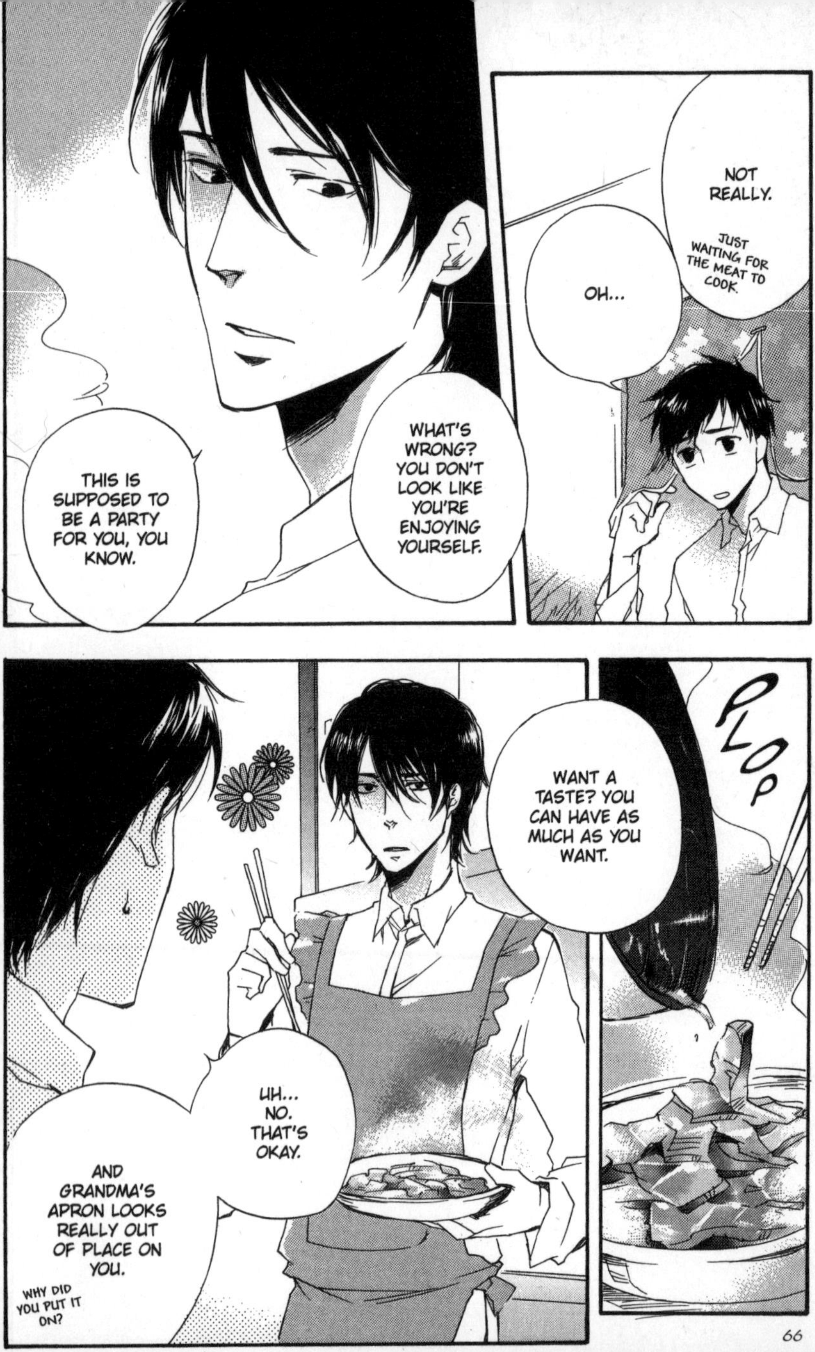
NOT REALLY.
JUST WAITING FOR THE MEAT TO COOK.
OH...
WHAT'S WRONG? YOU DON'T LOOK LIKE YOU'RE ENJOYING YOURSELF.
THIS IS SUPPOSED TO BE A PARTY FOR YOU, YOU KNOW.
PLOP
WANT A TASTE? YOU CAN HAVE AS MUCH AS YOU WANT.
UH... NO. THAT'S OKAY.
AND GRANDMA'S APRON LOOKS REALLY OUT OF PLACE ON YOU.
WHY DID YOU PUT IT ON?

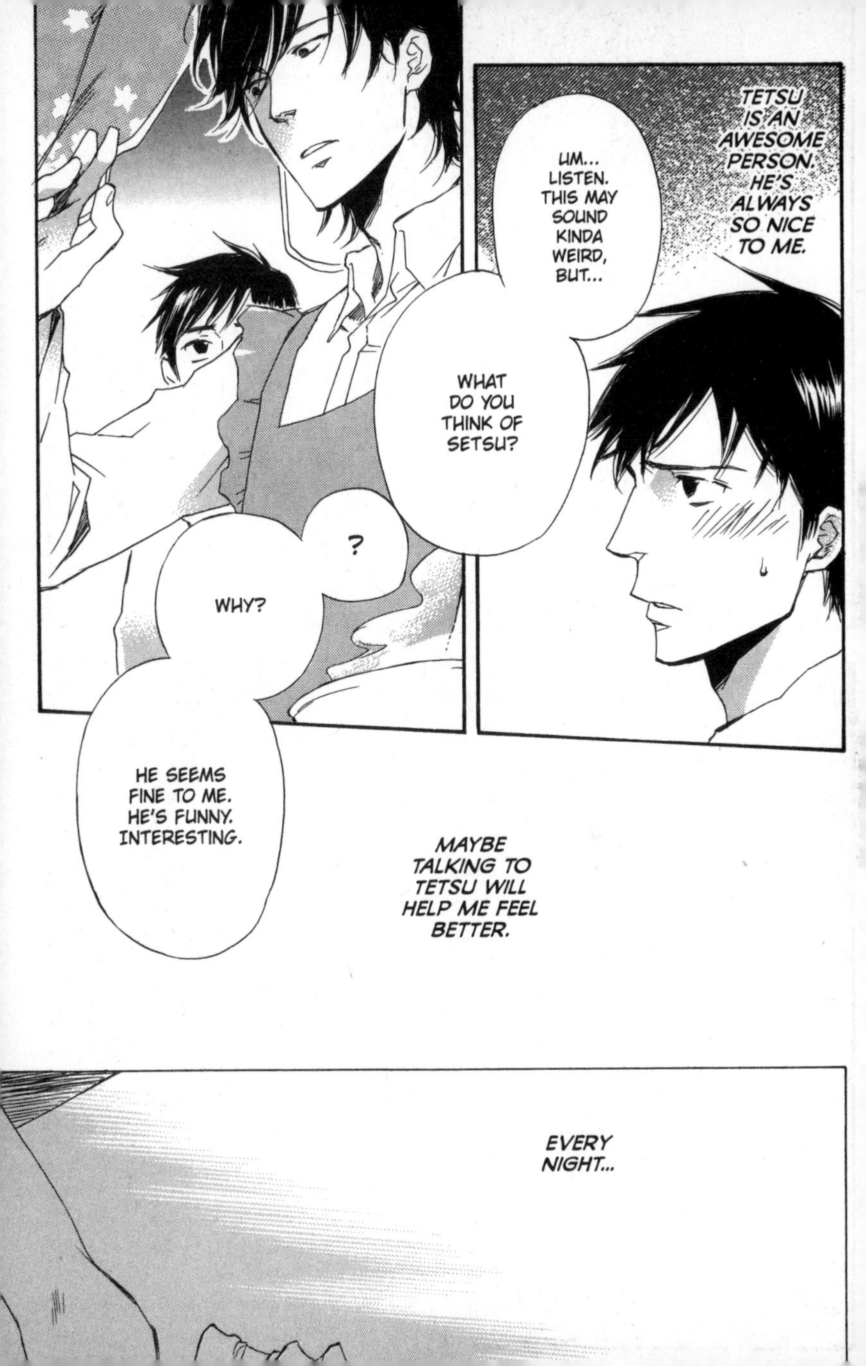
TETSU IS AN AWESOME PERSON. HE'S ALWAYS SO NICE TO ME.
UM... LISTEN. THIS MAY SOUND KINDA WEIRD, BUT...
WHAT DO YOU THINK OF SETSU?
?
WHY?
HE SEEMS FINE TO ME. HE'S FUNNY. INTERESTING.
MAYBE TALKING TO TETSU WILL HELP ME FEEL BETTER.
EVERY NIGHT...

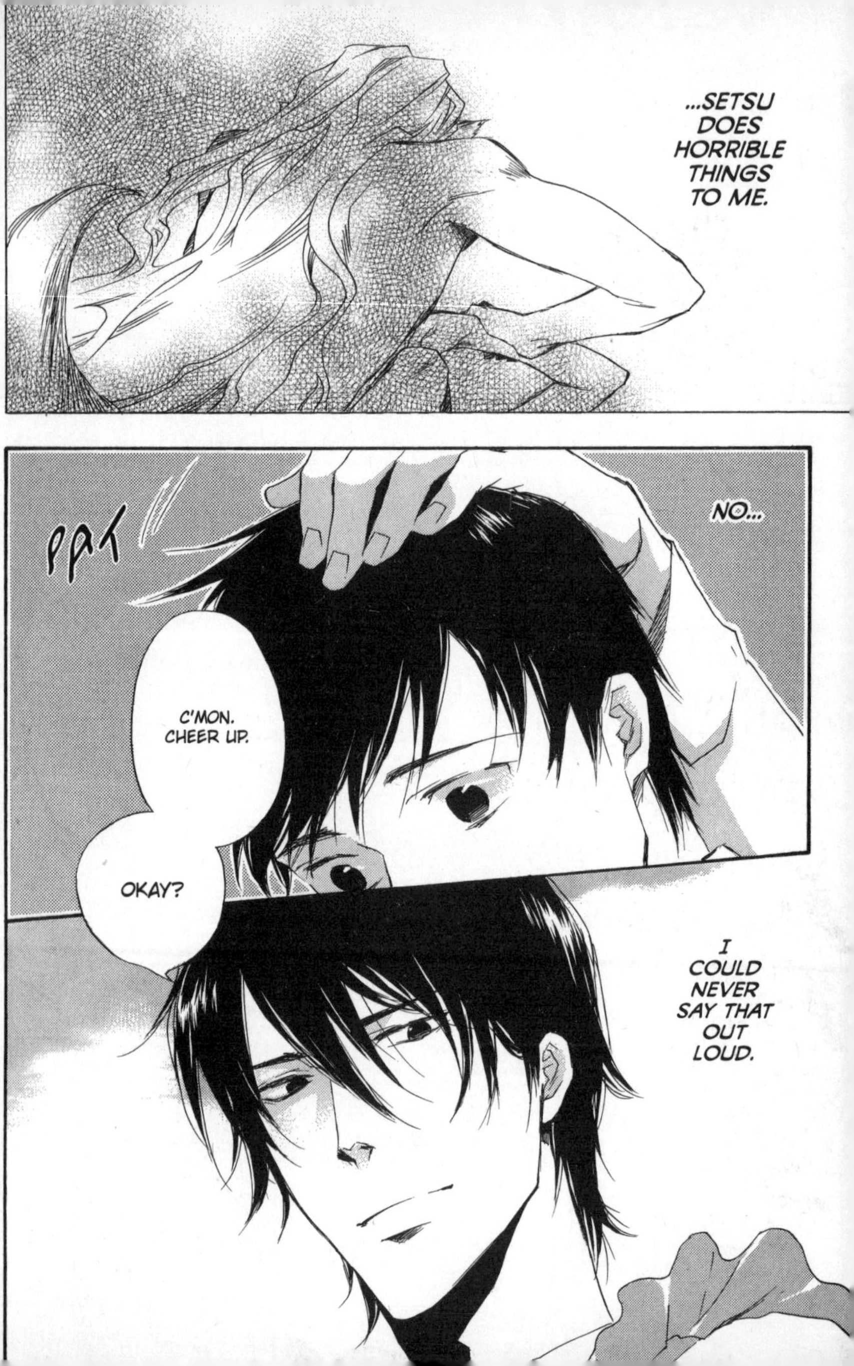
...SETSU DOES HORRIBLE THINGS TO ME.
NO...
PAT
C'MON. CHEER UP.
OKAY?
I COULD NEVER SAY THAT OUT LOUD.

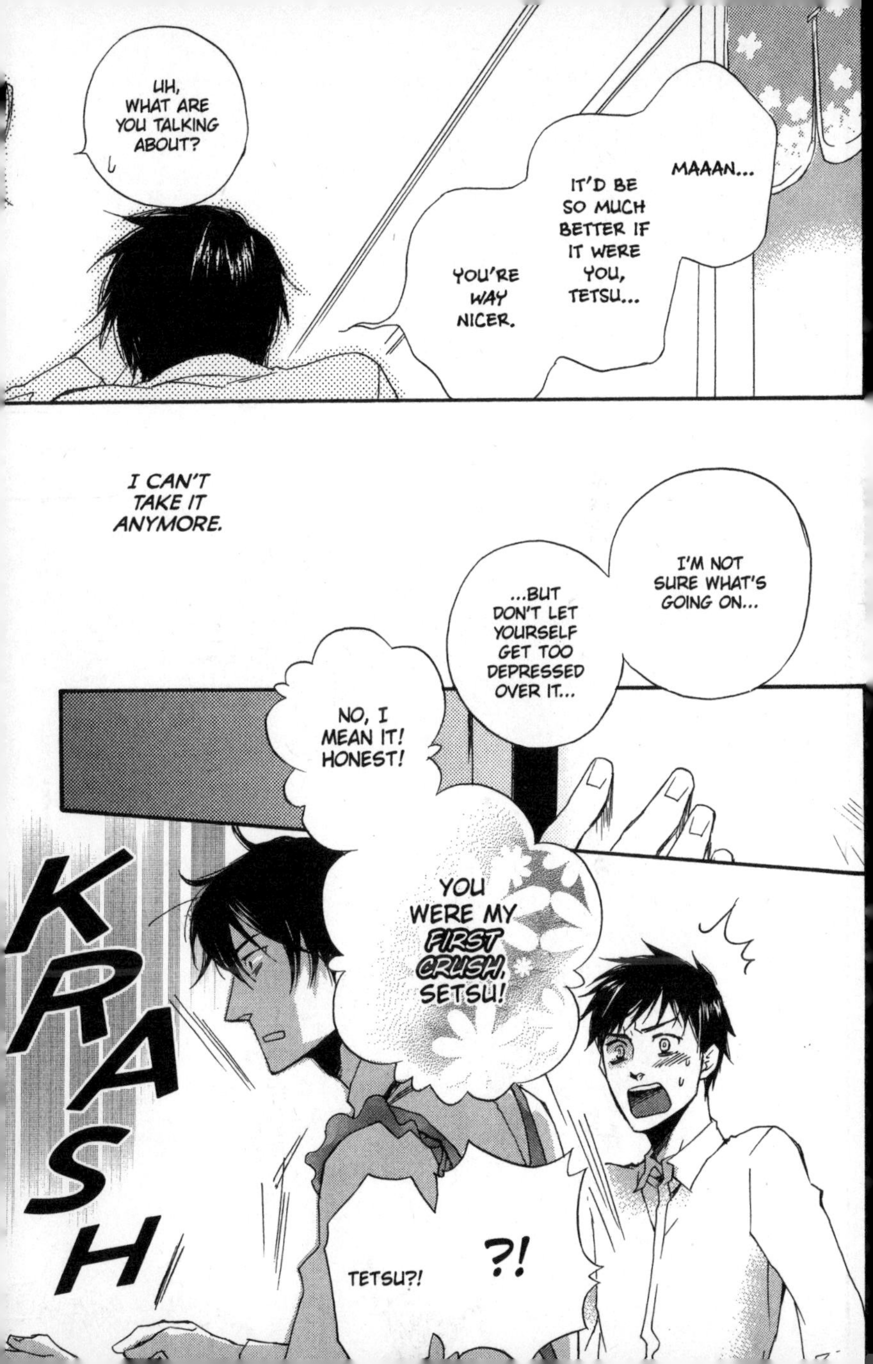
MAAAN...
IT'D BE SO MUCH BETTER IF IT WERE YOU, TETSU...
YOU'RE WAY NICER.
UH, WHAT ARE YOU TALKING ABOUT?
I'M NOT SURE WHAT'S GOING ON...
...BUT DON'T LET YOURSELF GET TOO DEPRESSED OVER IT...
I CAN'T TAKE IT ANYMORE.
NO, I MEAN IT! HONEST!
YOU WERE MY FIRST CRUSH, SETSU!
KRASH
?!
TETSU?!

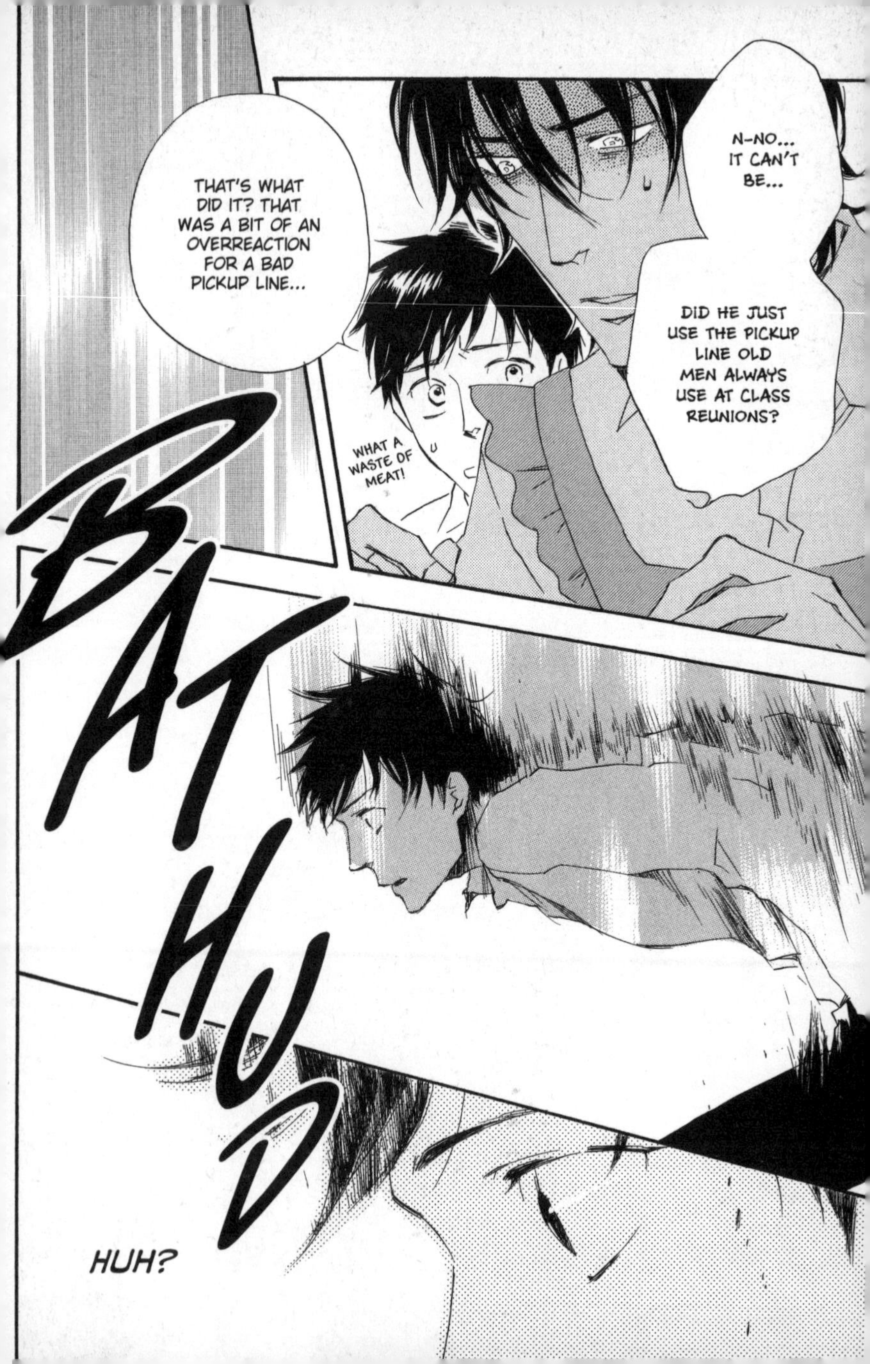
N-NO... IT CAN'T BE...
DID HE JUST USE THE PICKUP LINE OLD MEN ALWAYS USE AT CLASS REUNIONS?
THAT'S WHAT DID IT? THAT WAS A BIT OF AN OVERREACTION FOR A BAD PICKUP LINE...
WHAT A WASTE OF MEAT!
BATHUD
HUH?

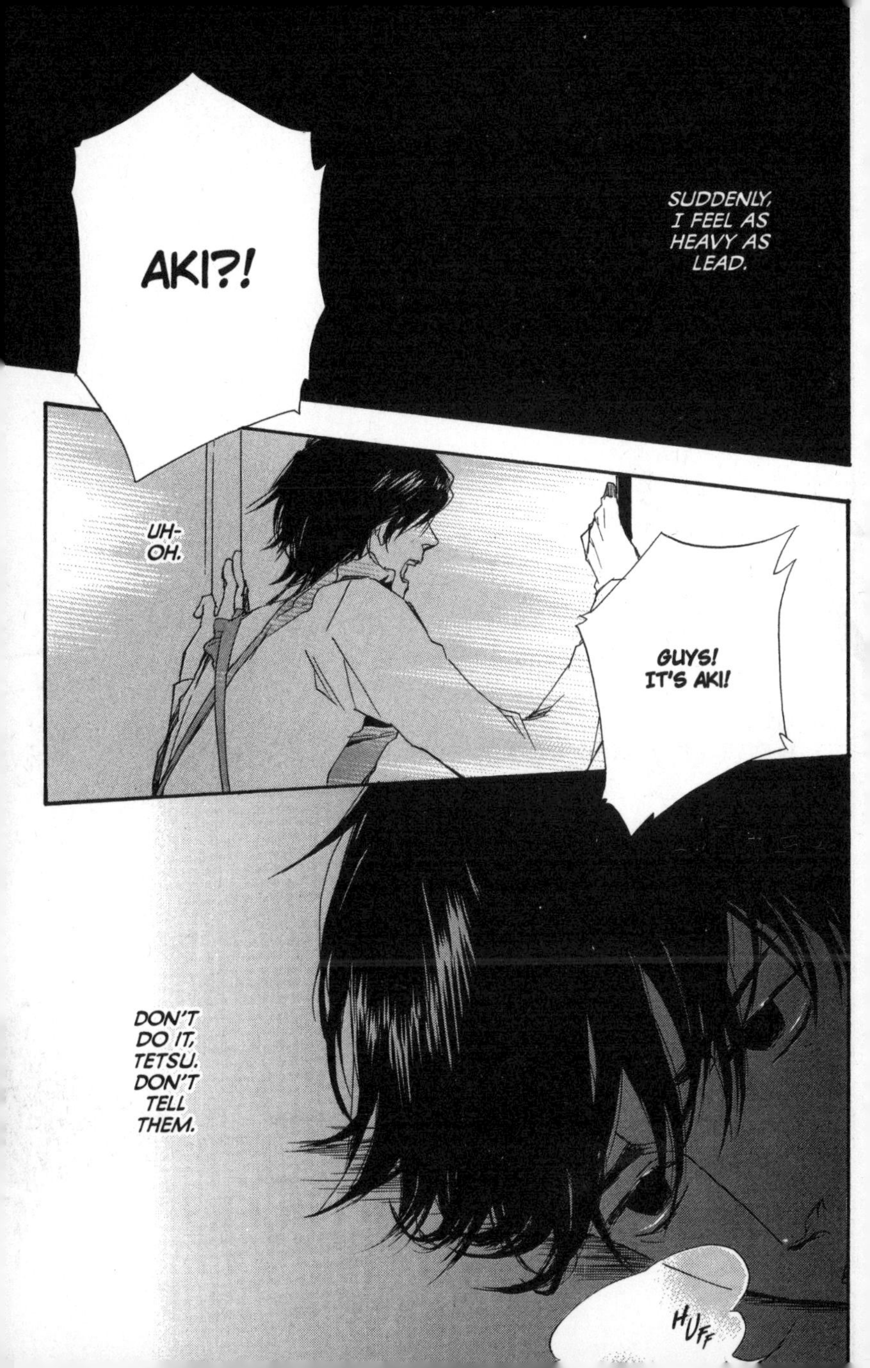
SUDDENLY, I FEEL AS HEAVY AS LEAD.
AKI?!
GUYS! IT'S AKI!
UH-OH.
DON'T DO IT, TETSU. DON'T TELL THEM.
HUFF

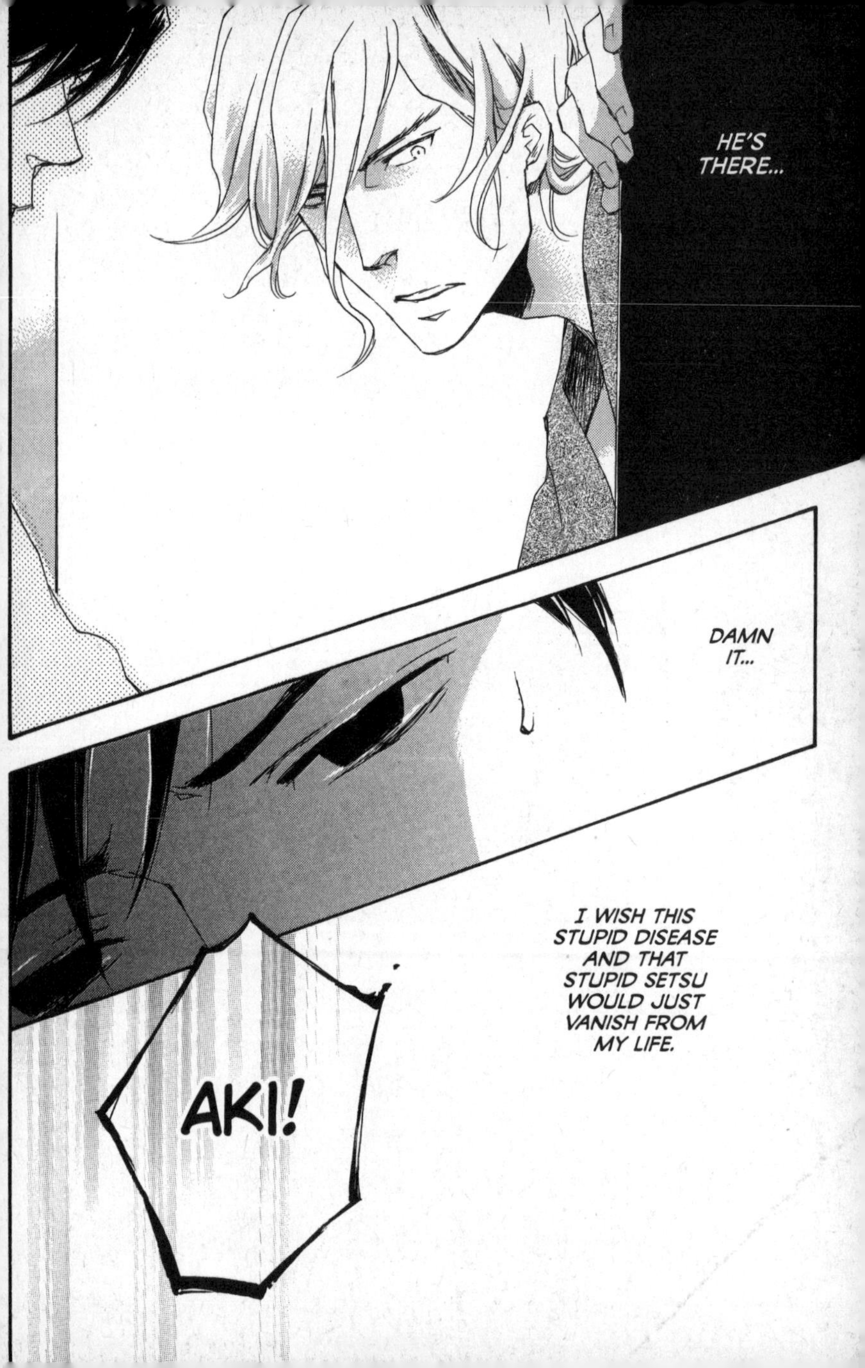
HE'S THERE...
DAMN IT...
I WISH THIS STUPID DISEASE AND THAT STUPID SETSU WOULD JUST VANISH FROM MY LIFE.
AKI!

A Strange & Mystifying Story

I ASKED HIM ONCE WHY HE DID THIS.

HE SAID, "I TOLD YOU. TO KILL TIME."

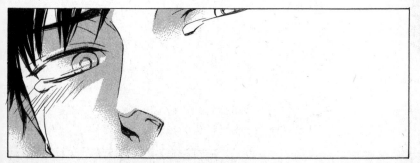

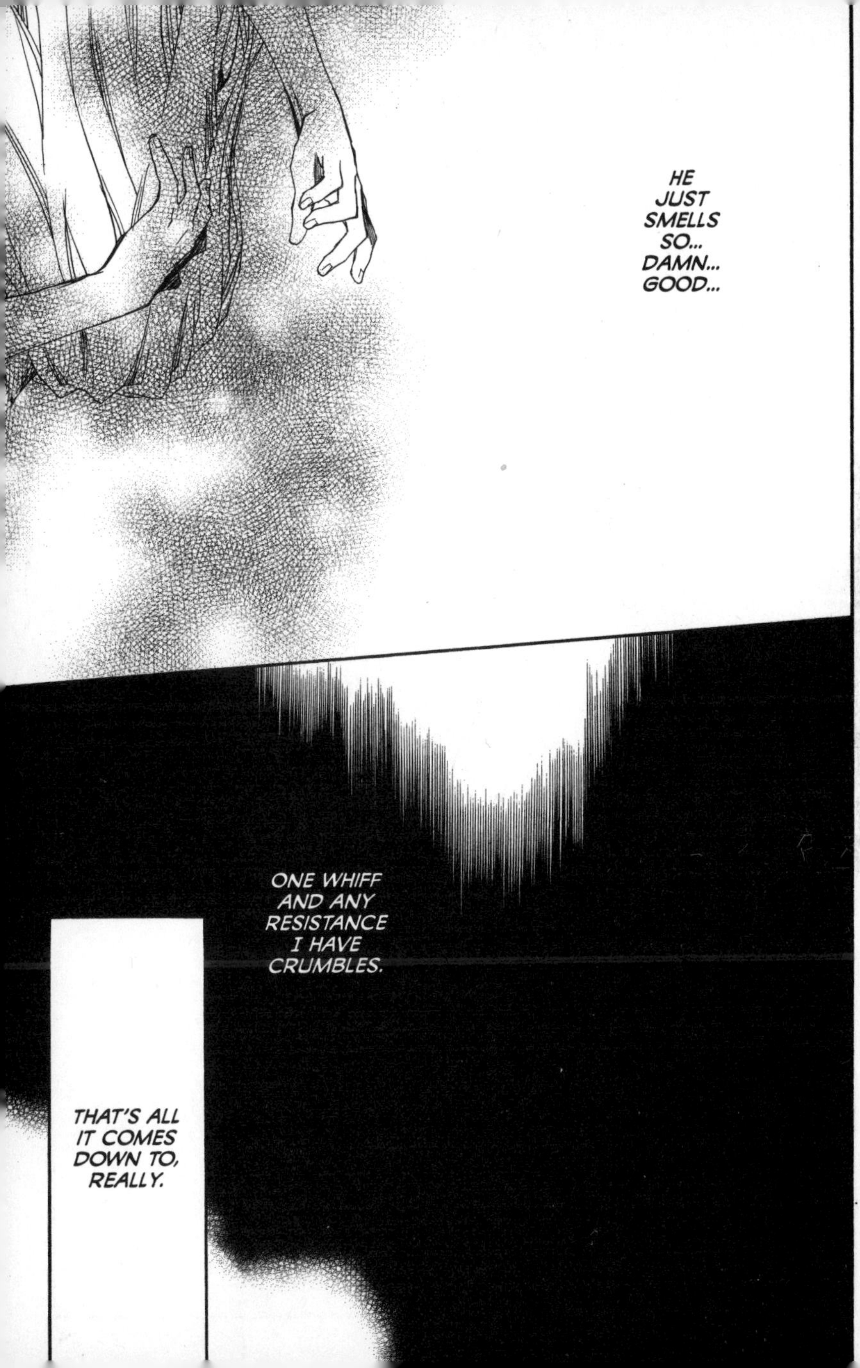
HE JUST SMELLS SO... DAMN... GOOD...
ONE WHIFF AND ANY RESISTANCE I HAVE CRUMBLES.
THAT'S ALL IT COMES DOWN TO, REALLY.

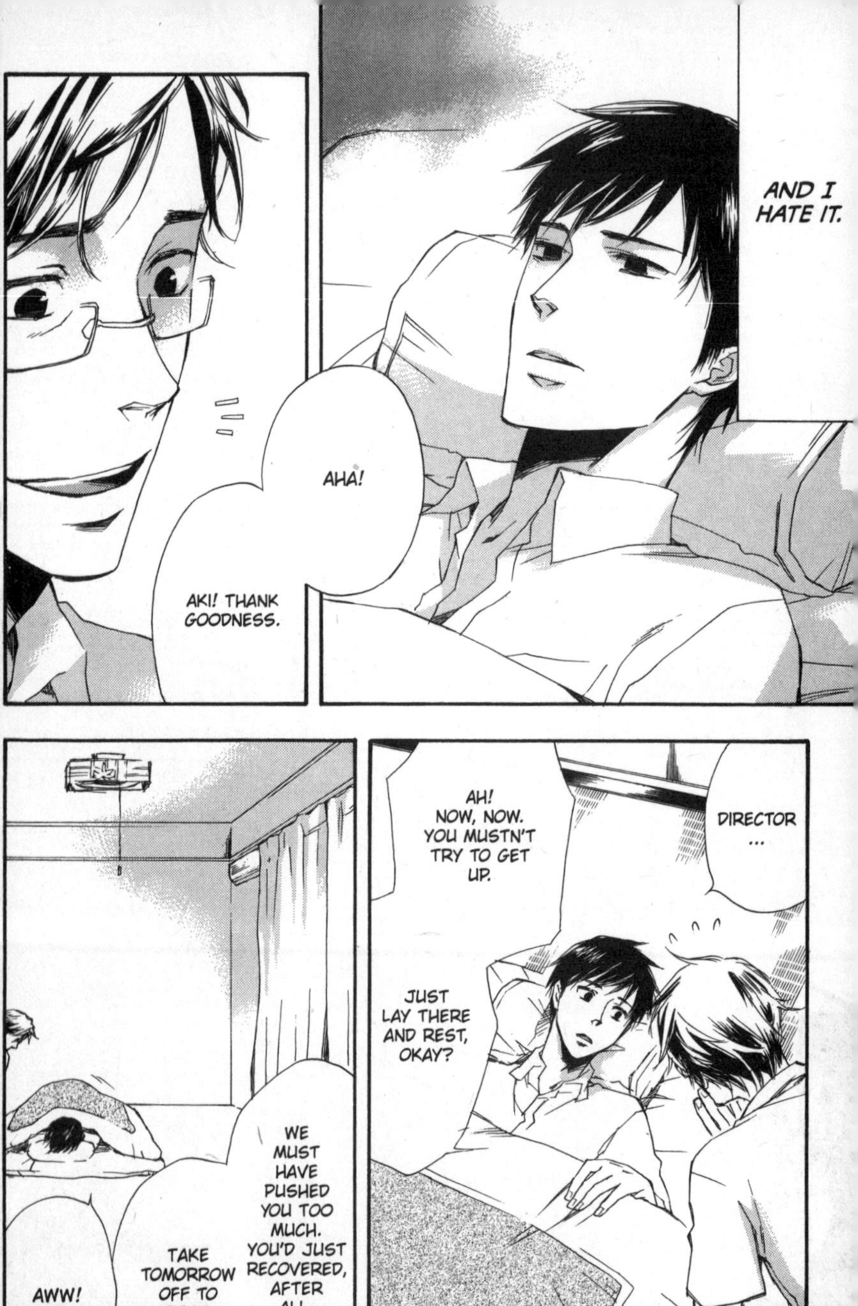
AND I HATE IT.
AHA!
AKI! THANK GOODNESS.
DIRECTOR ...
AH! NOW, NOW. YOU MUSTN'T TRY TO GET UP.
JUST LAY THERE AND REST, OKAY?
WE MUST HAVE PUSHED YOU TOO MUCH. YOU'D JUST RECOVERED, AFTER ALL.
TAKE TOMORROW OFF TO REST.
AWW!

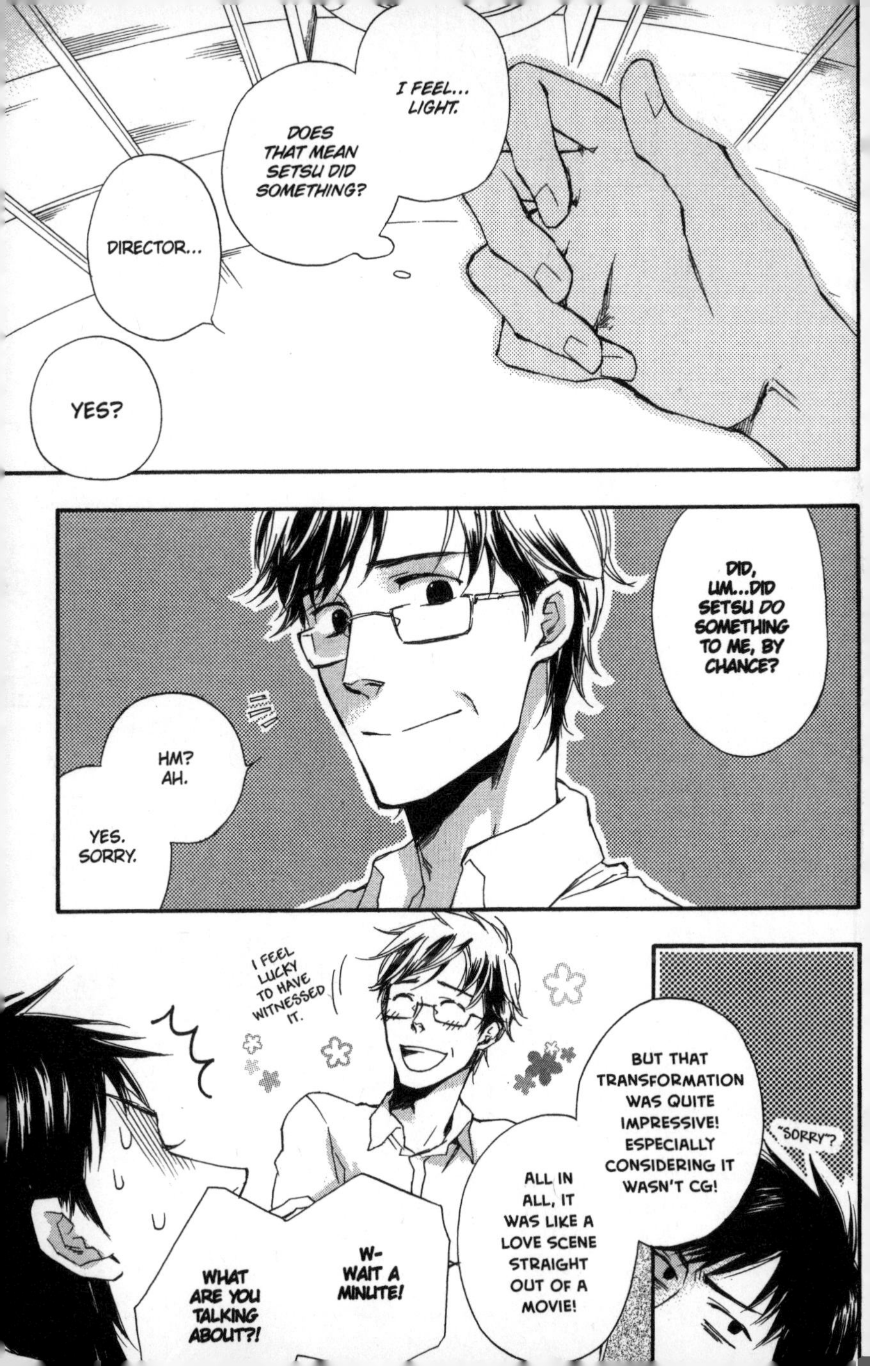
I FEEL... LIGHT.
DOES THAT MEAN SETSU DID SOMETHING?
DIRECTOR...
YES?
DID, UM...DID SETSU DO SOMETHING TO ME, BY CHANCE?
HM? AH.
YES. SORRY.
"SORRY"?
BUT THAT TRANSFORMATION WAS QUITE IMPRESSIVE! ESPECIALLY CONSIDERING IT WASN'T CG!
ALL IN ALL, IT WAS LIKE A LOVE SCENE STRAIGHT OUT OF A MOVIE!
I FEEL LUCKY TO HAVE WITNESSED IT.
W- WAIT A MINUTE!
WHAT ARE YOU TALKING ABOUT?!

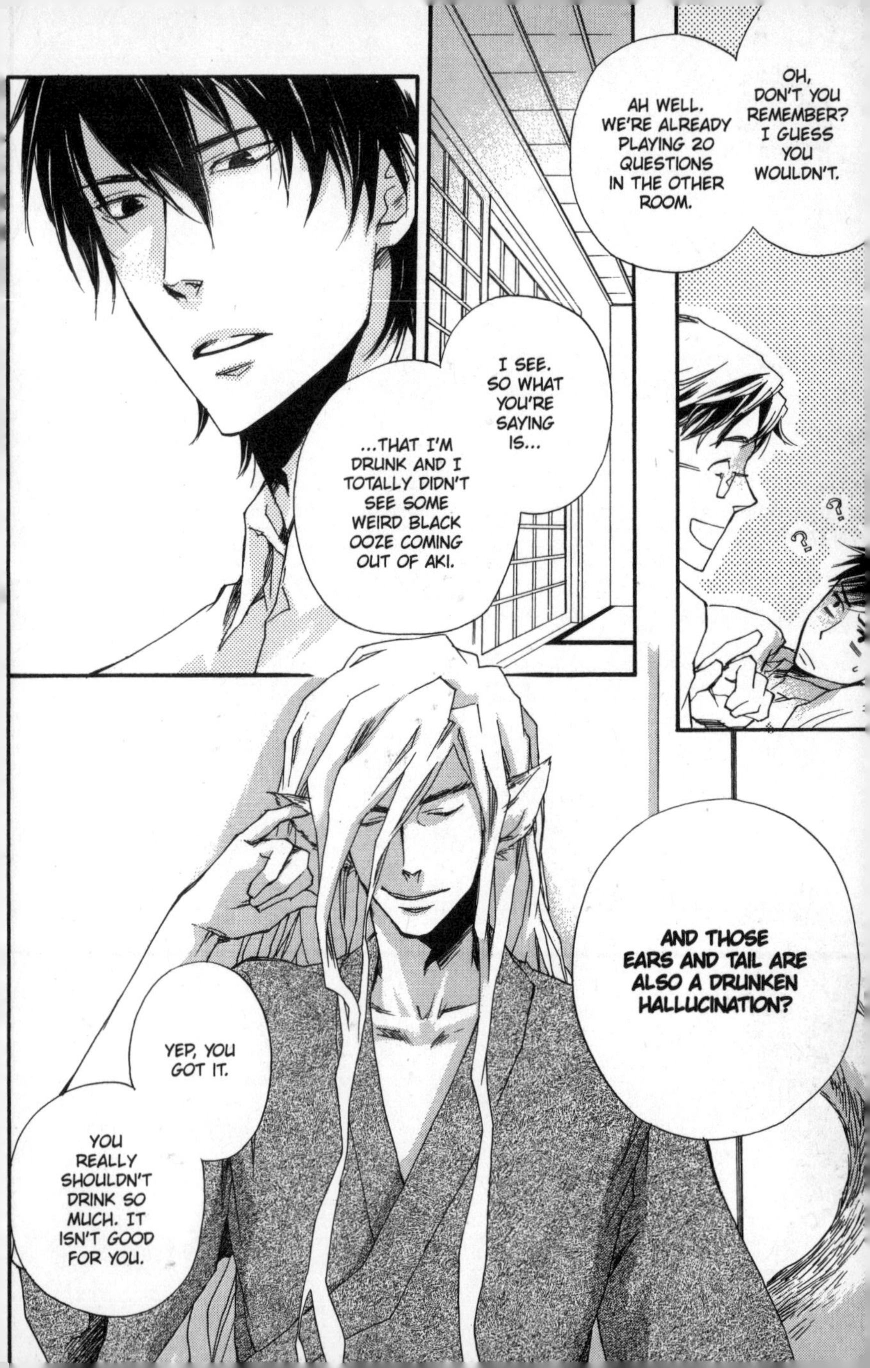
OH, DON'T YOU REMEMBER? I GUESS YOU WOULDN'T.
AH WELL. WE'RE ALREADY PLAYING 20 QUESTIONS IN THE OTHER ROOM.
I SEE. SO WHAT YOU'RE SAYING IS...
...THAT I'M DRUNK AND I TOTALLY DIDN'T SEE SOME WEIRD BLACK OOZE COMING OUT OF AKI.
??
AND THOSE EARS AND TAIL ARE ALSO A DRUNKEN HALLUCINATION?
YEP, YOU GOT IT.
YOU REALLY SHOULDN'T DRINK SO MUCH. IT ISN'T GOOD FOR YOU.

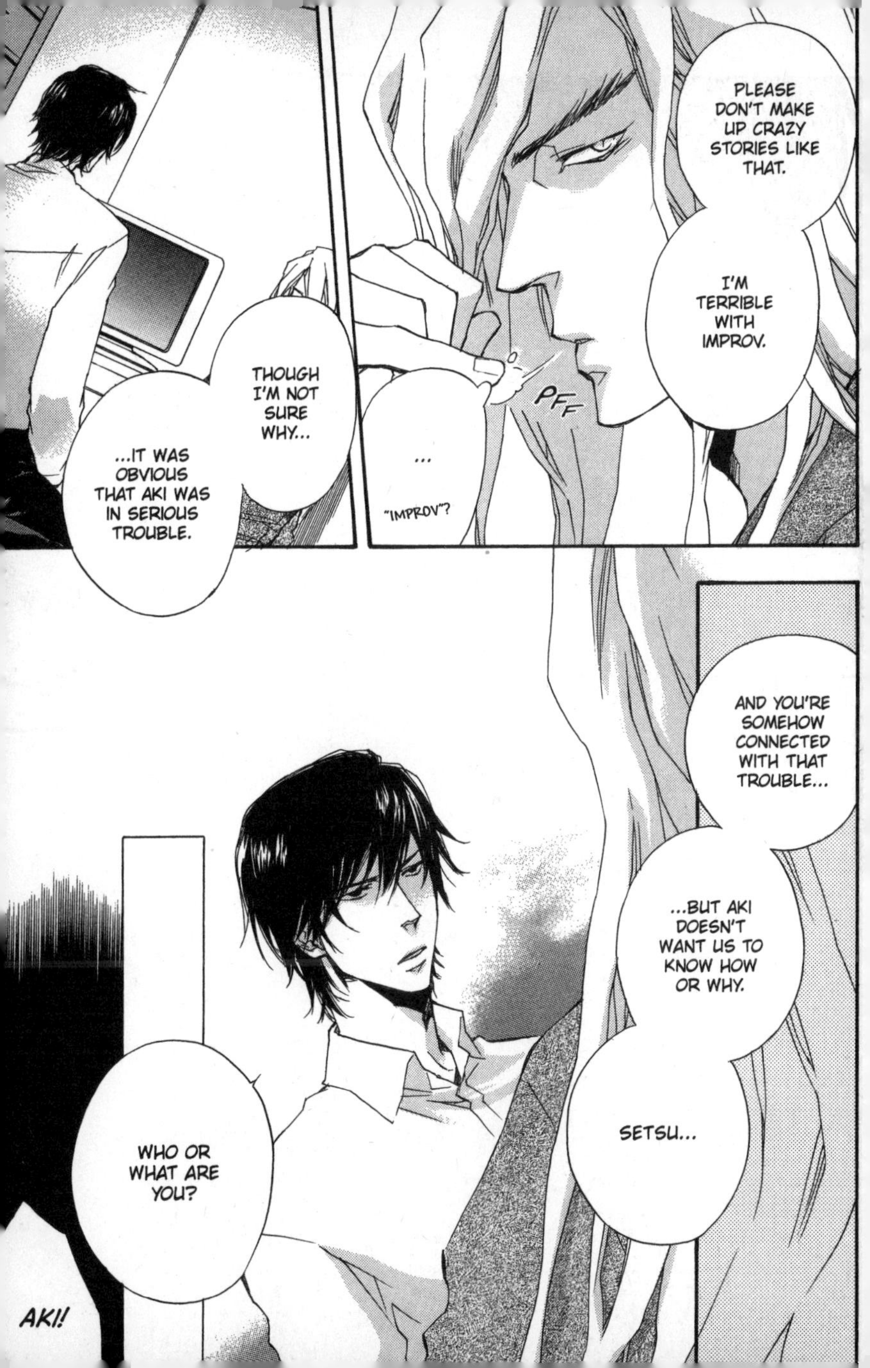
PLEASE DON'T MAKE UP CRAZY STORIES LIKE THAT.
I'M TERRIBLE WITH IMPROV.
PFF
...
"IMPROV"?
THOUGH I'M NOT SURE WHY...
...IT WAS OBVIOUS THAT AKI WAS IN SERIOUS TROUBLE.
AND YOU'RE SOMEHOW CONNECTED WITH THAT TROUBLE...
...BUT AKI DOESN'T WANT US TO KNOW HOW OR WHY.
SETSU...
WHO OR WHAT ARE YOU?
AKI!

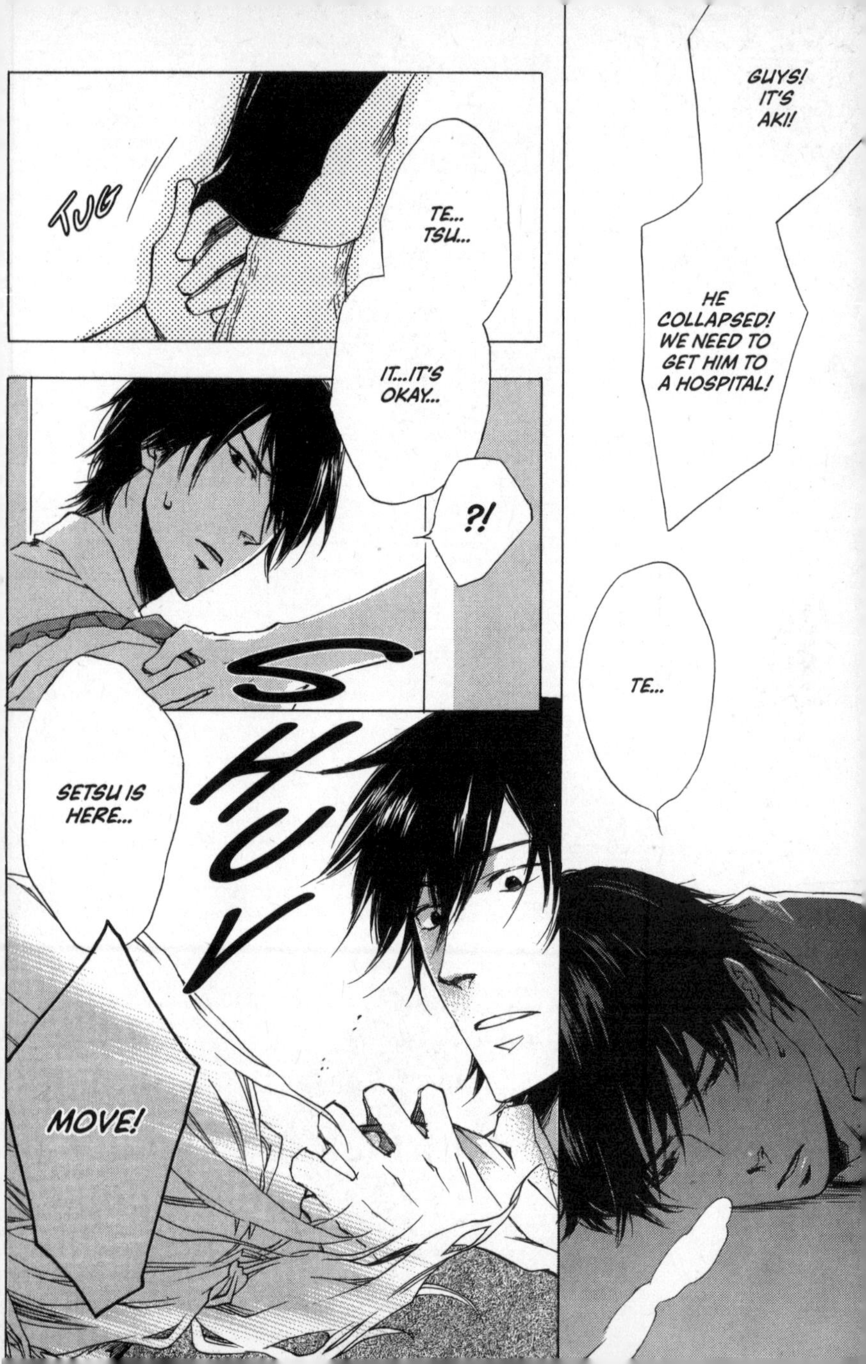
GUYS! IT'S AKI!
HE COLLAPSED! WE NEED TO GET HIM TO A HOSPITAL!
TE...
TUG
TE... TSU...
IT...IT'S OKAY...
?!
SHUV
SETSU IS HERE...
MOVE!

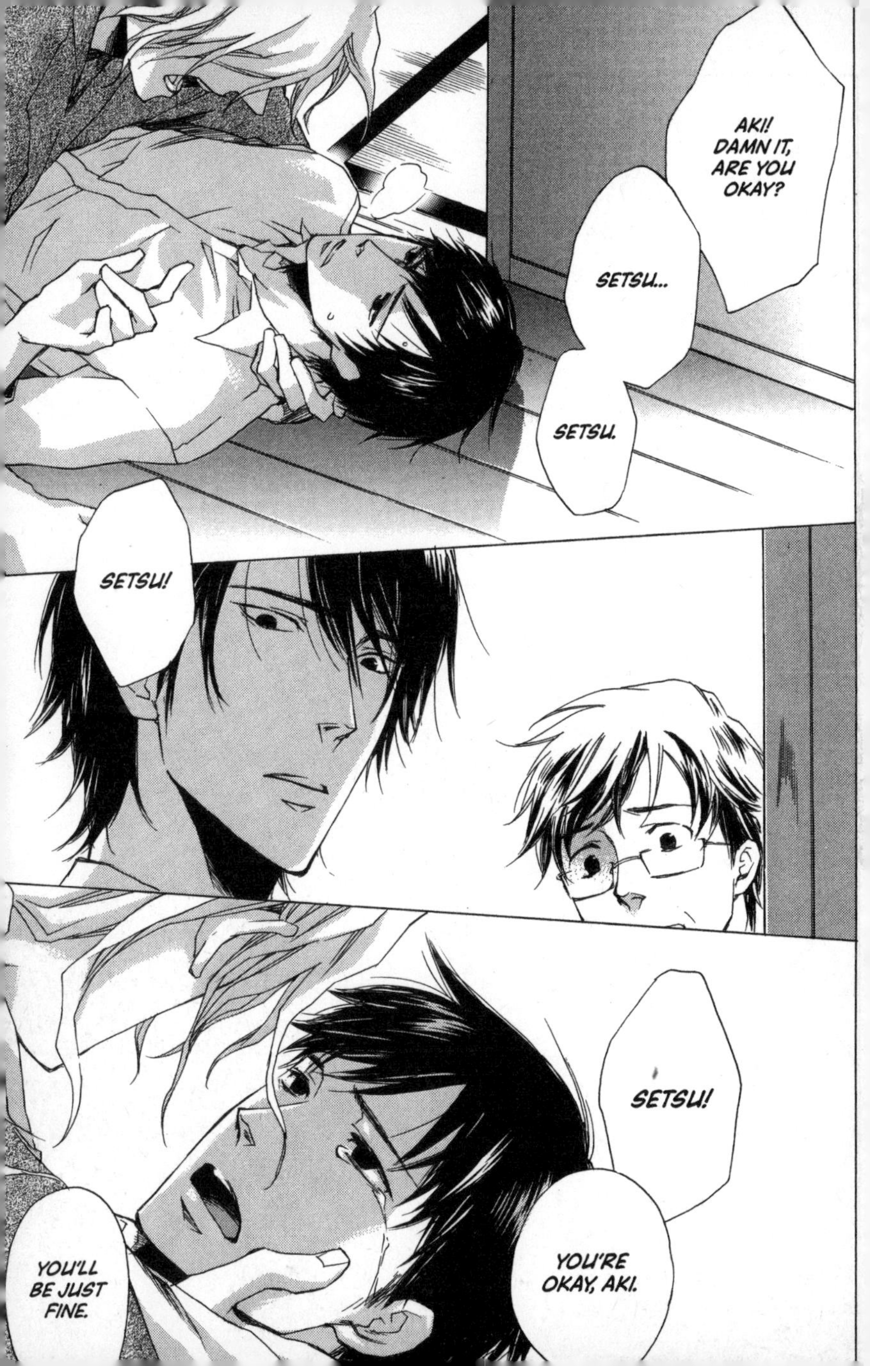
AKI! DAMN IT, ARE YOU OKAY?
SETSU...
SETSU.
SETSU!
SETSU!
YOU'RE OKAY, AKI.
YOU'LL BE JUST FINE.

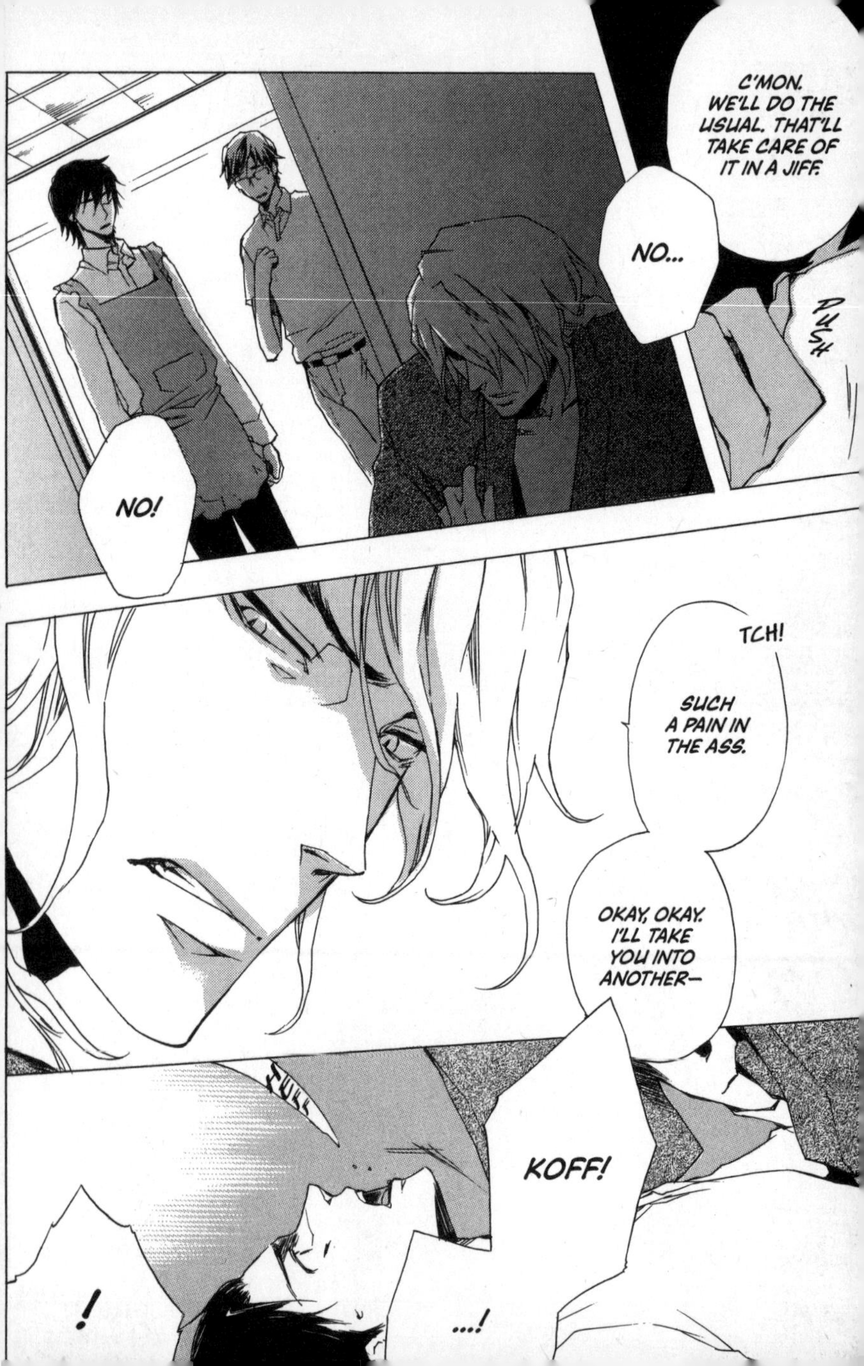
C'MON. WE'LL DO THE USUAL. THAT'LL TAKE CARE OF IT IN A JIFF.
PUSH
NO...
NO!
TCH!
SUCH A PAIN IN THE ASS.
OKAY, OKAY. I'LL TAKE YOU INTO ANOTHER—
KOFF!
...!
!

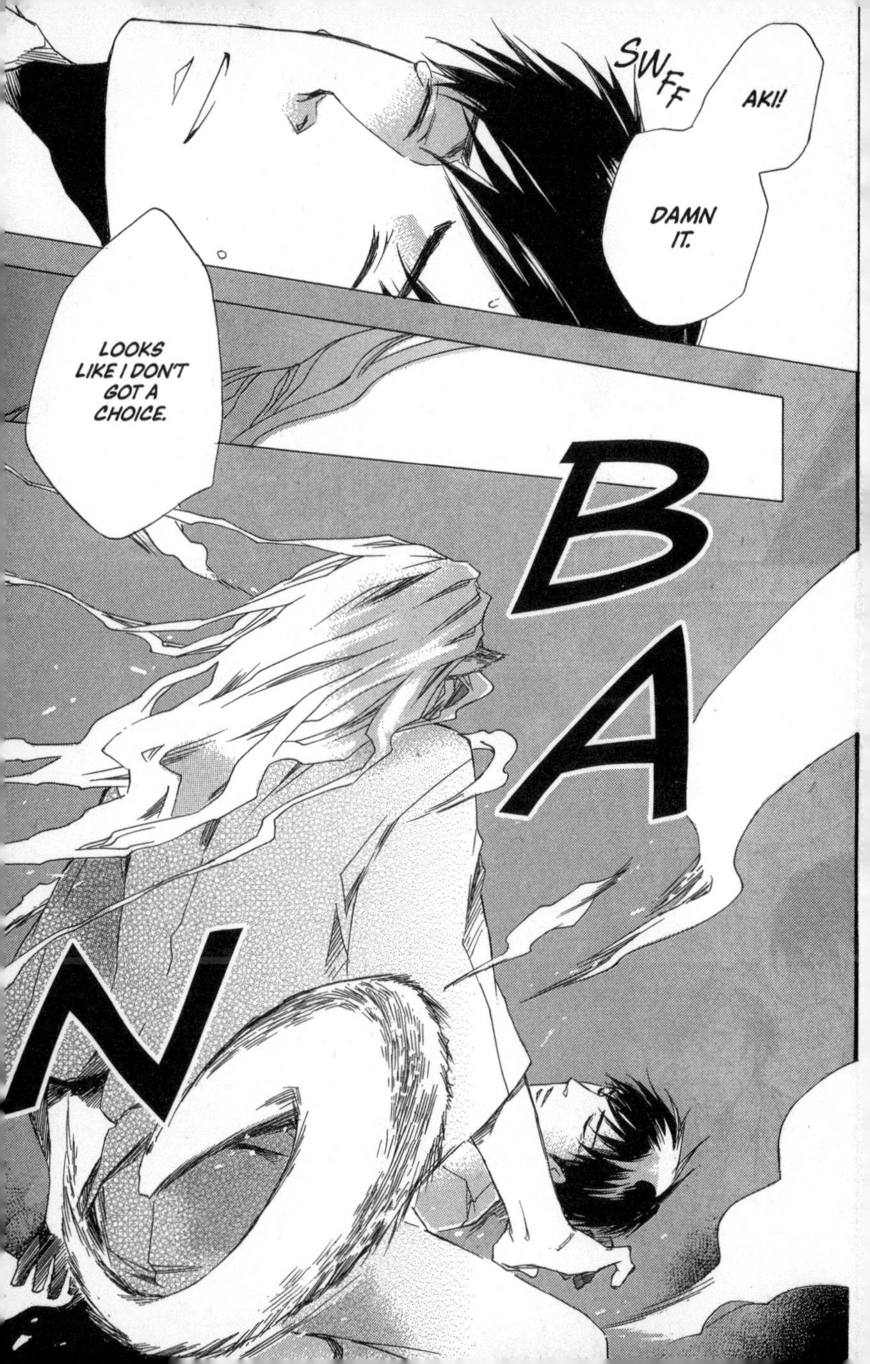
SWFF
AKI!
DAMN IT.
LOOKS LIKE I DON'T GOT A CHOICE.
BAN

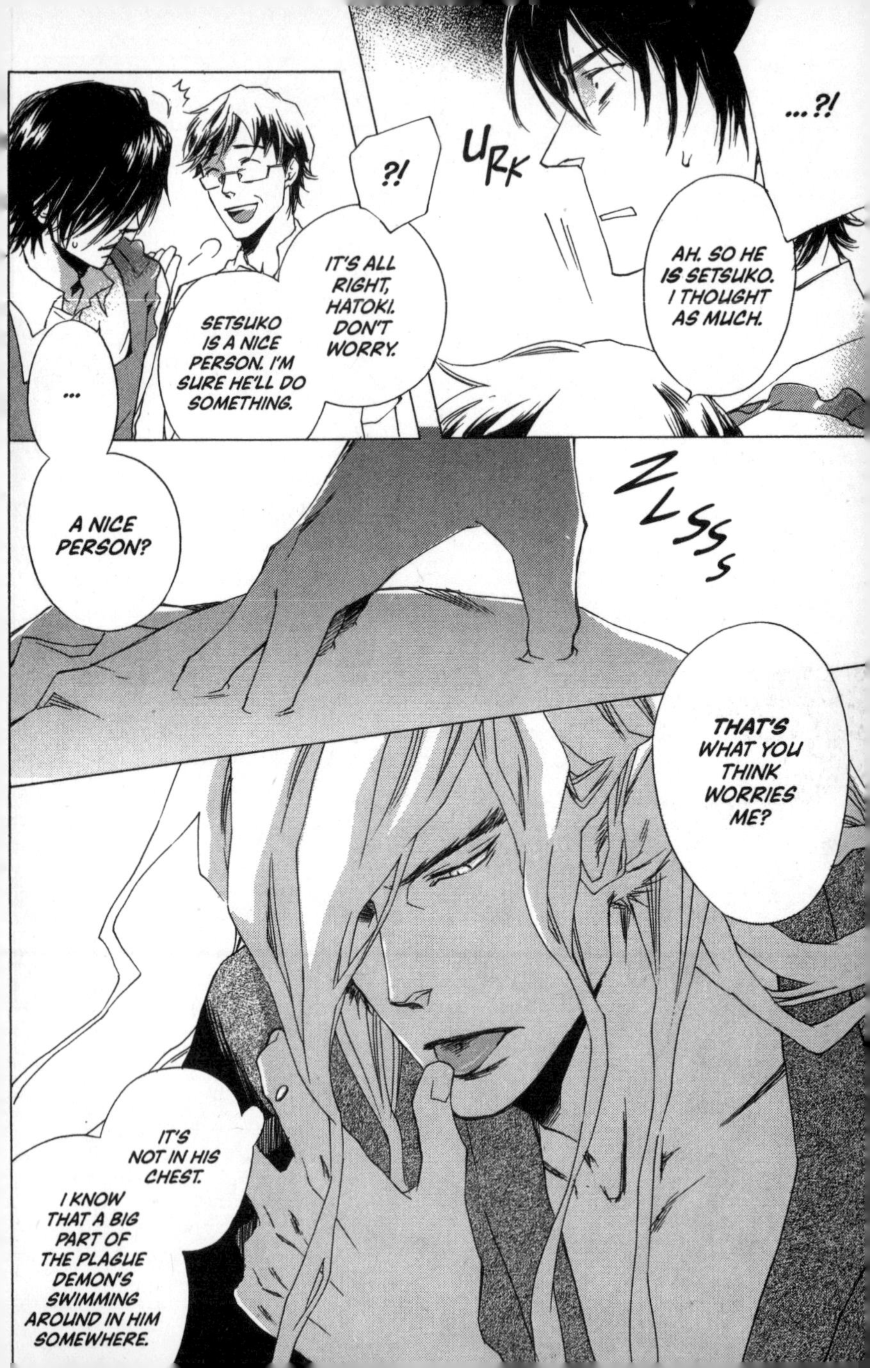
...?!
URK
AH. SO HE IS SETSUKO. I THOUGHT AS MUCH.
?!
IT'S ALL RIGHT, HATOKI. DON'T WORRY.
SETSUKO IS A NICE PERSON. I'M SURE HE'LL DO SOMETHING.
...
A NICE PERSON?
ZZSSSS
THAT'S WHAT YOU THINK WORRIES ME?
IT'S NOT IN HIS CHEST.
I KNOW THAT A BIG PART OF THE PLAGUE DEMON'S SWIMMING AROUND IN HIM SOMEWHERE.

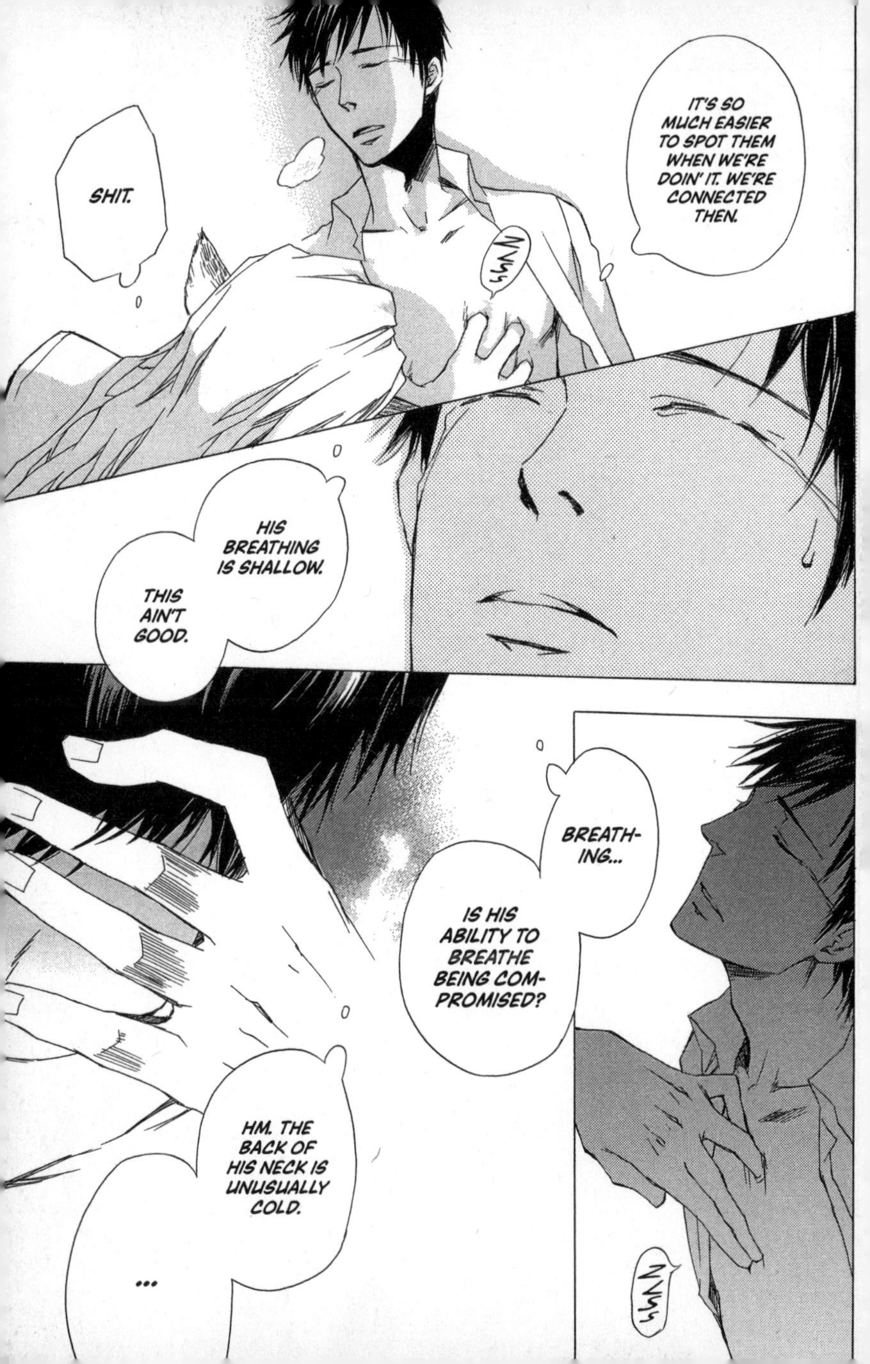
IT'S SO MUCH EASIER TO SPOT THEM WHEN WE'RE DOIN' IT. WE'RE CONNECTED THEN.
SHIT.
HIS BREATHING IS SHALLOW.
THIS AIN'T GOOD.
BREATH-ING...
IS HIS ABILITY TO BREATHE BEING COM-PROMISED?
HM. THE BACK OF HIS NECK IS UNUSUALLY COLD.
...

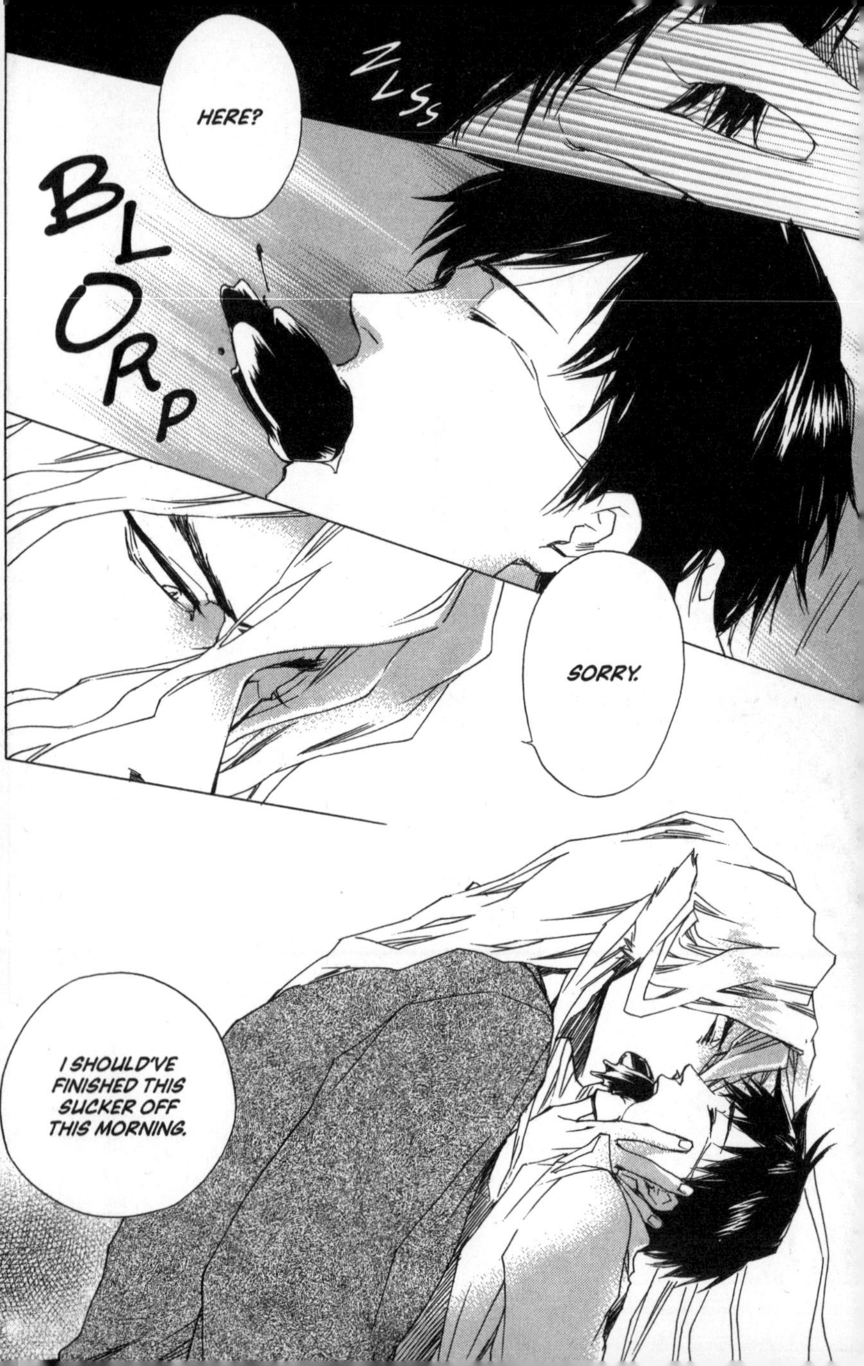
ZLSS
HERE?
BLORP
SORRY.
I SHOULD'VE FINISHED THIS SUCKER OFF THIS MORNING.

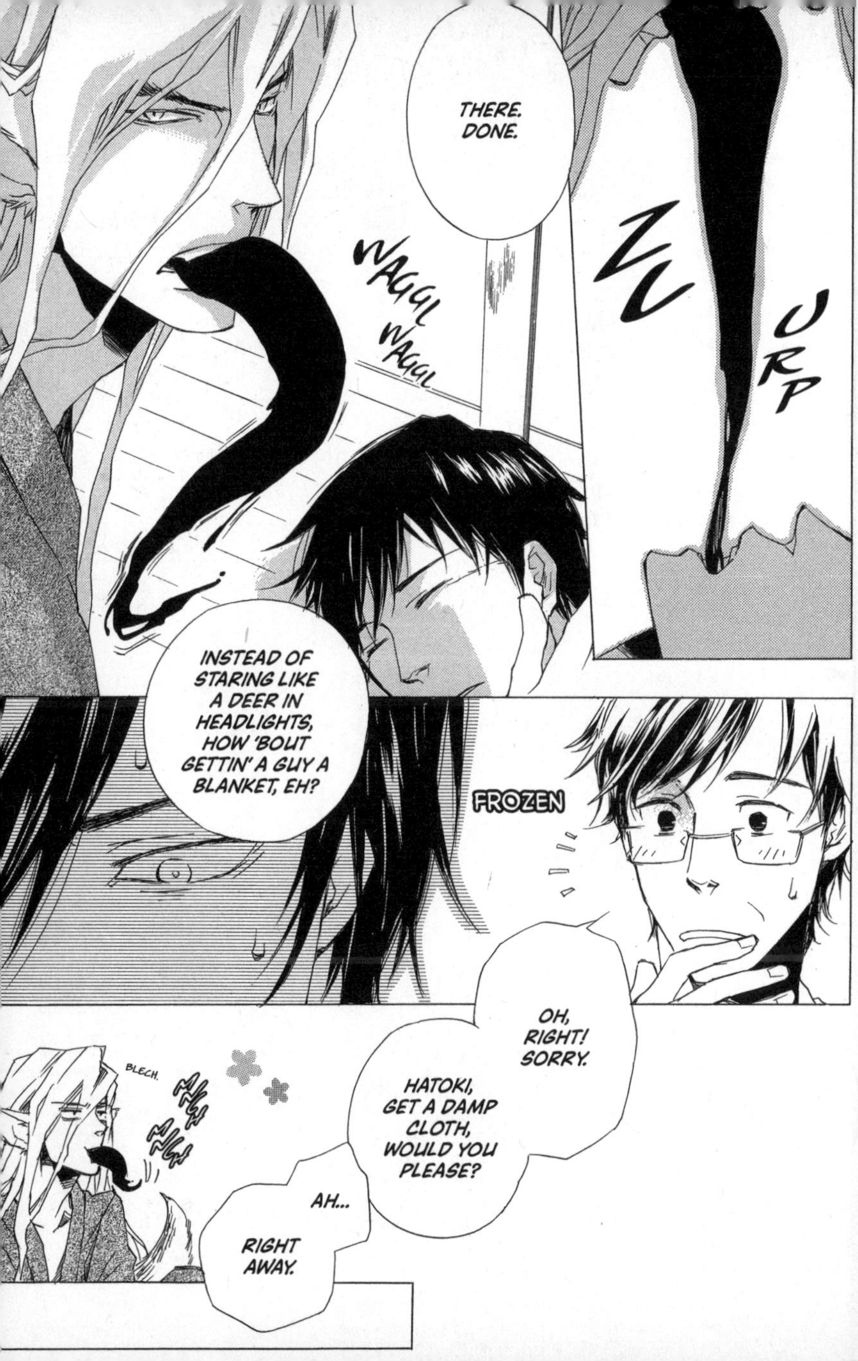
ZU
URP
THERE. DONE.
WAGGL WAGGL
INSTEAD OF STARING LIKE A DEER IN HEADLIGHTS, HOW 'BOUT GETTIN' A GUY A BLANKET, EH?
FROZEN
OH, RIGHT! SORRY.
HATOKI, GET A DAMP CLOTH, WOULD YOU PLEASE?
AH...
RIGHT AWAY.
BLECH.

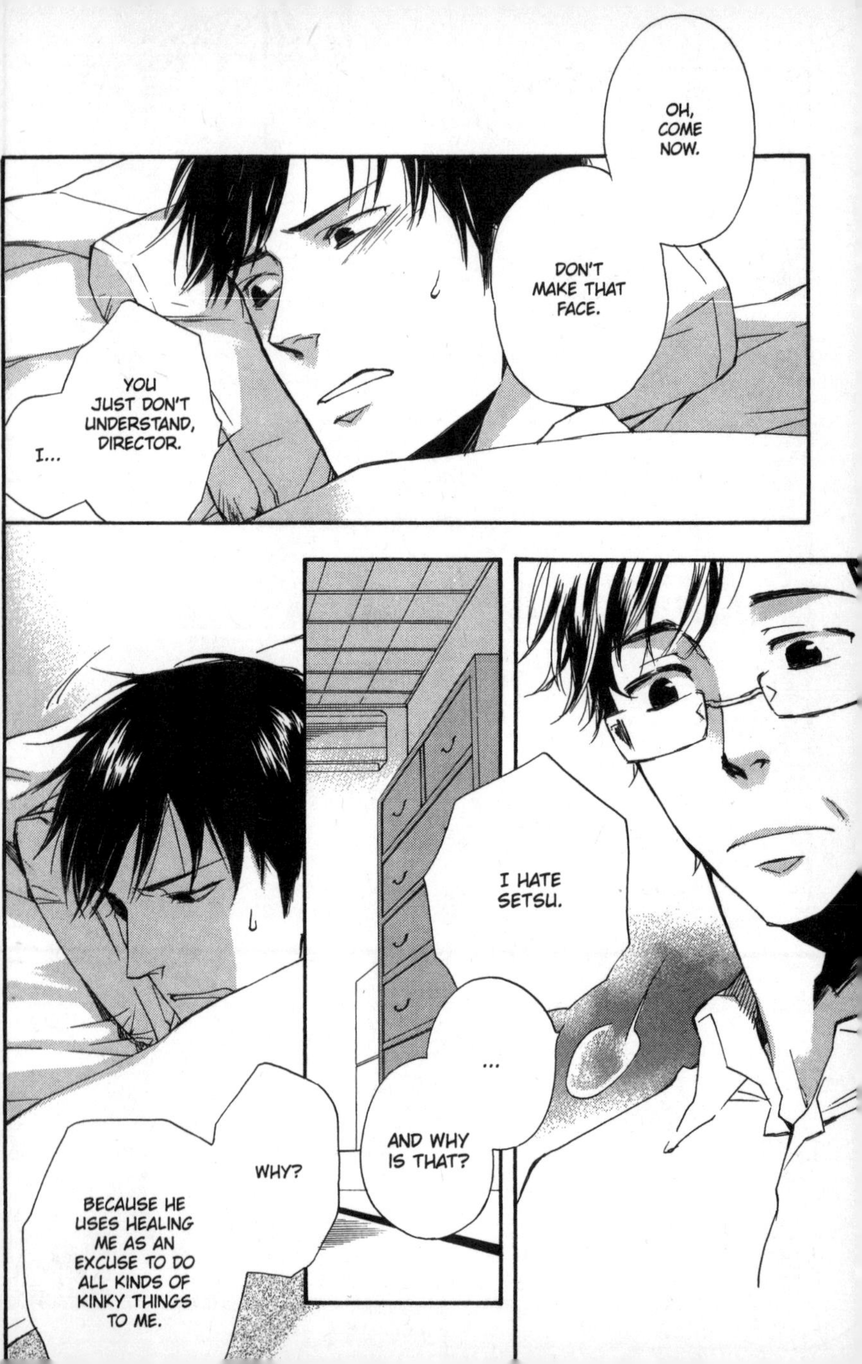
OH, COME NOW.
DON'T MAKE THAT FACE.
YOU JUST DON'T UNDERSTAND, DIRECTOR.
I...
I HATE SETSU.
...
AND WHY IS THAT?
WHY?
BECAUSE HE USES HEALING ME AS AN EXCUSE TO DO ALL KINDS OF KINKY THINGS TO ME.

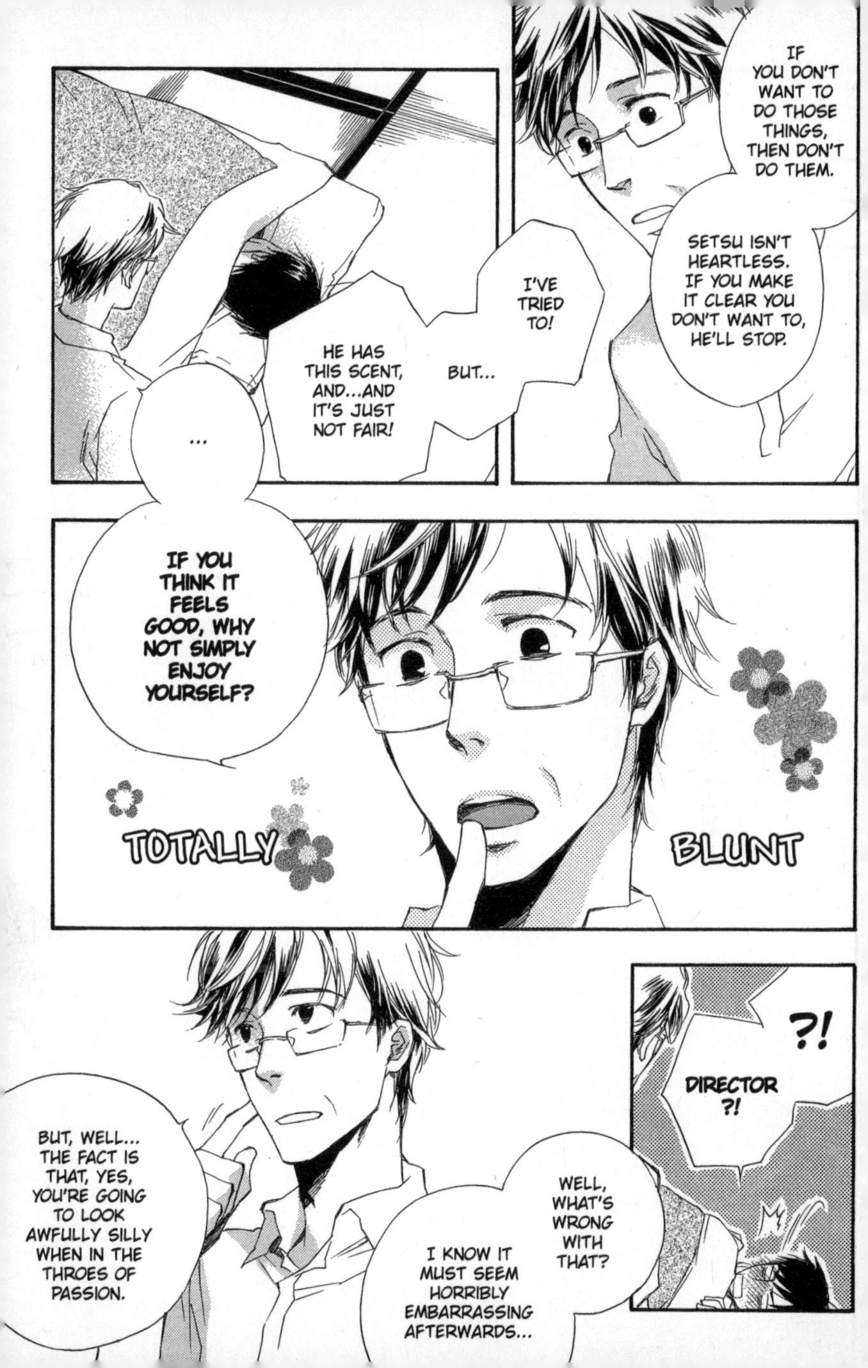
IF YOU DON'T WANT TO DO THOSE THINGS, THEN DON'T DO THEM.
SETSU ISN'T HEARTLESS. IF YOU MAKE IT CLEAR YOU DON'T WANT TO, HE'LL STOP.
I'VE TRIED TO!
BUT...
HE HAS THIS SCENT, AND...AND IT'S JUST NOT FAIR!
...
IF YOU THINK IT FEELS GOOD, WHY NOT SIMPLY ENJOY YOURSELF?
TOTALLY BLUNT
?!
DIRECTOR ?!
WELL, WHAT'S WRONG WITH THAT?
I KNOW IT MUST SEEM HORRIBLY EMBARRASSING AFTERWARDS...
BUT, WELL... THE FACT IS THAT, YES, YOU'RE GOING TO LOOK AWFULLY SILLY WHEN IN THE THROES OF PASSION.

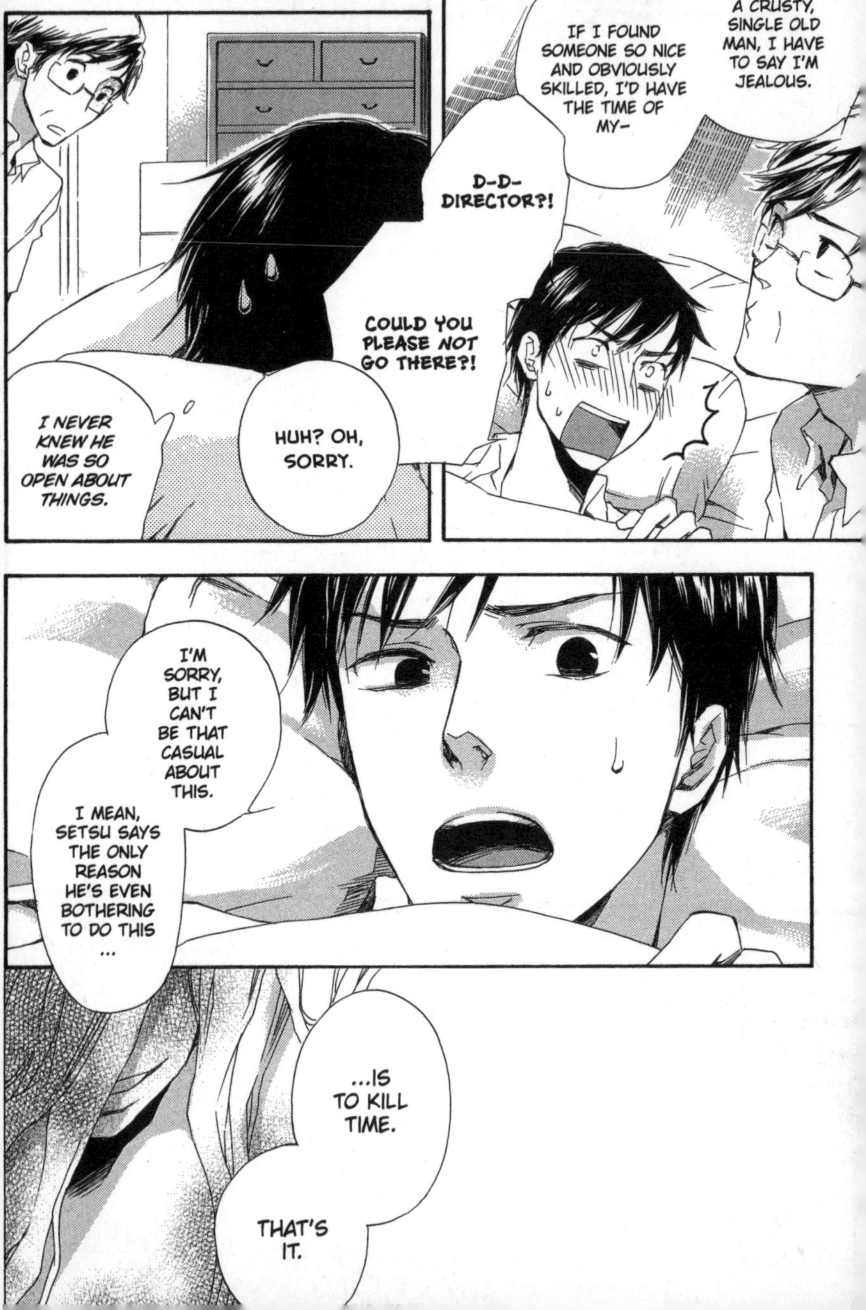
AND AS A CRUSTY, SINGLE OLD MAN, I HAVE TO SAY I'M JEALOUS.
IF I FOUND SOMEONE SO NICE AND OBVIOUSLY SKILLED, I'D HAVE THE TIME OF MY-
D-D-DIRECTOR?!
COULD YOU PLEASE NOT GO THERE?!
HUH? OH, SORRY.
I NEVER KNEW HE WAS SO OPEN ABOUT THINGS.
I'M SORRY, BUT I CAN'T BE THAT CASUAL ABOUT THIS.
I MEAN, SETSU SAYS THE ONLY REASON HE'S EVEN BOTHERING TO DO THIS ...
...IS TO KILL TIME.
THAT'S IT.

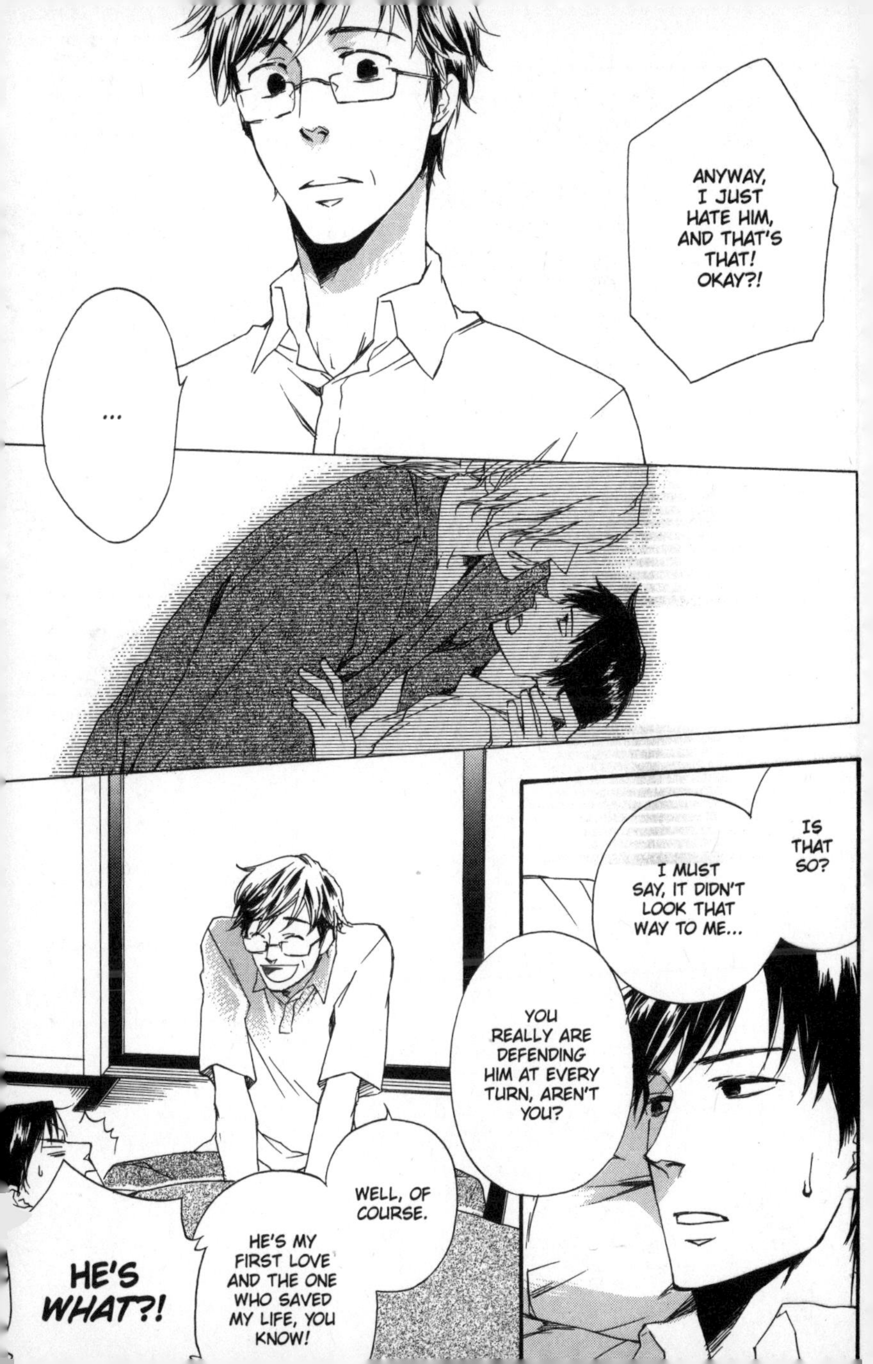
ANYWAY, I JUST HATE HIM, AND THAT'S THAT! OKAY?!
...
IS THAT SO?
I MUST SAY, IT DIDN'T LOOK THAT WAY TO ME...
YOU REALLY ARE DEFENDING HIM AT EVERY TURN, AREN'T YOU?
WELL, OF COURSE.
HE'S MY FIRST LOVE AND THE ONE WHO SAVED MY LIFE, YOU KNOW!
HE'S WHAT?!

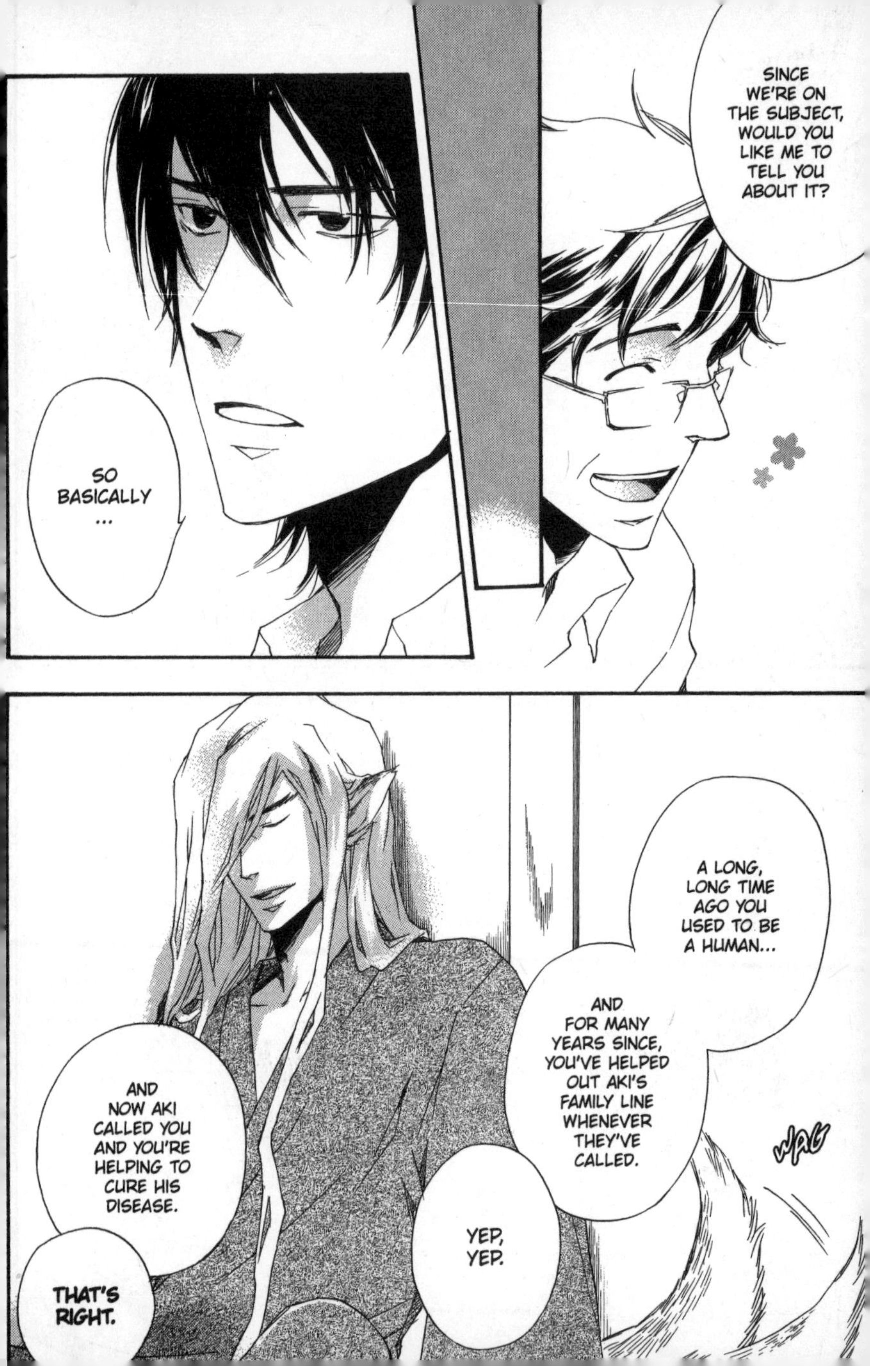
SINCE WE'RE ON THE SUBJECT, WOULD YOU LIKE ME TO TELL YOU ABOUT IT?
SO BASICALLY ...
A LONG, LONG TIME AGO YOU USED TO BE A HUMAN...
AND FOR MANY YEARS SINCE, YOU'VE HELPED OUT AKI'S FAMILY LINE WHENEVER THEY'VE CALLED.
WAG
YEP, YEP.
AND NOW AKI CALLED YOU AND YOU'RE HELPING TO CURE HIS DISEASE.
THAT'S RIGHT.

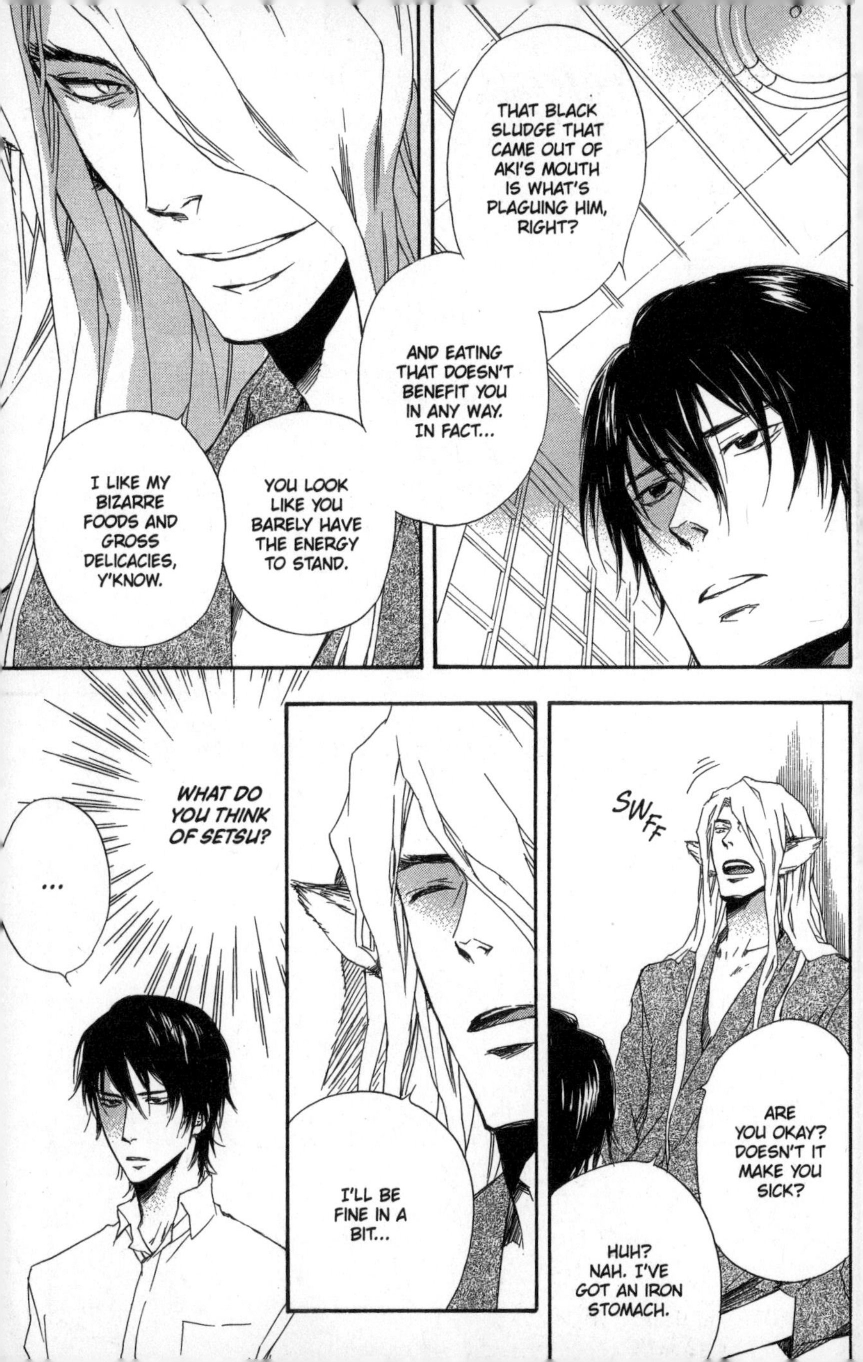
THAT BLACK SLUDGE THAT CAME OUT OF AKI'S MOUTH IS WHAT'S PLAGUING HIM, RIGHT?
AND EATING THAT DOESN'T BENEFIT YOU IN ANY WAY. IN FACT...
YOU LOOK LIKE YOU BARELY HAVE THE ENERGY TO STAND.
I LIKE MY BIZARRE FOODS AND GROSS DELICACIES, Y'KNOW.
SWFF
ARE YOU OKAY? DOESN'T IT MAKE YOU SICK?
HUH? NAH. I'VE GOT AN IRON STOMACH.
I'LL BE FINE IN A BIT...
WHAT DO YOU THINK OF SETSU?
...

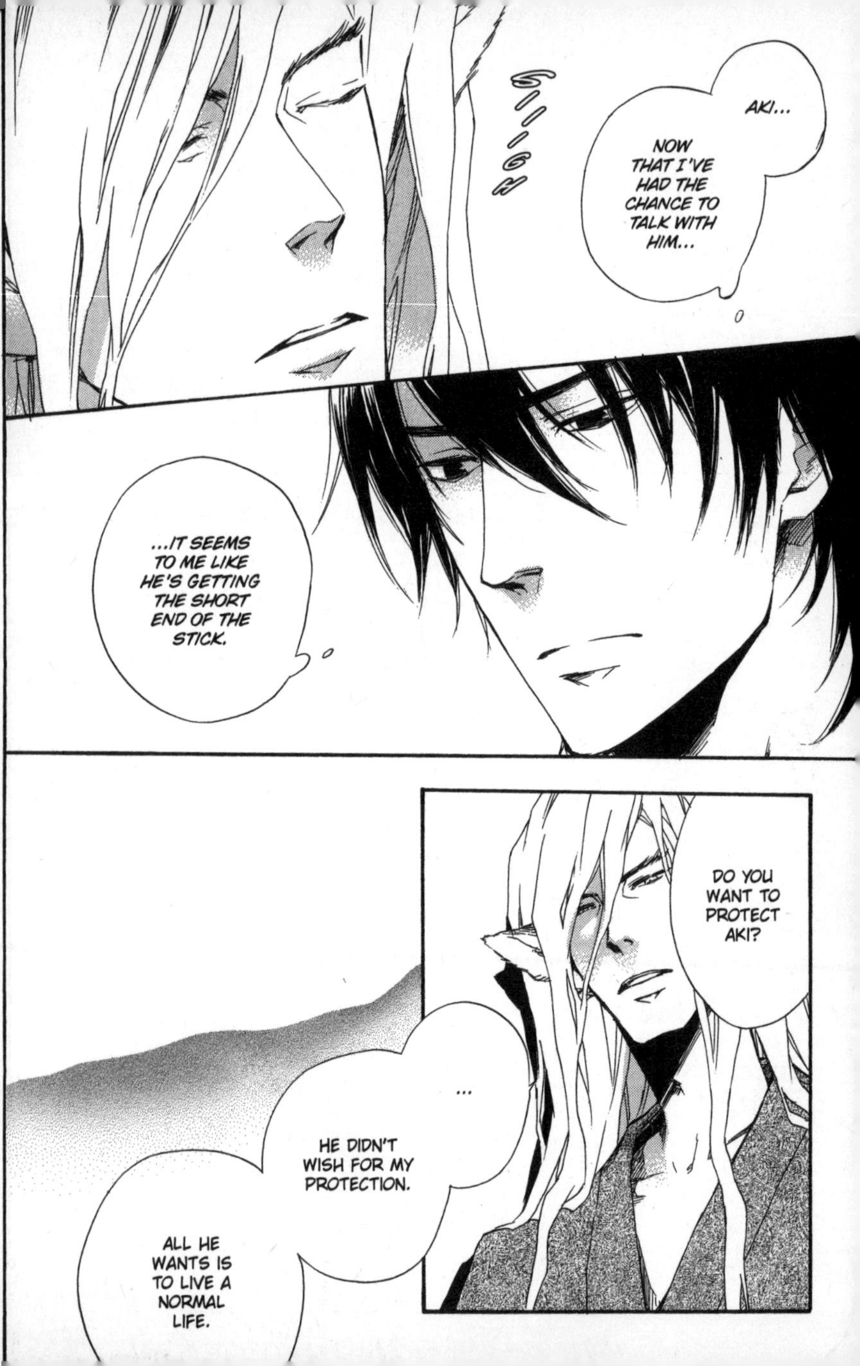
SIIIIGH
AKI...
NOW THAT I'VE HAD THE CHANCE TO TALK WITH HIM...
...IT SEEMS TO ME LIKE HE'S GETTING THE SHORT END OF THE STICK.
DO YOU WANT TO PROTECT AKI?
...
HE DIDN'T WISH FOR MY PROTECTION.
ALL HE WANTS IS TO LIVE A NORMAL LIFE.

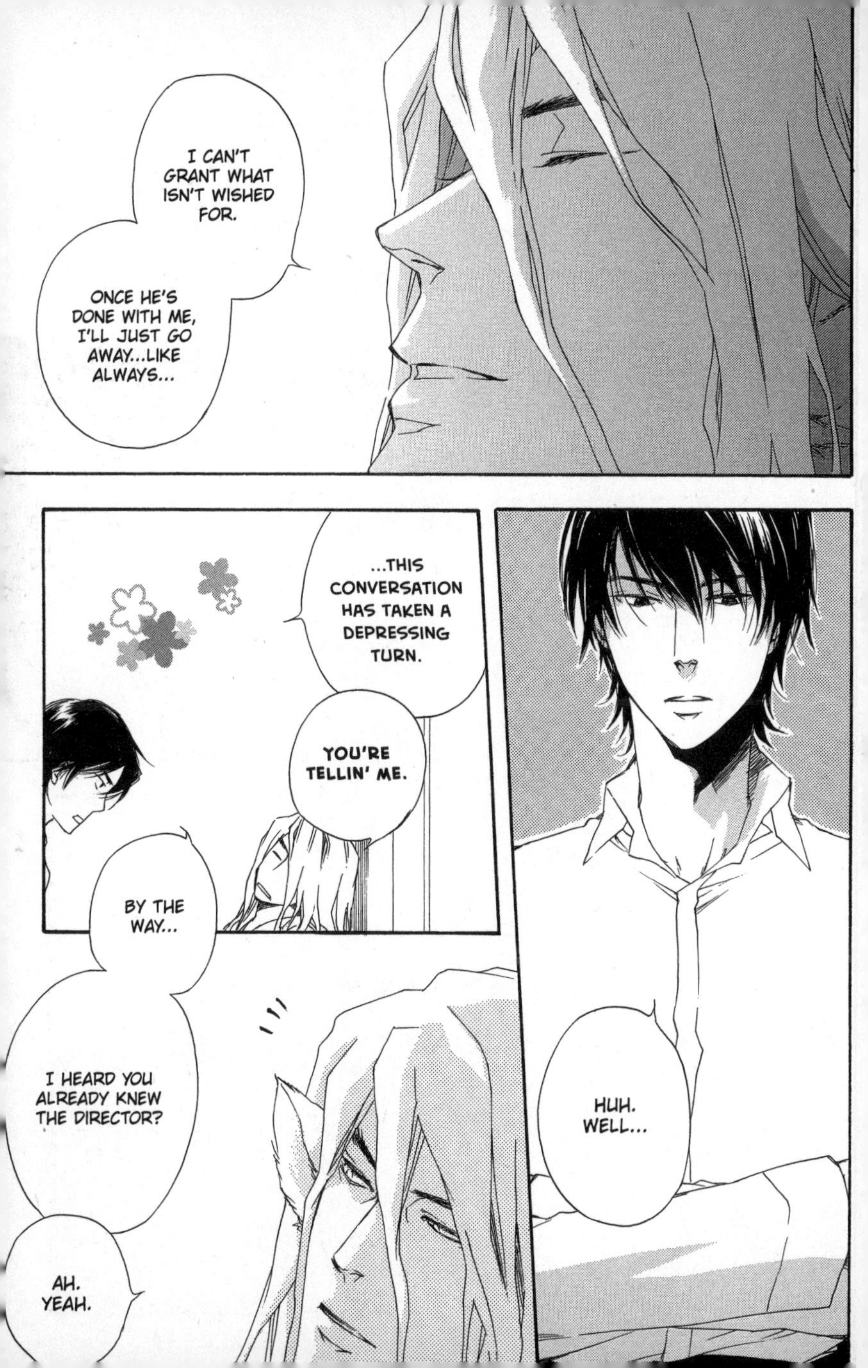
I CAN'T GRANT WHAT ISN'T WISHED FOR.
ONCE HE'S DONE WITH ME, I'LL JUST GO AWAY...LIKE ALWAYS...
HUH. WELL...
...THIS CONVERSATION HAS TAKEN A DEPRESSING TURN.
YOU'RE TELLIN' ME.
BY THE WAY...
I HEARD YOU ALREADY KNEW THE DIRECTOR?
AH. YEAH.

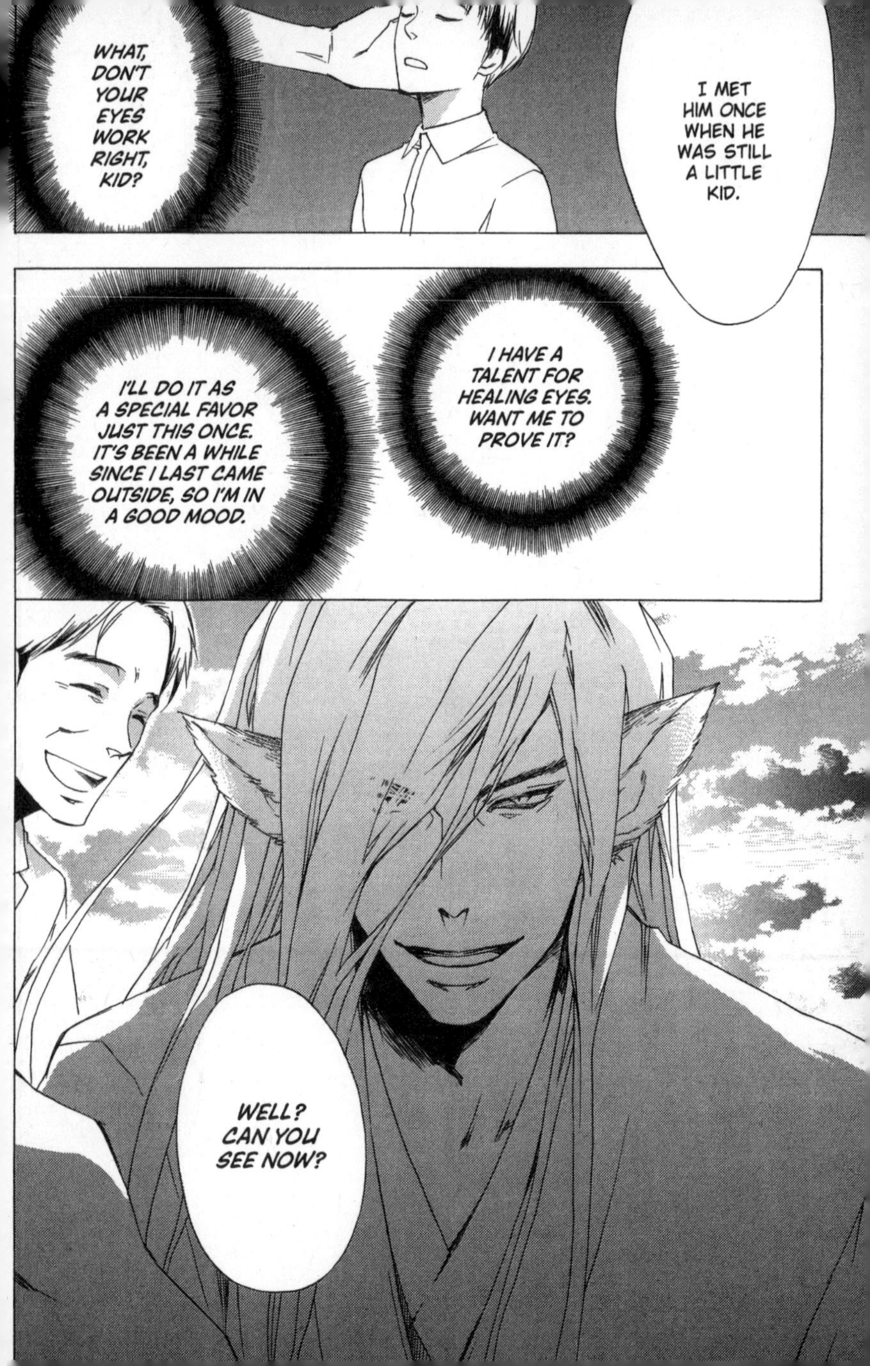
I MET HIM ONCE WHEN HE WAS STILL A LITTLE KID.
WHAT, DON'T YOUR EYES WORK RIGHT, KID?
I HAVE A TALENT FOR HEALING EYES. WANT ME TO PROVE IT?
I'LL DO IT AS A SPECIAL FAVOR JUST THIS ONCE. IT'S BEEN A WHILE SINCE I LAST CAME OUTSIDE, SO I'M IN A GOOD MOOD.
WELL? CAN YOU SEE NOW?

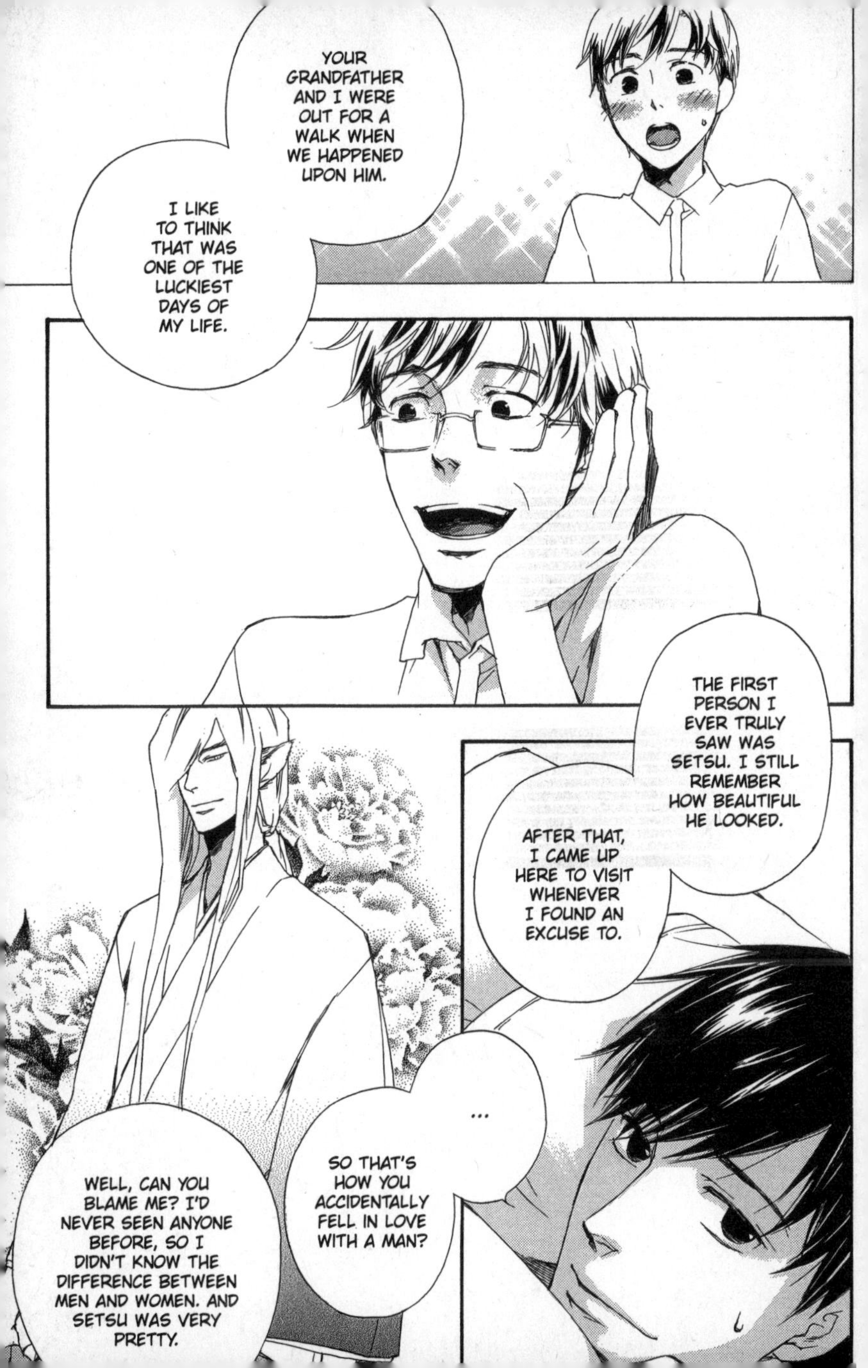
YOUR GRANDFATHER AND I WERE OUT FOR A WALK WHEN WE HAPPENED UPON HIM.
I LIKE TO THINK THAT WAS ONE OF THE LUCKIEST DAYS OF MY LIFE.
THE FIRST PERSON I EVER TRULY SAW WAS SETSU. I STILL REMEMBER HOW BEAUTIFUL HE LOOKED.
AFTER THAT, I CAME UP HERE TO VISIT WHENEVER I FOUND AN EXCUSE TO.
...
SO THAT'S HOW YOU ACCIDENTALLY FELL IN LOVE WITH A MAN?
WELL, CAN YOU BLAME ME? I'D NEVER SEEN ANYONE BEFORE, SO I DIDN'T KNOW THE DIFFERENCE BETWEEN MEN AND WOMEN. AND SETSU WAS VERY PRETTY.

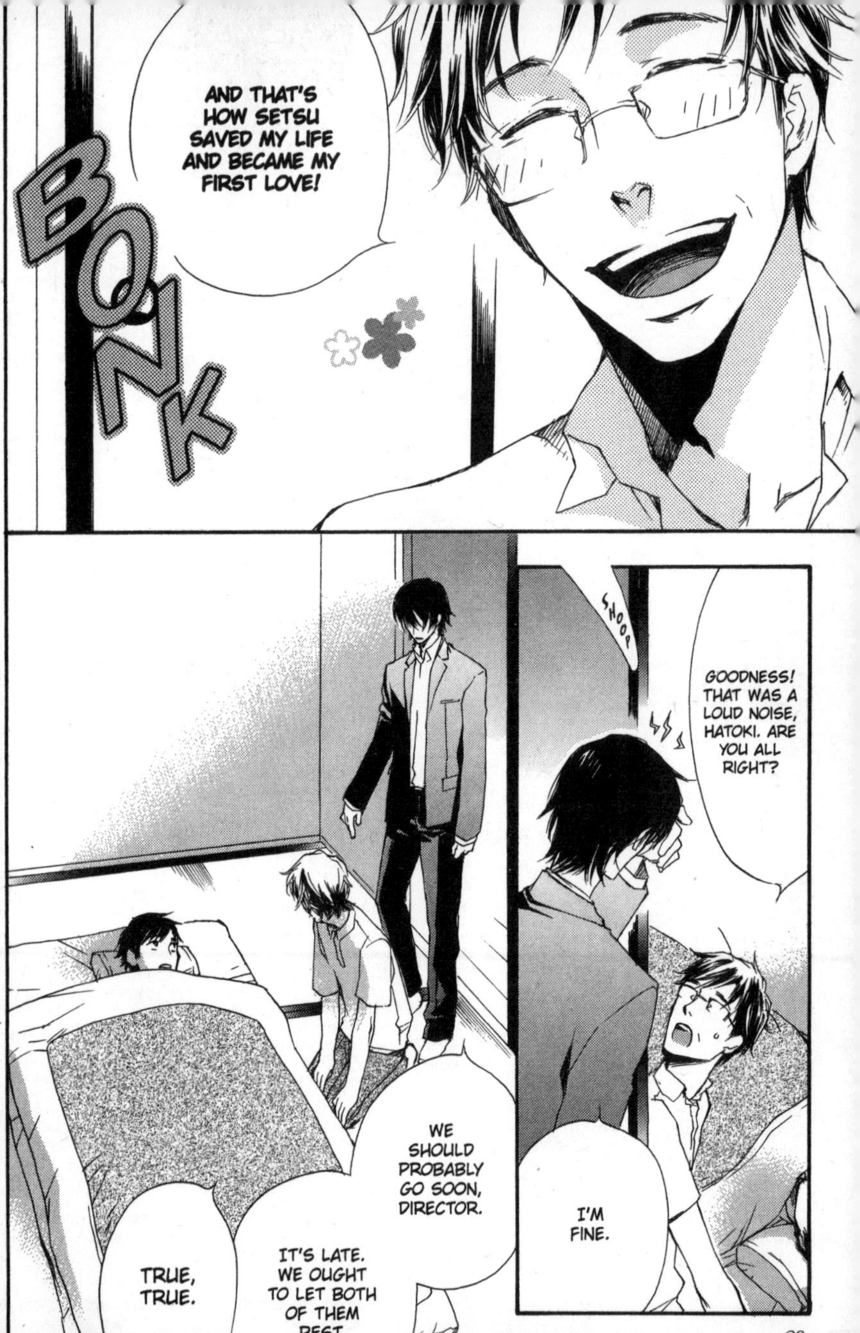
AND THAT'S HOW SETSU SAVED MY LIFE AND BECAME MY FIRST LOVE!
BONK
SHOOP
GOODNESS! THAT WAS A LOUD NOISE, HATOKI. ARE YOU ALL RIGHT?
I'M FINE.
WE SHOULD PROBABLY GO SOON, DIRECTOR.
IT'S LATE. WE OUGHT TO LET BOTH OF THEM REST.
TRUE, TRUE.

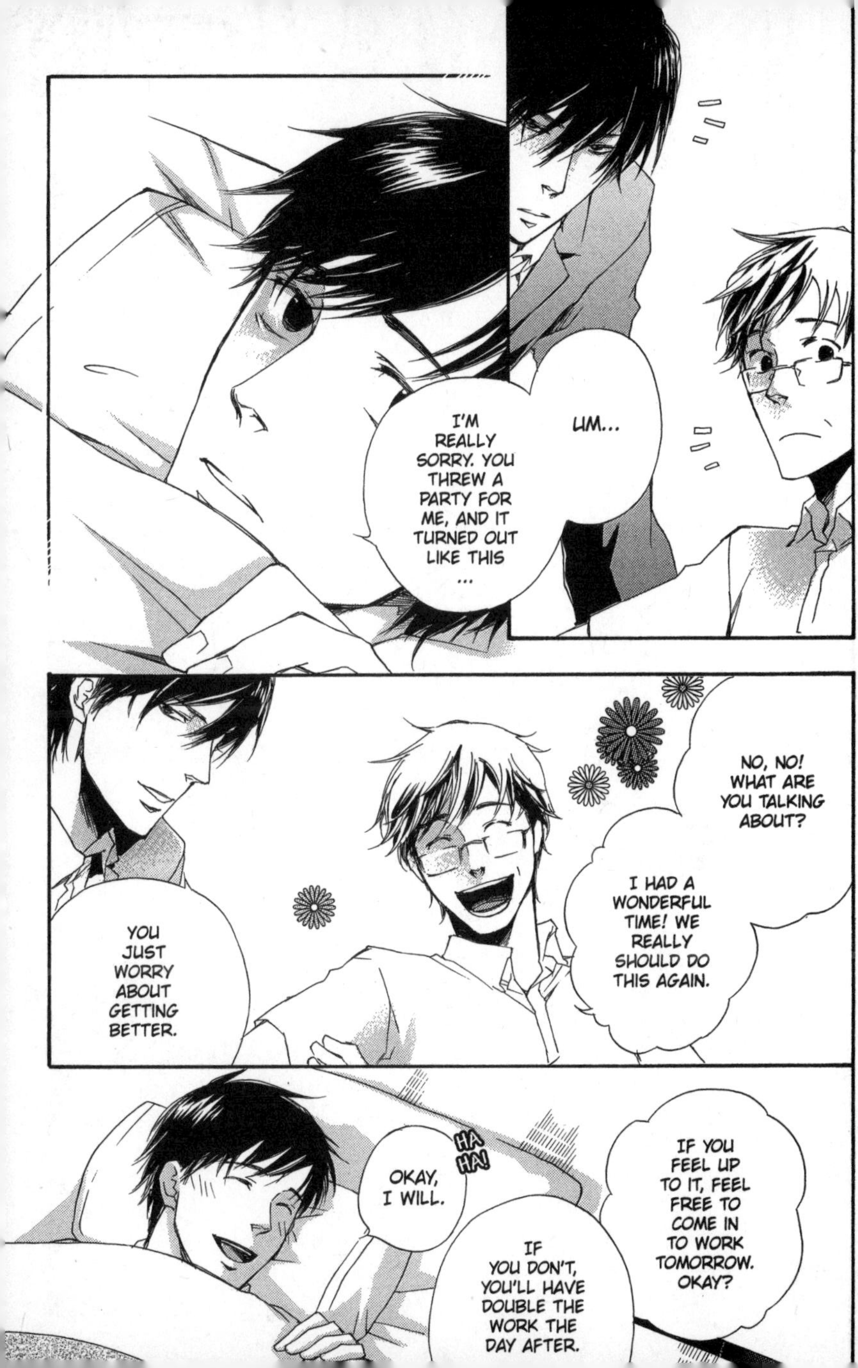
UM...
I'M REALLY SORRY. YOU THREW A PARTY FOR ME, AND IT TURNED OUT LIKE THIS ...
NO, NO! WHAT ARE YOU TALKING ABOUT?
I HAD A WONDERFUL TIME! WE REALLY SHOULD DO THIS AGAIN.
YOU JUST WORRY ABOUT GETTING BETTER.
IF YOU FEEL UP TO IT, FEEL FREE TO COME IN TO WORK TOMORROW. OKAY?
IF YOU DON'T, YOU'LL HAVE DOUBLE THE WORK THE DAY AFTER.
HA HA!
OKAY, I WILL.

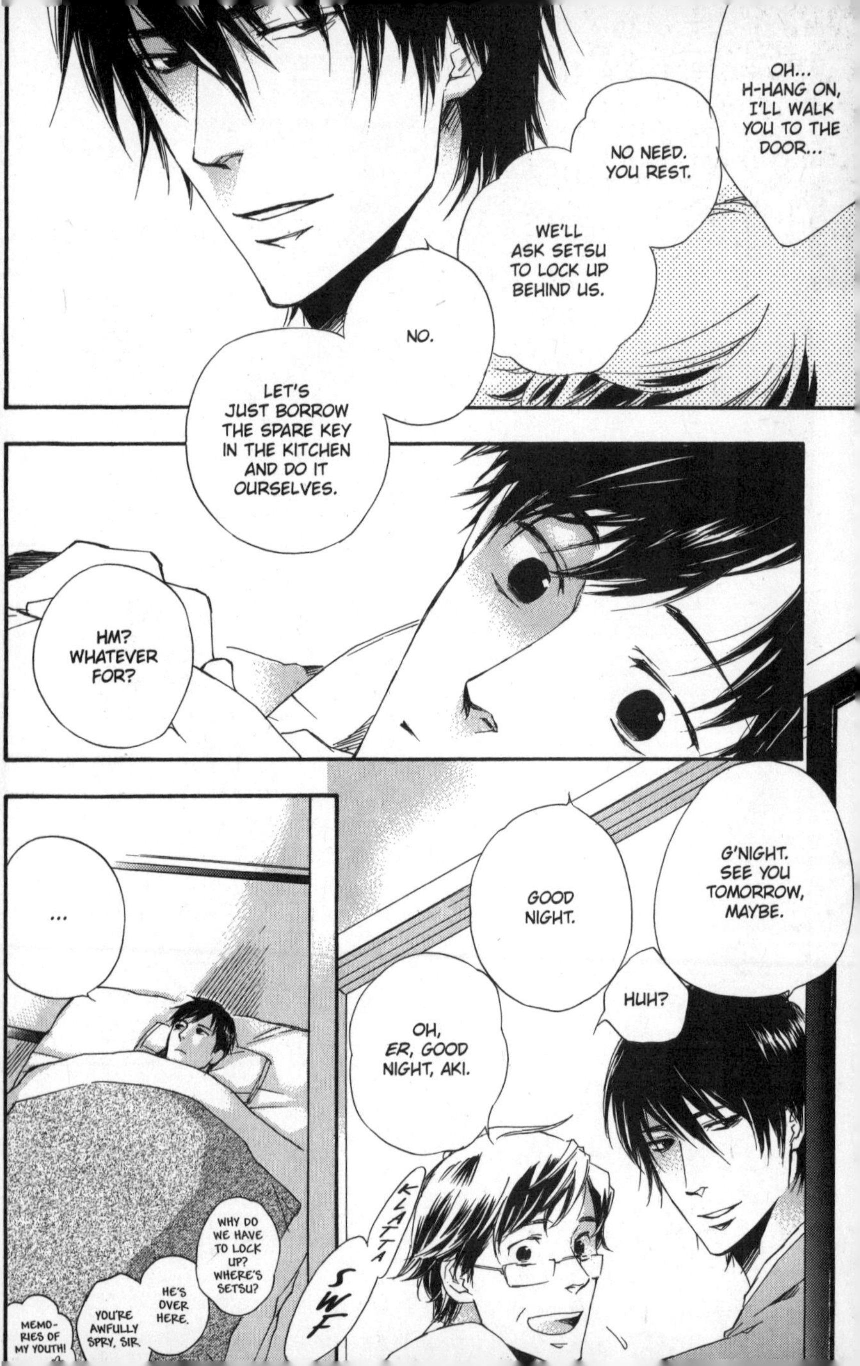
OH... H-HANG ON, I'LL WALK YOU TO THE DOOR...
NO NEED. YOU REST.
WE'LL ASK SETSU TO LOCK UP BEHIND US.
NO.
LET'S JUST BORROW THE SPARE KEY IN THE KITCHEN AND DO IT OURSELVES.
HM? WHATEVER FOR?
G'NIGHT. SEE YOU TOMORROW, MAYBE.
GOOD NIGHT.
HUH?
OH, ER, GOOD NIGHT, AKI.
KLATTA
SWF
...
WHY DO WE HAVE TO LOCK UP? WHERE'S SETSU?
HE'S OVER HERE.
YOU'RE AWFULLY SPRY, SIR.
MEMO-RIES OF MY YOUTH!

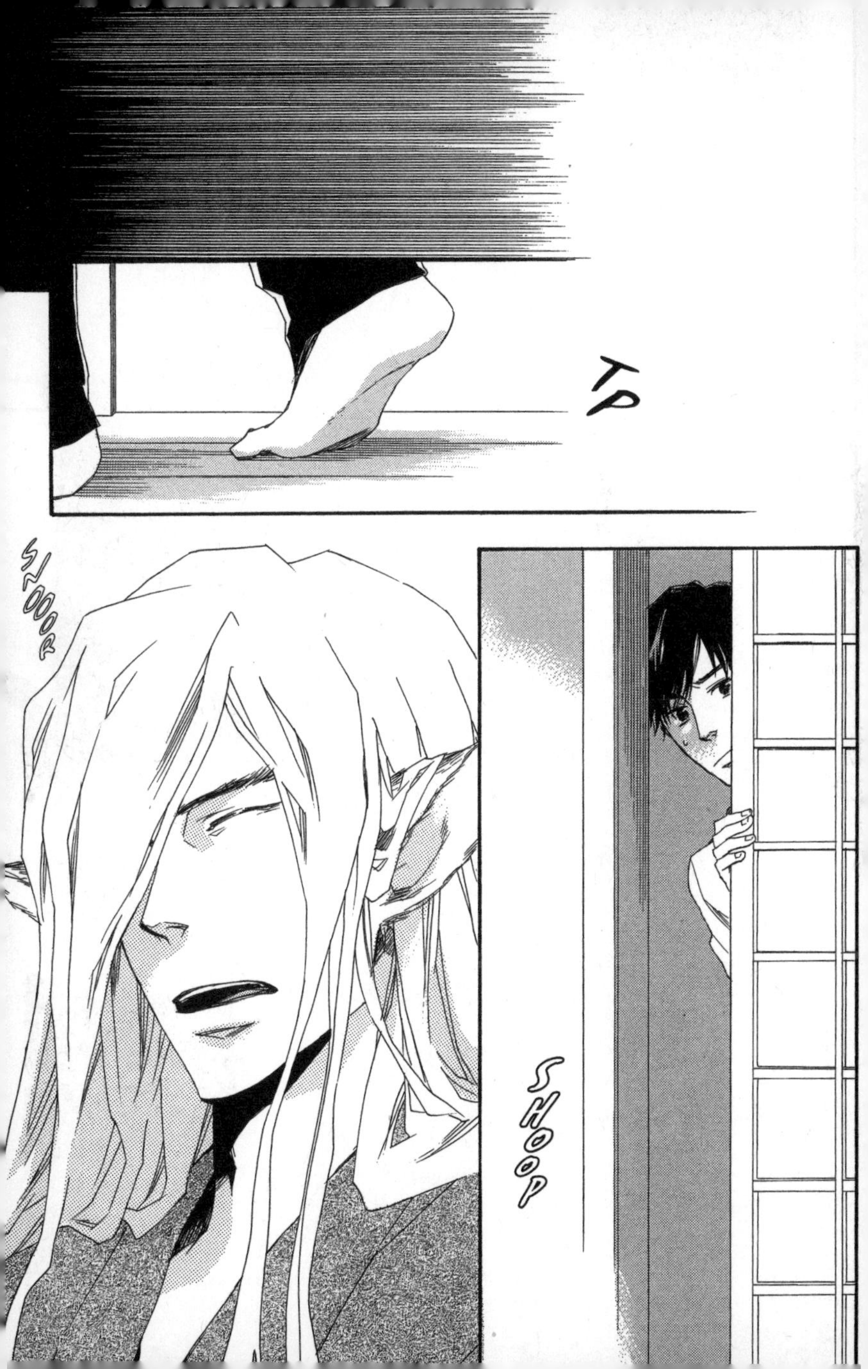
TP
SHOOP
SNOOOR

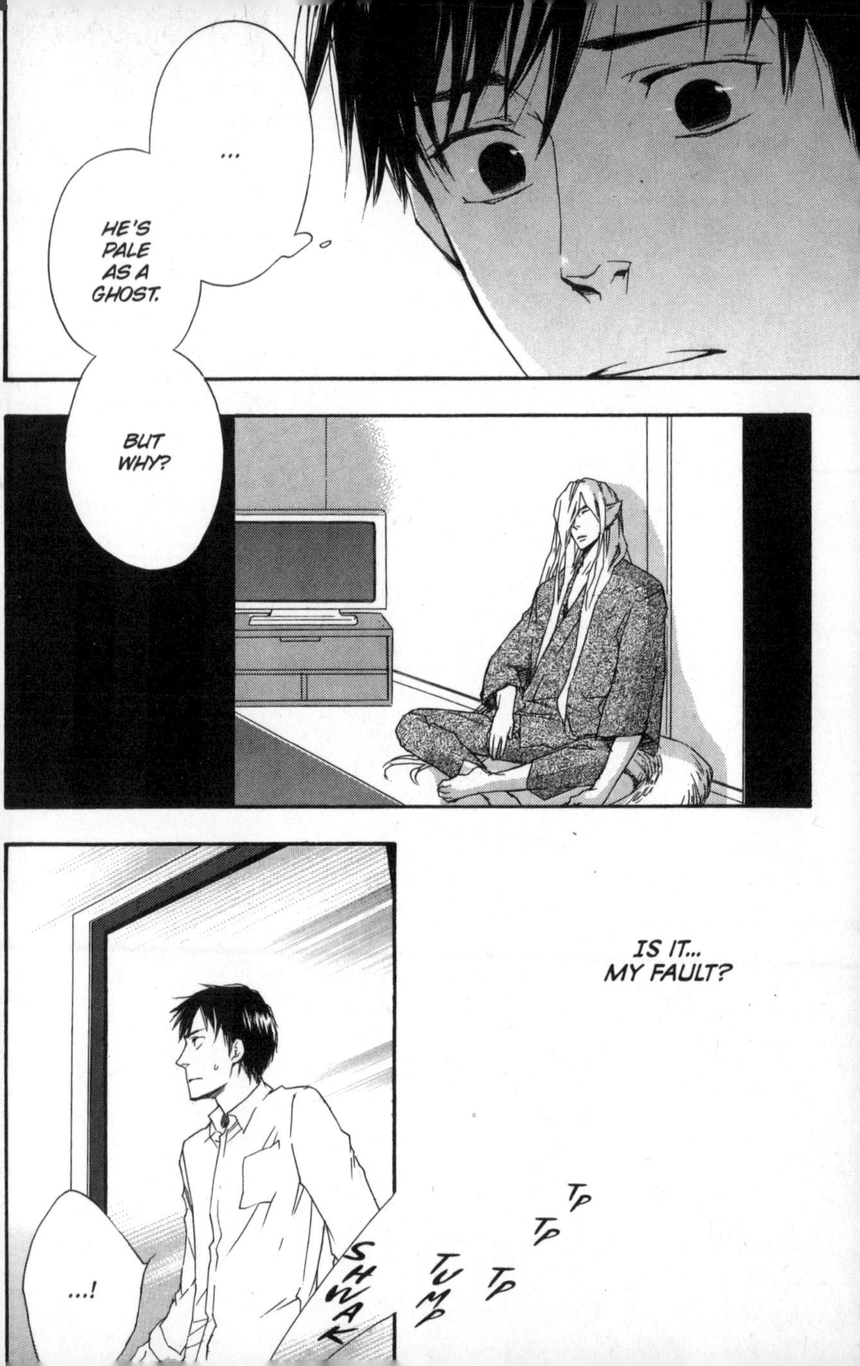
...
HE'S PALE AS A GHOST.
BUT WHY?
IS IT... MY FAULT?
TP TP TP
TUMP
SHWAK
...!

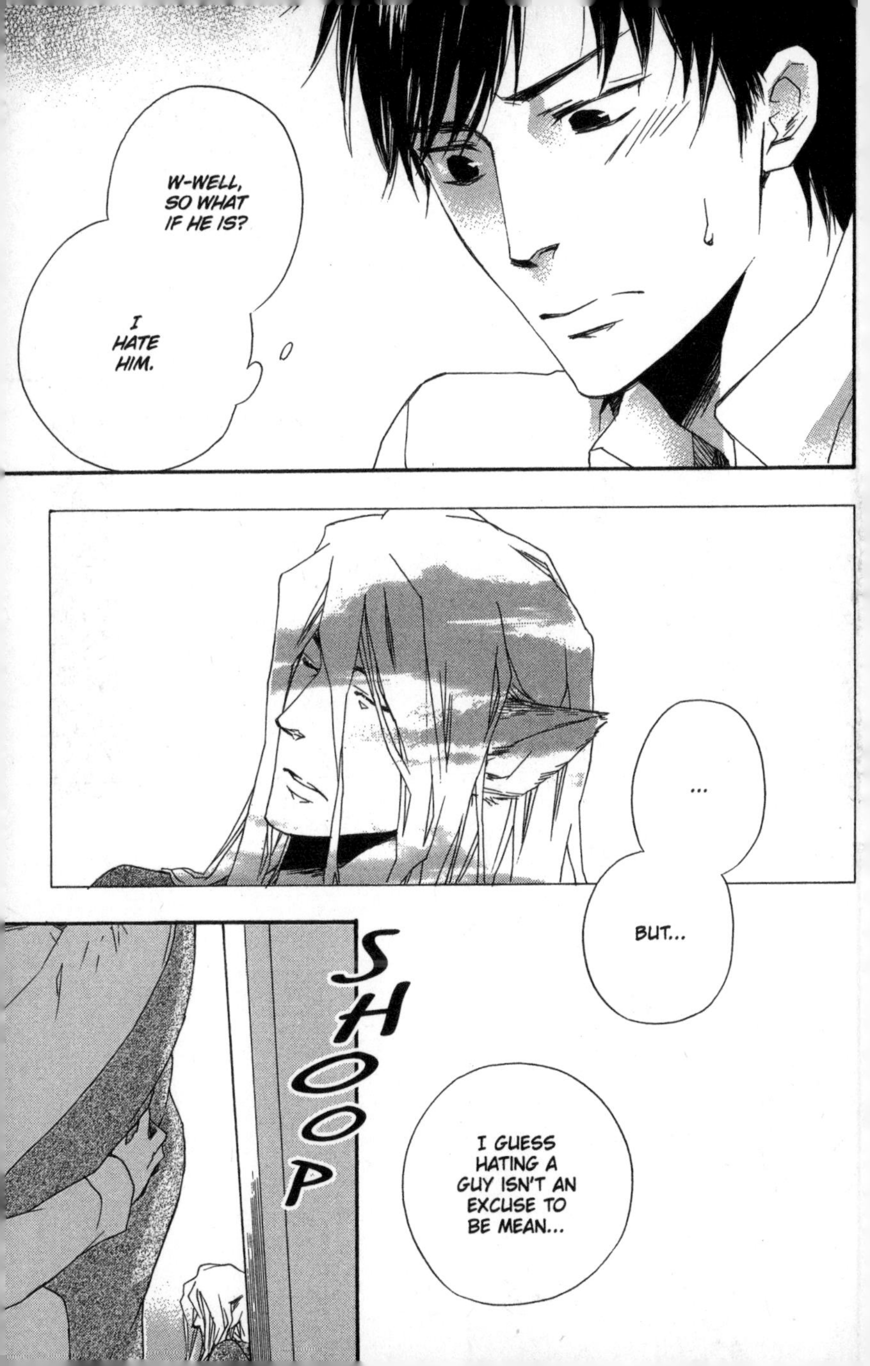
W-WELL, SO WHAT IF HE IS?
I HATE HIM.
...
BUT...
I GUESS HATING A GUY ISN'T AN EXCUSE TO BE MEAN...
SHOOP

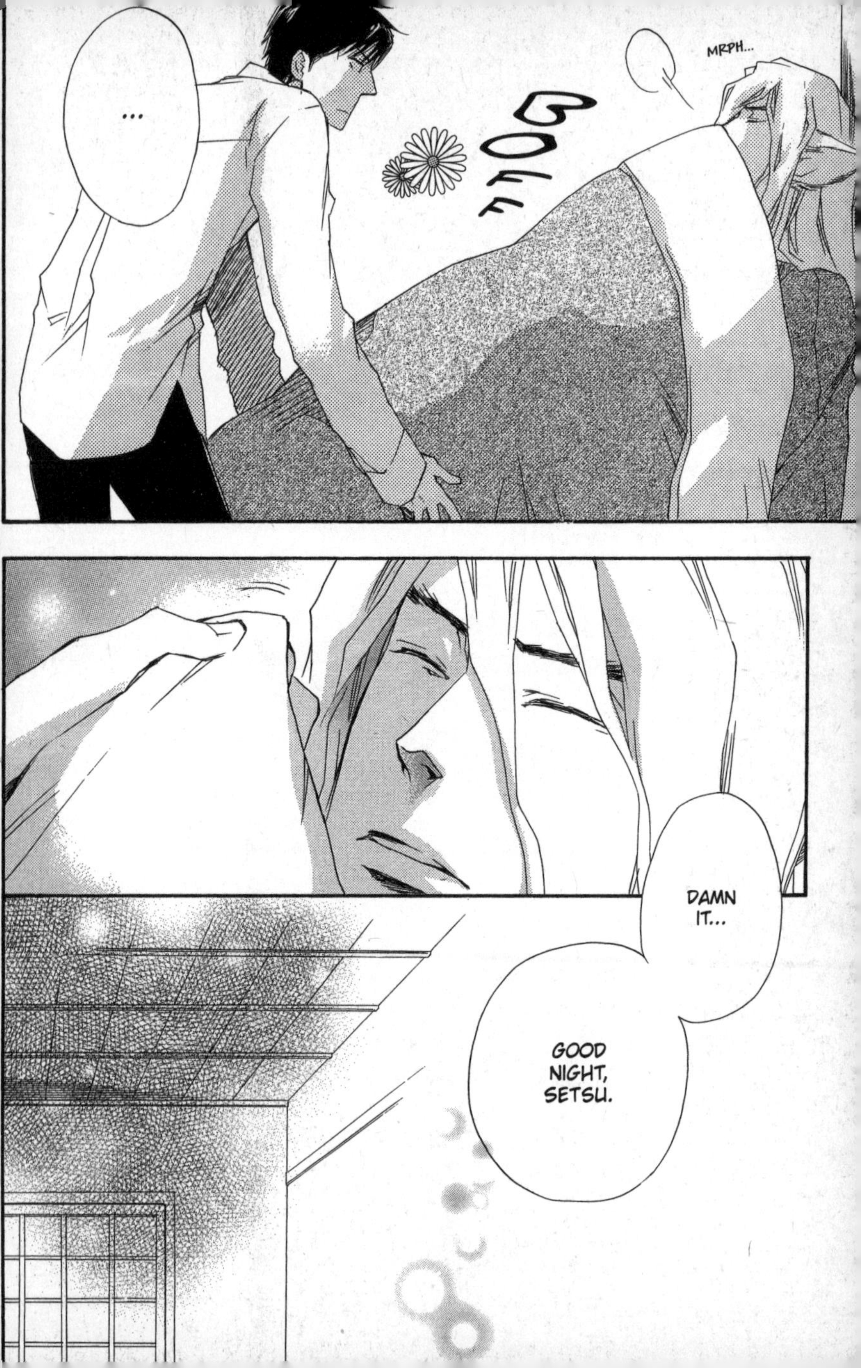
MRPH...
BOFF
...
DAMN IT...
GOOD NIGHT, SETSU.

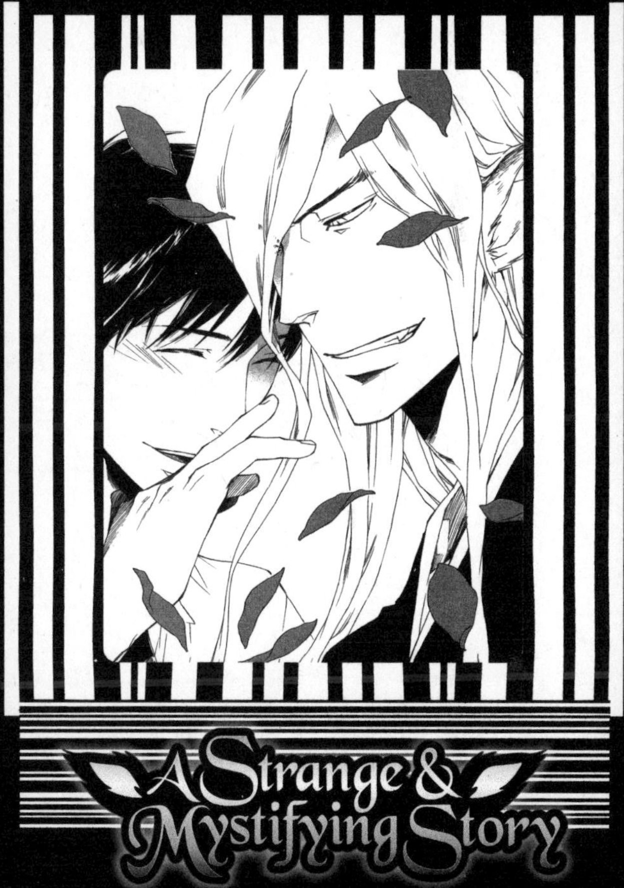
A Strange &
Mystifying Story

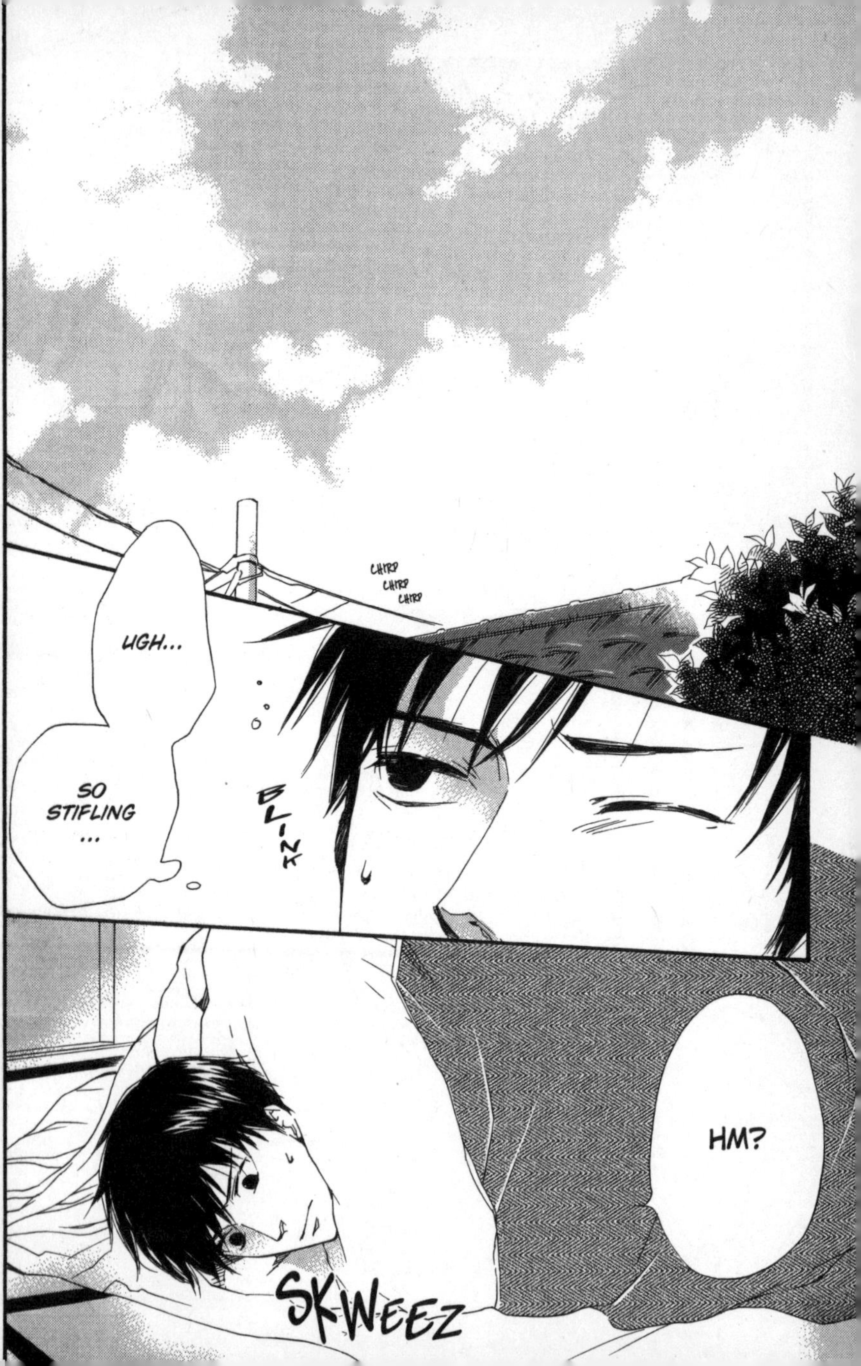
CHIRP
CHIRP
CHIRP
UGH...
SO STIFLING ...
BLINK
HM?
SKWEEZ

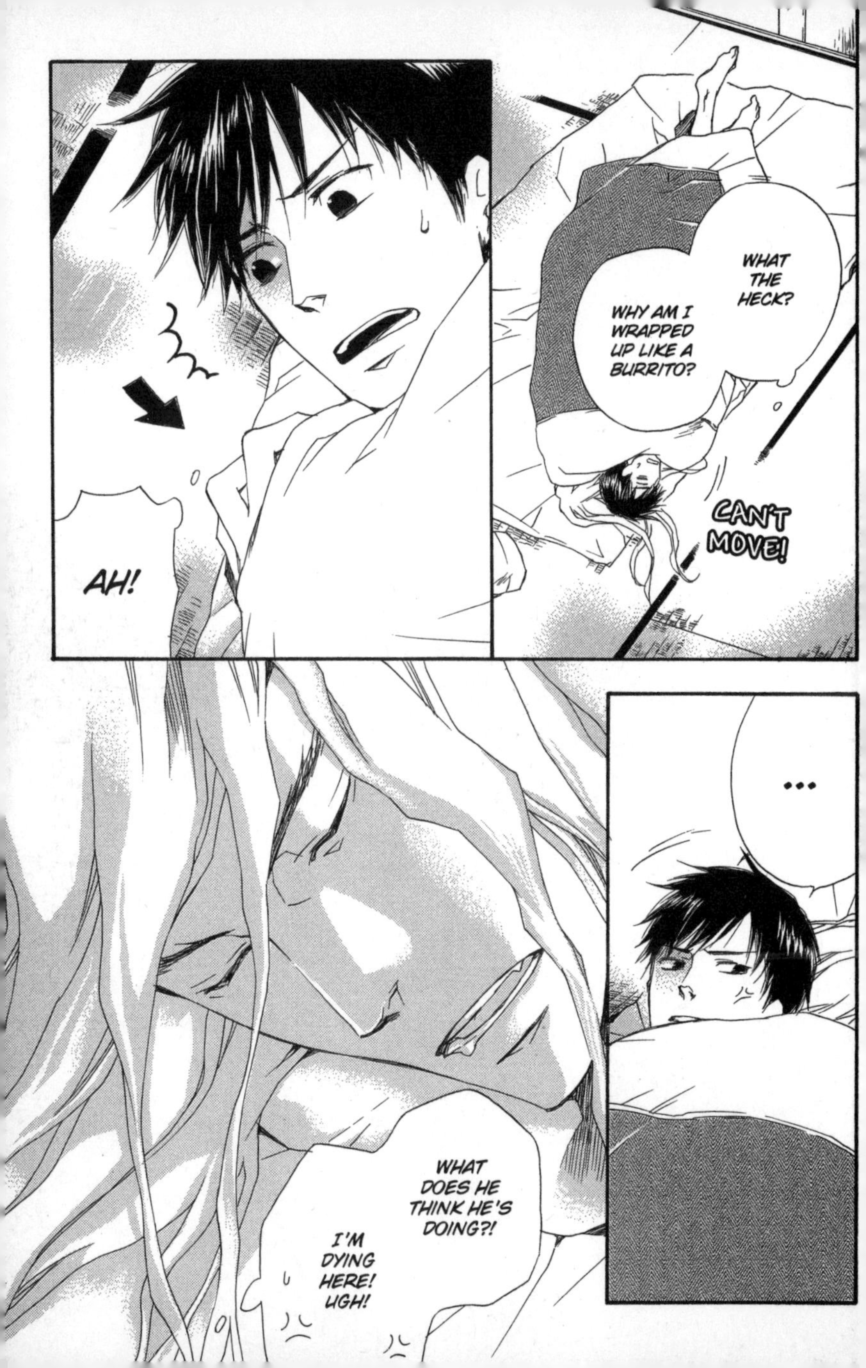
WHAT THE HECK?
WHY AM I WRAPPED UP LIKE A BURRITO?
CAN'T MOVE!
AH!
...
WHAT DOES HE THINK HE'S DOING?!
I'M DYING HERE! UGH!

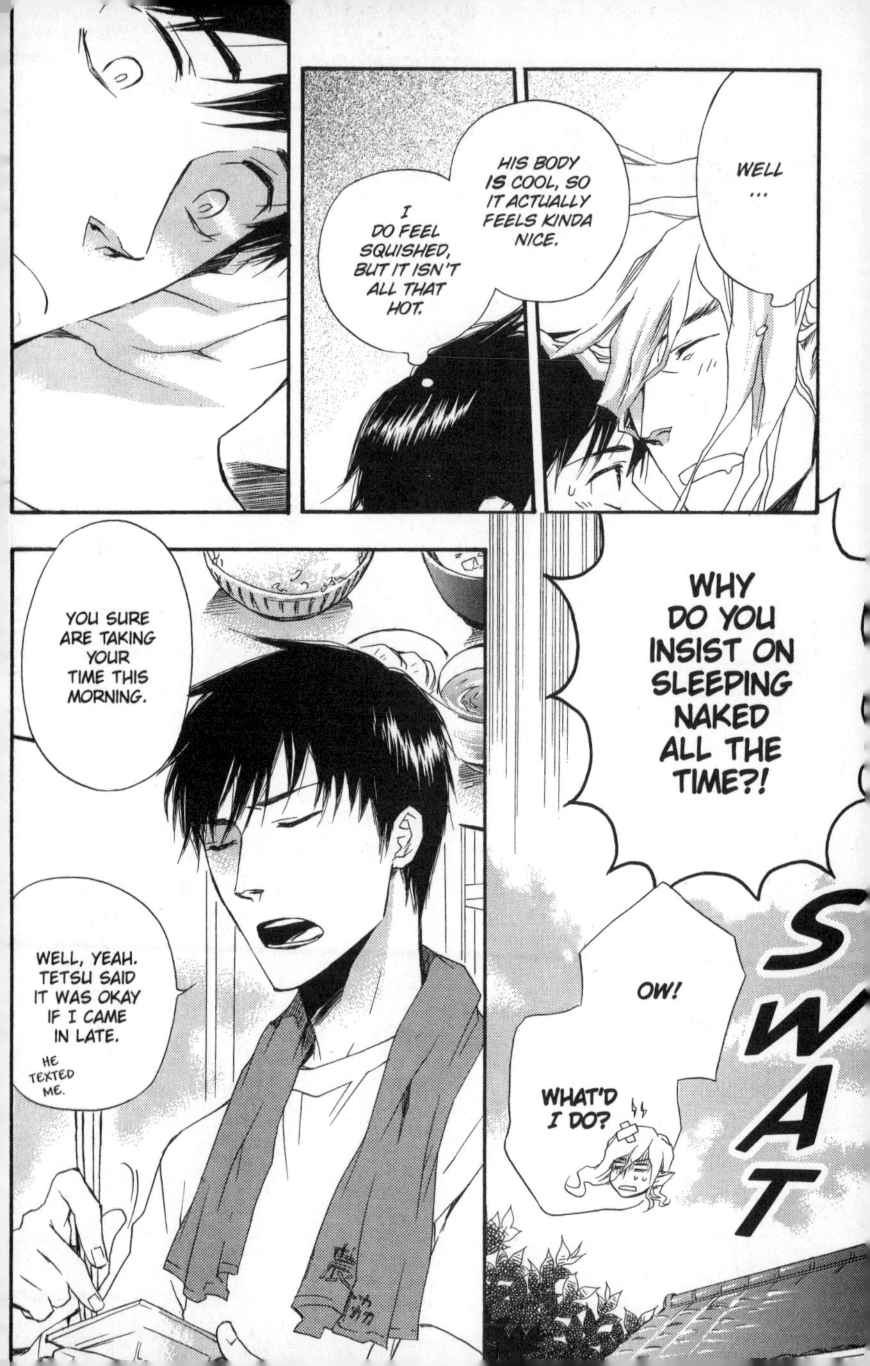
WELL ...
HIS BODY IS COOL, SO IT ACTUALLY FEELS KINDA NICE.
I DO FEEL SQUISHED, BUT IT ISN'T ALL THAT HOT.
WHY DO YOU INSIST ON SLEEPING NAKED ALL THE TIME?!
SWAT
OW!
WHAT'D I DO?
YOU SURE ARE TAKING YOUR TIME THIS MORNING.
WELL, YEAH. TETSU SAID IT WAS OKAY IF I CAME IN LATE.
HE TEXTED ME.

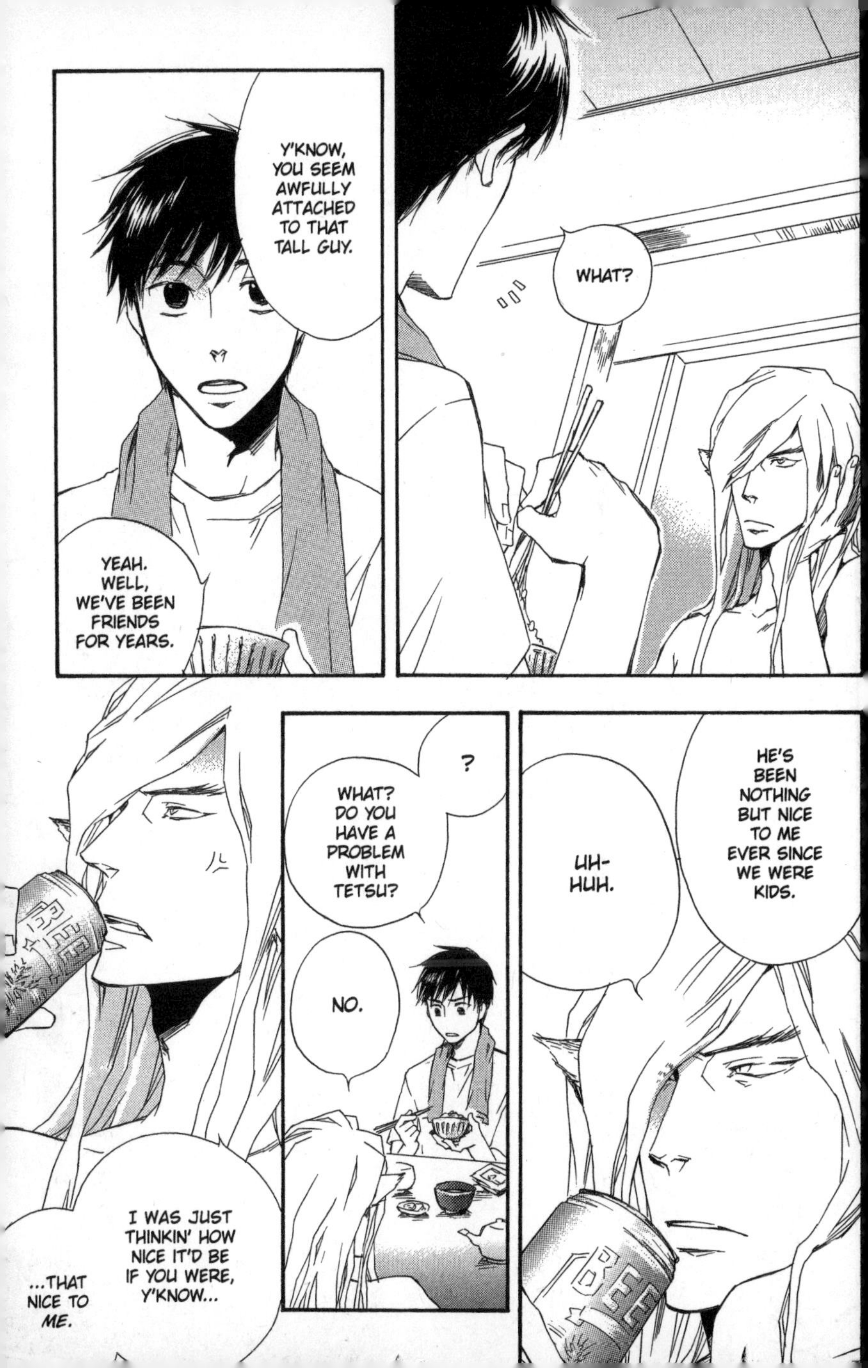
WHAT?
Y'KNOW, YOU SEEM AWFULLY ATTACHED TO THAT TALL GUY.
YEAH. WELL, WE'VE BEEN FRIENDS FOR YEARS.
HE'S BEEN NOTHING BUT NICE TO ME EVER SINCE WE WERE KIDS.
UH-HUH.
?
WHAT? DO YOU HAVE A PROBLEM WITH TETSU?
NO.
I WAS JUST THINKIN' HOW NICE IT'D BE IF YOU WERE, Y'KNOW...
...THAT NICE TO *ME*.

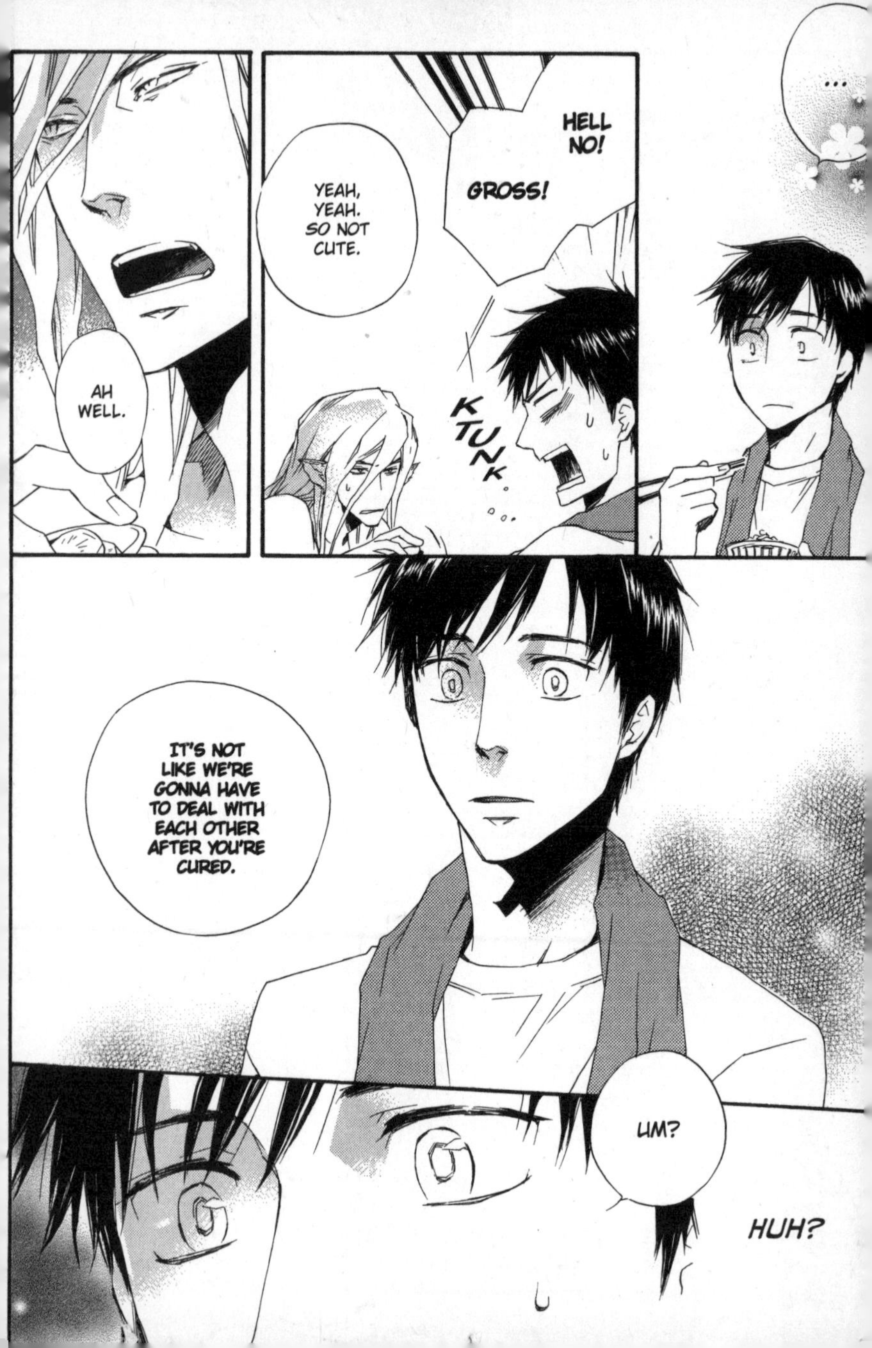
...
HELL NO!
GROSS!
YEAH, YEAH. SO NOT CUTE.
KTUNK
AH WELL.
IT'S NOT LIKE WE'RE GONNA HAVE TO DEAL WITH EACH OTHER AFTER YOU'RE CURED.
UM?
HUH?

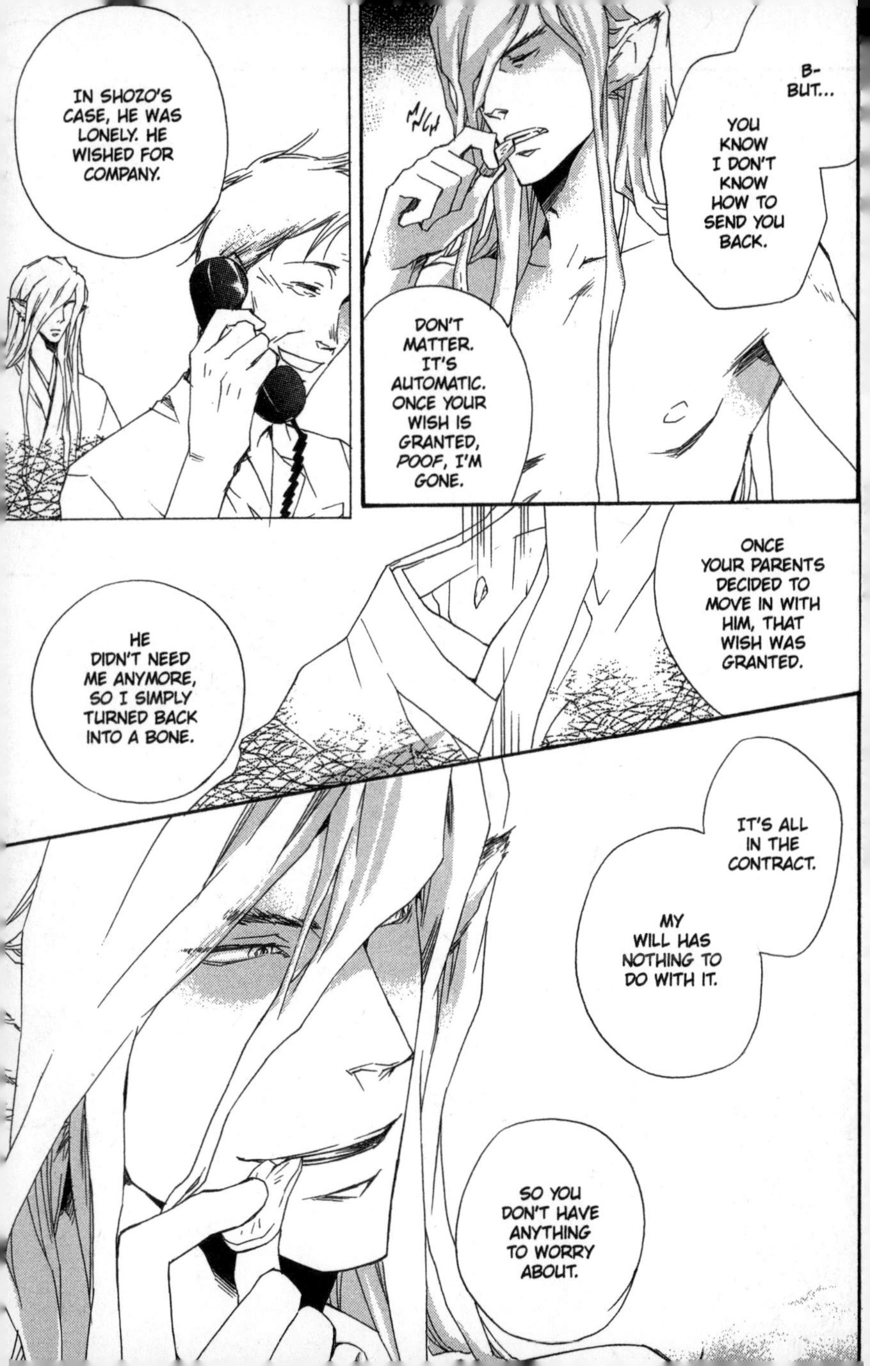
B-BUT...
YOU KNOW I DON'T KNOW HOW TO SEND YOU BACK.
DON'T MATTER. IT'S AUTOMATIC. ONCE YOUR WISH IS GRANTED, *POOF*, I'M GONE.
IN SHOZO'S CASE, HE WAS LONELY. HE WISHED FOR COMPANY.
ONCE YOUR PARENTS DECIDED TO MOVE IN WITH HIM, THAT WISH WAS GRANTED.
HE DIDN'T NEED ME ANYMORE, SO I SIMPLY TURNED BACK INTO A BONE.
IT'S ALL IN THE CONTRACT.
MY WILL HAS NOTHING TO DO WITH IT.
SO YOU DON'T HAVE ANYTHING TO WORRY ABOUT.

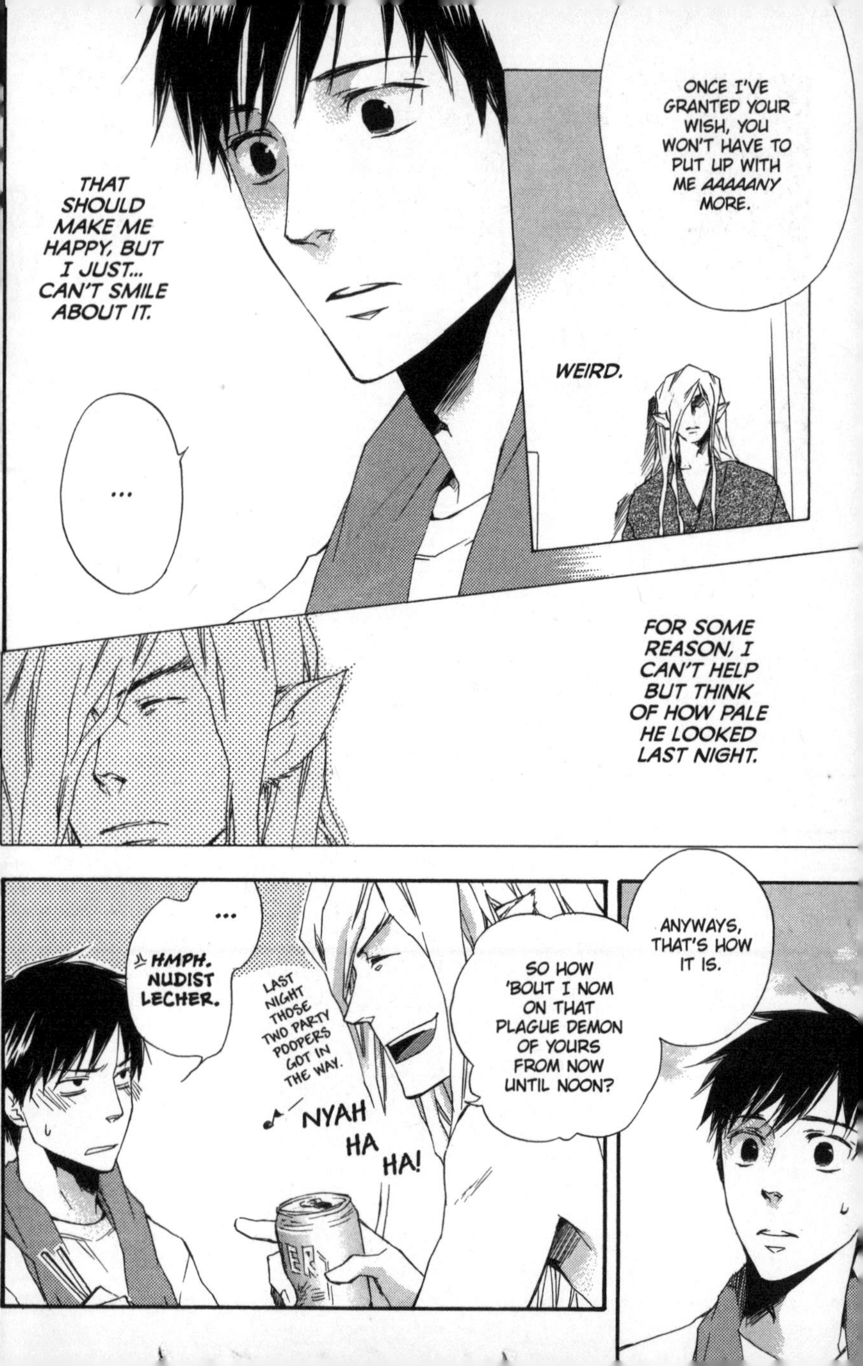
ONCE I'VE GRANTED YOUR WISH, YOU WON'T HAVE TO PUT UP WITH ME AAAAANY MORE.
WEIRD.
THAT SHOULD MAKE ME HAPPY, BUT I JUST... CAN'T SMILE ABOUT IT.
...
FOR SOME REASON, I CAN'T HELP BUT THINK OF HOW PALE HE LOOKED LAST NIGHT.
ANYWAYS, THAT'S HOW IT IS.
SO HOW 'BOUT I NOM ON THAT PLAGUE DEMON OF YOURS FROM NOW UNTIL NOON?
LAST NIGHT THOSE TWO PARTY POOPERS GOT IN THE WAY.
NYAH HA HA!
...
HMPH. NUDIST LECHER.

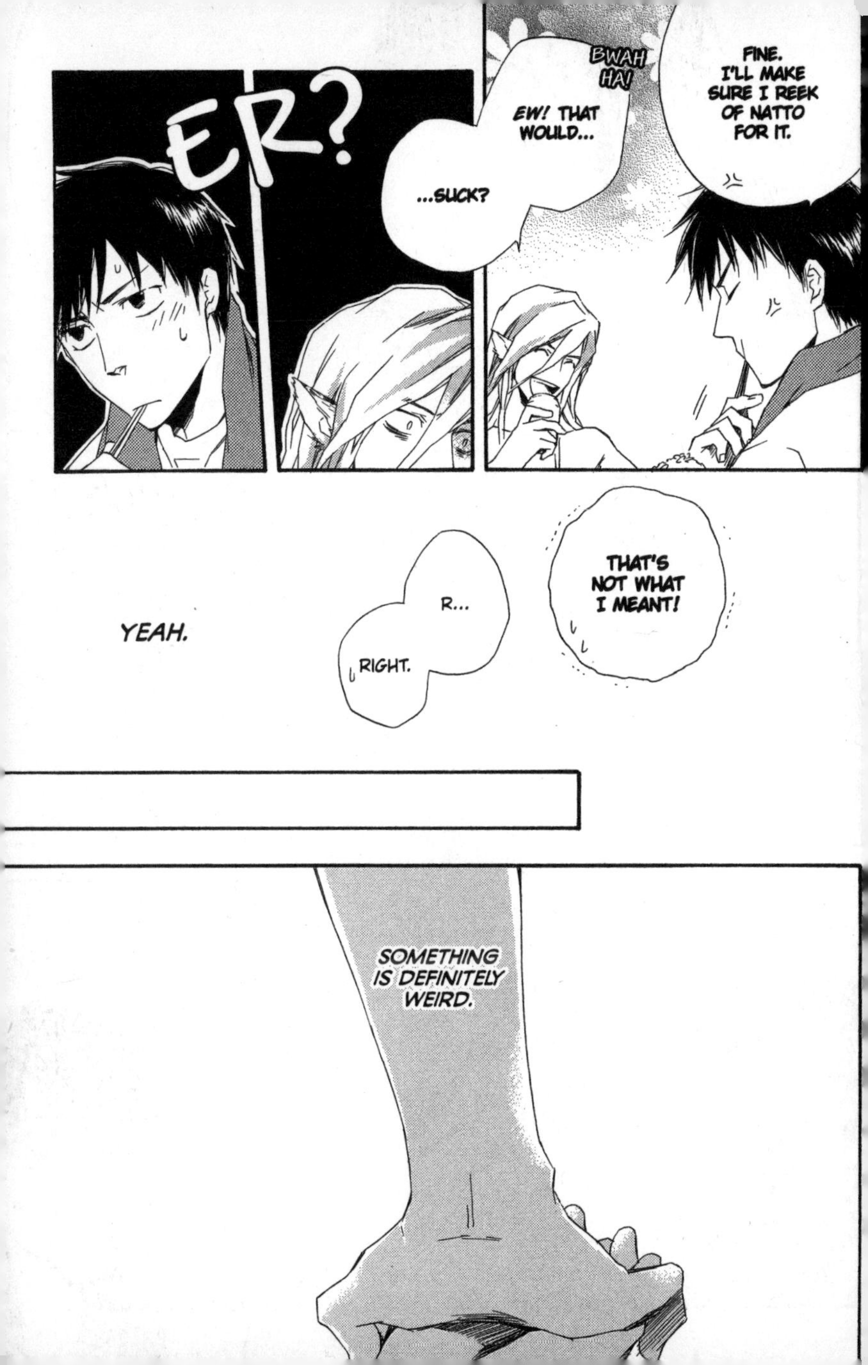
FINE. I'LL MAKE SURE I REEK OF NATTO FOR IT.
BWAH HA!
EW! THAT WOULD...
...SUCK?
ER?
THAT'S NOT WHAT I MEANT!
R...
RIGHT.
YEAH.
SOMETHING IS DEFINITELY WEIRD.

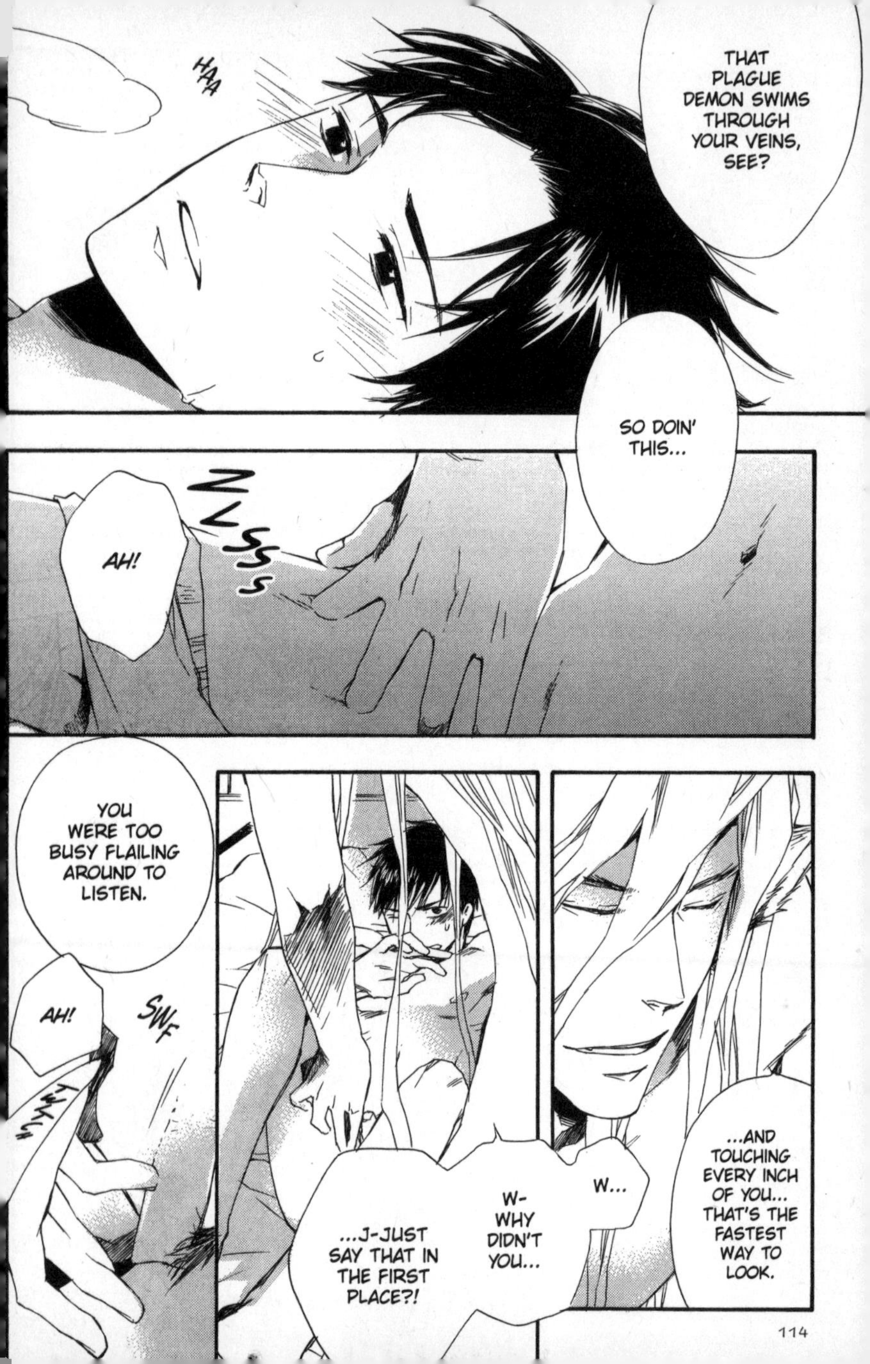
THAT PLAGUE DEMON SWIMS THROUGH YOUR VEINS, SEE?
HAA
SO DOIN' THIS...
AH!
...AND TOUCHING EVERY INCH OF YOU... THAT'S THE FASTEST WAY TO LOOK.
W...
W- WHY DIDN'T YOU...
...J-JUST SAY THAT IN THE FIRST PLACE?!
YOU WERE TOO BUSY FLAILING AROUND TO LISTEN.
AH!
SWF

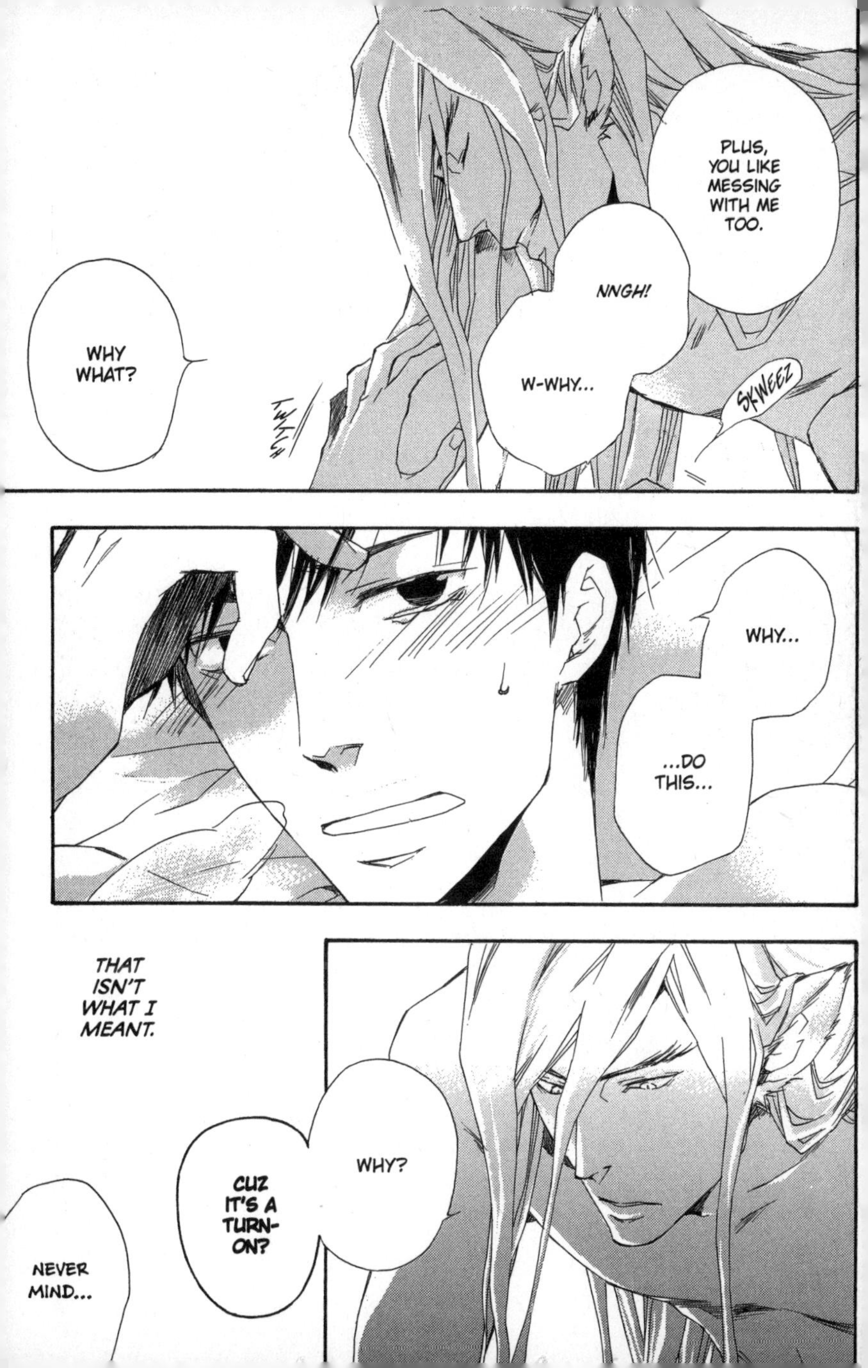
PLUS, YOU LIKE MESSING WITH ME TOO.
NNGH!
W-WHY...
SKWEEZ
WHY WHAT?
TWITCH
WHY...
...DO THIS...
THAT ISN'T WHAT I MEANT.
WHY?
CUZ IT'S A TURN-ON?
NEVER MIND...

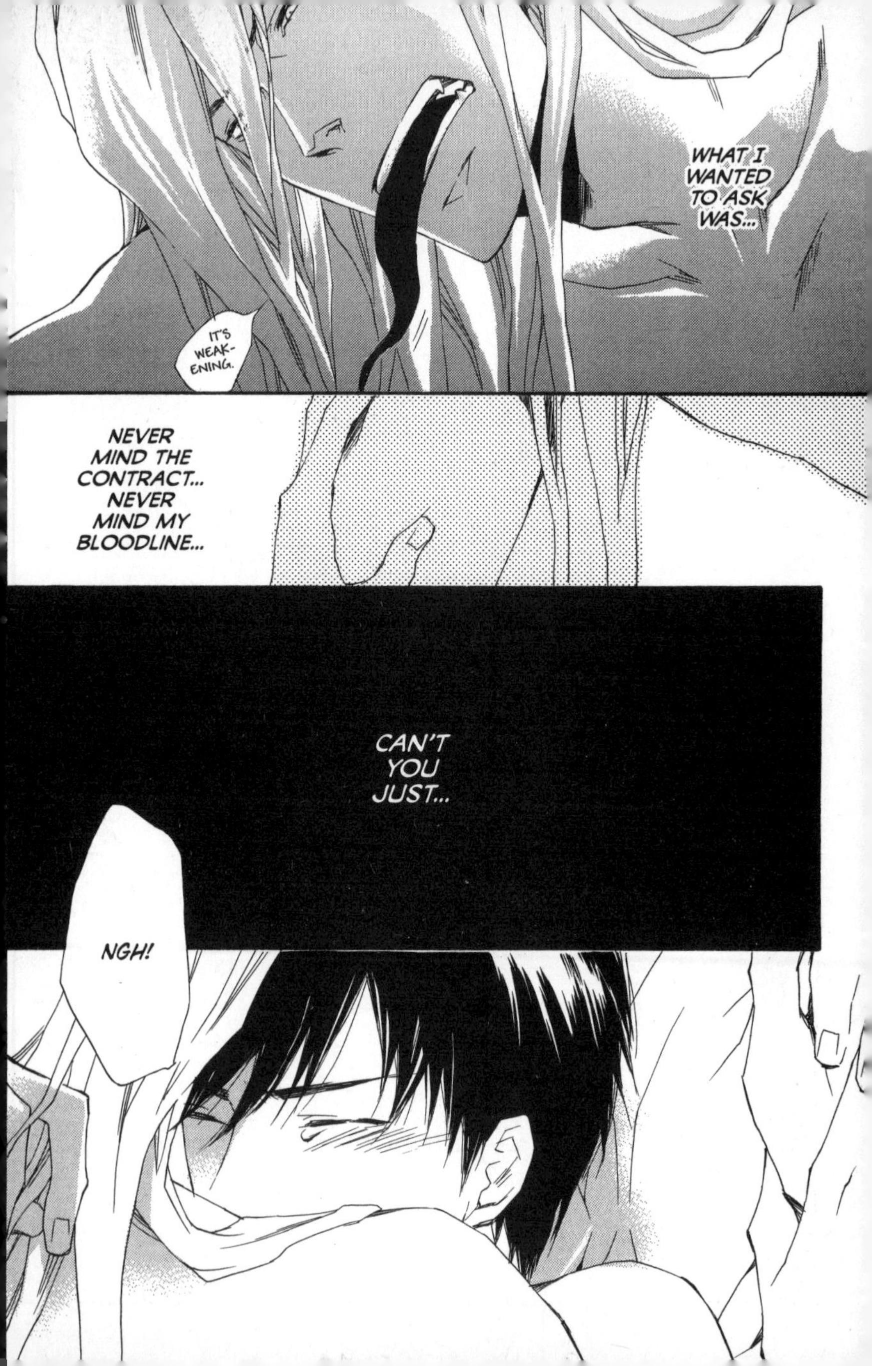
WHAT I WANTED TO ASK WAS...
IT'S WEAK-ENING.
NEVER MIND THE CONTRACT... NEVER MIND MY BLOODLINE...
CAN'T YOU JUST...
NGH!

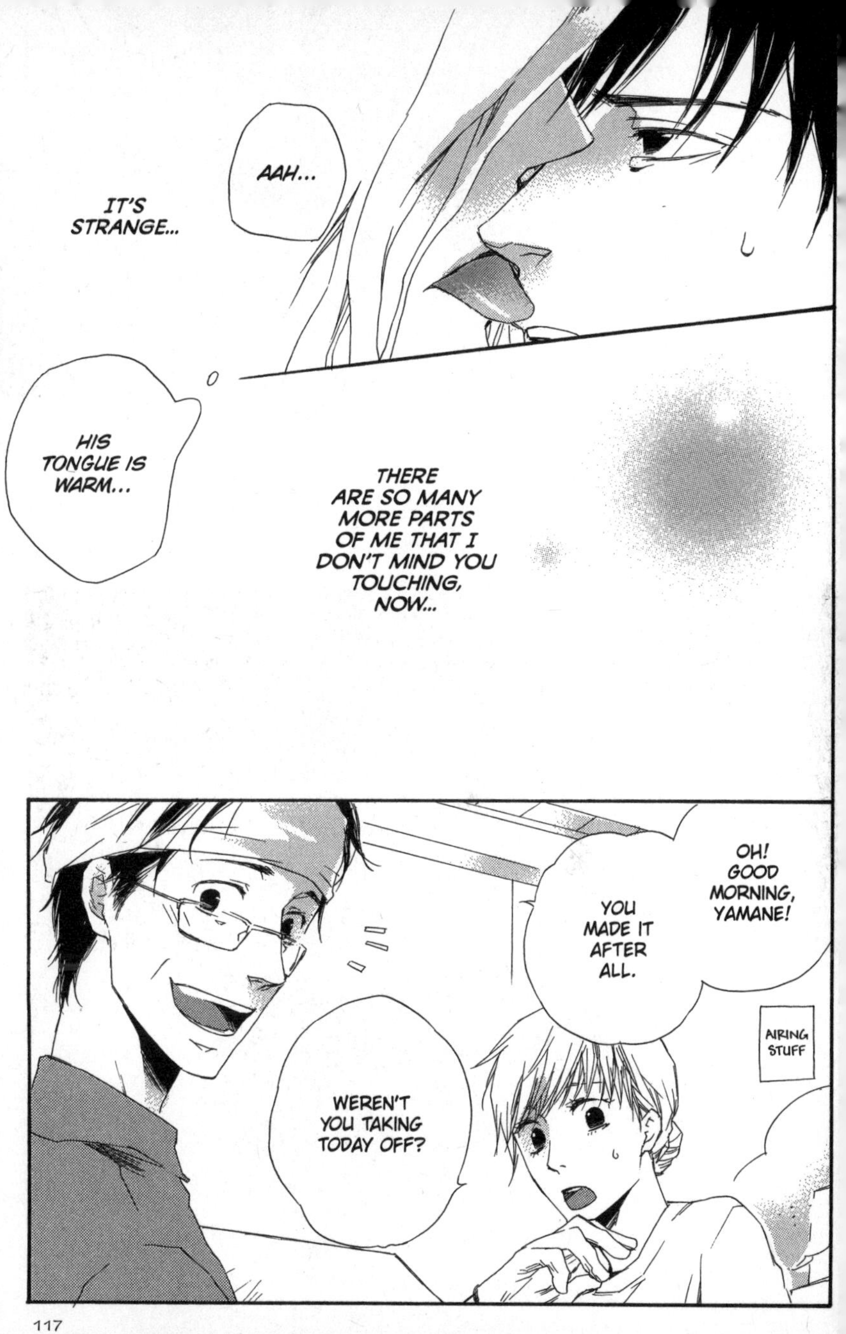

AAH...
IT'S STRANGE...
HIS TONGUE IS WARM...
THERE ARE SO MANY MORE PARTS OF ME THAT I DON'T MIND YOU TOUCHING, NOW...
OH! GOOD MORNING, YAMANE!
YOU MADE IT AFTER ALL.
AIRING STUFF
WEREN'T YOU TAKING TODAY OFF?

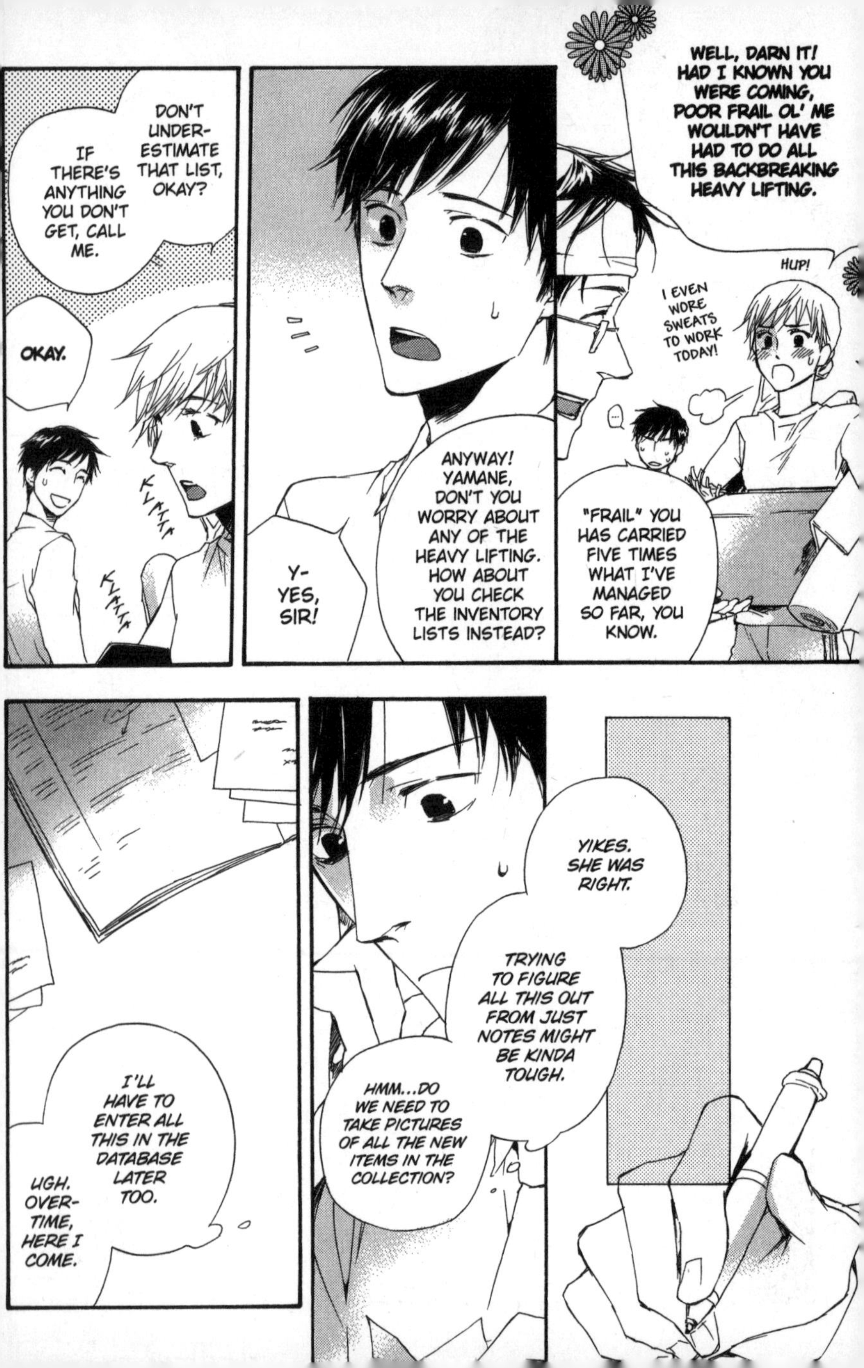
WELL, DARN IT! HAD I KNOWN YOU WERE COMING, POOR FRAIL OL' ME WOULDN'T HAVE HAD TO DO ALL THIS BACKBREAKING HEAVY LIFTING.
HUP!
I EVEN WORE SWEATS TO WORK TODAY!
...
"FRAIL" YOU HAS CARRIED FIVE TIMES WHAT I'VE MANAGED SO FAR, YOU KNOW.
ANYWAY! YAMANE, DON'T YOU WORRY ABOUT ANY OF THE HEAVY LIFTING. HOW ABOUT YOU CHECK THE INVENTORY LISTS INSTEAD?
Y- YES, SIR!
DON'T UNDER-ESTIMATE THAT LIST, OKAY?
IF THERE'S ANYTHING YOU DON'T GET, CALL ME.
OKAY.
YIKES. SHE WAS RIGHT.
TRYING TO FIGURE ALL THIS OUT FROM JUST NOTES MIGHT BE KINDA TOUGH.
HMM...DO WE NEED TO TAKE PICTURES OF ALL THE NEW ITEMS IN THE COLLECTION?
I'LL HAVE TO ENTER ALL THIS IN THE DATABASE LATER TOO.
UGH. OVER-TIME, HERE I COME.

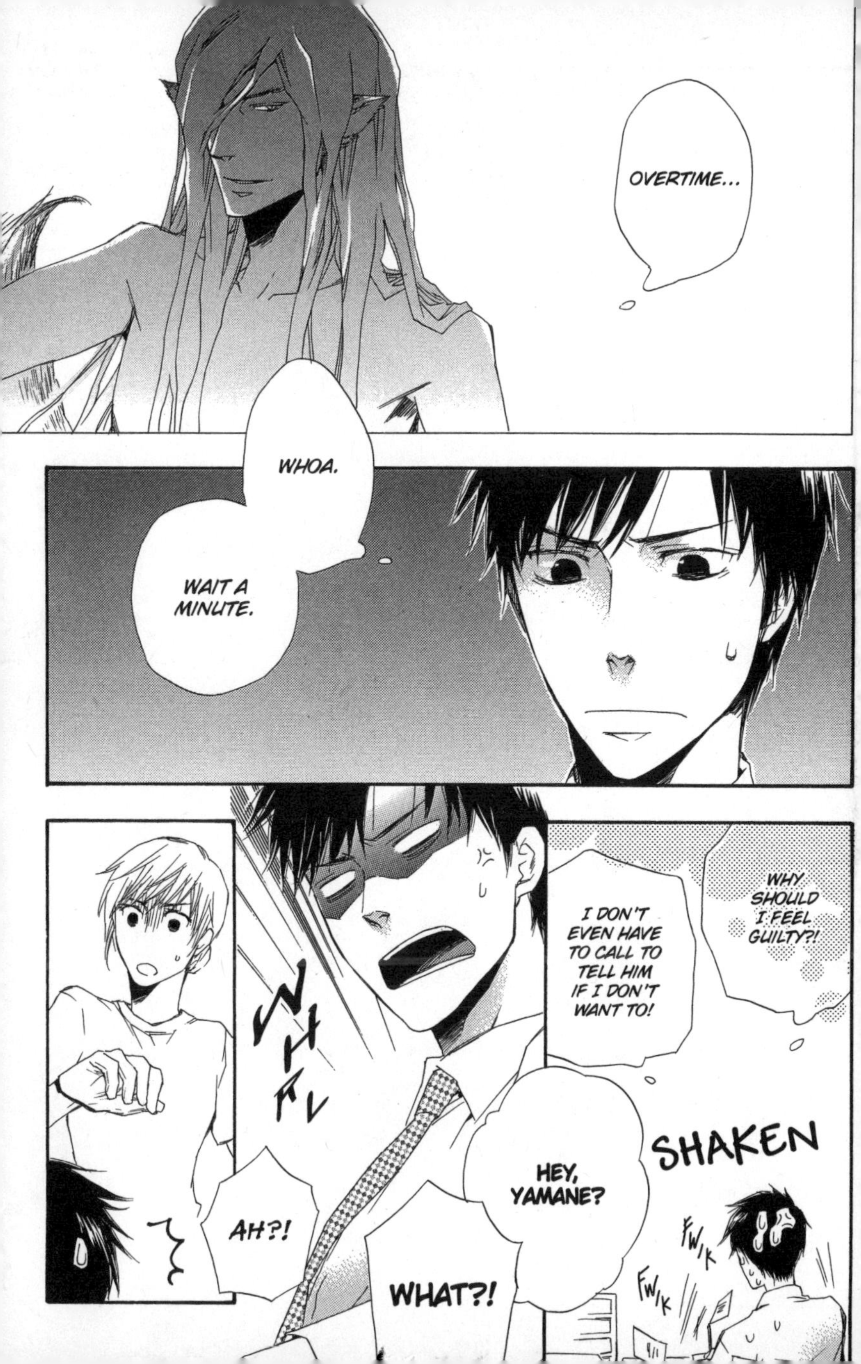
OVERTIME...
WHOA.
WAIT A MINUTE.
WHY SHOULD I FEEL GUILTY?!
I DON'T EVEN HAVE TO CALL TO TELL HIM IF I DON'T WANT TO!
SHAKEN
FWIK
FWIK
HEY, YAMANE?
WHAT?!
AH?!

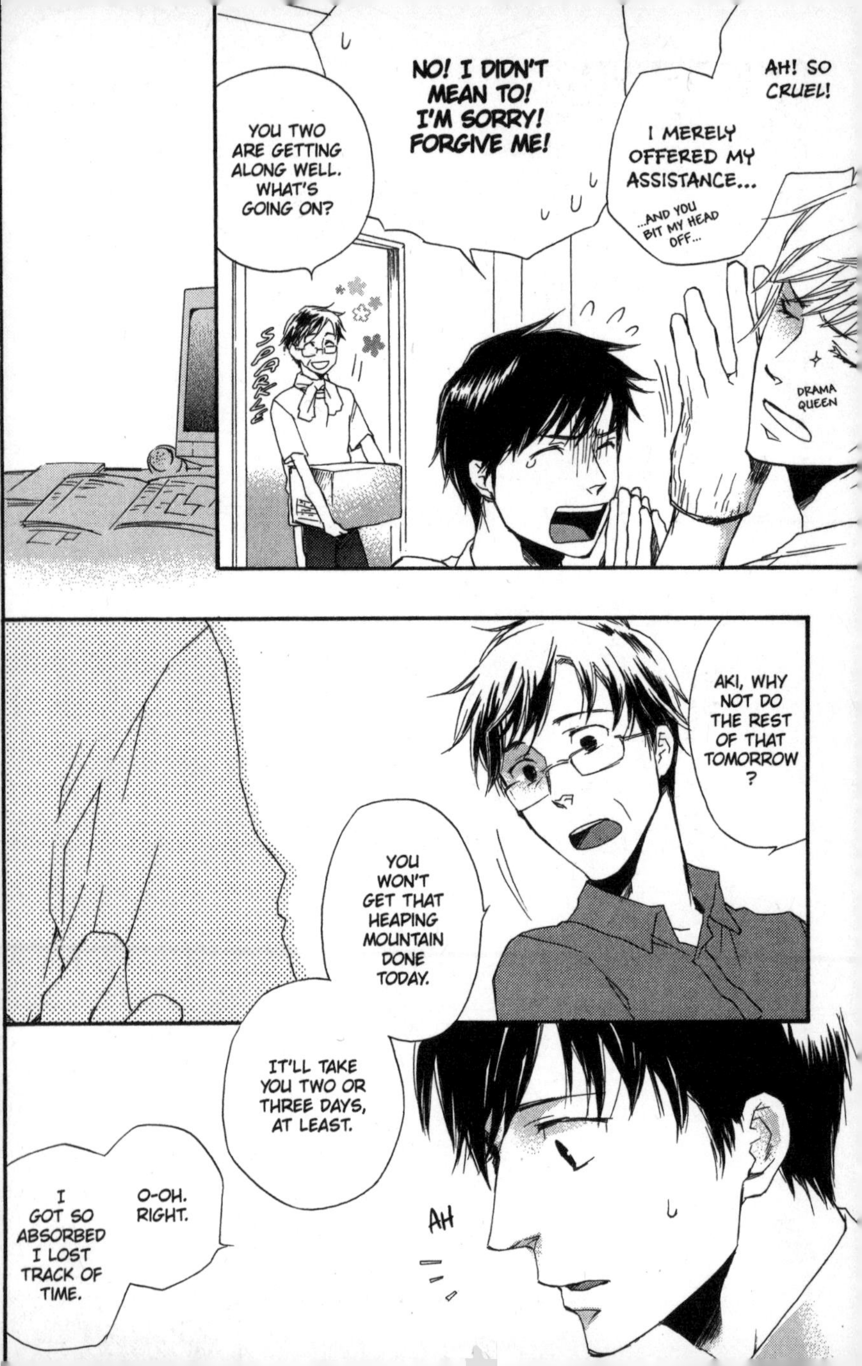
AH! SO CRUEL!
I MERELY OFFERED MY ASSISTANCE...
...AND YOU BIT MY HEAD OFF...
DRAMA QUEEN
NO! I DIDN'T MEAN TO! I'M SORRY! FORGIVE ME!
YOU TWO ARE GETTING ALONG WELL. WHAT'S GOING ON?
SPARKLE
AKI, WHY NOT DO THE REST OF THAT TOMORROW?
YOU WON'T GET THAT HEAPING MOUNTAIN DONE TODAY.
IT'LL TAKE YOU TWO OR THREE DAYS, AT LEAST.
AH
O-OH. RIGHT.
I GOT SO ABSORBED I LOST TRACK OF TIME.

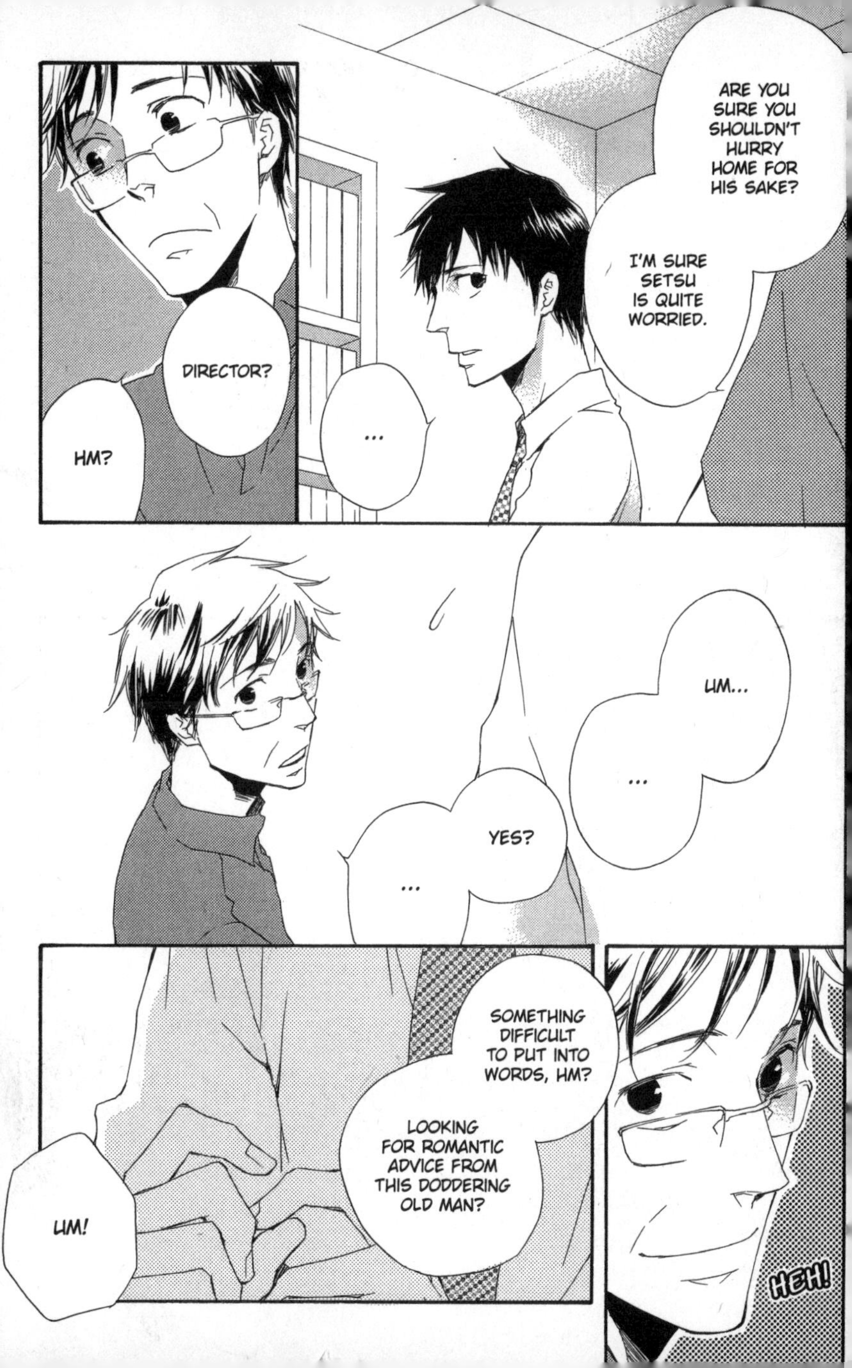
ARE YOU SURE YOU SHOULDN'T HURRY HOME FOR HIS SAKE?
I'M SURE SETSU IS QUITE WORRIED.
...
DIRECTOR?
HM?
UM...
...
YES?
...
HEH!
SOMETHING DIFFICULT TO PUT INTO WORDS, HM?
LOOKING FOR ROMANTIC ADVICE FROM THIS DODDERING OLD MAN?
UM!

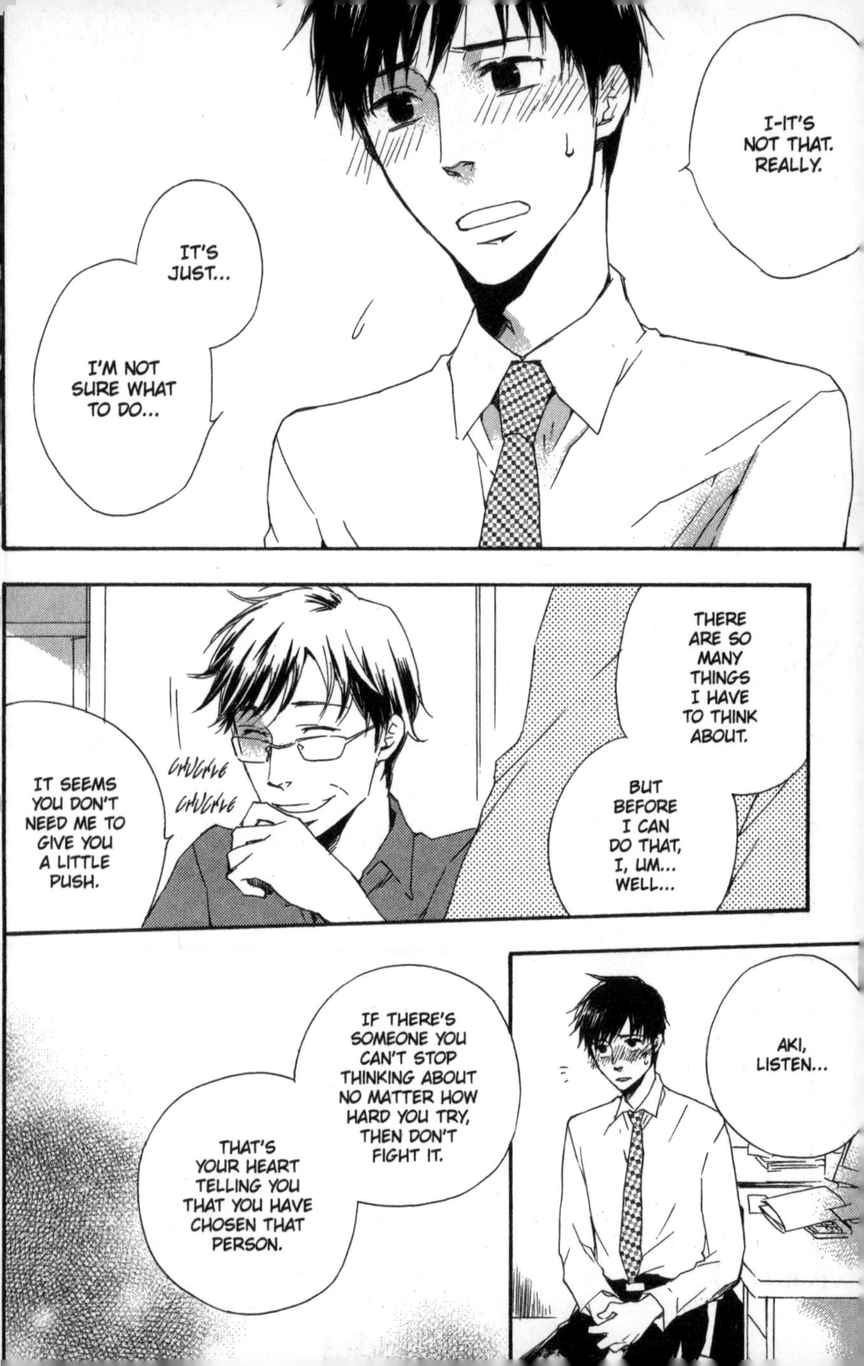
I-IT'S NOT THAT. REALLY.
IT'S JUST...
I'M NOT SURE WHAT TO DO...
THERE ARE SO MANY THINGS I HAVE TO THINK ABOUT.
BUT BEFORE I CAN DO THAT, I, UM... WELL...
CHUCKLE
CHUCKLE
IT SEEMS YOU DON'T NEED ME TO GIVE YOU A LITTLE PUSH.
AKI, LISTEN...
IF THERE'S SOMEONE YOU CAN'T STOP THINKING ABOUT NO MATTER HOW HARD YOU TRY, THEN DON'T FIGHT IT.
THAT'S YOUR HEART TELLING YOU THAT YOU HAVE CHOSEN THAT PERSON.

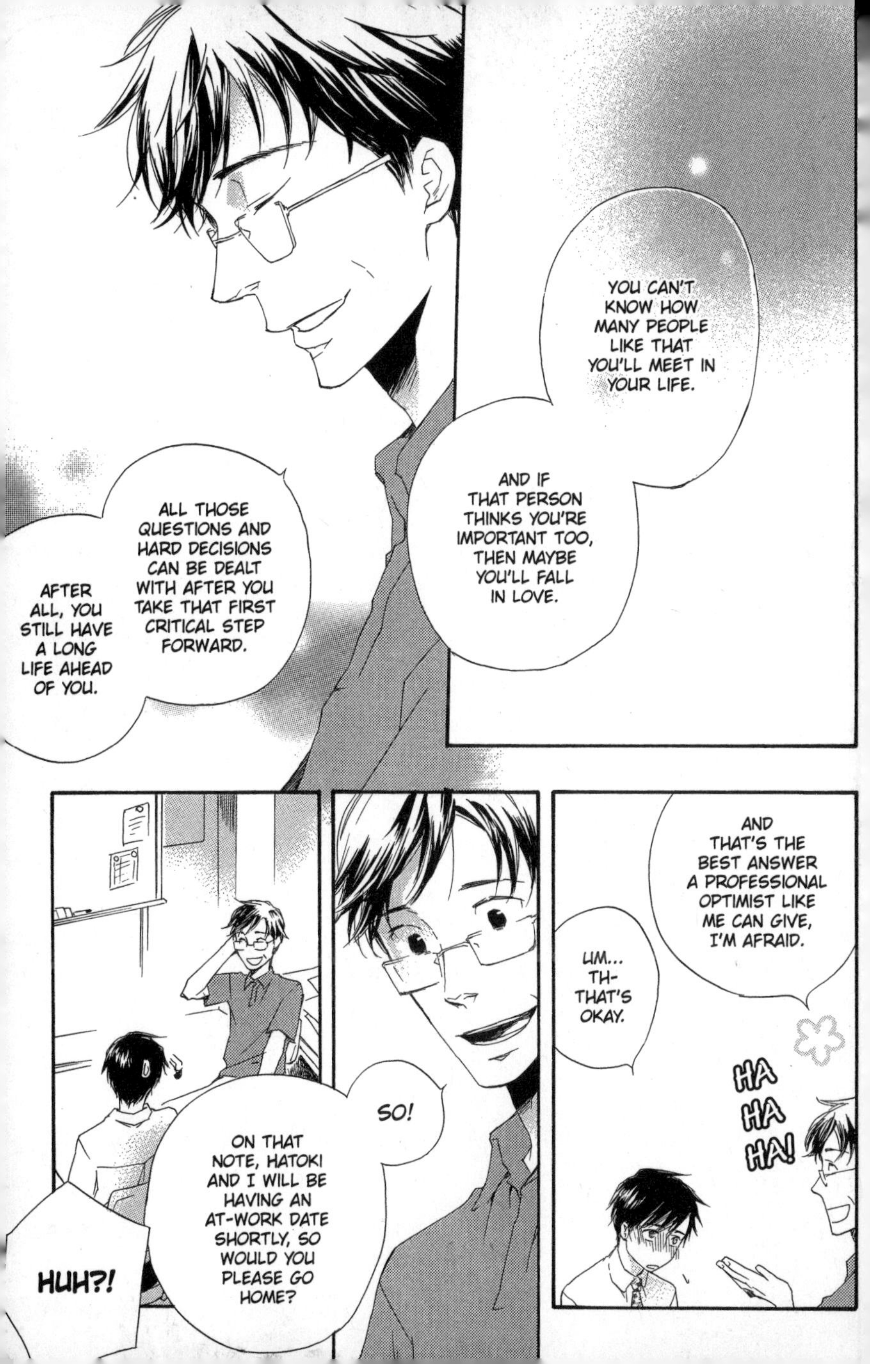
YOU CAN'T KNOW HOW MANY PEOPLE LIKE THAT YOU'LL MEET IN YOUR LIFE.
AND IF THAT PERSON THINKS YOU'RE IMPORTANT TOO, THEN MAYBE YOU'LL FALL IN LOVE.
ALL THOSE QUESTIONS AND HARD DECISIONS CAN BE DEALT WITH AFTER YOU TAKE THAT FIRST CRITICAL STEP FORWARD.
AFTER ALL, YOU STILL HAVE A LONG LIFE AHEAD OF YOU.
AND THAT'S THE BEST ANSWER A PROFESSIONAL OPTIMIST LIKE ME CAN GIVE, I'M AFRAID.
UM... TH- THAT'S OKAY.
HA HA HA!
SO!
ON THAT NOTE, HATOKI AND I WILL BE HAVING AN AT-WORK DATE SHORTLY, SO WOULD YOU PLEASE GO HOME?
HUH?!

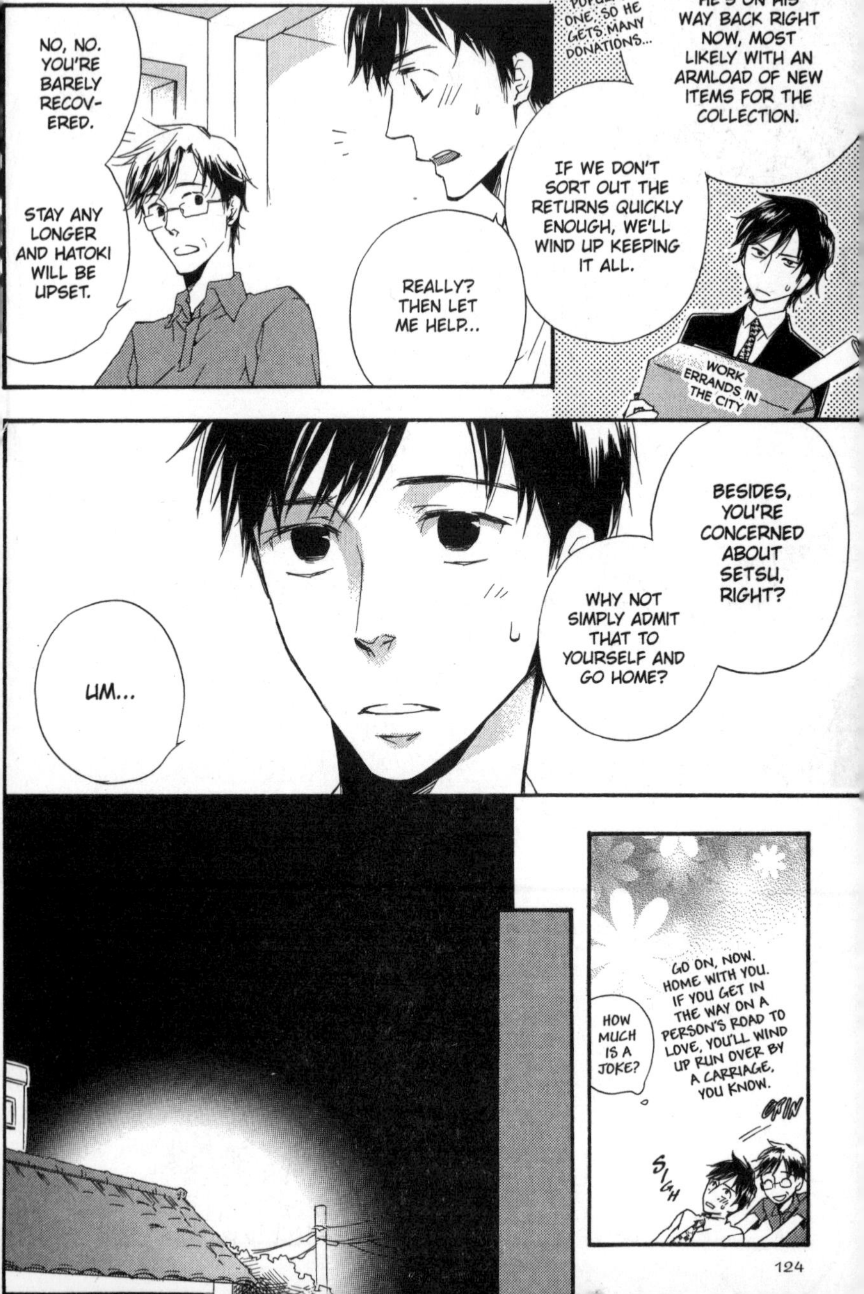
YEP! HE'S ON HIS WAY BACK RIGHT NOW, MOST LIKELY WITH AN ARMLOAD OF NEW ITEMS FOR THE COLLECTION.
HE'S A POPULAR ONE, SO HE GETS MANY DONATIONS...
WORK ERRANDS IN THE CITY
IF WE DON'T SORT OUT THE RETURNS QUICKLY ENOUGH, WE'LL WIND UP KEEPING IT ALL.
REALLY? THEN LET ME HELP...
NO, NO. YOU'RE BARELY RECOVERED.
STAY ANY LONGER AND HATOKI WILL BE UPSET.
BESIDES, YOU'RE CONCERNED ABOUT SETSU, RIGHT?
WHY NOT SIMPLY ADMIT THAT TO YOURSELF AND GO HOME?
UM...
GO ON, NOW. HOME WITH YOU. IF YOU GET IN THE WAY ON A PERSON'S ROAD TO LOVE, YOU'LL WIND UP RUN OVER BY A CARRIAGE, YOU KNOW.
HOW MUCH IS A JOKE?
GRIN
SIGH

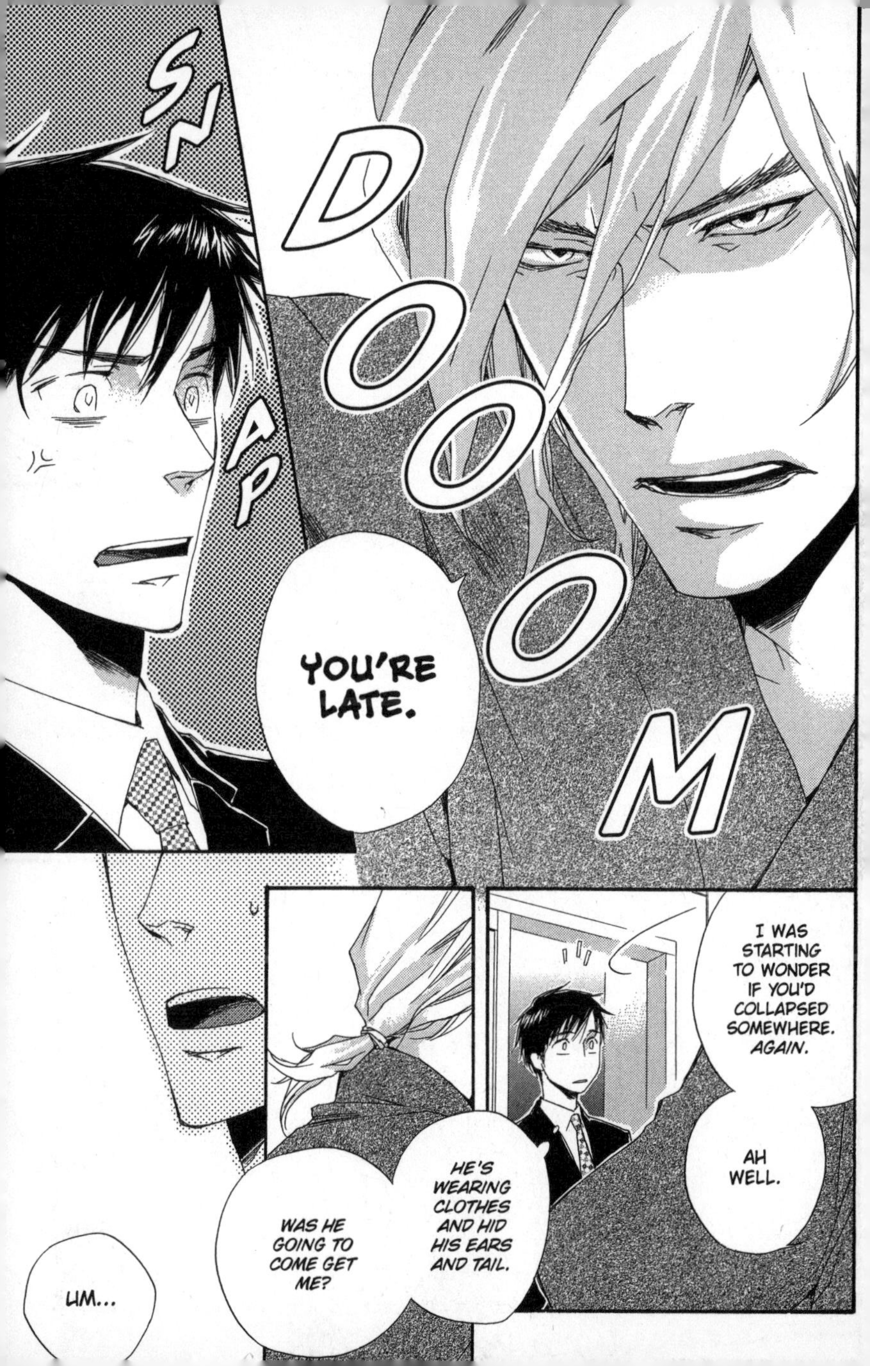
DOOOM
YOU'RE LATE.
SNAP
I WAS STARTING TO WONDER IF YOU'D COLLAPSED SOMEWHERE. AGAIN.
AH WELL.
HE'S WEARING CLOTHES AND HID HIS EARS AND TAIL.
WAS HE GOING TO COME GET ME?
UM...

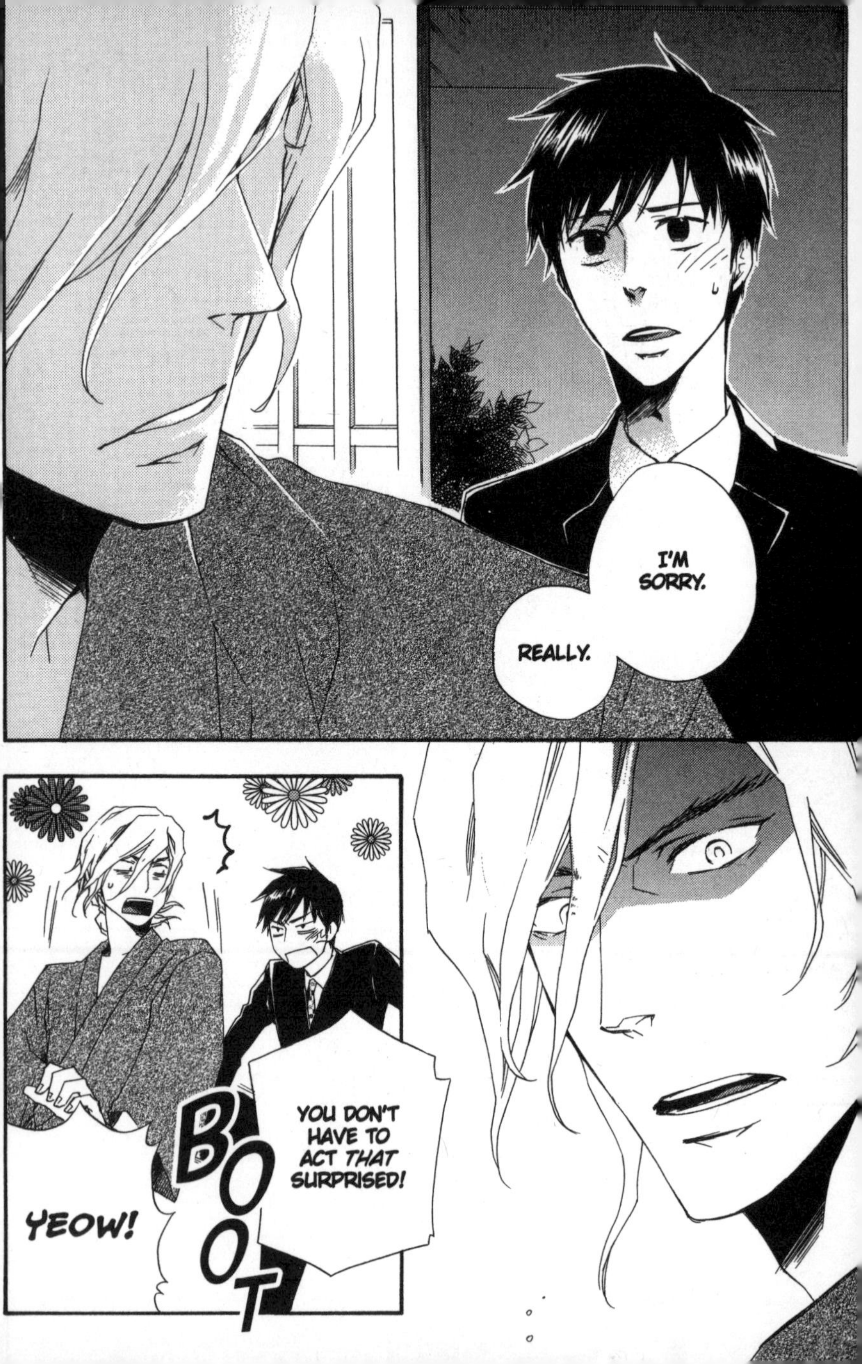
I'M SORRY.
REALLY.
YOU DON'T HAVE TO ACT *THAT* SURPRISED!
BOOT
YEOW!

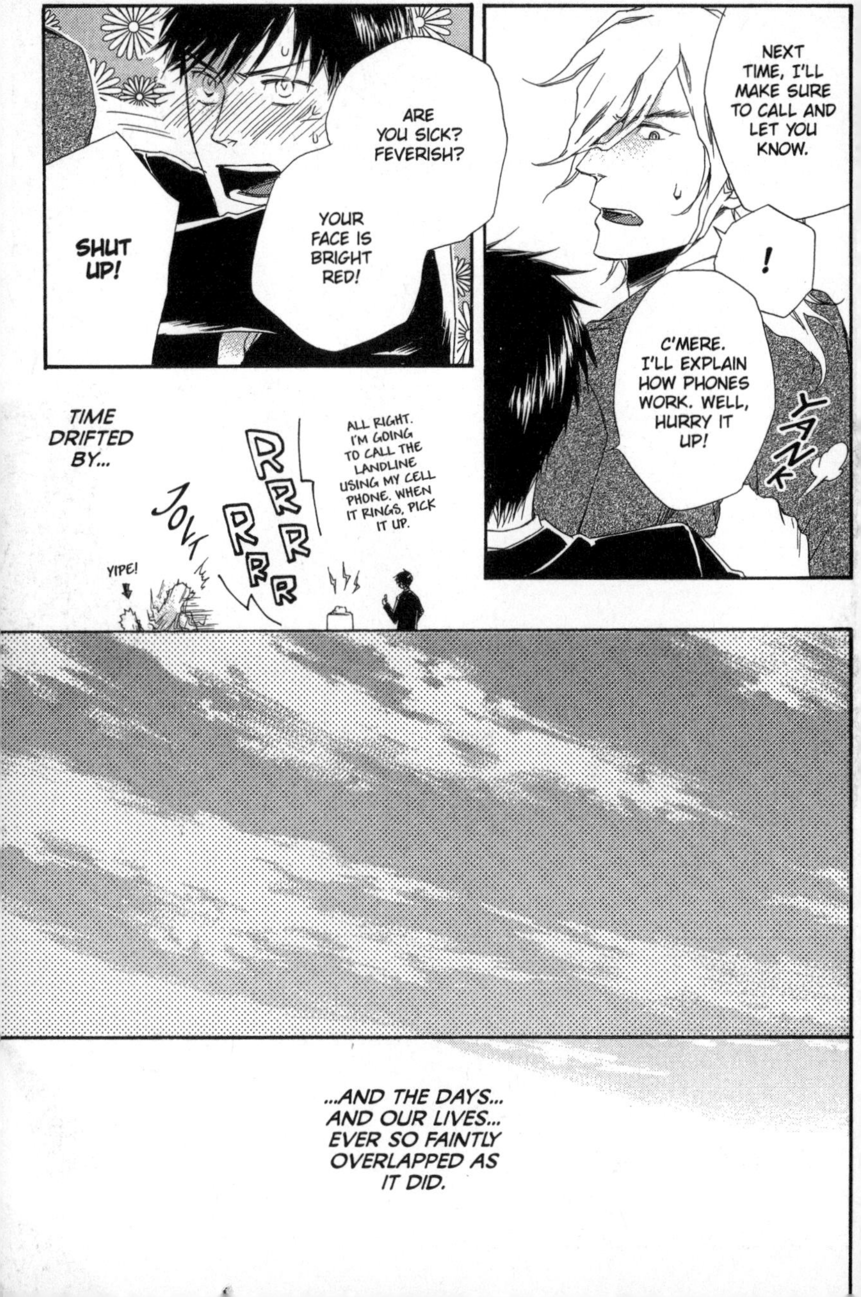
NEXT TIME, I'LL MAKE SURE TO CALL AND LET YOU KNOW.
!
C'MERE. I'LL EXPLAIN HOW PHONES WORK. WELL, HURRY IT UP!
YANK
ARE YOU SICK? FEVERISH?
YOUR FACE IS BRIGHT RED!
SHUT UP!
TIME DRIFTED BY...
ALL RIGHT. I'M GOING TO CALL THE LANDLINE USING MY CELL PHONE. WHEN IT RINGS, PICK IT UP.
RRRR
RRRR
JOLT
YIPE!
...AND THE DAYS... AND OUR LIVES... EVER SO FAINTLY OVERLAPPED AS IT DID.

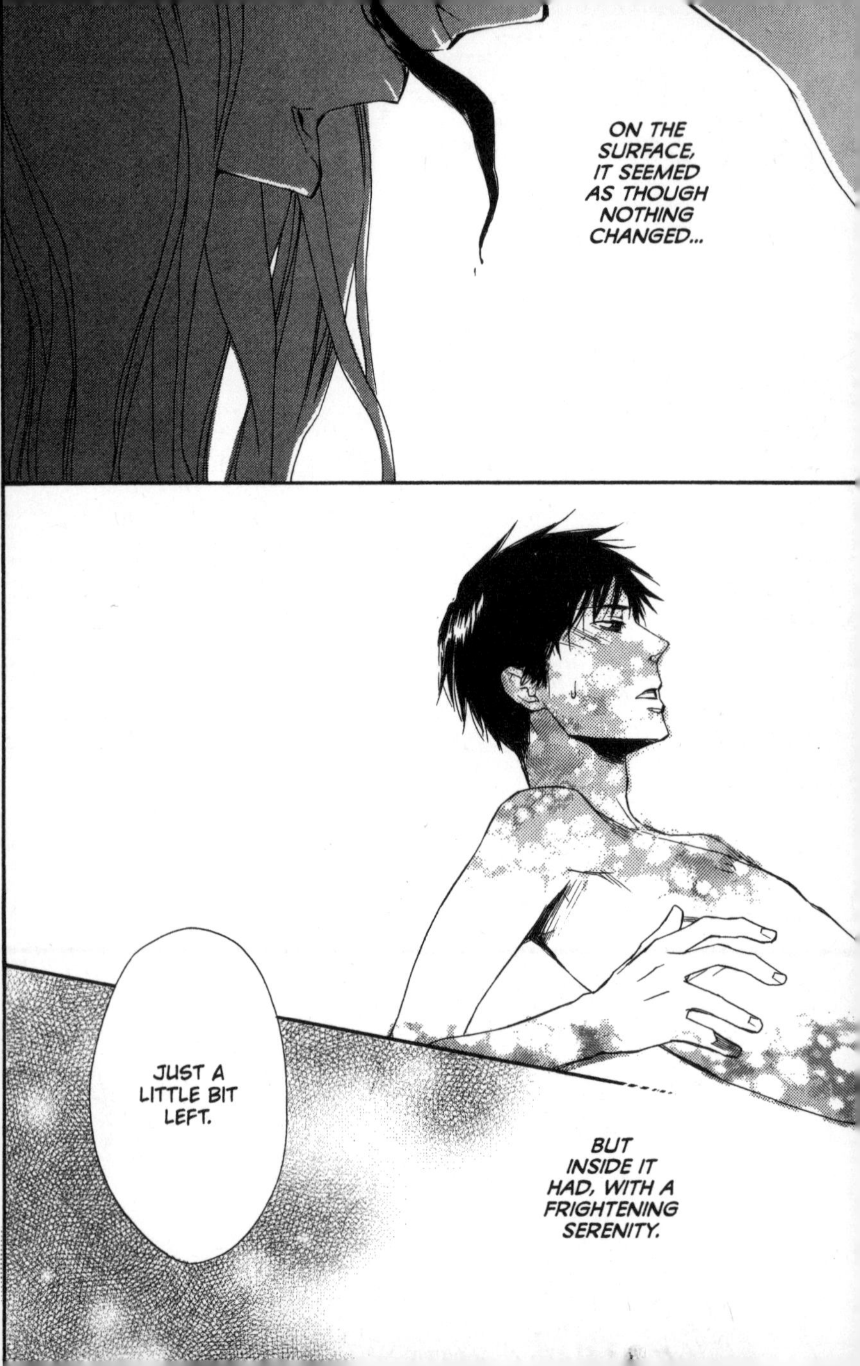
ON THE SURFACE, IT SEEMED AS THOUGH NOTHING CHANGED...
BUT INSIDE IT HAD, WITH A FRIGHTENING SERENITY.
JUST A LITTLE BIT LEFT.

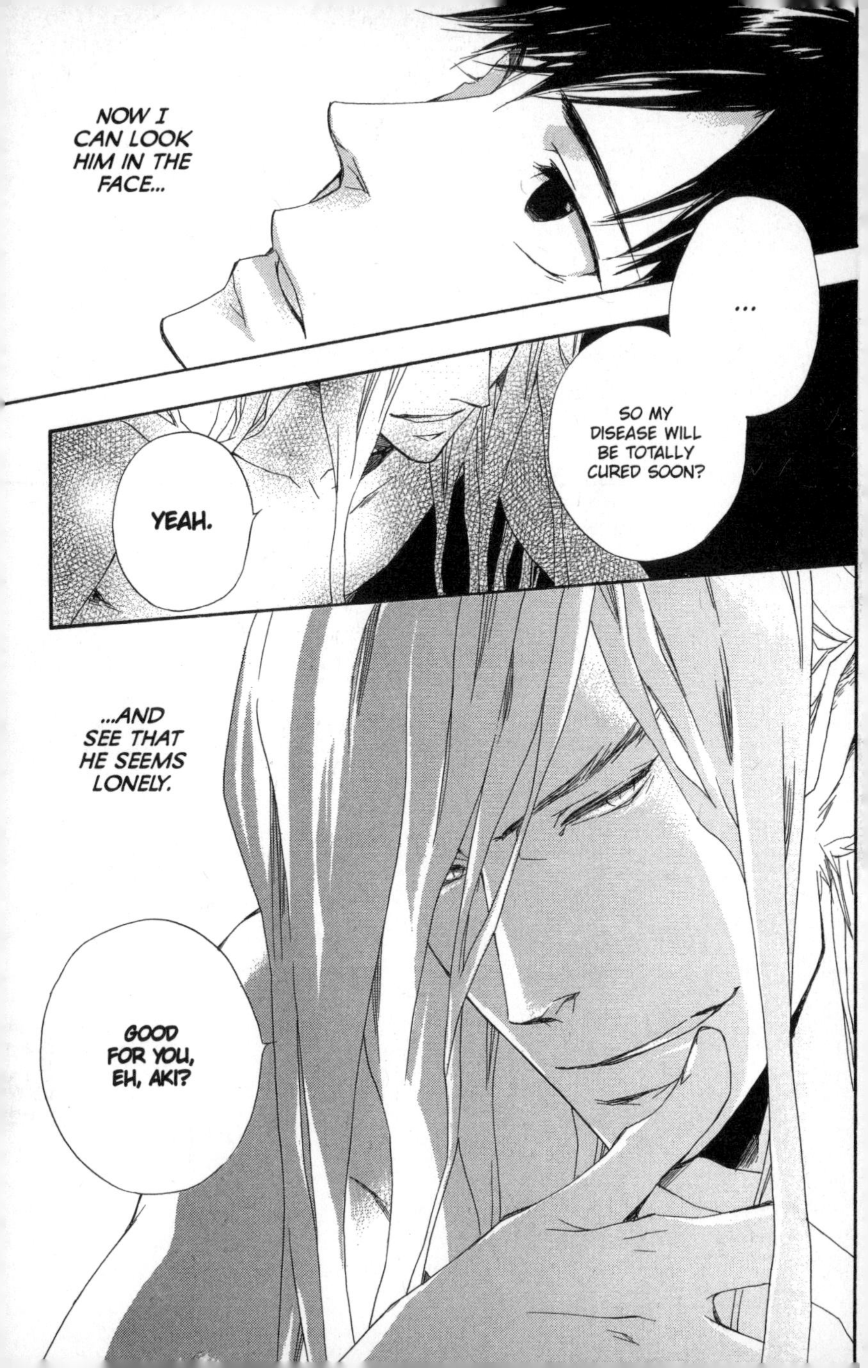
NOW I CAN LOOK HIM IN THE FACE...
...
SO MY DISEASE WILL BE TOTALLY CURED SOON?
YEAH.
...AND SEE THAT HE SEEMS LONELY.
GOOD FOR YOU, EH, AKI?

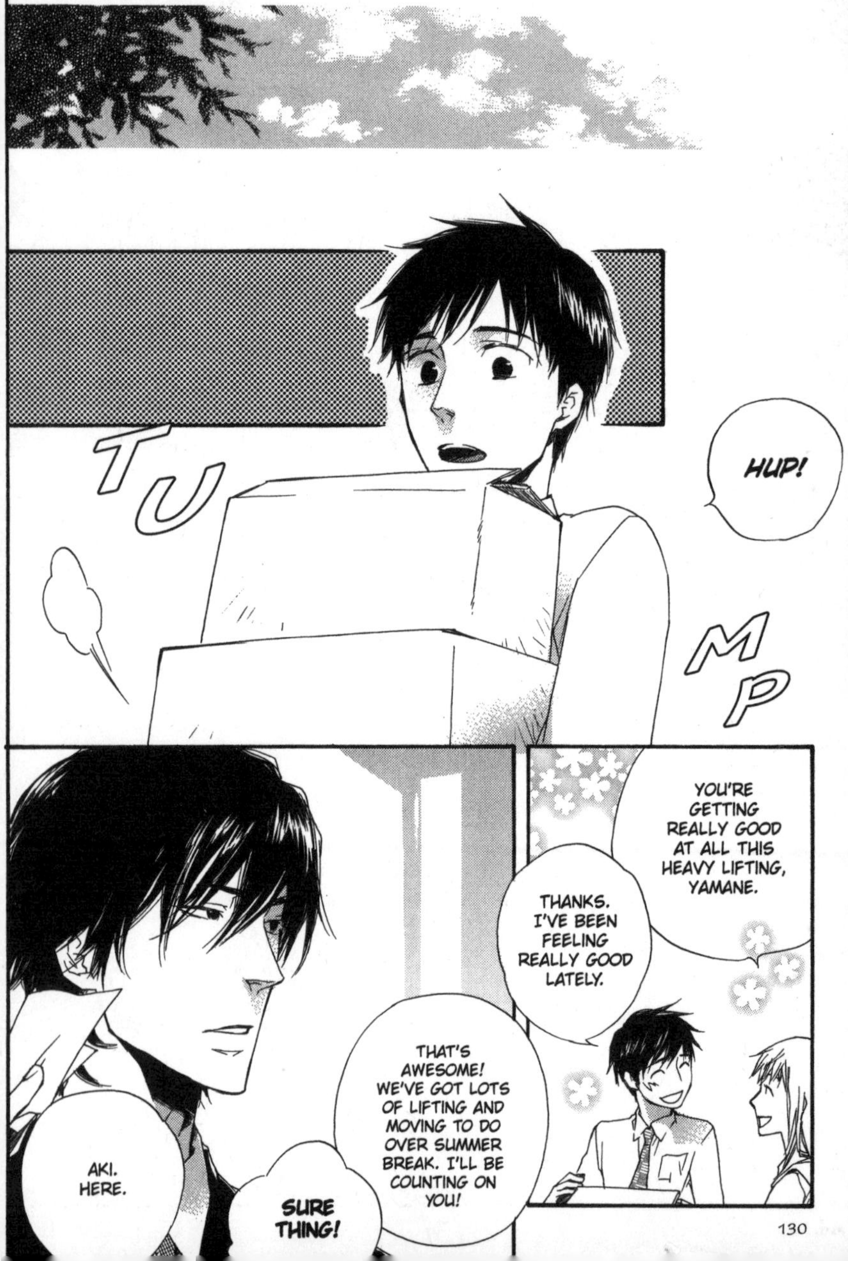
HUP!
TUMP
YOU'RE GETTING REALLY GOOD AT ALL THIS HEAVY LIFTING, YAMANE.
THANKS. I'VE BEEN FEELING REALLY GOOD LATELY.
THAT'S AWESOME! WE'VE GOT LOTS OF LIFTING AND MOVING TO DO OVER SUMMER BREAK. I'LL BE COUNTING ON YOU!
SURE THING!
AKI. HERE.

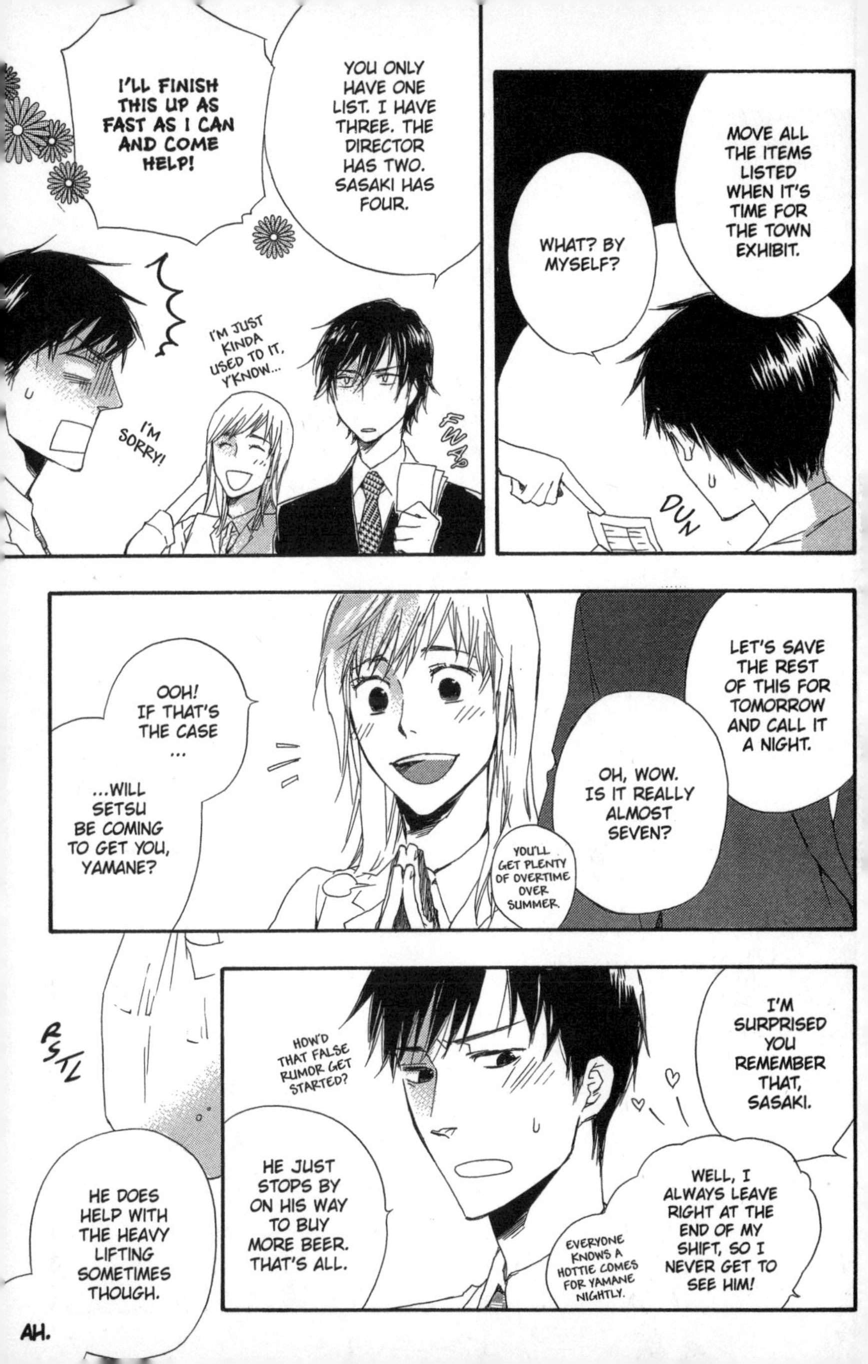
MOVE ALL THE ITEMS LISTED WHEN IT'S TIME FOR THE TOWN EXHIBIT.
WHAT? BY MYSELF?
DUN
YOU ONLY HAVE ONE LIST. I HAVE THREE. THE DIRECTOR HAS TWO. SASAKI HAS FOUR.
I'LL FINISH THIS UP AS FAST AS I CAN AND COME HELP!
FWAP
I'M JUST KINDA USED TO IT, Y'KNOW...
I'M SORRY!
LET'S SAVE THE REST OF THIS FOR TOMORROW AND CALL IT A NIGHT.
OH, WOW. IS IT REALLY ALMOST SEVEN?
YOU'LL GET PLENTY OF OVERTIME OVER SUMMER.
OOH! IF THAT'S THE CASE ...
...WILL SETSU BE COMING TO GET YOU, YAMANE?
I'M SURPRISED YOU REMEMBER THAT, SASAKI.
WELL, I ALWAYS LEAVE RIGHT AT THE END OF MY SHIFT, SO I NEVER GET TO SEE HIM!
EVERYONE KNOWS A HOTTIE COMES FOR YAMANE NIGHTLY.
HOW'D THAT FALSE RUMOR GET STARTED?
HE JUST STOPS BY ON HIS WAY TO BUY MORE BEER. THAT'S ALL.
RSTL
HE DOES HELP WITH THE HEAVY LIFTING SOMETIMES THOUGH.
AH.

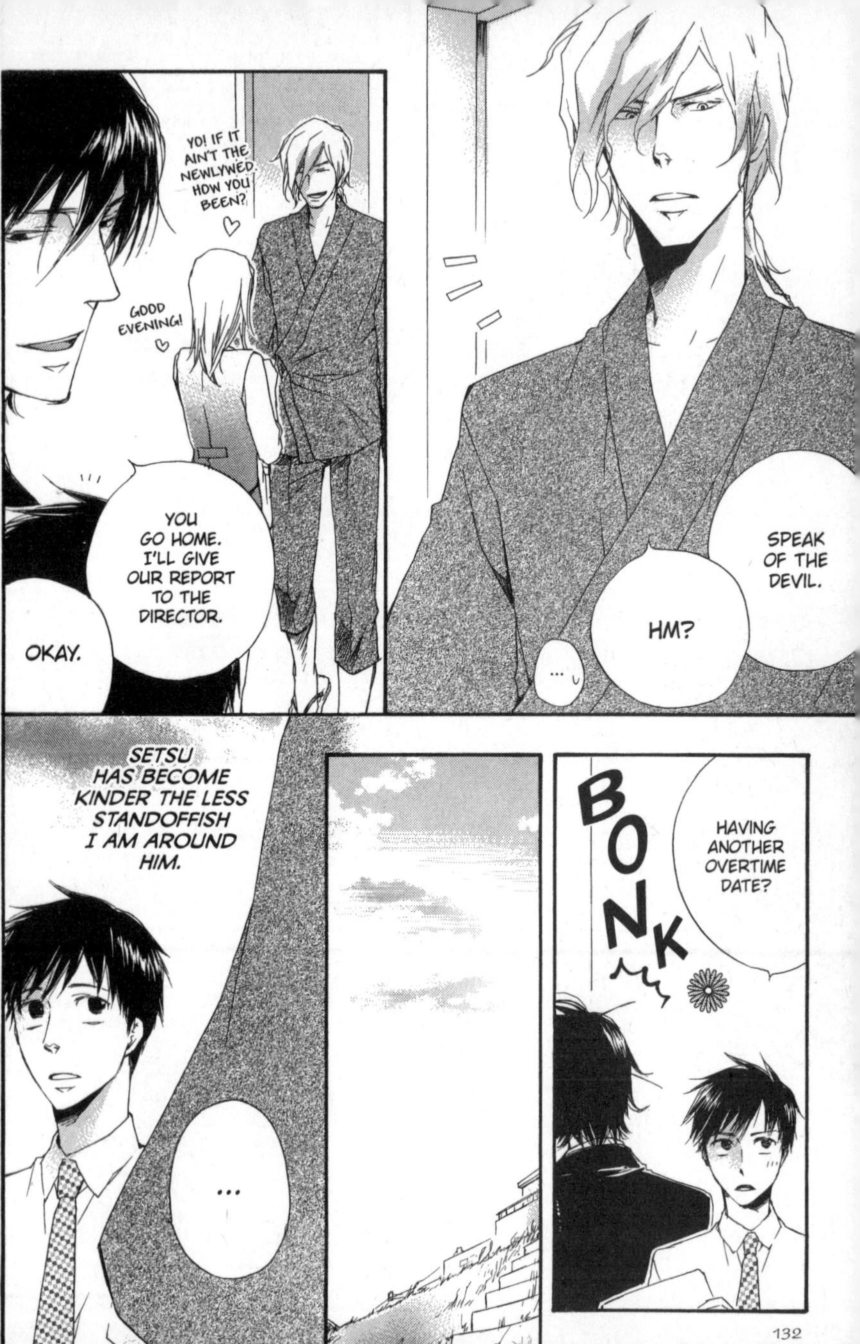
SPEAK OF THE DEVIL.
HM?
...
YO! IF IT AIN'T THE NEWLYWED. HOW YOU BEEN?
GOOD EVENING!
YOU GO HOME. I'LL GIVE OUR REPORT TO THE DIRECTOR.
OKAY.
HAVING ANOTHER OVERTIME DATE?
BONK
SETSU HAS BECOME KINDER THE LESS STANDOFFISH I AM AROUND HIM.
...

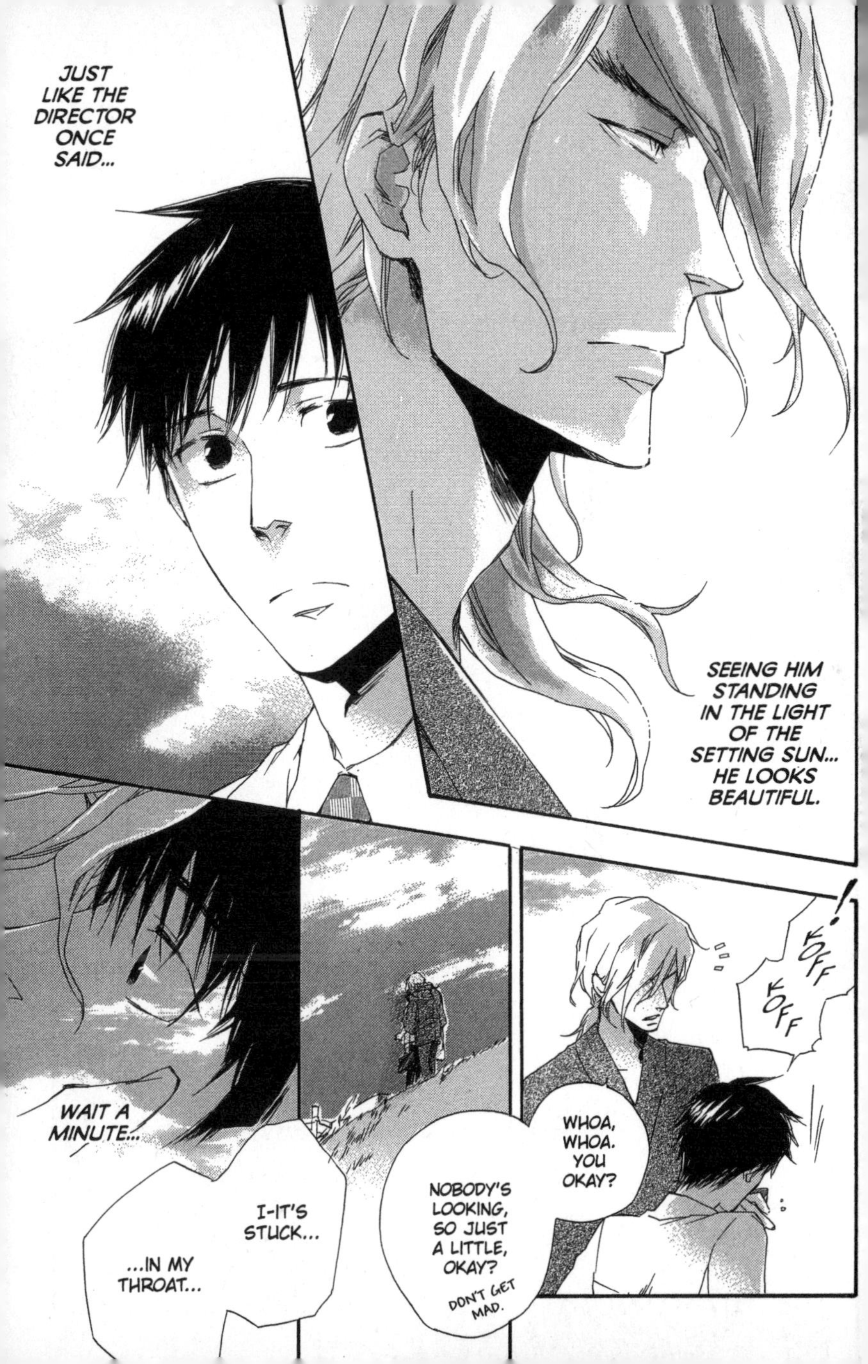
SEEING HIM STANDING IN THE LIGHT OF THE SETTING SUN... HE LOOKS BEAUTIFUL.
JUST LIKE THE DIRECTOR ONCE SAID...
!
KOFF KOFF
WHOA, WHOA. YOU OKAY?
WAIT A MINUTE...
I-IT'S STUCK...
...IN MY THROAT...
NOBODY'S LOOKING, SO JUST A LITTLE, OKAY?
DON'T GET MAD.

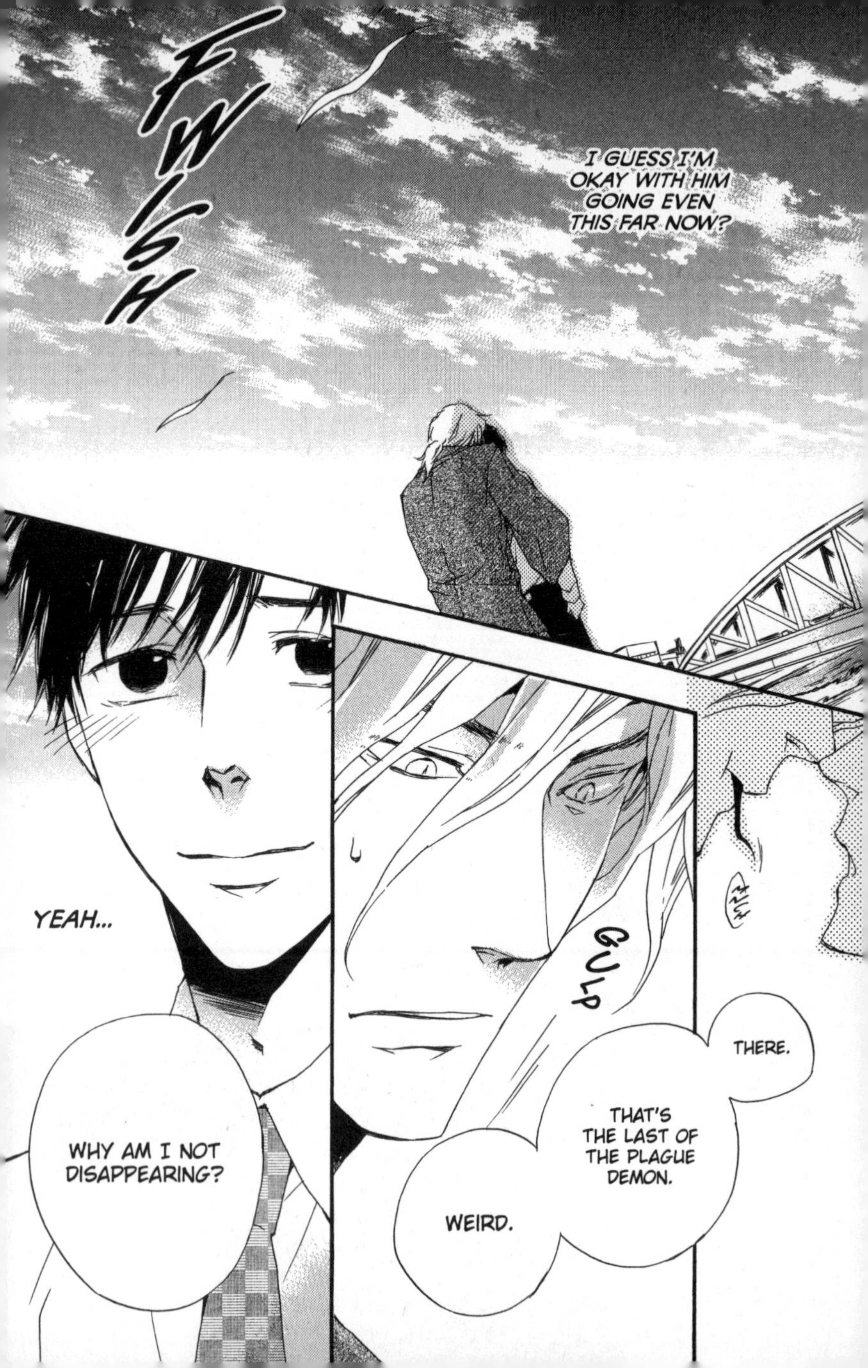
I GUESS I'M OKAY WITH HIM GOING EVEN THIS FAR NOW?
FWISH
GULP
THERE.
THAT'S THE LAST OF THE PLAGUE DEMON.
WEIRD.
YEAH...
WHY AM I NOT DISAPPEARING?

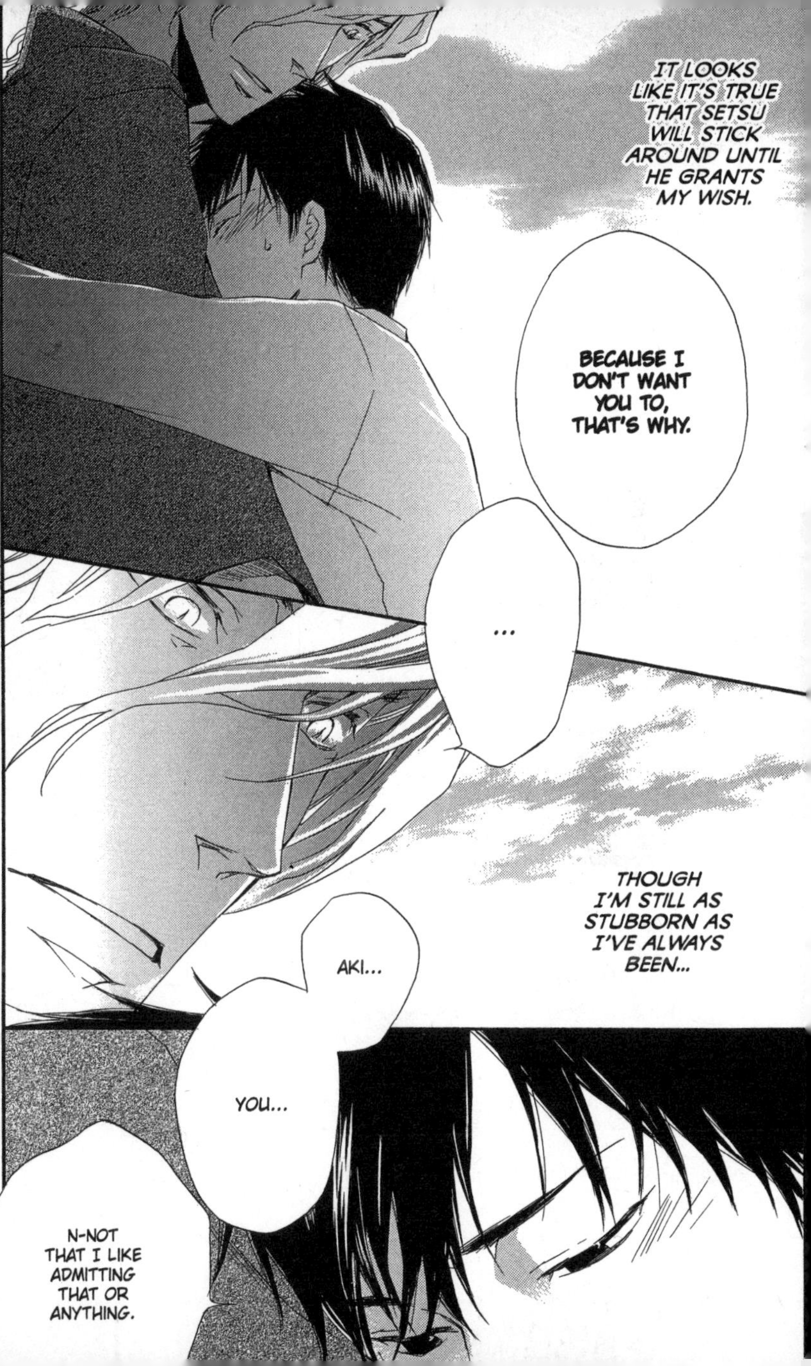
IT LOOKS LIKE IT'S TRUE THAT SETSU WILL STICK AROUND UNTIL HE GRANTS MY WISH.
BECAUSE I DON'T WANT YOU TO, THAT'S WHY.
...
THOUGH I'M STILL AS STUBBORN AS I'VE ALWAYS BEEN...
AKI...
YOU...
N-NOT THAT I LIKE ADMITTING THAT OR ANYTHING.

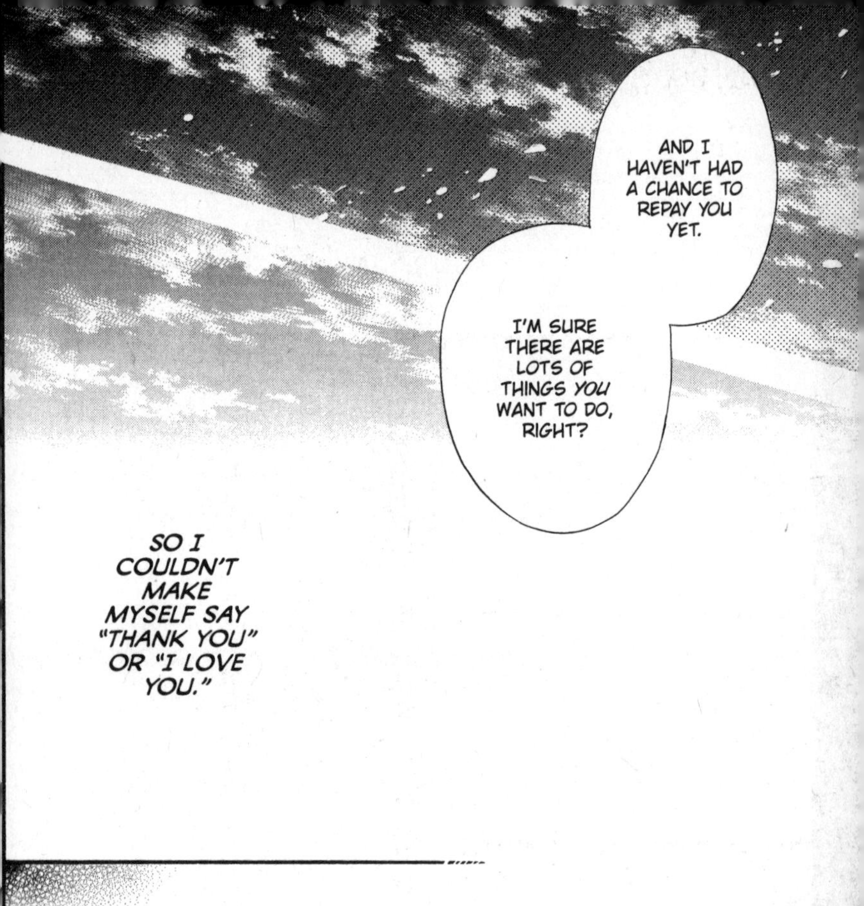
AND I HAVEN'T HAD A CHANCE TO REPAY YOU YET.
I'M SURE THERE ARE LOTS OF THINGS *YOU* WANT TO DO, RIGHT?
SO I COULDN'T MAKE MYSELF SAY "THANK YOU" OR "I LOVE YOU."

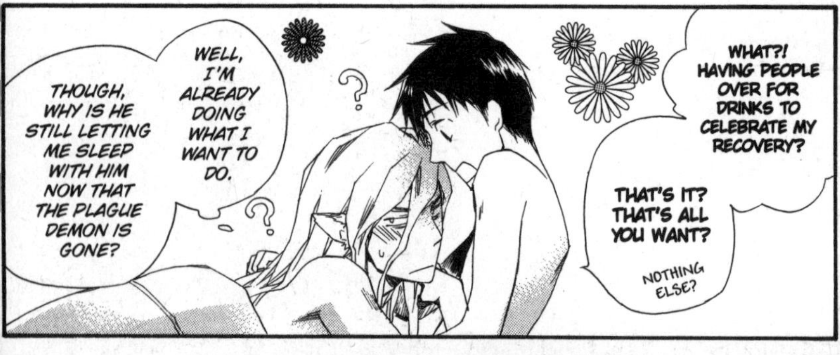
WHAT?! HAVING PEOPLE OVER FOR DRINKS TO CELEBRATE MY RECOVERY?
THAT'S IT? THAT'S ALL YOU WANT?
NOTHING ELSE?
WELL, I'M ALREADY DOING WHAT I WANT TO DO.
THOUGH, WHY IS HE STILL LETTING ME SLEEP WITH HIM NOW THAT THE PLAGUE DEMON IS GONE?

A Strange & Mystifying Story, Chapter 2 / END

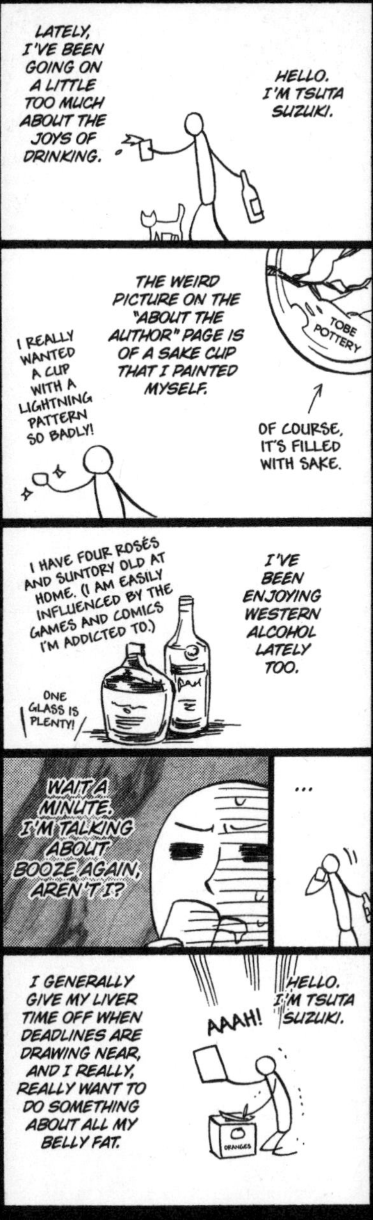
HELLO. I'M TSUTA SUZUKI.
LATELY, I'VE BEEN GOING ON A LITTLE TOO MUCH ABOUT THE JOYS OF DRINKING.
TOBE POTTERY
THE WEIRD PICTURE ON THE "ABOUT THE AUTHOR" PAGE IS OF A SAKE CUP THAT I PAINTED MYSELF.
OF COURSE, IT'S FILLED WITH SAKE.
I REALLY WANTED A CUP WITH A LIGHTNING PATTERN SO BADLY!
I'VE BEEN ENJOYING WESTERN ALCOHOL LATELY TOO.
I HAVE FOUR ROSES AND SUNTORY OLD AT HOME. (I AM EASILY INFLUENCED BY THE GAMES AND COMICS I'M ADDICTED TO.)
ONE GLASS IS PLENTY!
...
WAIT A MINUTE. I'M TALKING ABOUT BOOZE AGAIN, AREN'T I?
HELLO. I'M TSUTA SUZUKI.
AAAH!
ORANGES
I GENERALLY GIVE MY LIVER TIME OFF WHEN DEADLINES ARE DRAWING NEAR, AND I REALLY, REALLY WANT TO DO SOMETHING ABOUT ALL MY BELLY FAT.

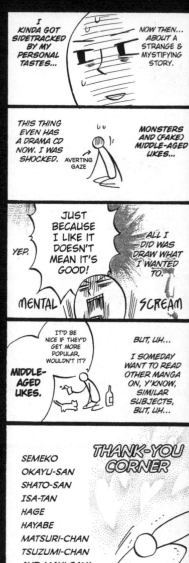

NOW THEN... ABOUT A STRANGE & MYSTIFYING STORY.
I KINDA GOT SIDETRACKED BY MY PERSONAL TASTES...
MONSTERS AND (FAKE) MIDDLE-AGED UKES...
AVERTING GAZE
THIS THING EVEN HAS A DRAMA CD NOW. I WAS SHOCKED.
ALL I DID WAS DRAW WHAT I WANTED TO.
JUST BECAUSE I LIKE IT DOESN'T MEAN IT'S GOOD!
YEP.
MENTAL SCREAM
BUT, UH...
I SOMEDAY WANT TO READ OTHER MANGA ON, Y'KNOW, SIMILAR SUBJECTS, BUT, UH...
IT'D BE NICE IF THEY'D GET MORE POPULAR, WOULDN'T IT?
MIDDLE-AGED UKES.
THANK-YOU CORNER
SEMEKO
OKAYU-SAN
SHATO-SAN
ISA-TAN
HAGE
HAYABE
MATSURI-CHAN
TSUZUMI-CHAN
AND MAKI-SAN!
THIS NOTE IS DRAGGING ON... RIGHT?
THANK YOU FOR EVERYTHING
I APOLOGIZE FOR BEING A TERRIBLE HUMAN BEING.
<END>

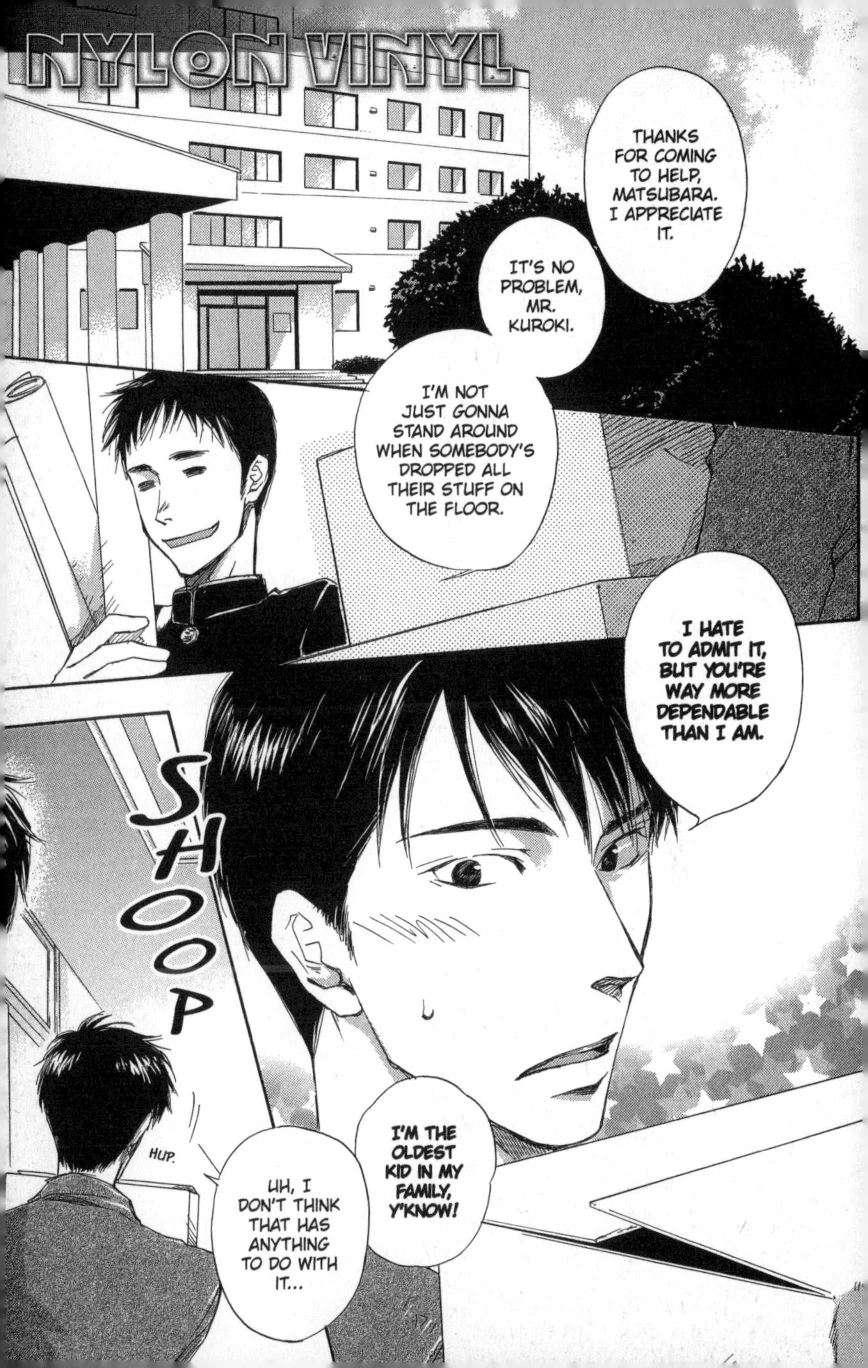
NYLON VINYL
THANKS FOR COMING TO HELP, MATSUBARA. I APPRECIATE IT.
IT'S NO PROBLEM, MR. KUROKI.
I'M NOT JUST GONNA STAND AROUND WHEN SOMEBODY'S DROPPED ALL THEIR STUFF ON THE FLOOR.
I HATE TO ADMIT IT, BUT YOU'RE WAY MORE DEPENDABLE THAN I AM.
SHOOP
I'M THE OLDEST KID IN MY FAMILY, Y'KNOW!
HUP.
UH, I DON'T THINK THAT HAS ANYTHING TO DO WITH IT...

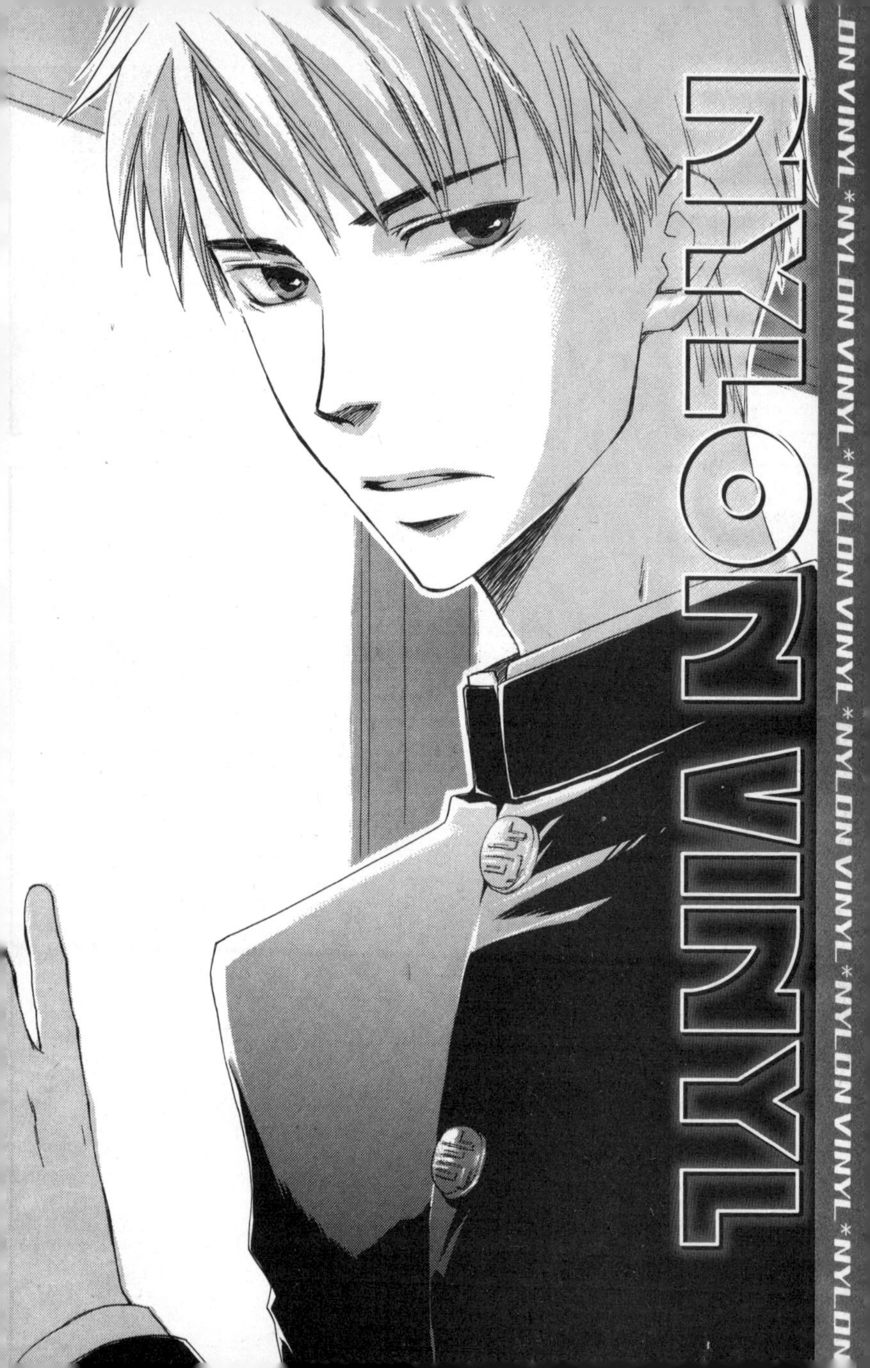
NYLON VINYL
_ON VINYL*NYLON VINYL*NYLON VINYL*NYLON VINYL*NYLON VINYL*NYLON

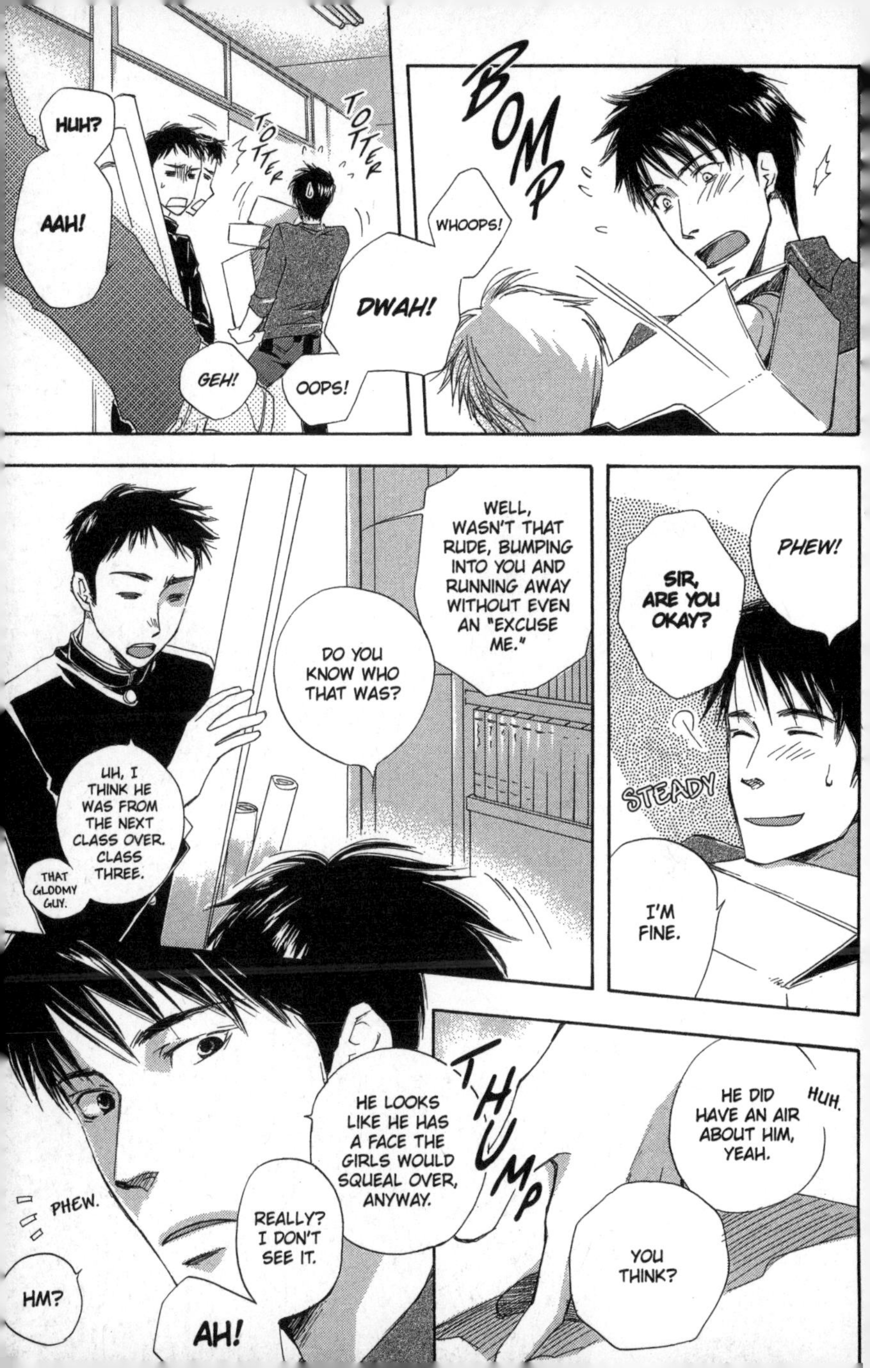
BOMP
WHOOPS!
DWAH!
TOTTER
TOTTER
HUH?
AAH!
OOPS!
GEH!
PHEW!
SIR, ARE YOU OKAY?
STEADY
I'M FINE.
WELL, WASN'T THAT RUDE, BUMPING INTO YOU AND RUNNING AWAY WITHOUT EVEN AN "EXCUSE ME."
DO YOU KNOW WHO THAT WAS?
UH, I THINK HE WAS FROM THE NEXT CLASS OVER. CLASS THREE.
THAT GLOOMY GUY.
HUH.
HE DID HAVE AN AIR ABOUT HIM, YEAH.
YOU THINK?
THUMP
HE LOOKS LIKE HE HAS A FACE THE GIRLS WOULD SQUEAL OVER, ANYWAY.
REALLY? I DON'T SEE IT.
PHEW.
HM?
AH!

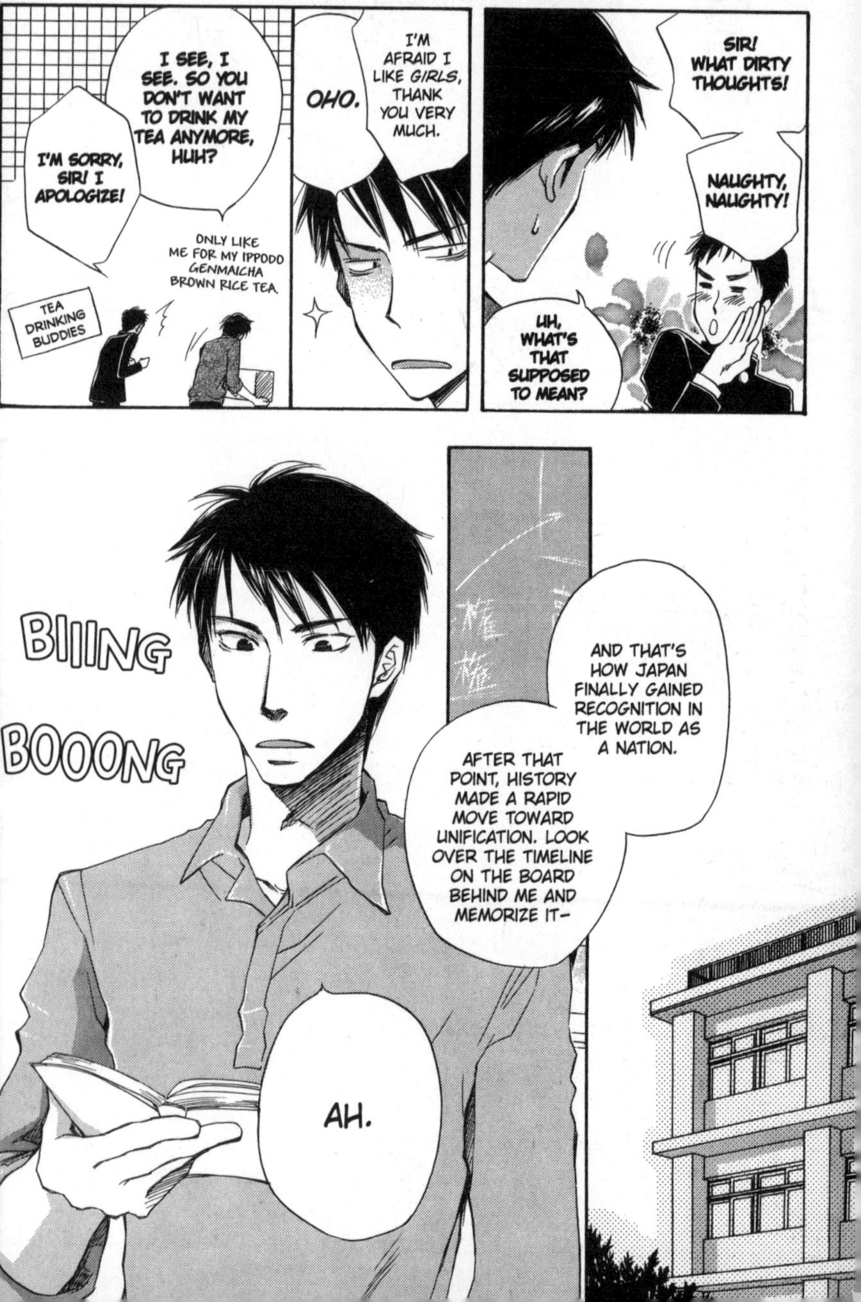
SIR! WHAT DIRTY THOUGHTS!
NAUGHTY, NAUGHTY!
UH, WHAT'S THAT SUPPOSED TO MEAN?
I'M AFRAID I LIKE *GIRLS*, THANK YOU VERY MUCH.
OHO.
I SEE, I SEE. SO YOU DON'T WANT TO DRINK MY TEA ANYMORE, HUH?
I'M SORRY, SIR! I APOLOGIZE!
ONLY LIKE ME FOR MY IPPODO GENMAICHA BROWN RICE TEA.
TEA DRINKING BUDDIES
AND THAT'S HOW JAPAN FINALLY GAINED RECOGNITION IN THE WORLD AS A NATION.
AFTER THAT POINT, HISTORY MADE A RAPID MOVE TOWARD UNIFICATION. LOOK OVER THE TIMELINE ON THE BOARD BEHIND ME AND MEMORIZE IT—
AH.
BIIING
BOOONG

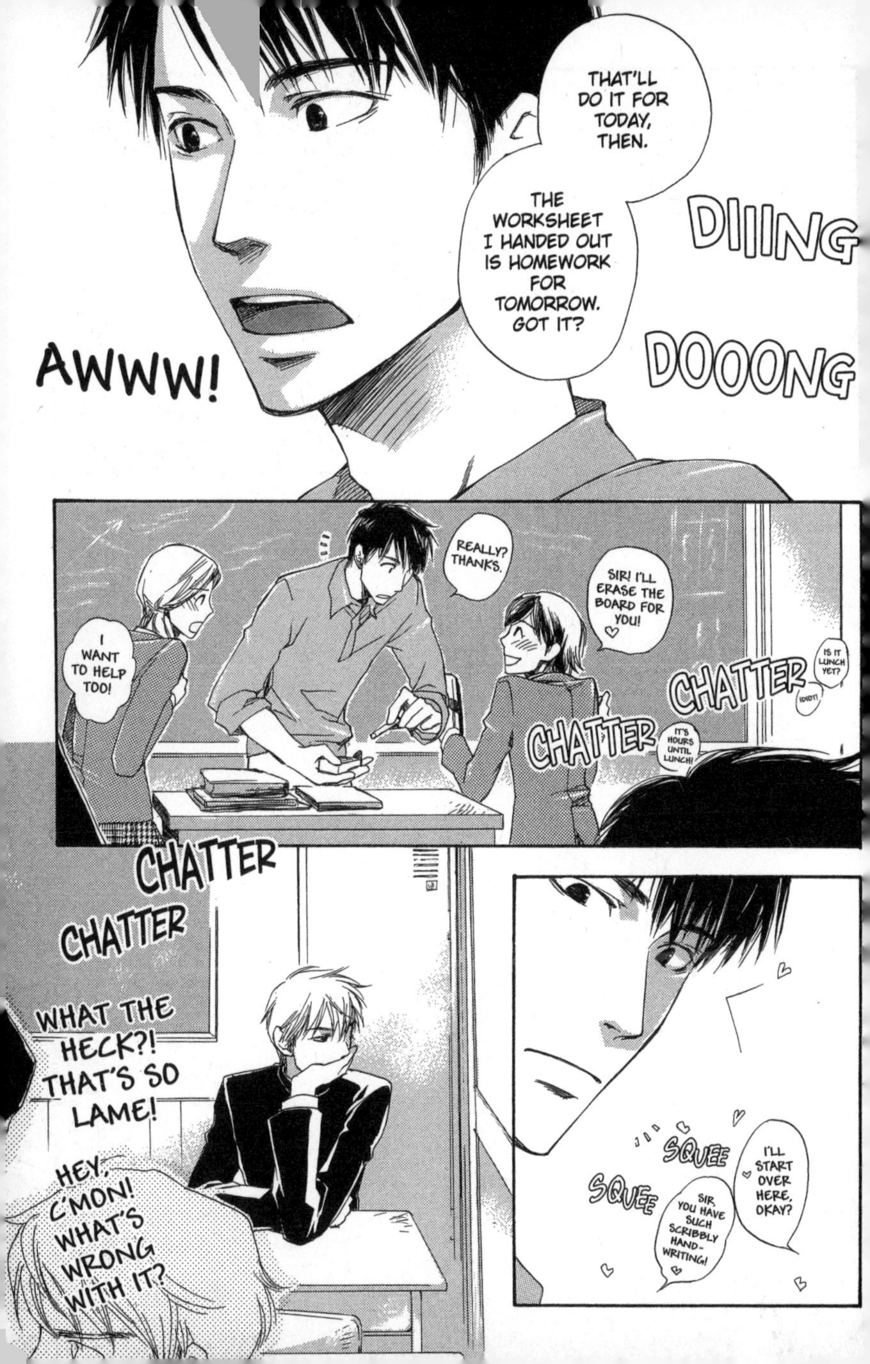
DIIING
DOOONG
THAT'LL DO IT FOR TODAY, THEN.
THE WORKSHEET I HANDED OUT IS HOMEWORK FOR TOMORROW. GOT IT?
AWWW!
IS IT LUNCH YET?
IDIOT!
CHATTER
IT'S HOURS UNTIL LUNCH!
CHATTER
SIR! I'LL ERASE THE BOARD FOR YOU!
REALLY? THANKS.
I WANT TO HELP TOO!
I'LL START OVER HERE, OKAY?
SIR, YOU HAVE SUCH SCRIBBLY HAND-WRITING!
SQUEE
SQUEE
CHATTER
CHATTER
WHAT THE HECK?! THAT'S SO LAME!
HEY, C'MON! WHAT'S WRONG WITH IT?

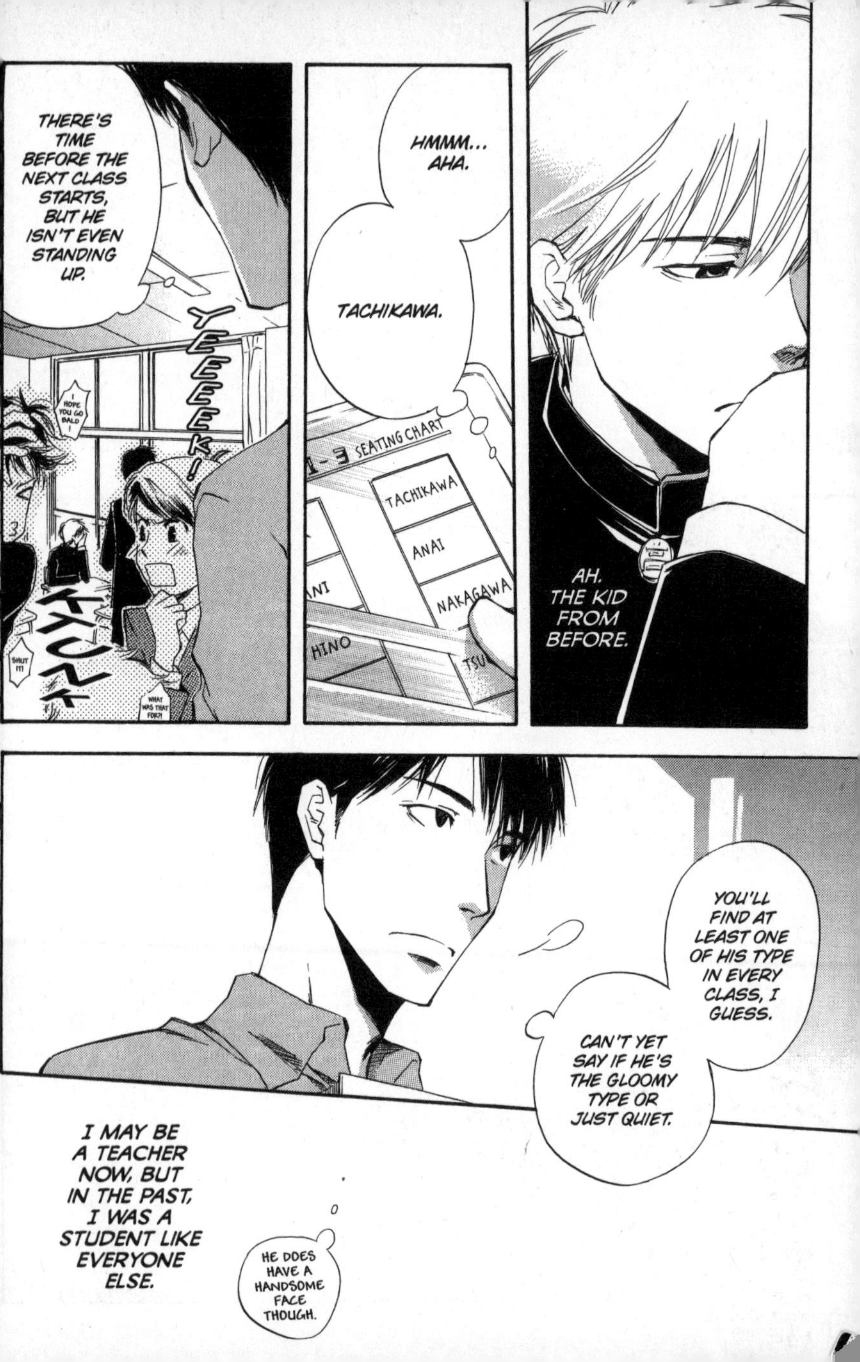
AH. THE KID FROM BEFORE.
HMMM... AHA.
TACHIKAWA.
1-3 SEATING CHART
TACHIKAWA
ANAI
NAKAGAWA
HINO
THERE'S TIME BEFORE THE NEXT CLASS STARTS, BUT HE ISN'T EVEN STANDING UP.
YEEEEK!
I HOPE YOU GO BALD!
KYUN
SHUT IT!
WHAT WAS THAT FOR?!
YOU'LL FIND AT LEAST ONE OF HIS TYPE IN EVERY CLASS, I GUESS.
CAN'T YET SAY IF HE'S THE GLOOMY TYPE OR JUST QUIET.
I MAY BE A TEACHER NOW, BUT IN THE PAST, I WAS A STUDENT LIKE EVERYONE ELSE.
HE DOES HAVE A HANDSOME FACE THOUGH.

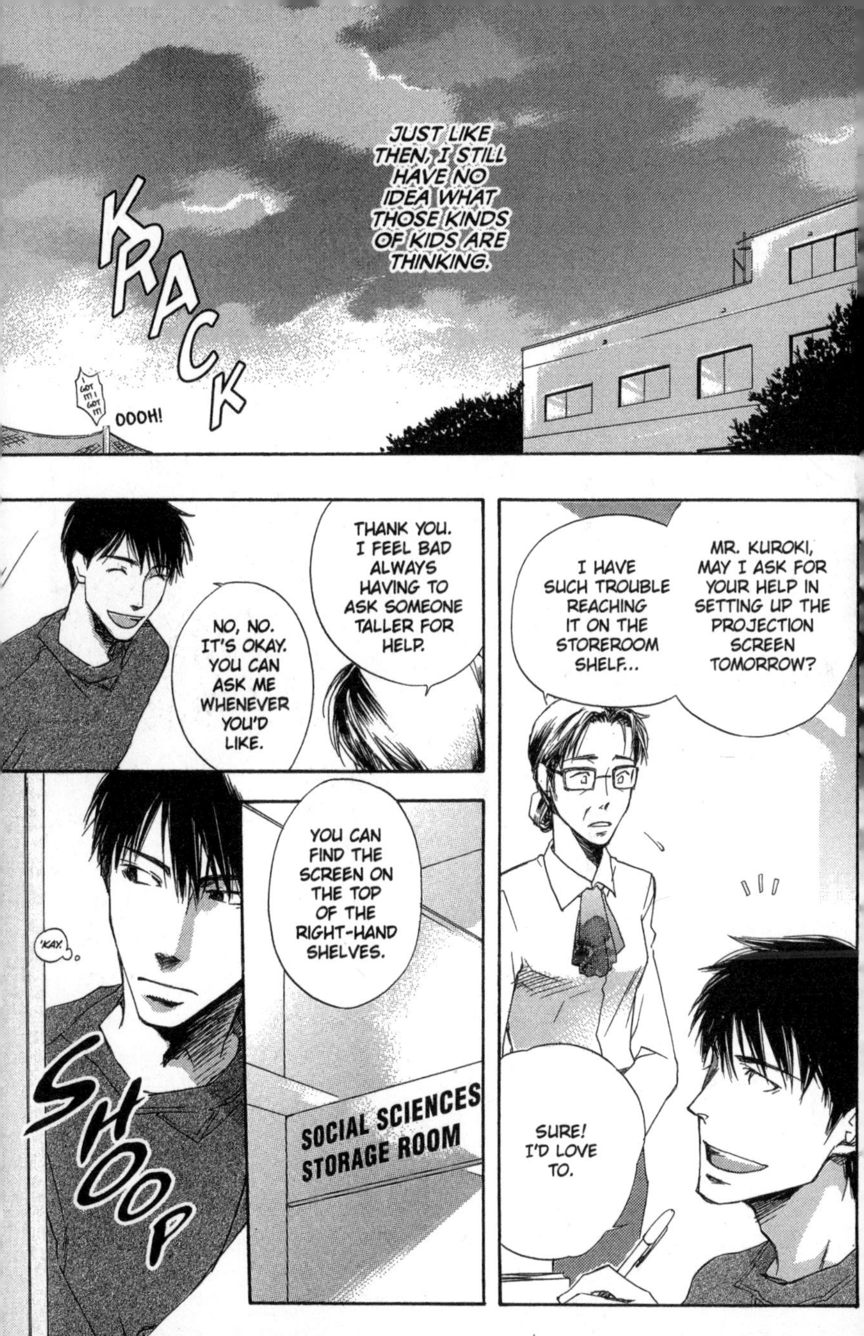
JUST LIKE THEN, I STILL HAVE NO IDEA WHAT THOSE KINDS OF KIDS ARE THINKING.
KRACK
I GOT IT! I GOT IT!
OOOH!
MR. KUROKI, MAY I ASK FOR YOUR HELP IN SETTING UP THE PROJECTION SCREEN TOMORROW?
I HAVE SUCH TROUBLE REACHING IT ON THE STOREROOM SHELF...
SURE! I'D LOVE TO.
THANK YOU. I FEEL BAD ALWAYS HAVING TO ASK SOMEONE TALLER FOR HELP.
NO, NO. IT'S OKAY. YOU CAN ASK ME WHENEVER YOU'D LIKE.
YOU CAN FIND THE SCREEN ON THE TOP OF THE RIGHT-HAND SHELVES.
SOCIAL SCIENCES STORAGE ROOM
'KAY.
SHOOP

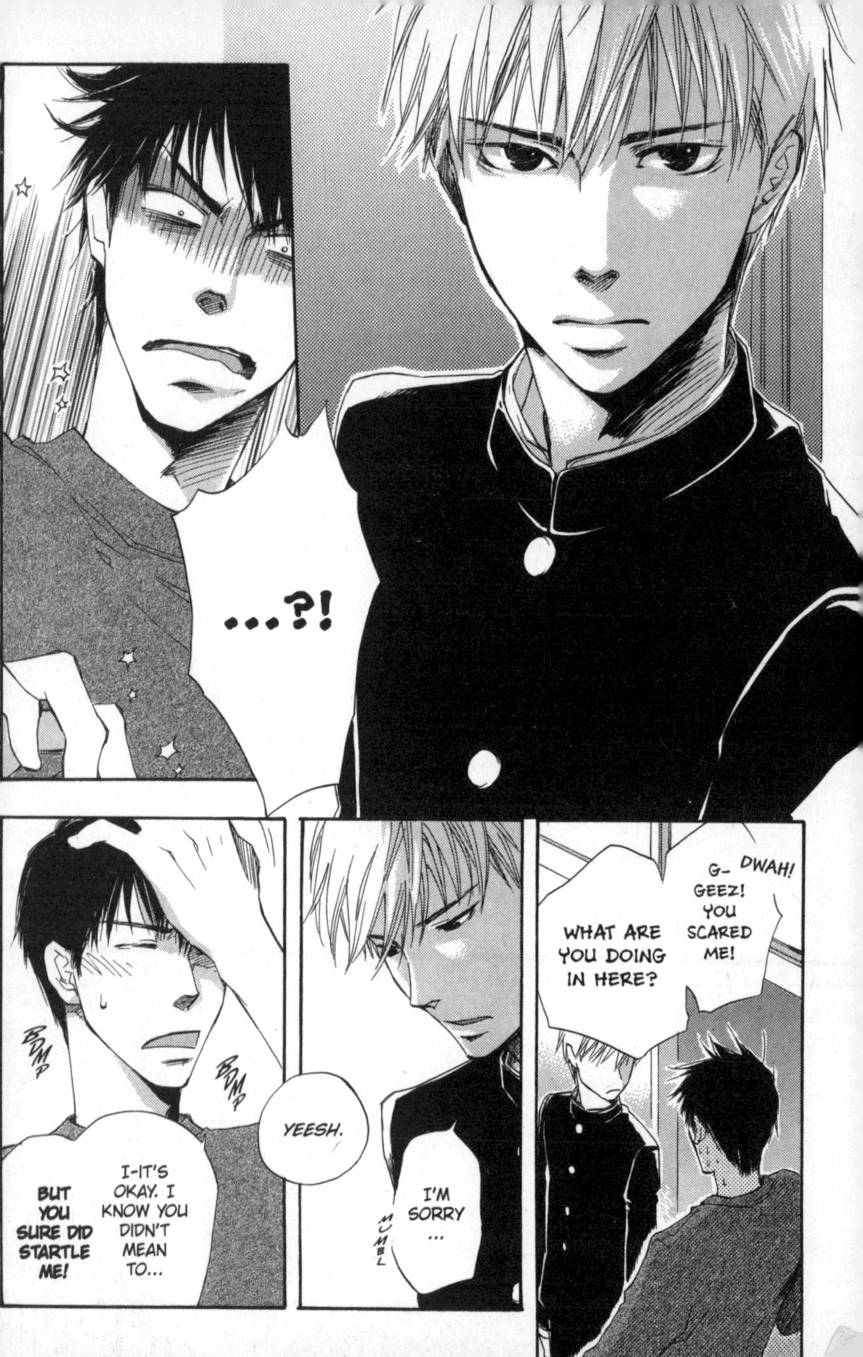
...?!
DWAH!
G- GEEZ! YOU SCARED ME!
WHAT ARE YOU DOING IN HERE?
YEESH.
I'M SORRY ...
MUMBL
BDMP
BDMP
I-IT'S OKAY. I KNOW YOU DIDN'T MEAN TO...
BUT YOU SURE DID STARTLE ME!

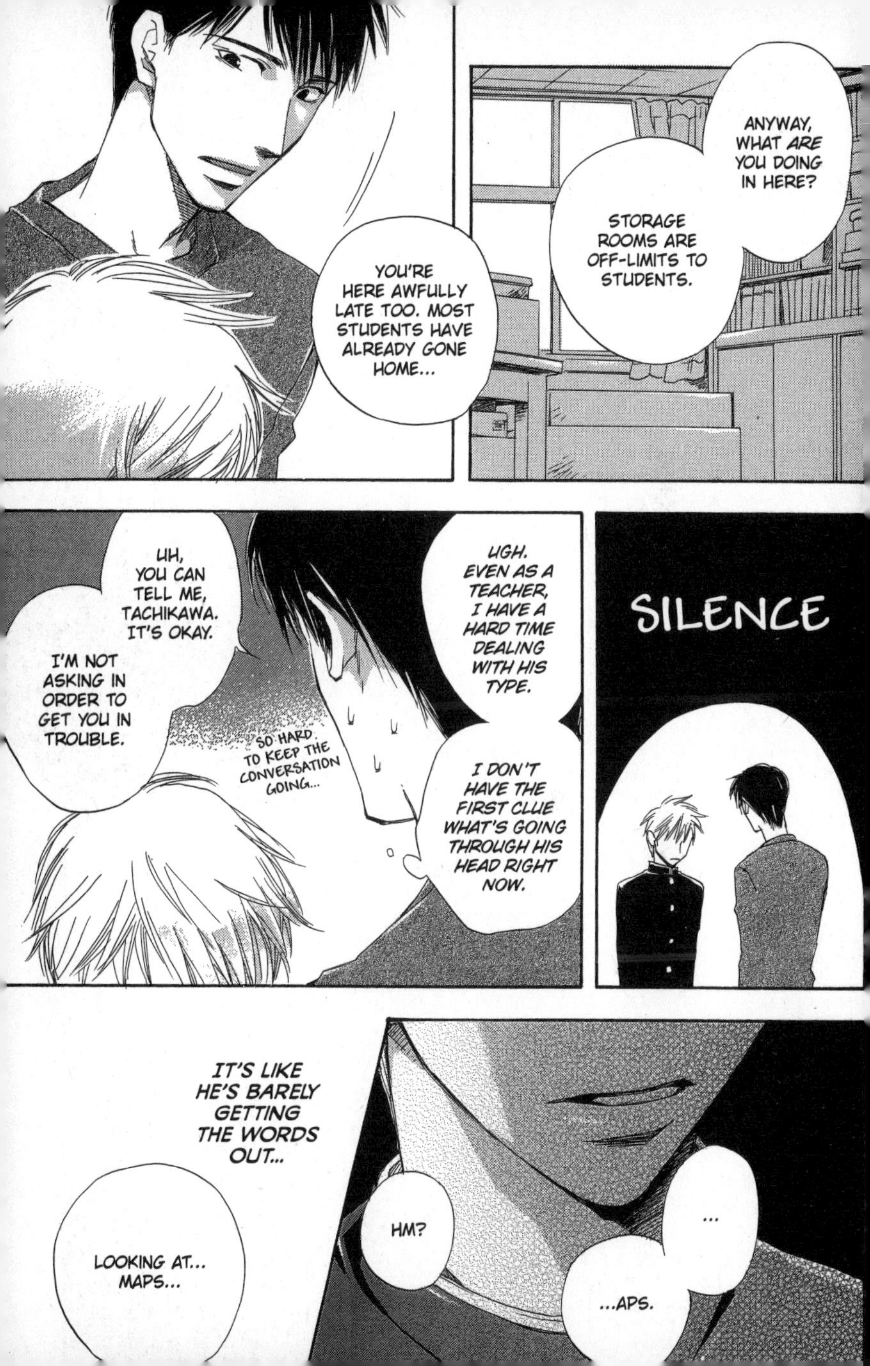
ANYWAY, WHAT ARE YOU DOING IN HERE?
STORAGE ROOMS ARE OFF-LIMITS TO STUDENTS.
YOU'RE HERE AWFULLY LATE TOO. MOST STUDENTS HAVE ALREADY GONE HOME...
SILENCE
UGH. EVEN AS A TEACHER, I HAVE A HARD TIME DEALING WITH HIS TYPE.
I DON'T HAVE THE FIRST CLUE WHAT'S GOING THROUGH HIS HEAD RIGHT NOW.
UH, YOU CAN TELL ME, TACHIKAWA. IT'S OKAY.
I'M NOT ASKING IN ORDER TO GET YOU IN TROUBLE.
SO HARD TO KEEP THE CONVERSATION GOING...
...
...APS.
HM?
IT'S LIKE HE'S BARELY GETTING THE WORDS OUT...
LOOKING AT... MAPS...

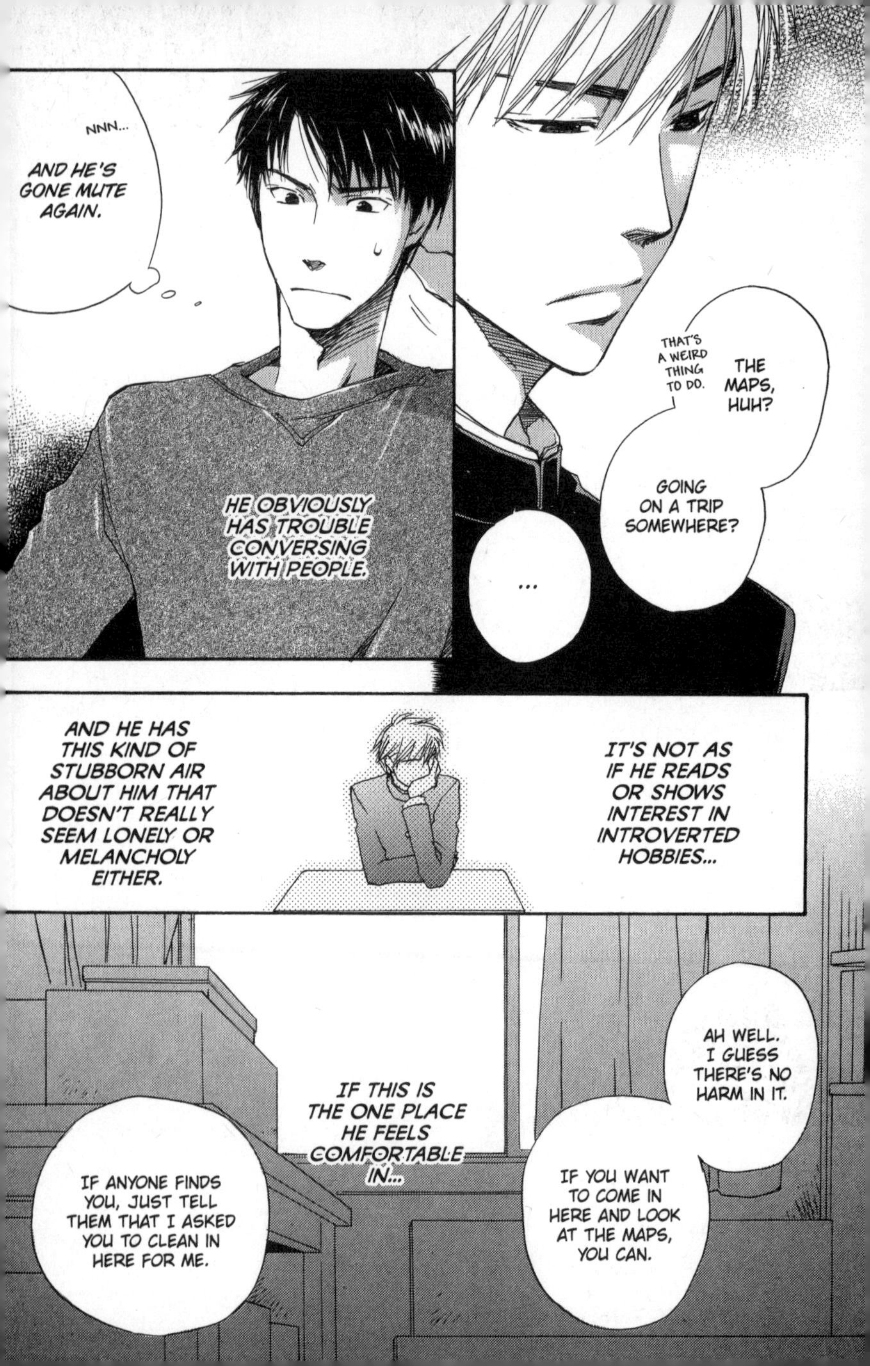

THAT'S A WEIRD THING TO DO.
THE MAPS, HUH?
GOING ON A TRIP SOMEWHERE?
...
NNN...
AND HE'S GONE MUTE AGAIN.
HE OBVIOUSLY HAS TROUBLE CONVERSING WITH PEOPLE.
IT'S NOT AS IF HE READS OR SHOWS INTEREST IN INTROVERTED HOBBIES...
AND HE HAS THIS KIND OF STUBBORN AIR ABOUT HIM THAT DOESN'T REALLY SEEM LONELY OR MELANCHOLY EITHER.
AH WELL. I GUESS THERE'S NO HARM IN IT.
IF THIS IS THE ONE PLACE HE FEELS COMFORTABLE IN...
IF YOU WANT TO COME IN HERE AND LOOK AT THE MAPS, YOU CAN.
IF ANYONE FINDS YOU, JUST TELL THEM THAT I ASKED YOU TO CLEAN IN HERE FOR ME.

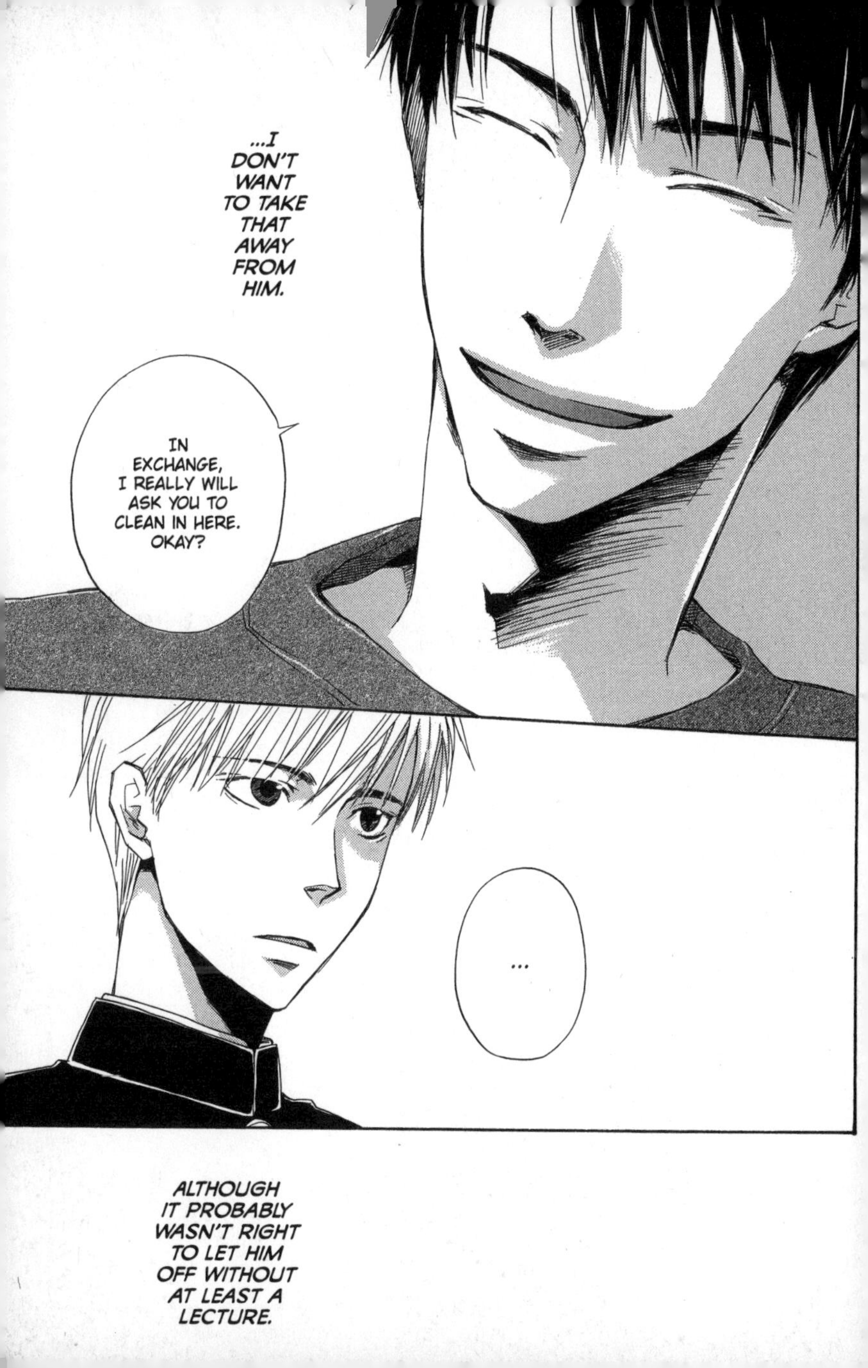
...I DON'T WANT TO TAKE THAT AWAY FROM HIM.
IN EXCHANGE, I REALLY WILL ASK YOU TO CLEAN IN HERE. OKAY?
...
ALTHOUGH IT PROBABLY WASN'T RIGHT TO LET HIM OFF WITHOUT AT LEAST A LECTURE.

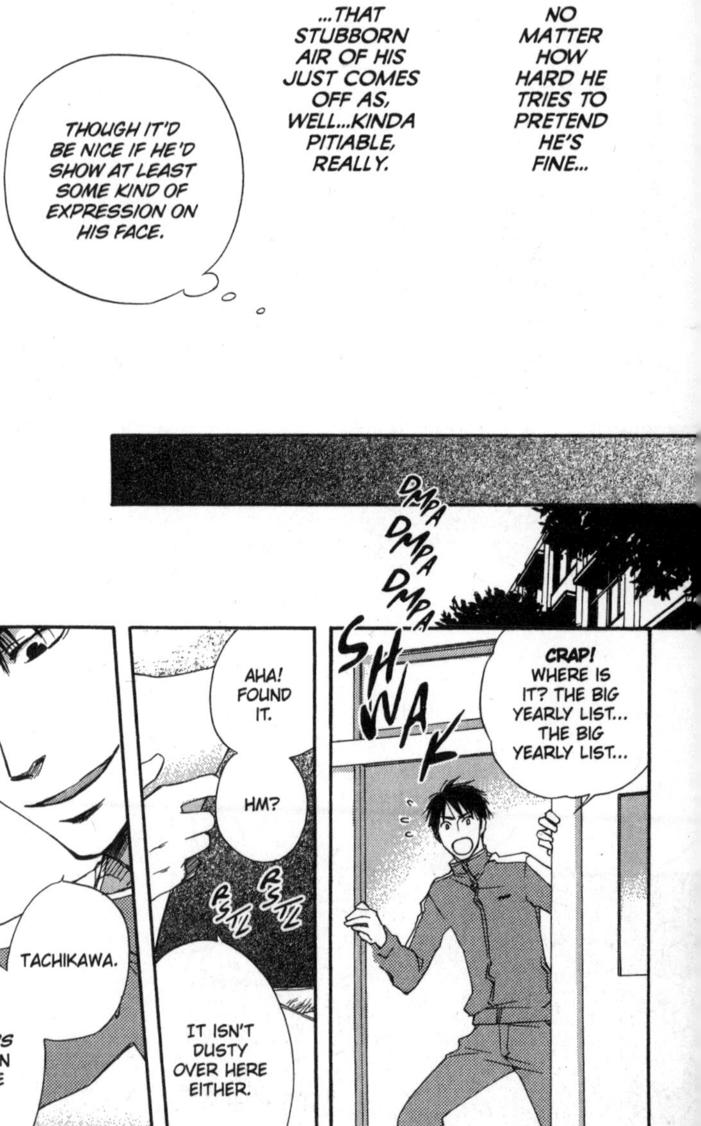
NO MATTER HOW HARD HE TRIES TO PRETEND HE'S FINE...
...THAT STUBBORN AIR OF HIS JUST COMES OFF AS, WELL...KINDA PITIABLE, REALLY.
THOUGH IT'D BE NICE IF HE'D SHOW AT LEAST SOME KIND OF EXPRESSION ON HIS FACE.
DMPA DMPA DMPA DMPA
SHWAK
CRAP! WHERE IS IT? THE BIG YEARLY LIST... THE BIG YEARLY LIST...
AHA! FOUND IT.
HM?
IT ISN'T DUSTY OVER HERE EITHER.
TACHIKAWA.
HE ACTUALLY *IS* CLEANING IN HERE, LIKE I ASKED.

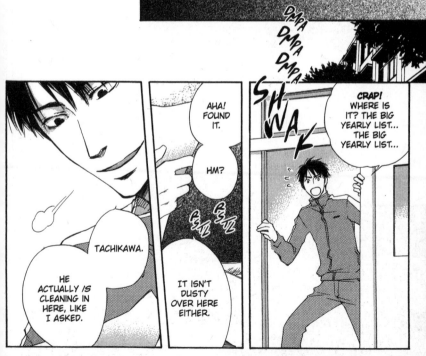

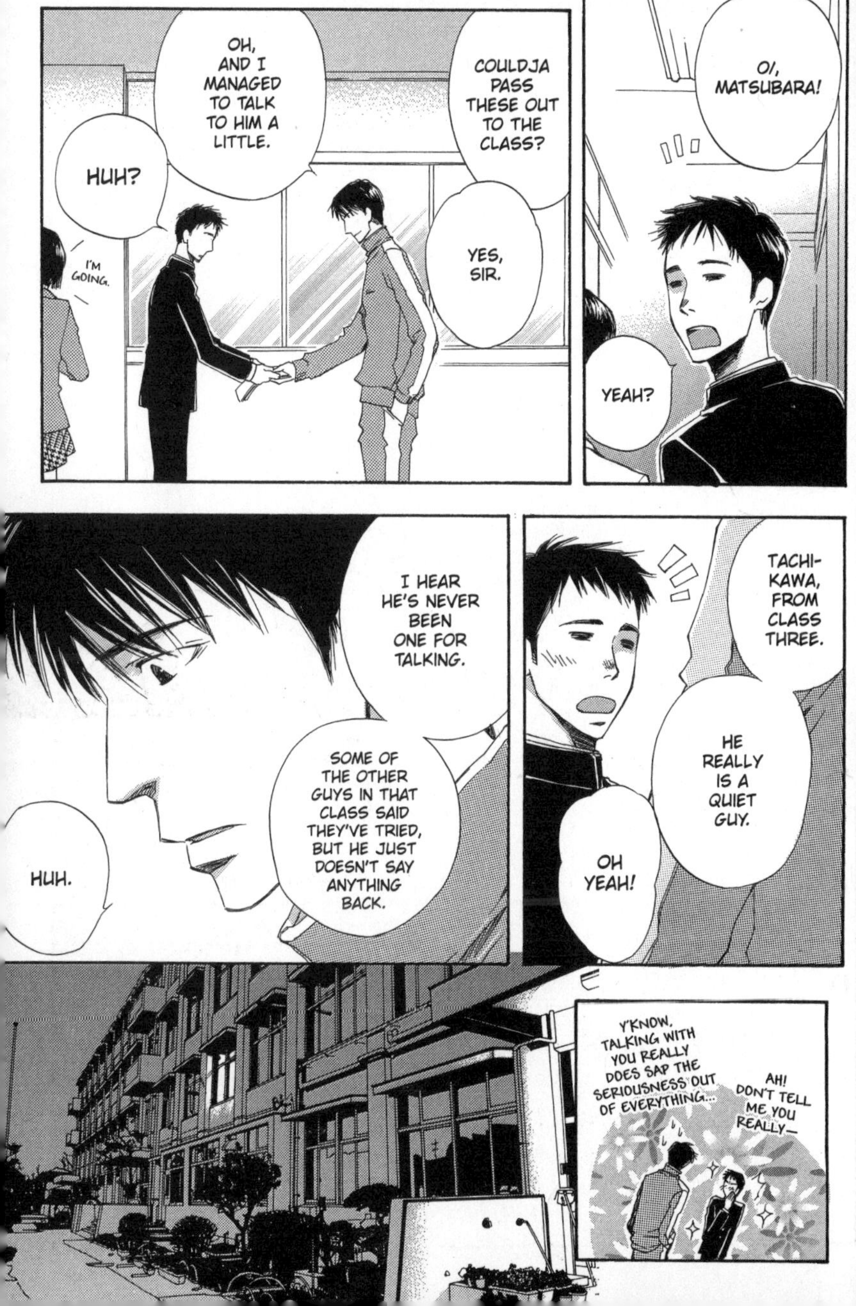
OI, MATSUBARA!
YEAH?
COULDJA PASS THESE OUT TO THE CLASS?
YES, SIR.
OH, AND I MANAGED TO TALK TO HIM A LITTLE.
HUH?
I'M GOING.
TACHI-KAWA, FROM CLASS THREE.
HE REALLY IS A QUIET GUY.
OH YEAH!
I HEAR HE'S NEVER BEEN ONE FOR TALKING.
SOME OF THE OTHER GUYS IN THAT CLASS SAID THEY'VE TRIED, BUT HE JUST DOESN'T SAY ANYTHING BACK.
HUH.
Y'KNOW, TALKING WITH YOU REALLY DOES SAP THE SERIOUSNESS OUT OF EVERYTHING...
AH! DON'T TELL ME YOU REALLY—

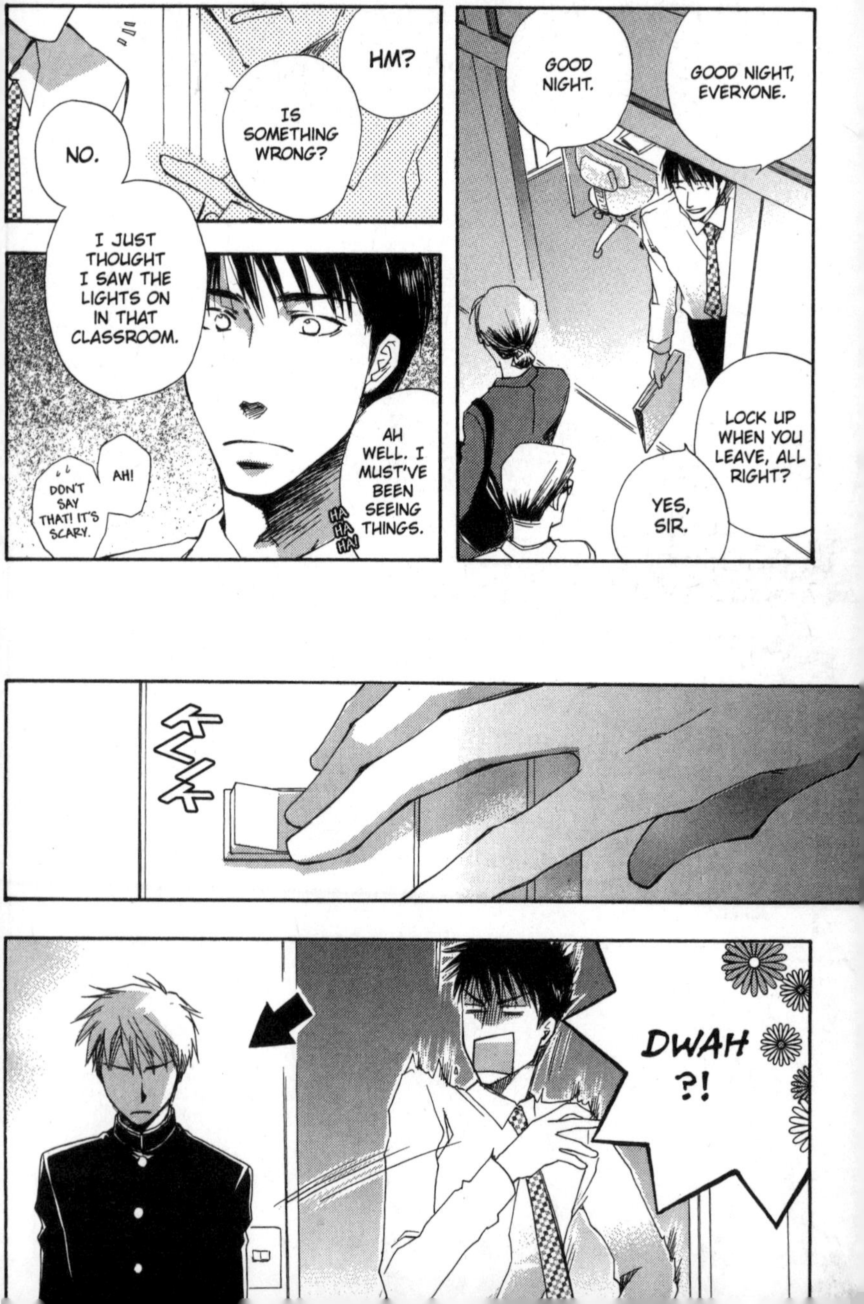
GOOD NIGHT, EVERYONE.
GOOD NIGHT.
LOCK UP WHEN YOU LEAVE, ALL RIGHT?
YES, SIR.
HM?
IS SOMETHING WRONG?
NO.
I JUST THOUGHT I SAW THE LIGHTS ON IN THAT CLASSROOM.
AH WELL. I MUST'VE BEEN SEEING THINGS.
HA HA HA!
AH!
DON'T SAY THAT! IT'S SCARY.
DWAH ?!

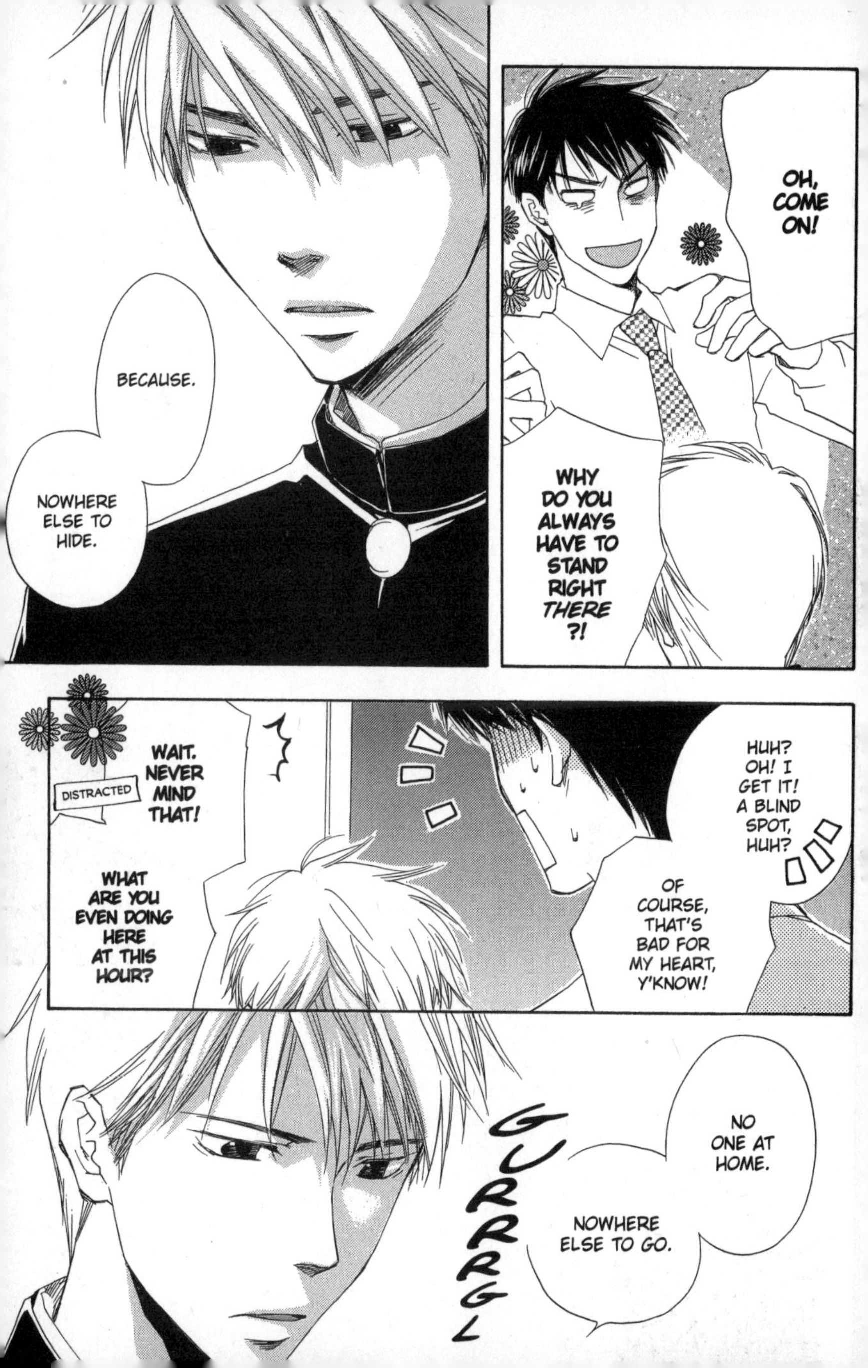
OH, COME ON!
WHY DO YOU ALWAYS HAVE TO STAND RIGHT *THERE* ?!
BECAUSE.
NOWHERE ELSE TO HIDE.
HUH? OH! I GET IT! A BLIND SPOT, HUH?
OF COURSE, THAT'S BAD FOR MY HEART, Y'KNOW!
WAIT. NEVER MIND THAT!
DISTRACTED
WHAT ARE YOU EVEN DOING HERE AT THIS HOUR?
NO ONE AT HOME.
NOWHERE ELSE TO GO.
GURRRGL

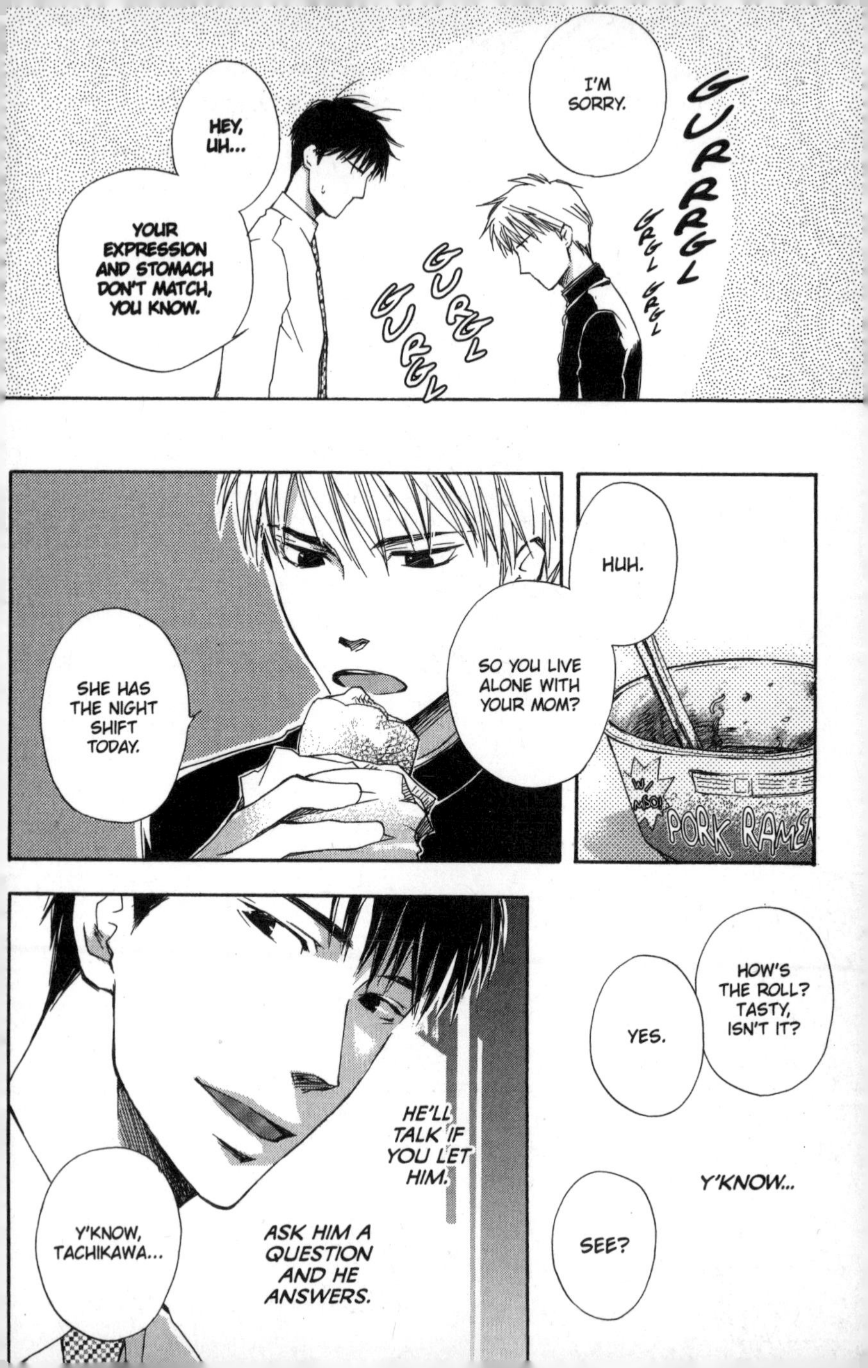
I'M SORRY.
GURRRGL
GRGL GRGL
GURGL
GURGL
HEY, UH...
YOUR EXPRESSION AND STOMACH DON'T MATCH, YOU KNOW.
HUH.
SO YOU LIVE ALONE WITH YOUR MOM?
PORK RAMEN
SHE HAS THE NIGHT SHIFT TODAY.
HOW'S THE ROLL? TASTY, ISN'T IT?
YES.
Y'KNOW...
SEE?
HE'LL TALK IF YOU LET HIM.
ASK HIM A QUESTION AND HE ANSWERS.
Y'KNOW, TACHIKAWA...

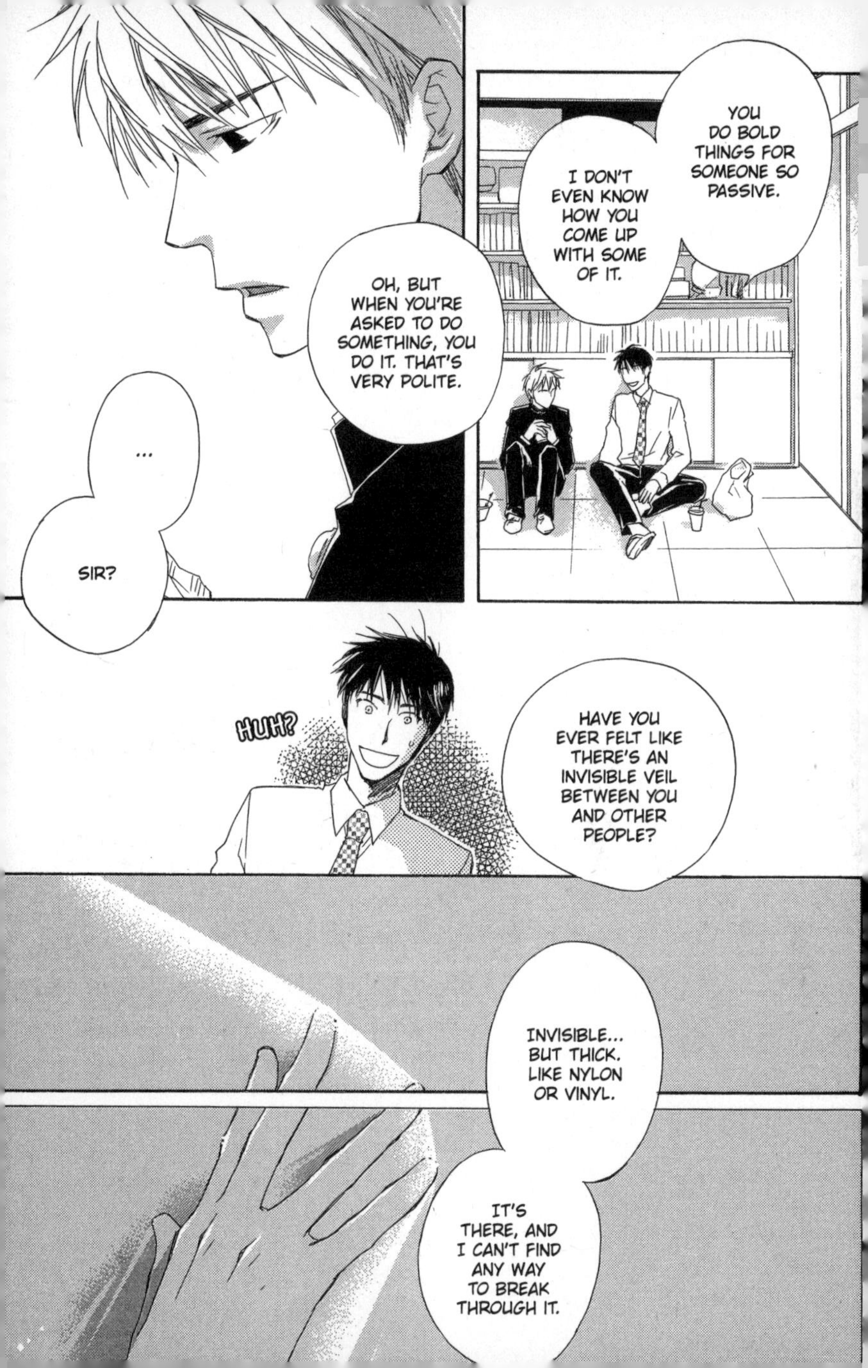
YOU DO BOLD THINGS FOR SOMEONE SO PASSIVE.
I DON'T EVEN KNOW HOW YOU COME UP WITH SOME OF IT.
OH, BUT WHEN YOU'RE ASKED TO DO SOMETHING, YOU DO IT. THAT'S VERY POLITE.
...
SIR?
HAVE YOU EVER FELT LIKE THERE'S AN INVISIBLE VEIL BETWEEN YOU AND OTHER PEOPLE?
HUH?
INVISIBLE... BUT THICK. LIKE NYLON OR VINYL.
IT'S THERE, AND I CAN'T FIND ANY WAY TO BREAK THROUGH IT.

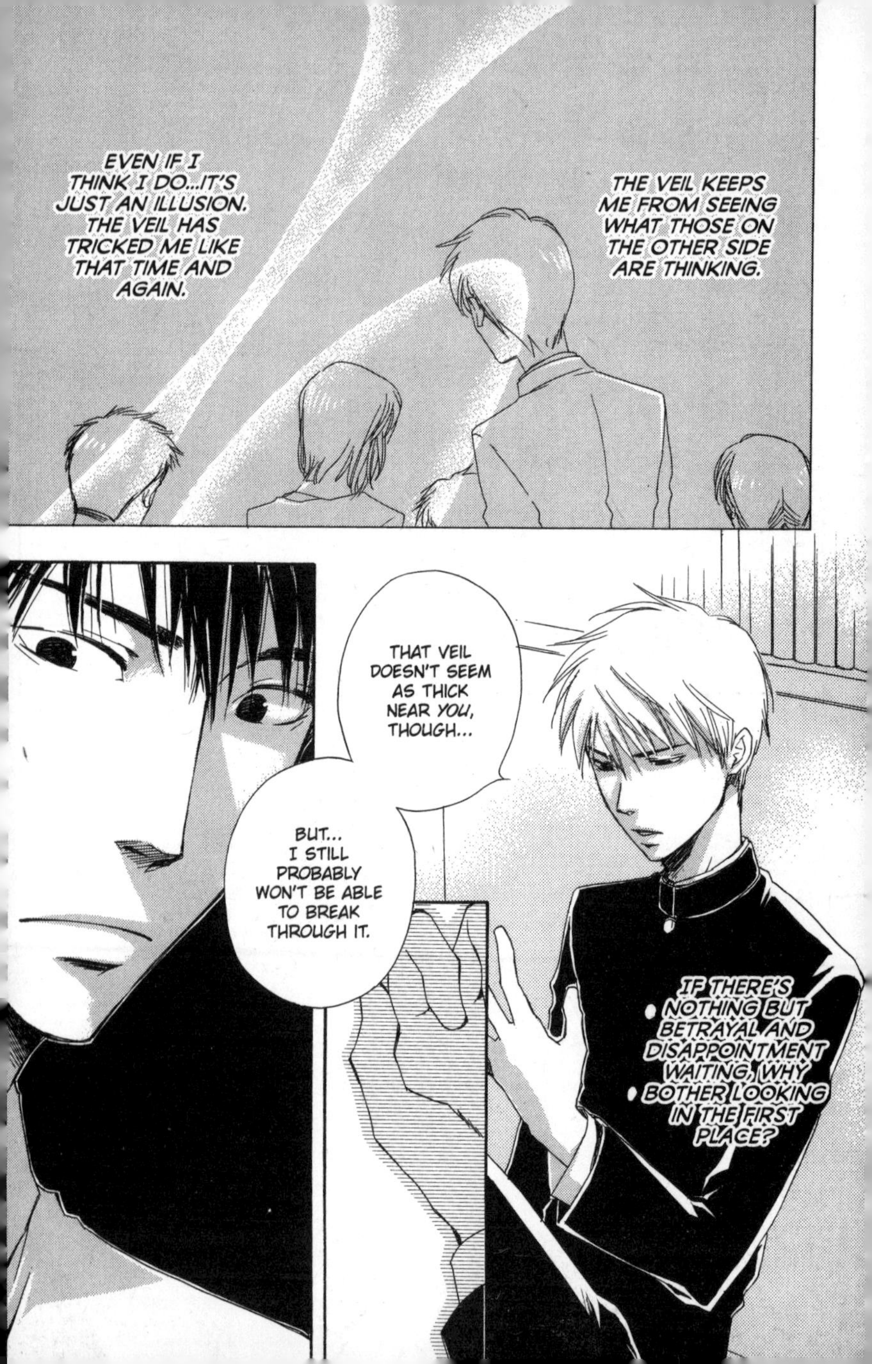
THE VEIL KEEPS ME FROM SEEING WHAT THOSE ON THE OTHER SIDE ARE THINKING.
EVEN IF I THINK I DO...IT'S JUST AN ILLUSION. THE VEIL HAS TRICKED ME LIKE THAT TIME AND AGAIN.
THAT VEIL DOESN'T SEEM AS THICK NEAR *YOU*, THOUGH...
BUT... I STILL PROBABLY WON'T BE ABLE TO BREAK THROUGH IT.
IF THERE'S NOTHING BUT BETRAYAL AND DISAPPOINTMENT WAITING, WHY BOTHER LOOKING IN THE FIRST PLACE?

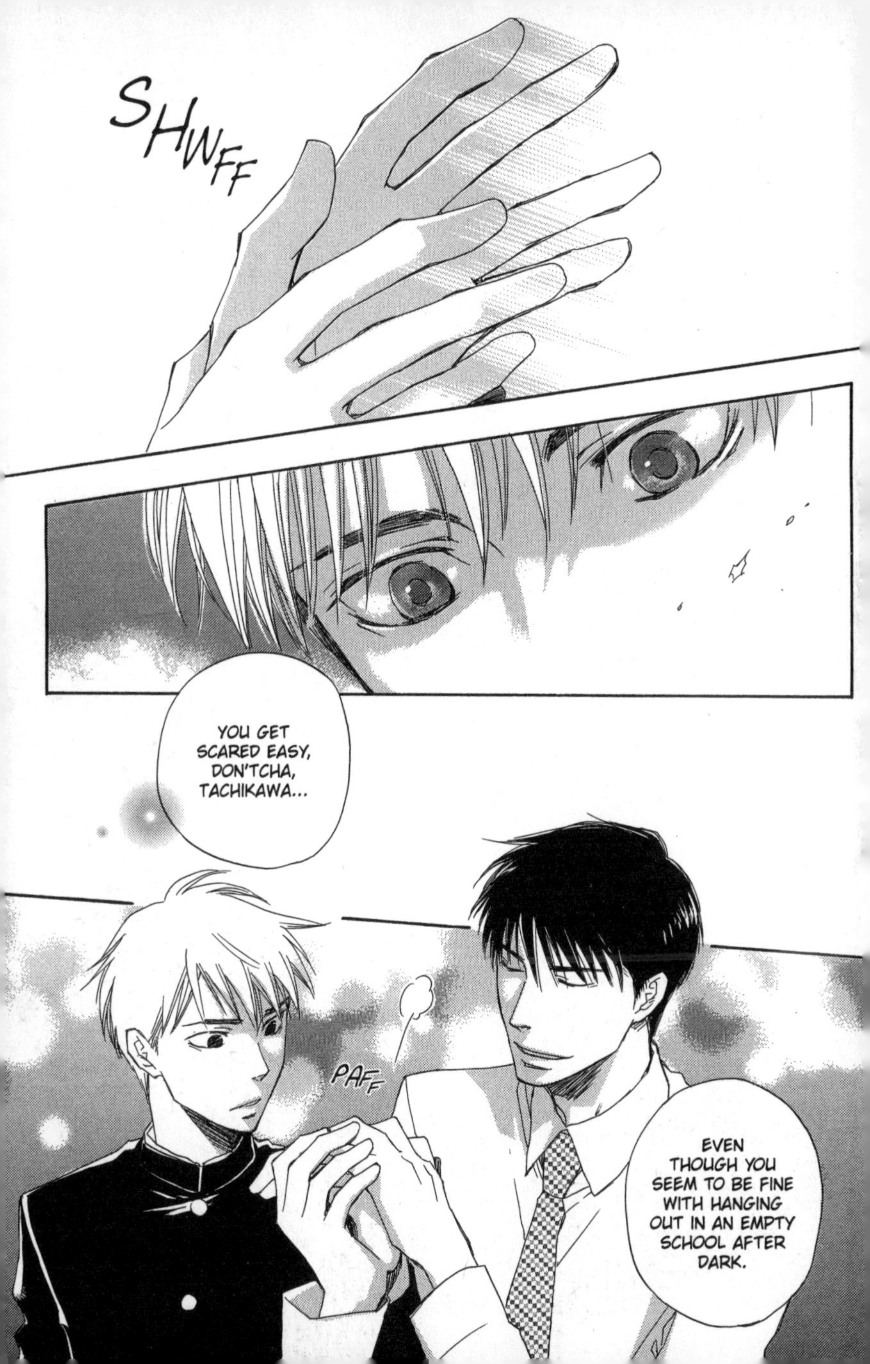
SHWFF
YOU GET SCARED EASY, DON'TCHA, TACHIKAWA...
PAFF
EVEN THOUGH YOU SEEM TO BE FINE WITH HANGING OUT IN AN EMPTY SCHOOL AFTER DARK.

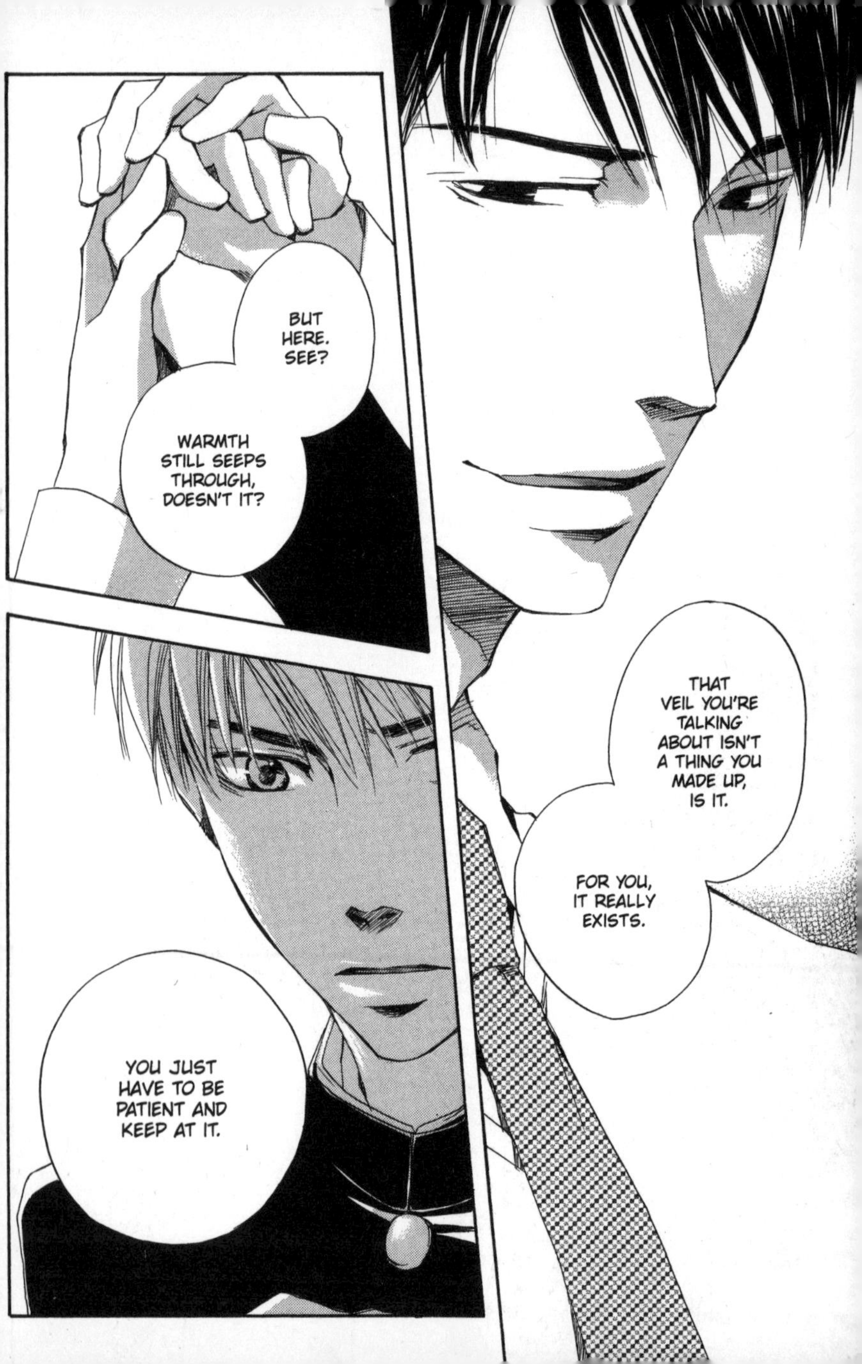
THAT VEIL YOU'RE TALKING ABOUT ISN'T A THING YOU MADE UP, IS IT.
FOR YOU, IT REALLY EXISTS.
BUT HERE. SEE?
WARMTH STILL SEEPS THROUGH, DOESN'T IT?
YOU JUST HAVE TO BE PATIENT AND KEEP AT IT.

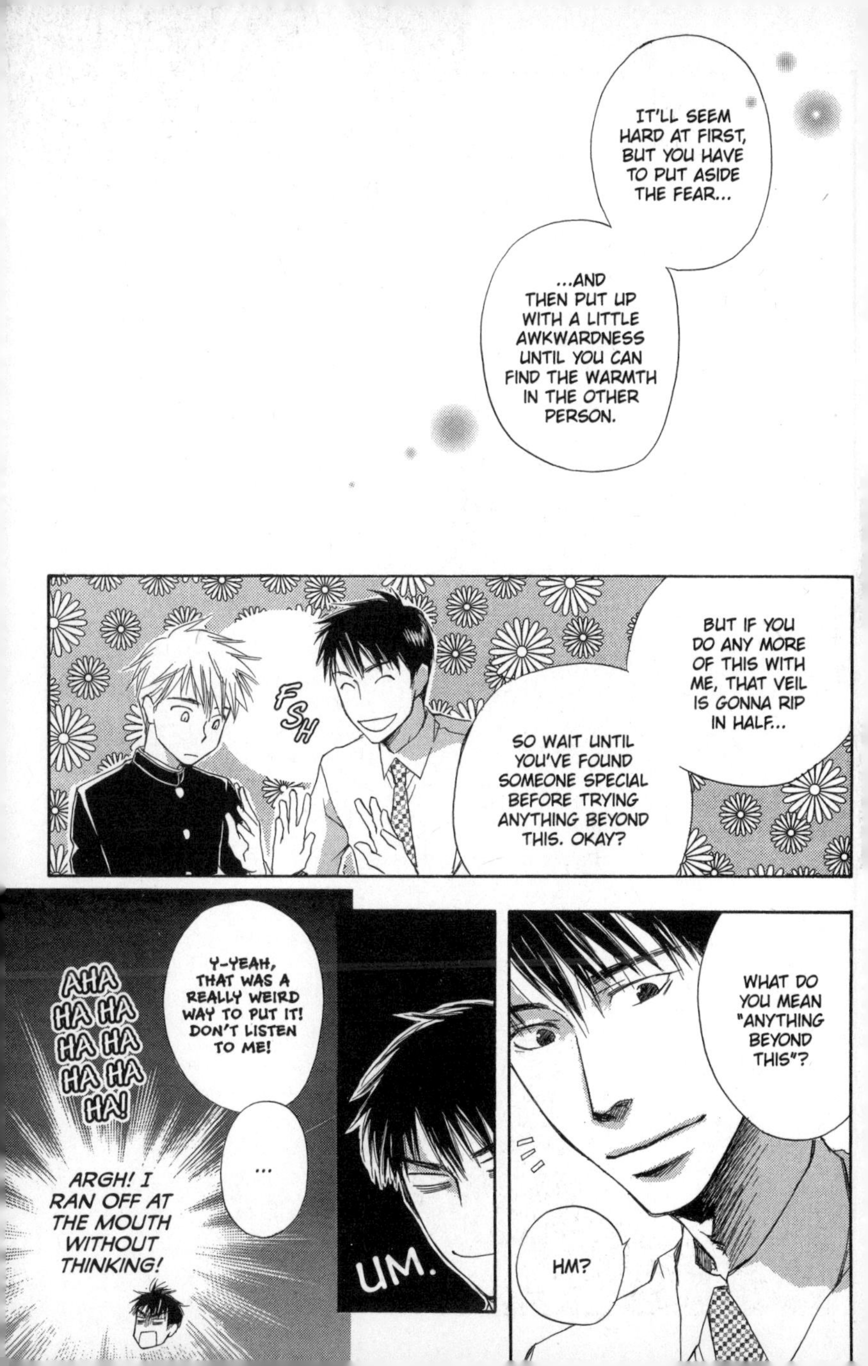
IT'LL SEEM HARD AT FIRST, BUT YOU HAVE TO PUT ASIDE THE FEAR...
...AND THEN PUT UP WITH A LITTLE AWKWARDNESS UNTIL YOU CAN FIND THE WARMTH IN THE OTHER PERSON.
BUT IF YOU DO ANY MORE OF THIS WITH ME, THAT VEIL IS GONNA RIP IN HALF...
SO WAIT UNTIL YOU'VE FOUND SOMEONE SPECIAL BEFORE TRYING ANYTHING BEYOND THIS. OKAY?
FSH
WHAT DO YOU MEAN "ANYTHING BEYOND THIS"?
HM?
UM.
...
Y-YEAH, THAT WAS A REALLY WEIRD WAY TO PUT IT! DON'T LISTEN TO ME!
AHA HA HA HA HA HA HA HA!
ARGH! I RAN OFF AT THE MOUTH WITHOUT THINKING!

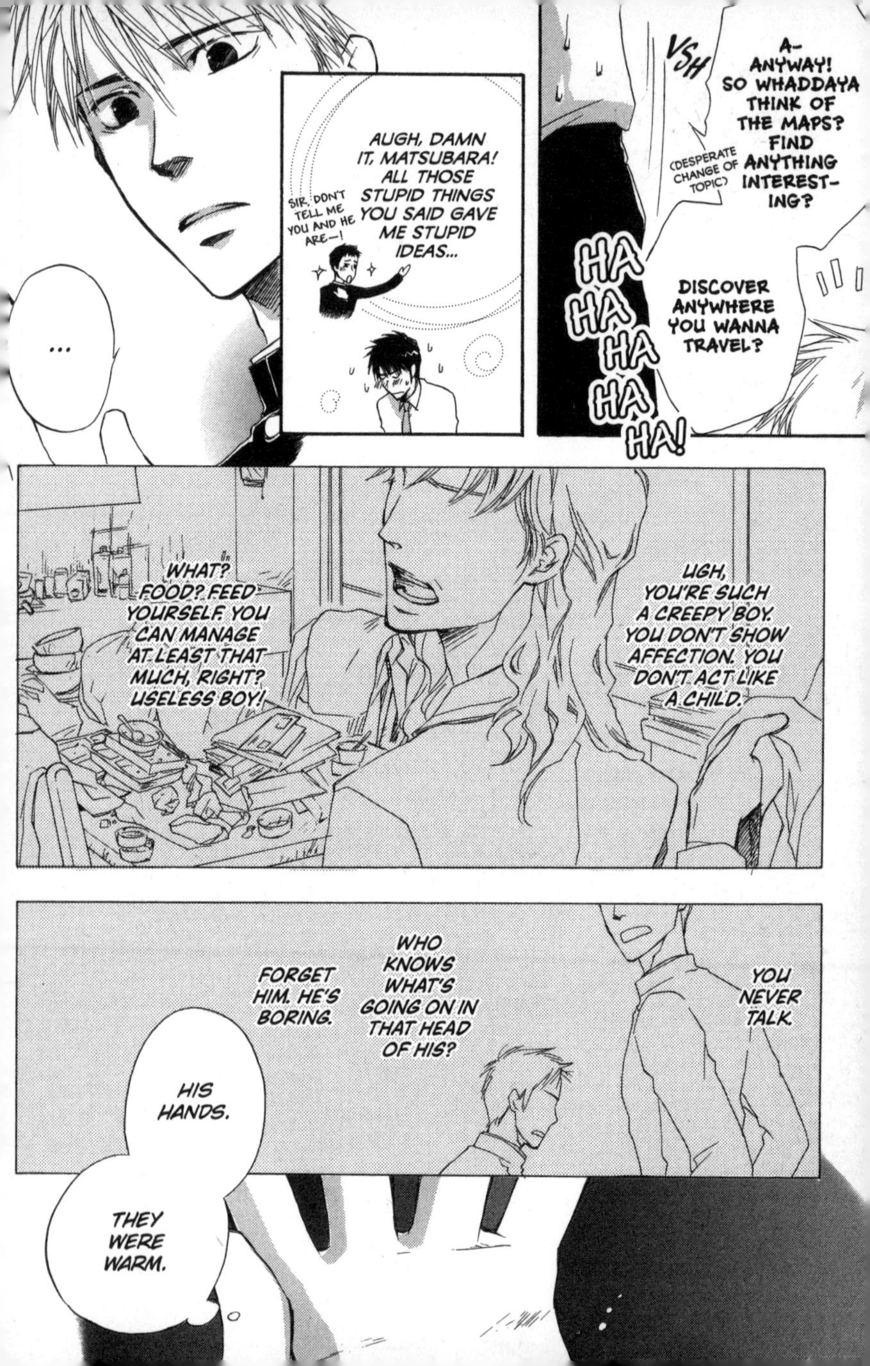
VSH
A- ANYWAY! SO WHADDAYA THINK OF THE MAPS? FIND ANYTHING INTEREST-ING?
(DESPERATE CHANGE OF TOPIC)
DISCOVER ANYWHERE YOU WANNA TRAVEL?
HA HA HA HA HA!
AUGH, DAMN IT, MATSUBARA! ALL THOSE STUPID THINGS YOU SAID GAVE ME STUPID IDEAS...
SIR, DON'T TELL ME YOU AND HE ARE—!
...
UGH, YOU'RE SUCH A CREEPY BOY. YOU DON'T SHOW AFFECTION. YOU DON'T ACT LIKE A CHILD.
WHAT? FOOD? FEED YOURSELF. YOU CAN MANAGE AT LEAST THAT MUCH, RIGHT? USELESS BOY!
YOU NEVER TALK.
WHO KNOWS WHAT'S GOING ON IN THAT HEAD OF HIS?
FORGET HIM. HE'S BORING.
HIS HANDS.
THEY WERE WARM.

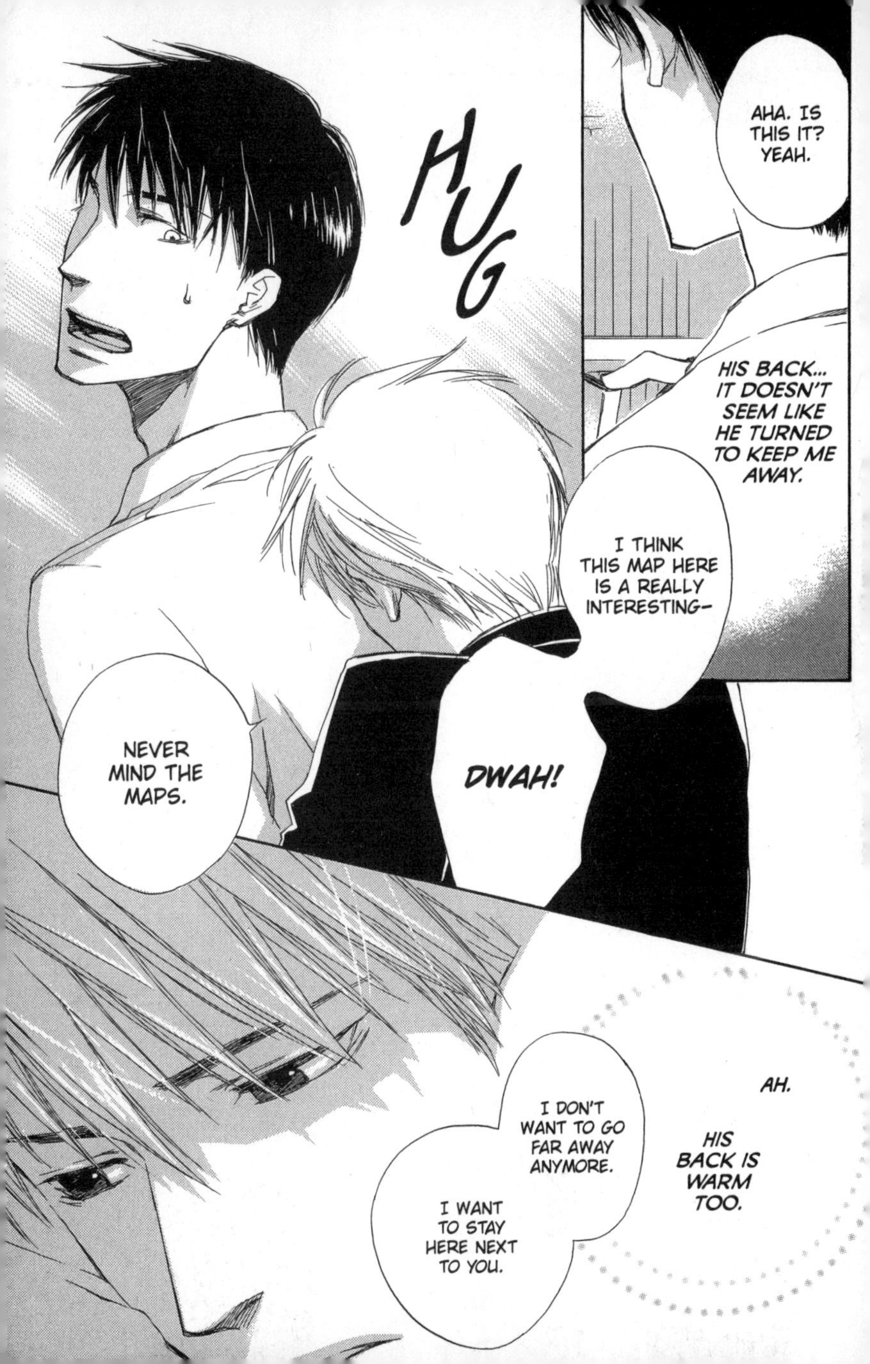
AHA. IS THIS IT? YEAH.
HIS BACK... IT DOESN'T SEEM LIKE HE TURNED TO KEEP ME AWAY.
I THINK THIS MAP HERE IS A REALLY INTERESTING–
HUG
DWAH!
NEVER MIND THE MAPS.
AH.
HIS BACK IS WARM TOO.
I DON'T WANT TO GO FAR AWAY ANYMORE.
I WANT TO STAY HERE NEXT TO YOU.

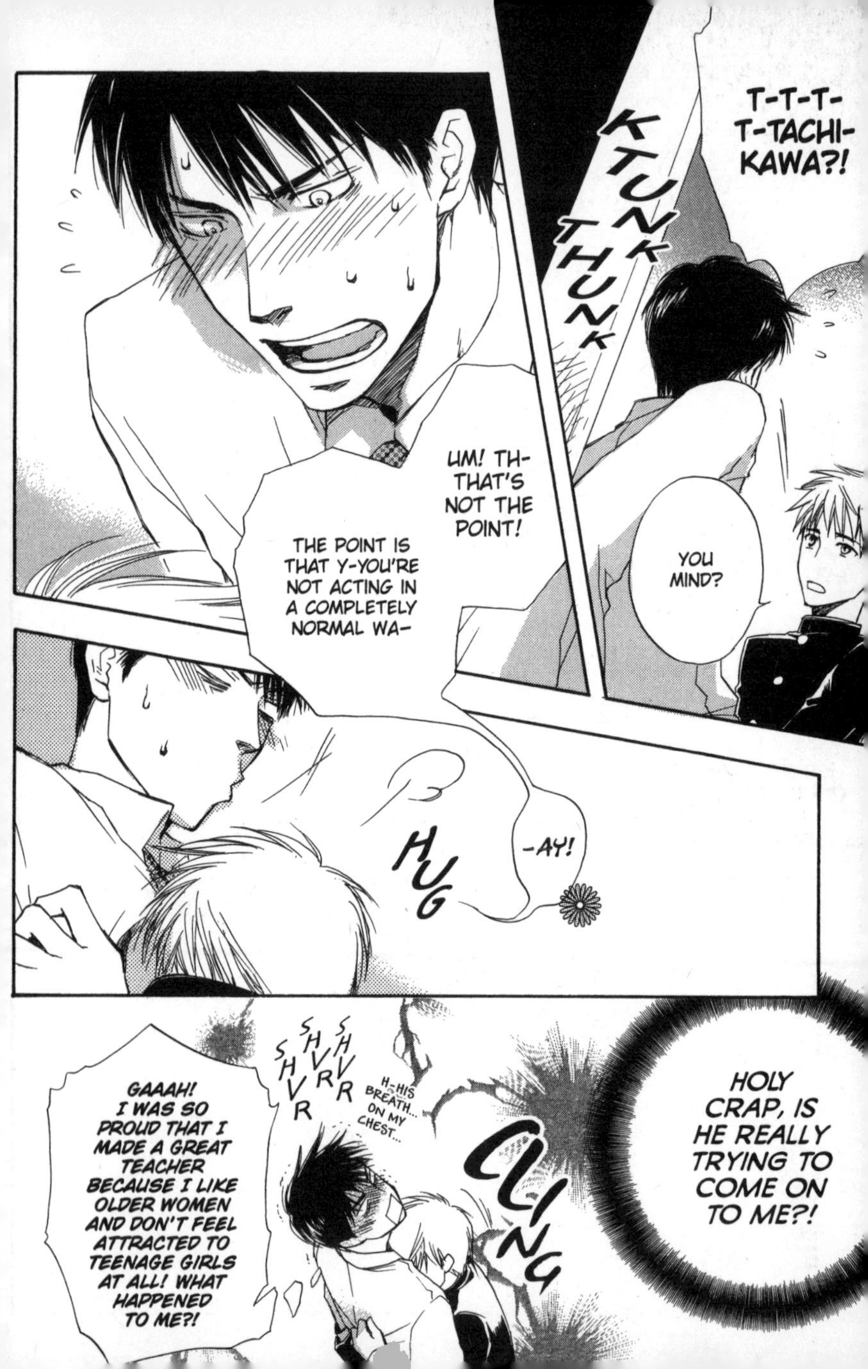
T-T-T-T-TACHI-KAWA?!
KTUNK
THUNK THUNK
YOU MIND?
UM! TH-THAT'S NOT THE POINT!
THE POINT IS THAT Y-YOU'RE NOT ACTING IN A COMPLETELY NORMAL WA-
-AY!
HUG
HOLY CRAP, IS HE REALLY TRYING TO COME ON TO ME?!
CLING
H-HIS BREATH... ON MY CHEST...
SHVR SHVR SHVR
GAAAH! I WAS SO PROUD THAT I MADE A GREAT TEACHER BECAUSE I LIKE OLDER WOMEN AND DON'T FEEL ATTRACTED TO TEENAGE GIRLS AT ALL! WHAT HAPPENED TO ME?!

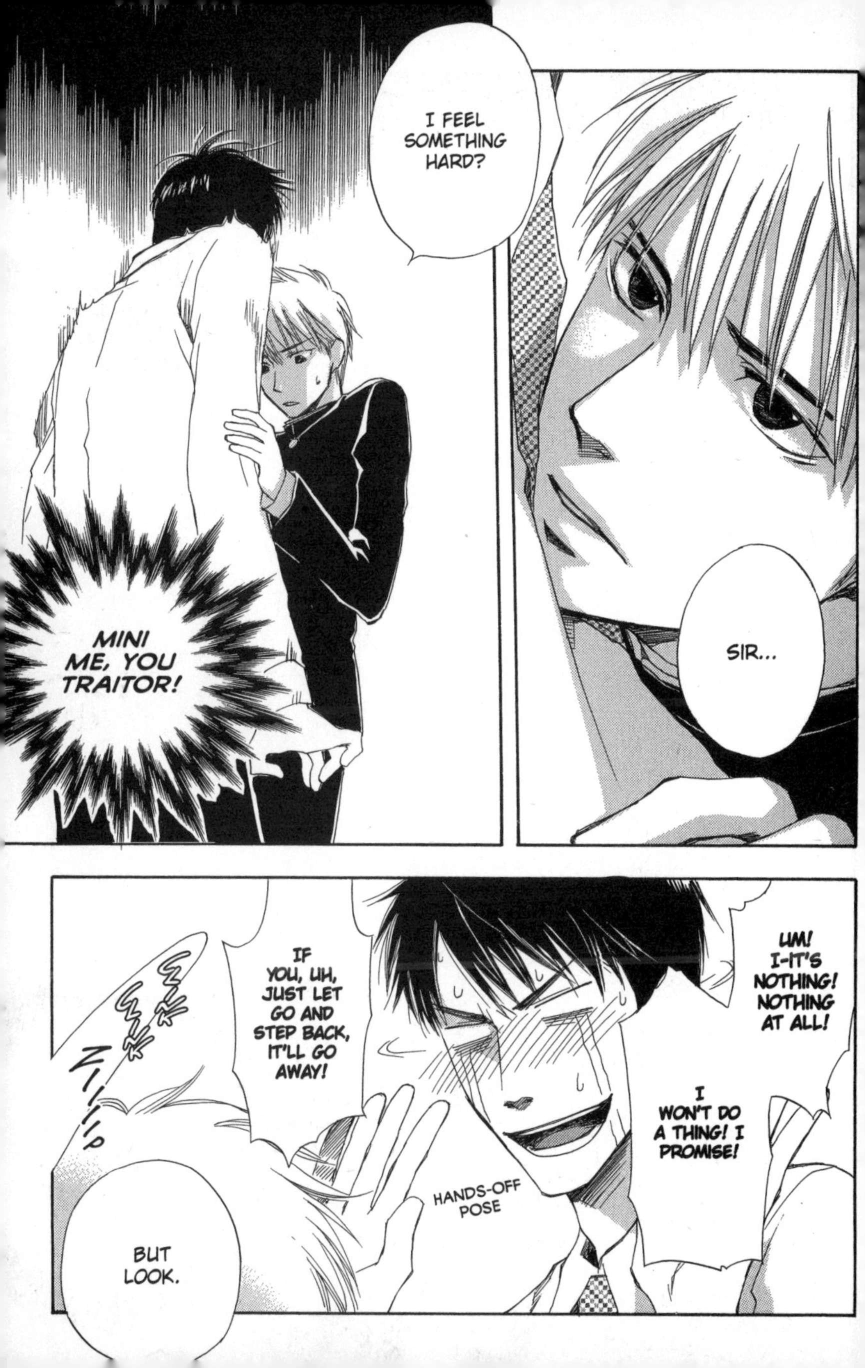
SIR...
I FEEL SOMETHING HARD?
MINI ME, YOU TRAITOR!
UM! I-IT'S NOTHING! NOTHING AT ALL!
I WON'T DO A THING! I PROMISE!
IF YOU, UH, JUST LET GO AND STEP BACK, IT'LL GO AWAY!
HANDS-OFF POSE
BUT LOOK.

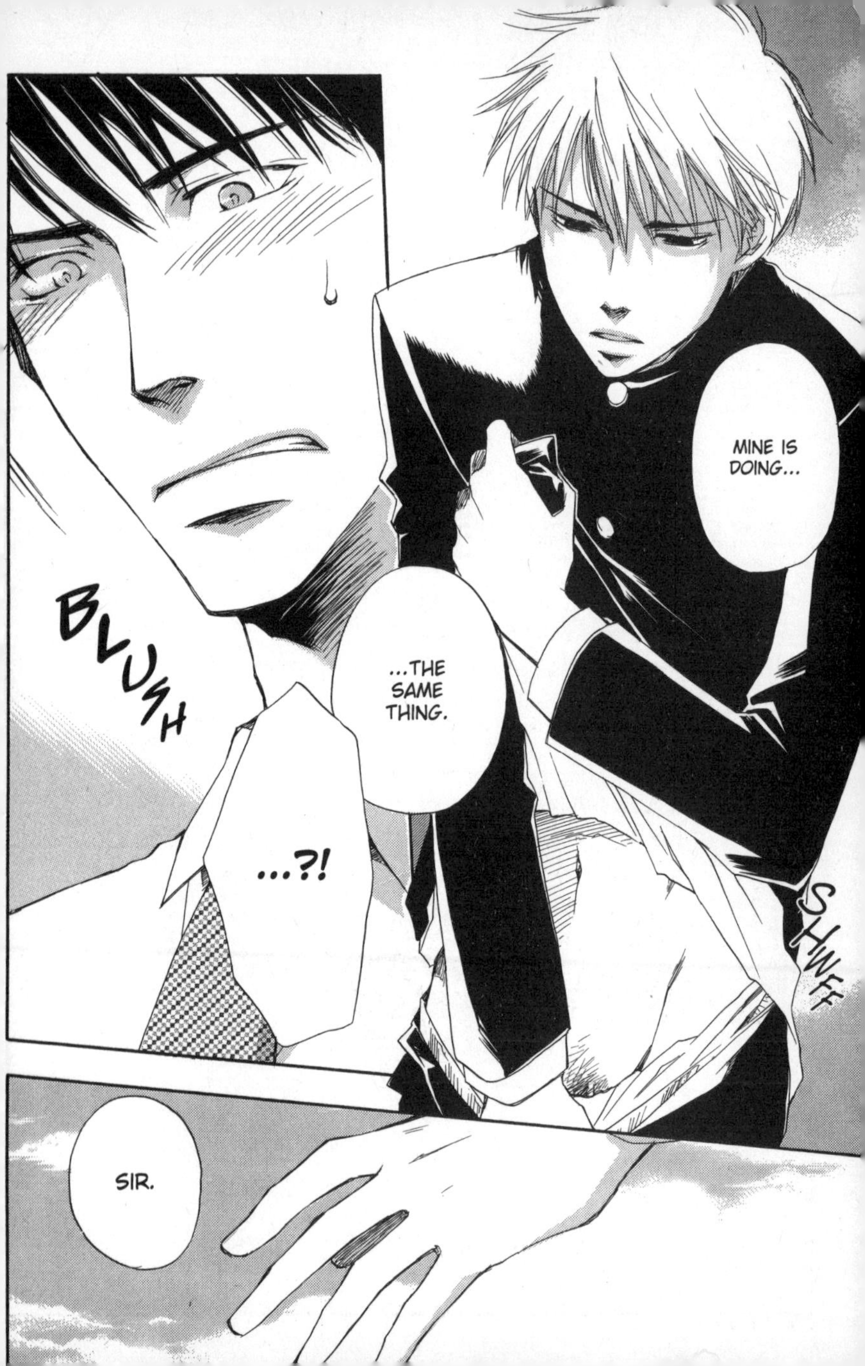
MINE IS DOING...
...THE SAME THING.
SHWFF
BLUSH
...?!
SIR.

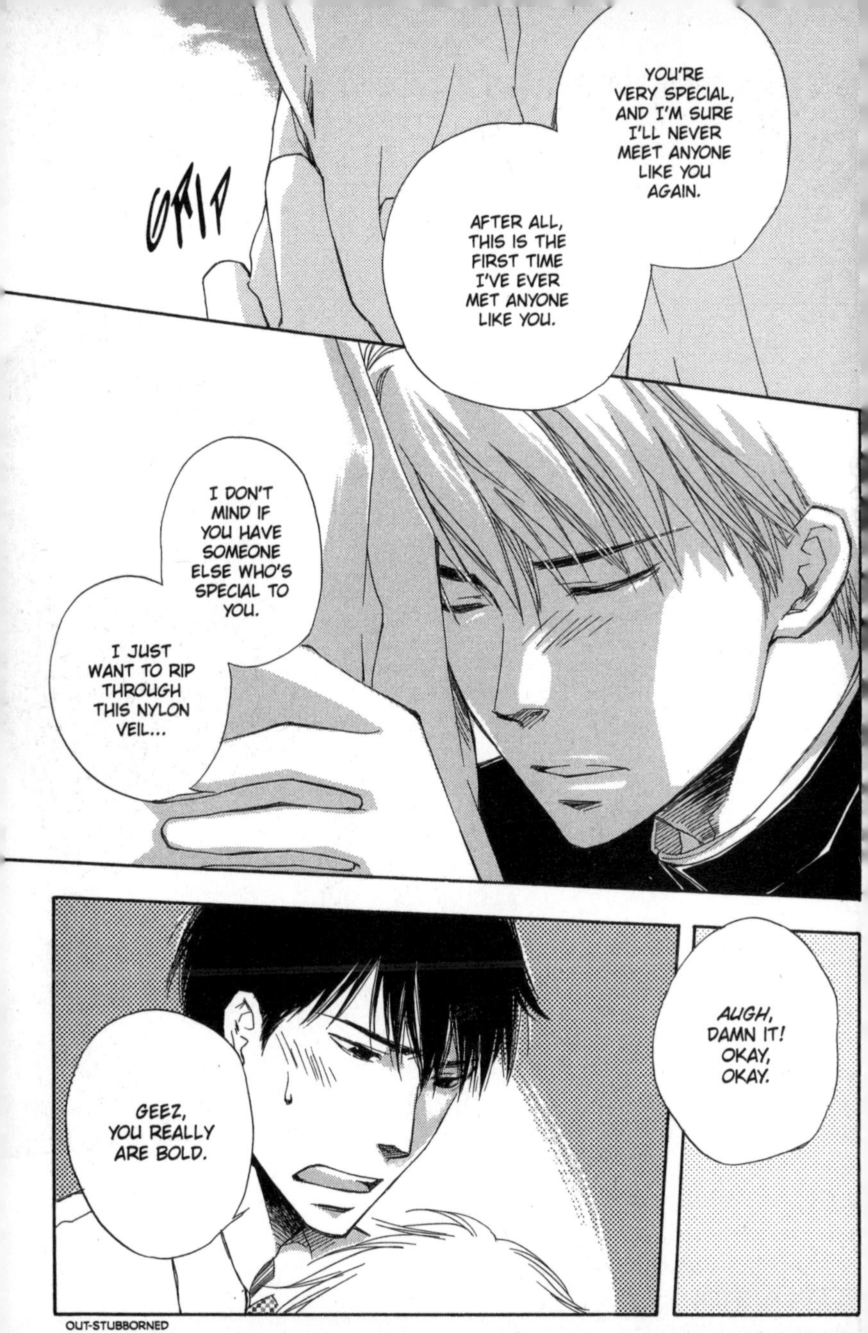
YOU'RE VERY SPECIAL, AND I'M SURE I'LL NEVER MEET ANYONE LIKE YOU AGAIN.
AFTER ALL, THIS IS THE FIRST TIME I'VE EVER MET ANYONE LIKE YOU.
GRIP
I DON'T MIND IF YOU HAVE SOMEONE ELSE WHO'S SPECIAL TO YOU.
I JUST WANT TO RIP THROUGH THIS NYLON VEIL...
AUGH, DAMN IT! OKAY, OKAY.
GEEZ, YOU REALLY ARE BOLD.
OUT-STUBBORNED

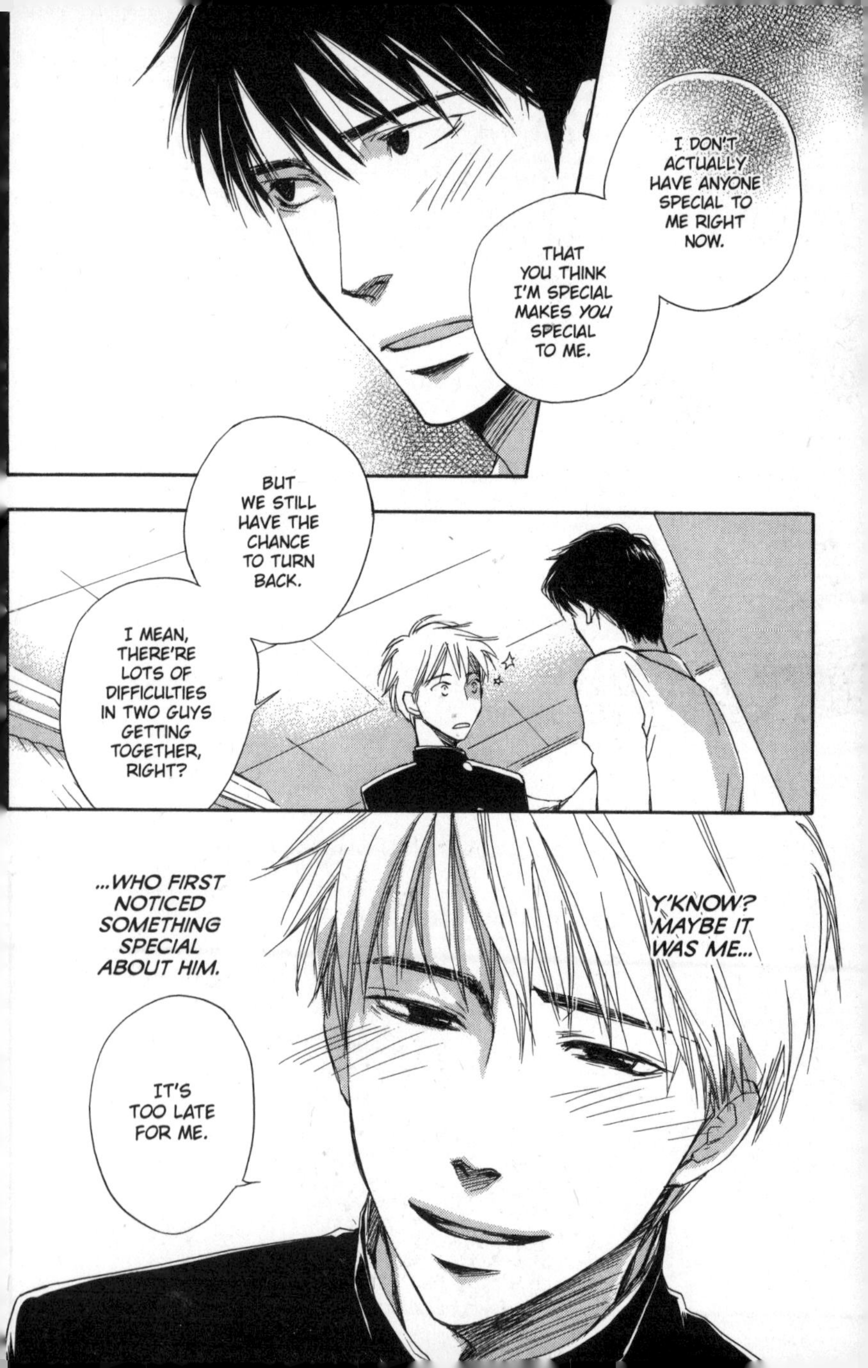
I DON'T ACTUALLY HAVE ANYONE SPECIAL TO ME RIGHT NOW.
THAT YOU THINK I'M SPECIAL MAKES *YOU* SPECIAL TO ME.
BUT WE STILL HAVE THE CHANCE TO TURN BACK.
I MEAN, THERE'RE LOTS OF DIFFICULTIES IN TWO GUYS GETTING TOGETHER, RIGHT?
Y'KNOW? MAYBE IT WAS ME...
...WHO FIRST NOTICED SOMETHING SPECIAL ABOUT HIM.
IT'S TOO LATE FOR ME.

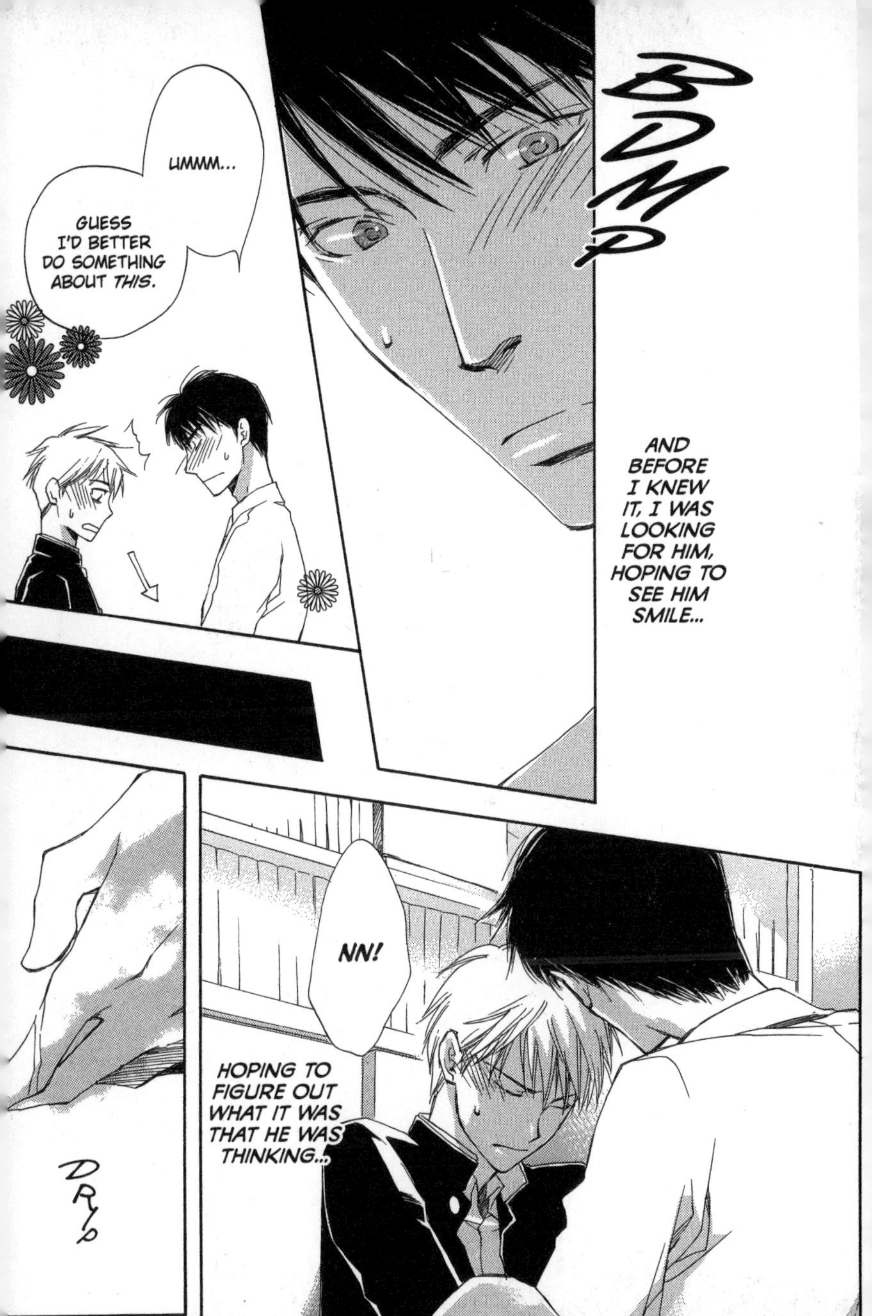
BDUMP
AND BEFORE I KNEW IT, I WAS LOOKING FOR HIM, HOPING TO SEE HIM SMILE...
UMMM...
GUESS I'D BETTER DO SOMETHING ABOUT *THIS*.
NN!
HOPING TO FIGURE OUT WHAT IT WAS THAT HE WAS THINKING...
DRIP

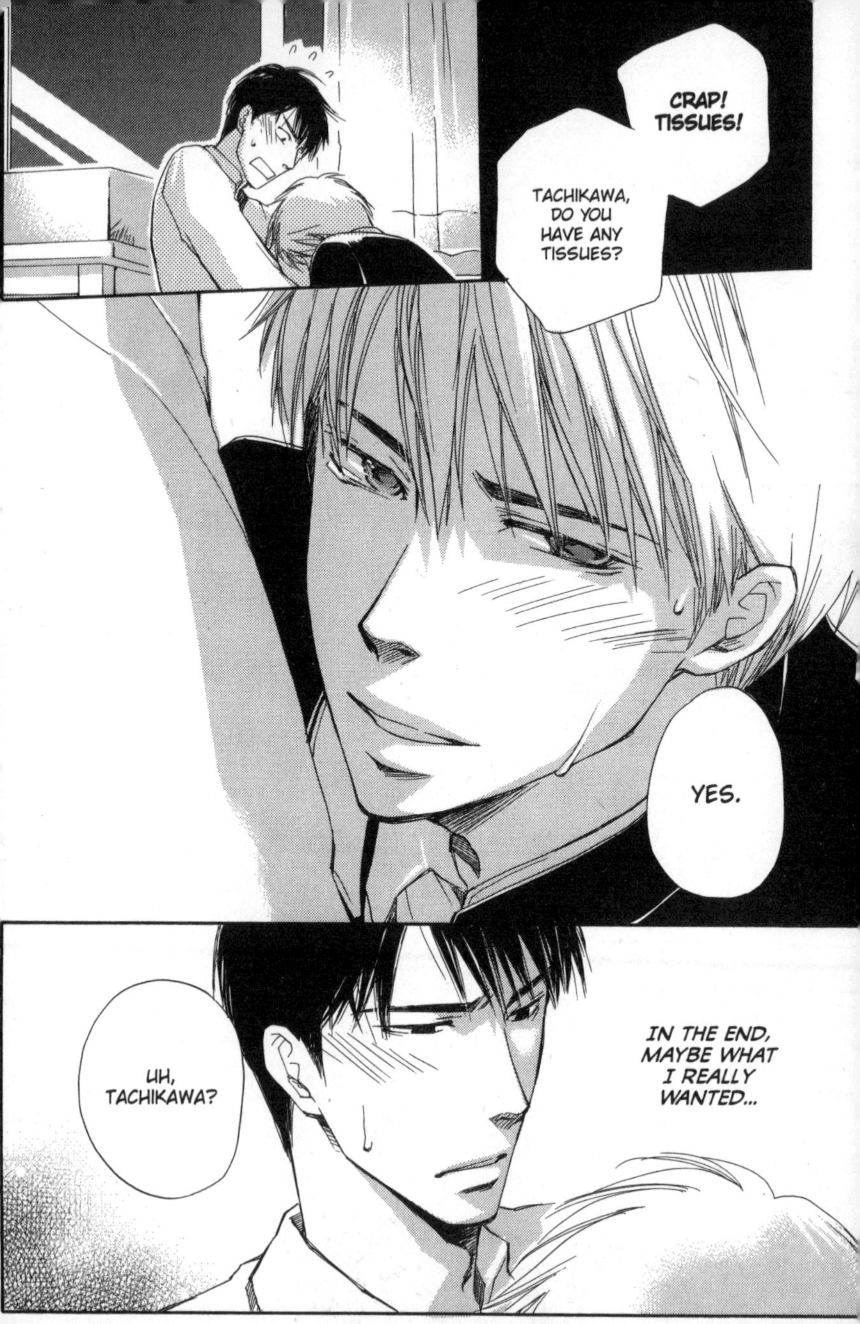
CRAP! TISSUES!
TACHIKAWA, DO YOU HAVE ANY TISSUES?
YES.
IN THE END, MAYBE WHAT I REALLY WANTED...
UH, TACHIKAWA?

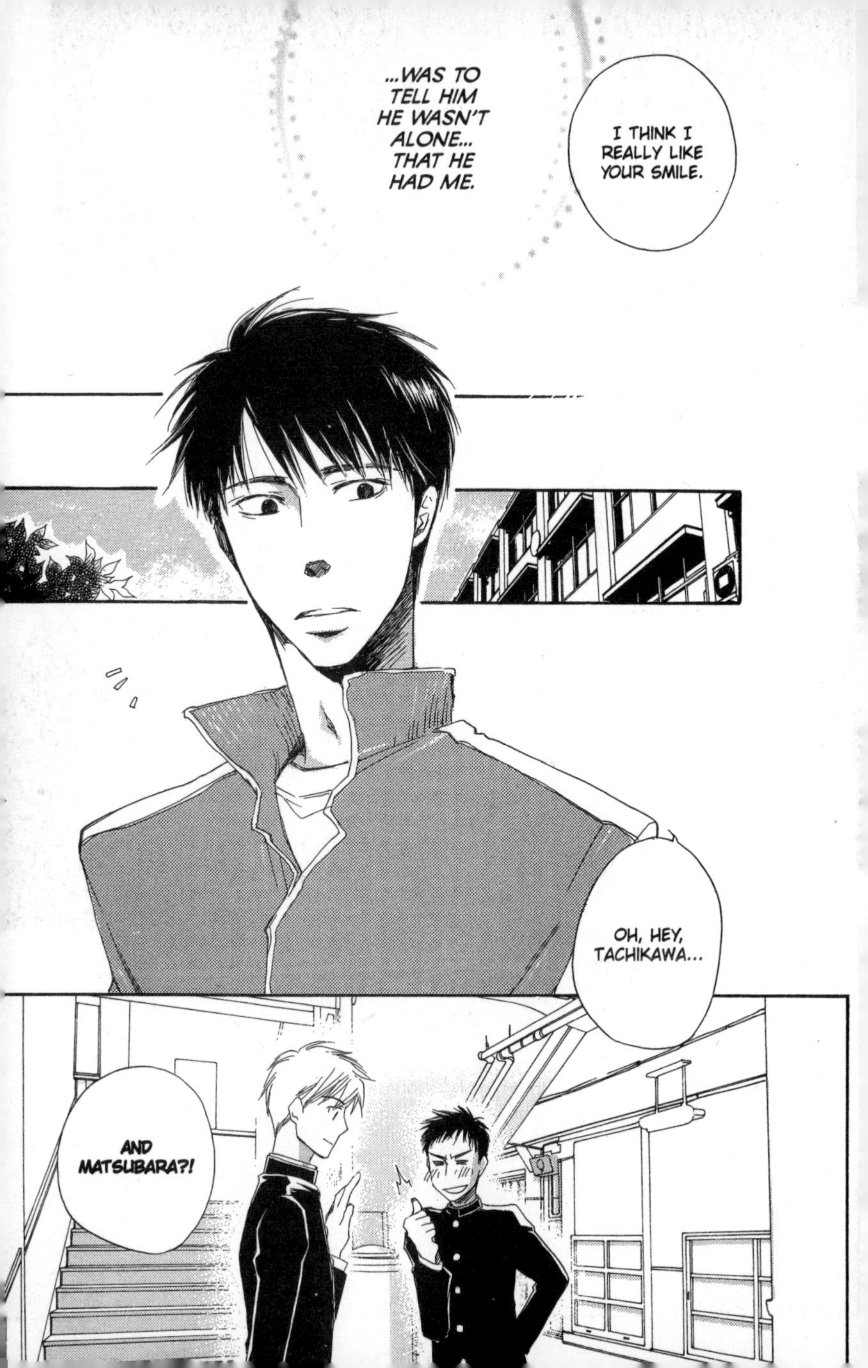
I THINK I REALLY LIKE YOUR SMILE.
...WAS TO TELL HIM HE WASN'T ALONE... THAT HE HAD ME.
OH, HEY, TACHIKAWA...
AND MATSUBARA?!

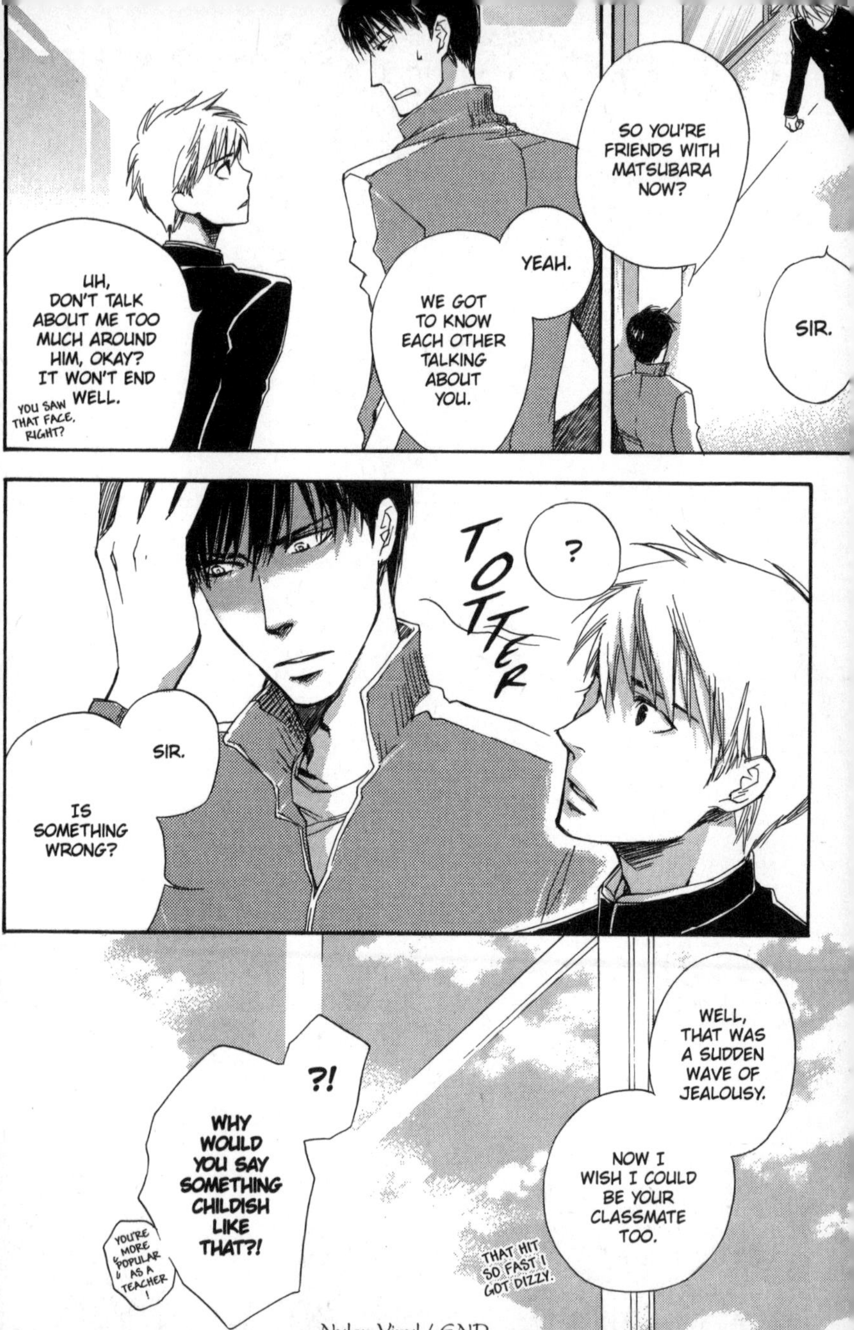
SO YOU'RE FRIENDS WITH MATSUBARA NOW?
SIR.
YEAH.
WE GOT TO KNOW EACH OTHER TALKING ABOUT YOU.
UH, DON'T TALK ABOUT ME TOO MUCH AROUND HIM, OKAY? IT WON'T END WELL.
YOU SAW THAT FACE, RIGHT?
?
TOTTER
SIR.
IS SOMETHING WRONG?
WELL, THAT WAS A SUDDEN WAVE OF JEALOUSY.
NOW I WISH I COULD BE YOUR CLASSMATE TOO.
THAT HIT SO FAST I GOT DIZZY.
?!
WHY WOULD YOU SAY SOMETHING CHILDISH LIKE THAT?!
YOU'RE MORE POPULAR AS A TEACHER!

THE GODS DON'T EXIST

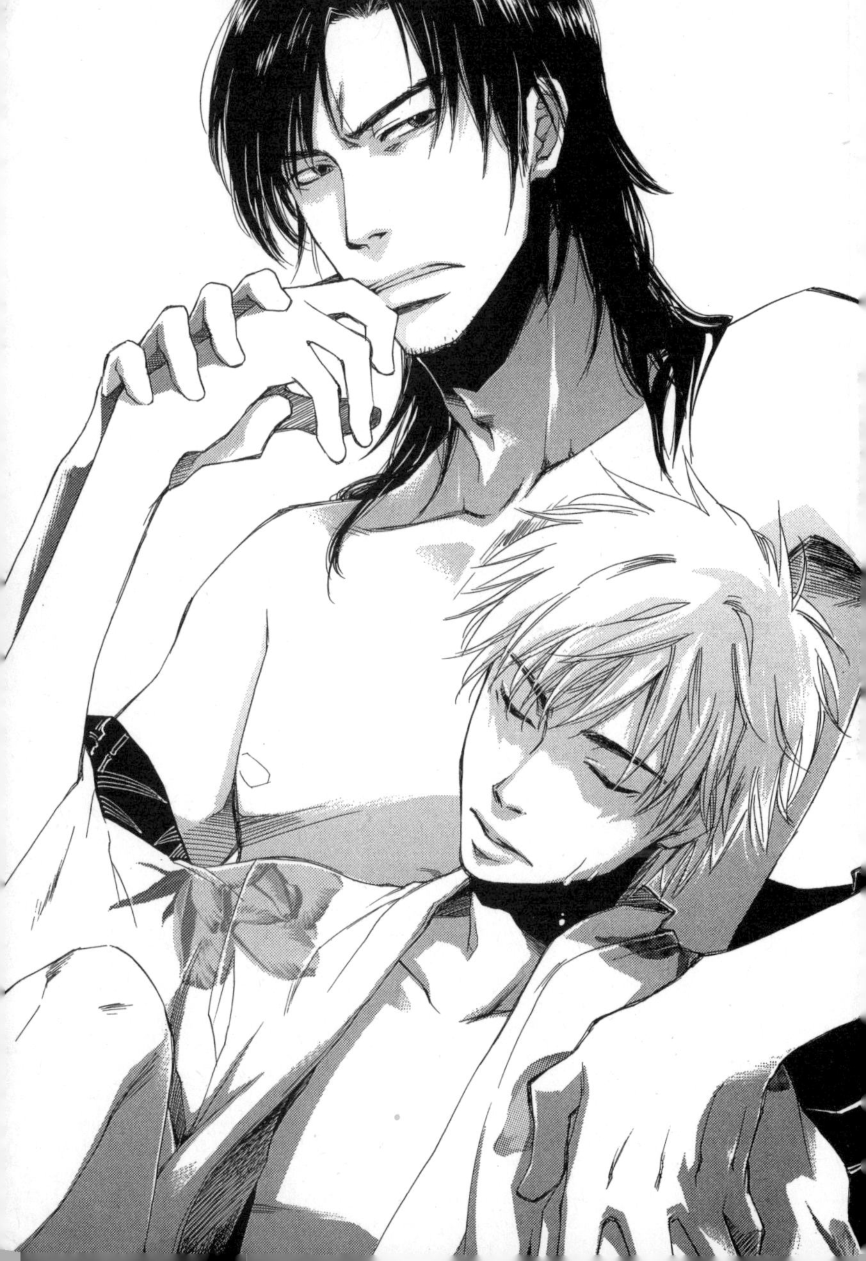

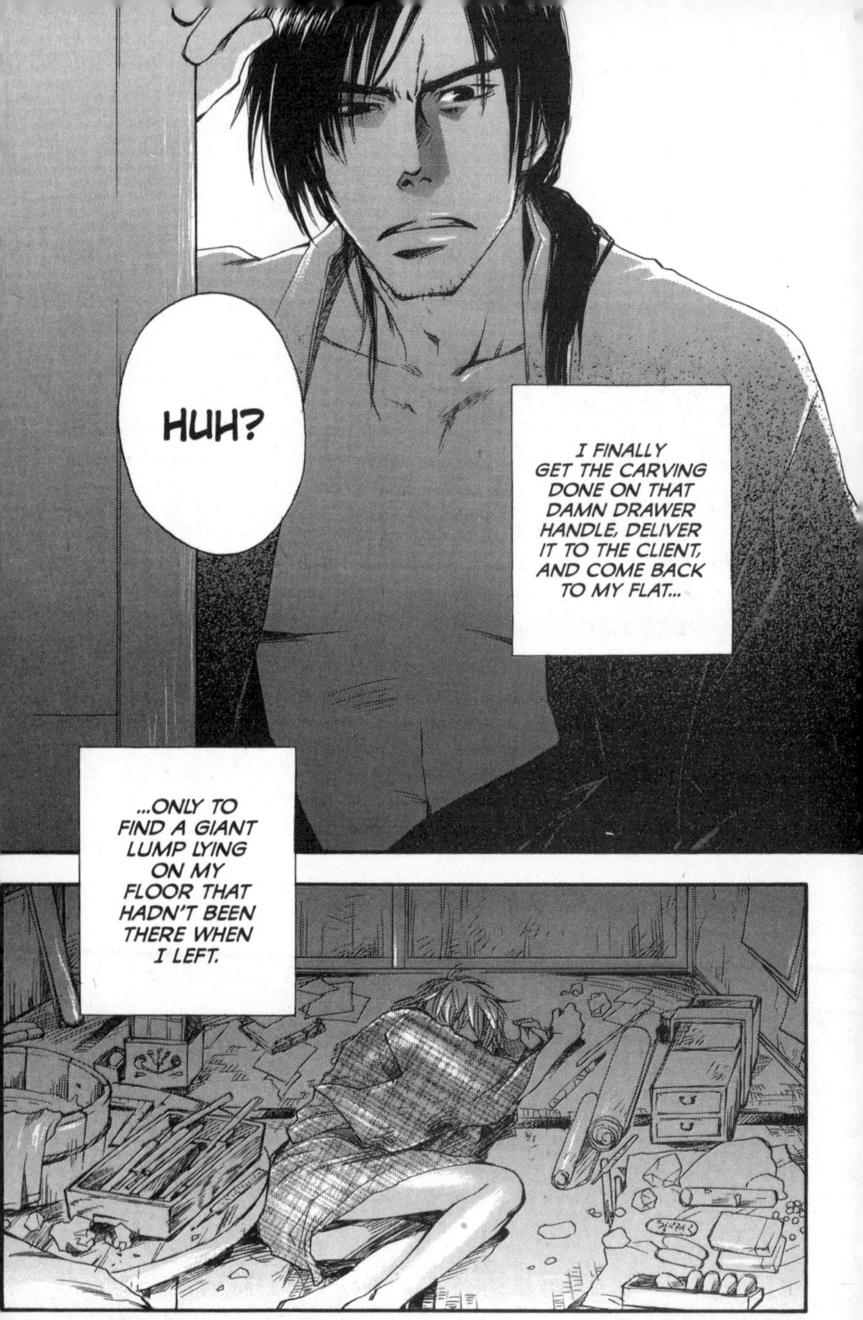
I FINALLY GET THE CARVING DONE ON THAT DAMN DRAWER HANDLE, DELIVER IT TO THE CLIENT, AND COME BACK TO MY FLAT...
HUH?
...ONLY TO FIND A GIANT LUMP LYING ON MY FLOOR THAT HADN'T BEEN THERE WHEN I LEFT.

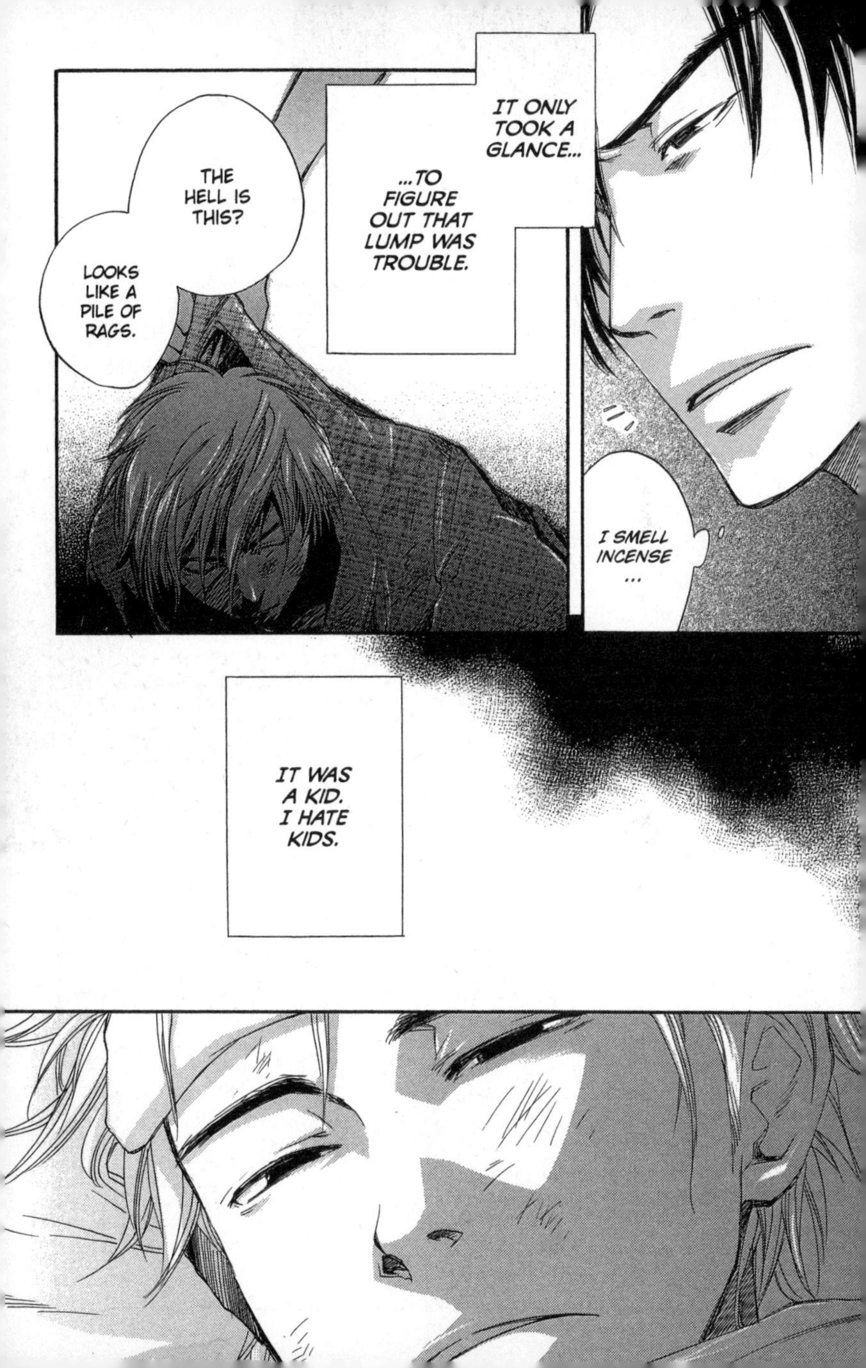
IT ONLY TOOK A GLANCE...
I SMELL INCENSE...
...TO FIGURE OUT THAT LUMP WAS TROUBLE.
THE HELL IS THIS?
LOOKS LIKE A PILE OF RAGS.
IT WAS A KID. I HATE KIDS.

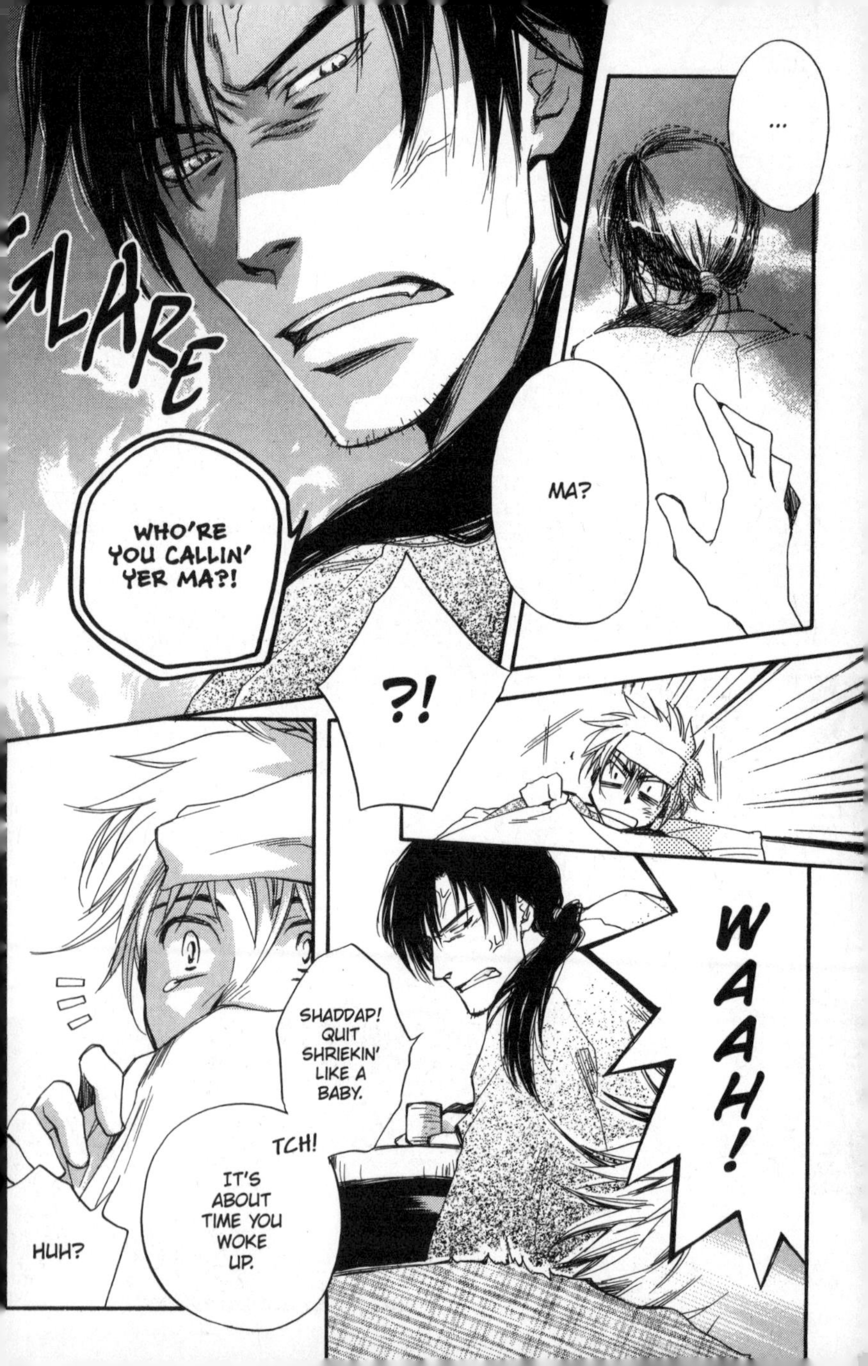
...
MA?
LARE
WHO'RE YOU CALLIN' YER MA?!
?!
WAAH!
SHADDAP! QUIT SHRIEKIN' LIKE A BABY.
TCH!
IT'S ABOUT TIME YOU WOKE UP.
HUH?

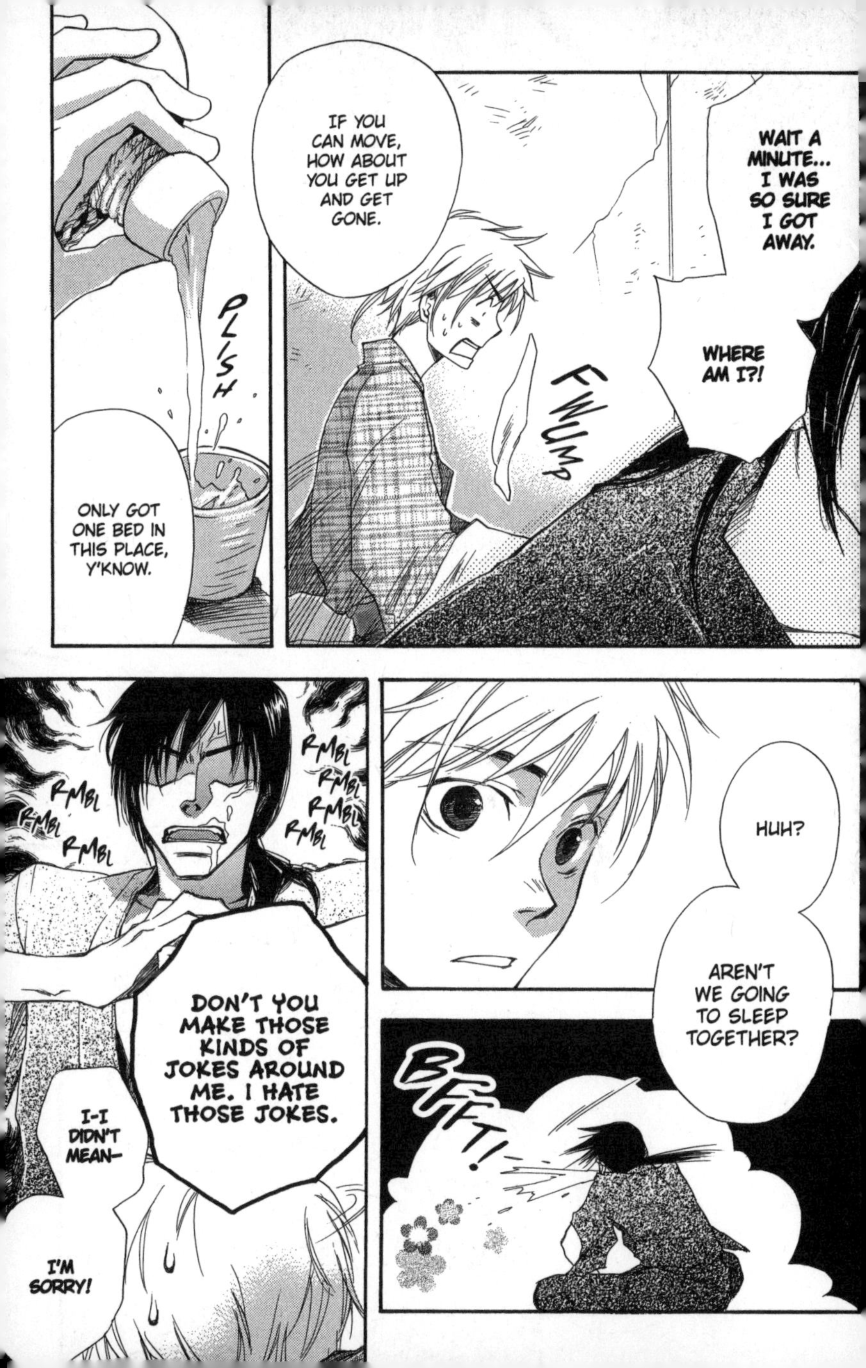
WAIT A MINUTE... I WAS SO SURE I GOT AWAY.
WHERE AM I?!
FWUMP
IF YOU CAN MOVE, HOW ABOUT YOU GET UP AND GET GONE.
PLISH
ONLY GOT ONE BED IN THIS PLACE, Y'KNOW.
HUH?
AREN'T WE GOING TO SLEEP TOGETHER?
BFFT!
RMBL RMBL RMBL RMBL RMBL RMBL RMBL RMBL
DON'T YOU MAKE THOSE KINDS OF JOKES AROUND ME. I HATE THOSE JOKES.
I-I DIDN'T MEAN-
I'M SORRY!

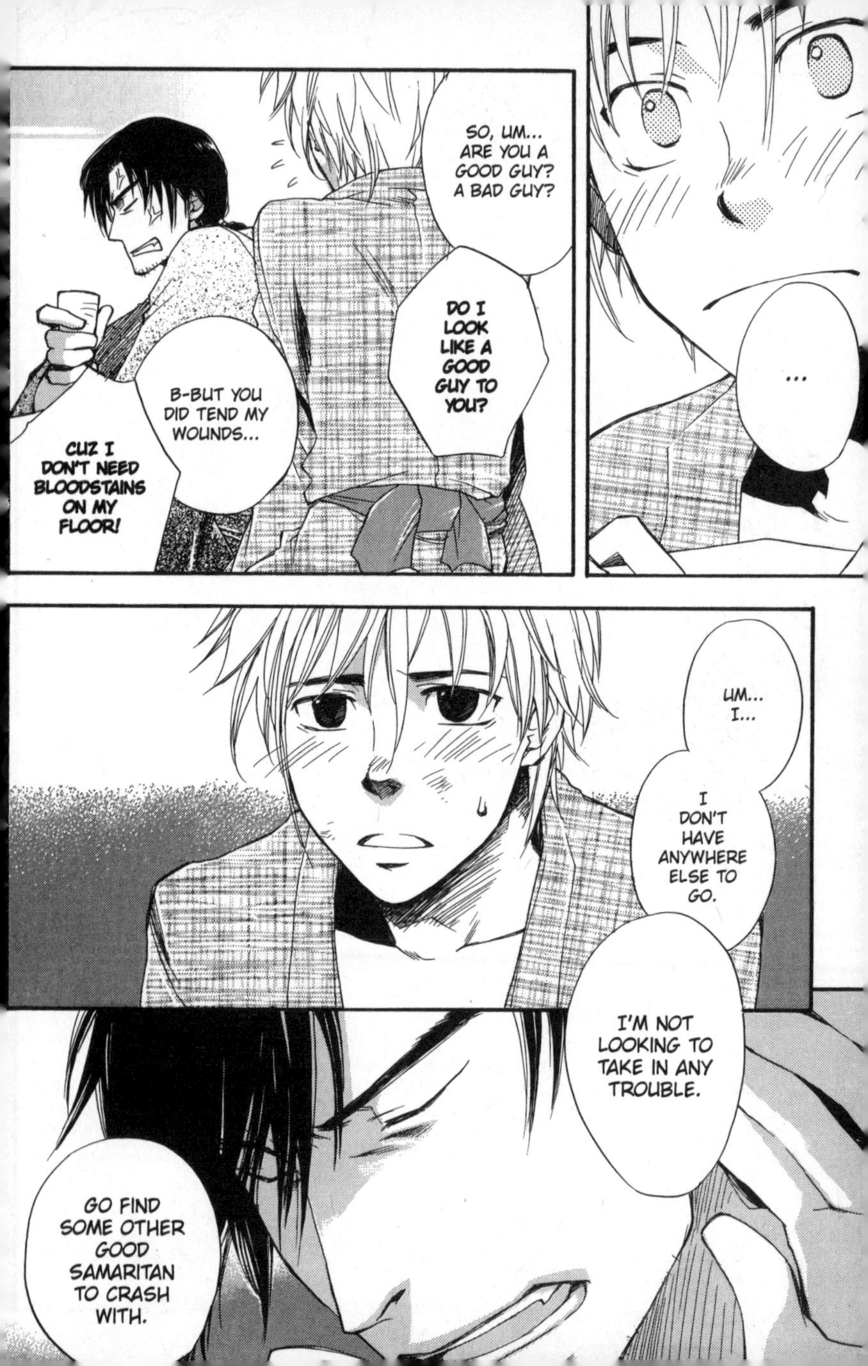
...
SO, UM... ARE YOU A GOOD GUY? A BAD GUY?
DO I LOOK LIKE A GOOD GUY TO YOU?
B-BUT YOU DID TEND MY WOUNDS...
CUZ I DON'T NEED BLOODSTAINS ON MY FLOOR!
UM... I...
I DON'T HAVE ANYWHERE ELSE TO GO.
I'M NOT LOOKING TO TAKE IN ANY TROUBLE.
GO FIND SOME OTHER GOOD SAMARITAN TO CRASH WITH.

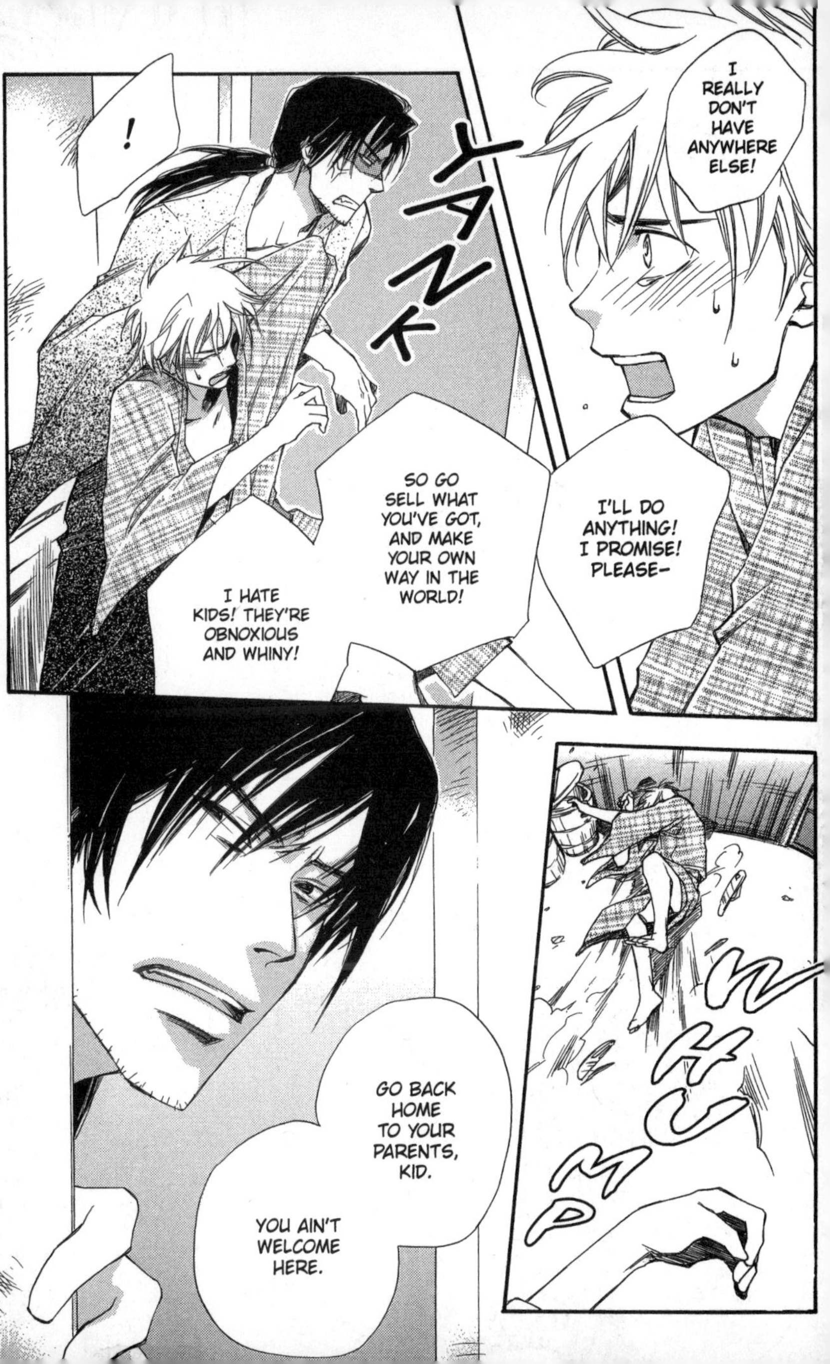
I REALLY DON'T HAVE ANYWHERE ELSE!
I'LL DO ANYTHING! I PROMISE! PLEASE-
YANK
!
SO GO SELL WHAT YOU'VE GOT, AND MAKE YOUR OWN WAY IN THE WORLD!
I HATE KIDS! THEY'RE OBNOXIOUS AND WHINY!
WHUMP
GO BACK HOME TO YOUR PARENTS, KID.
YOU AIN'T WELCOME HERE.

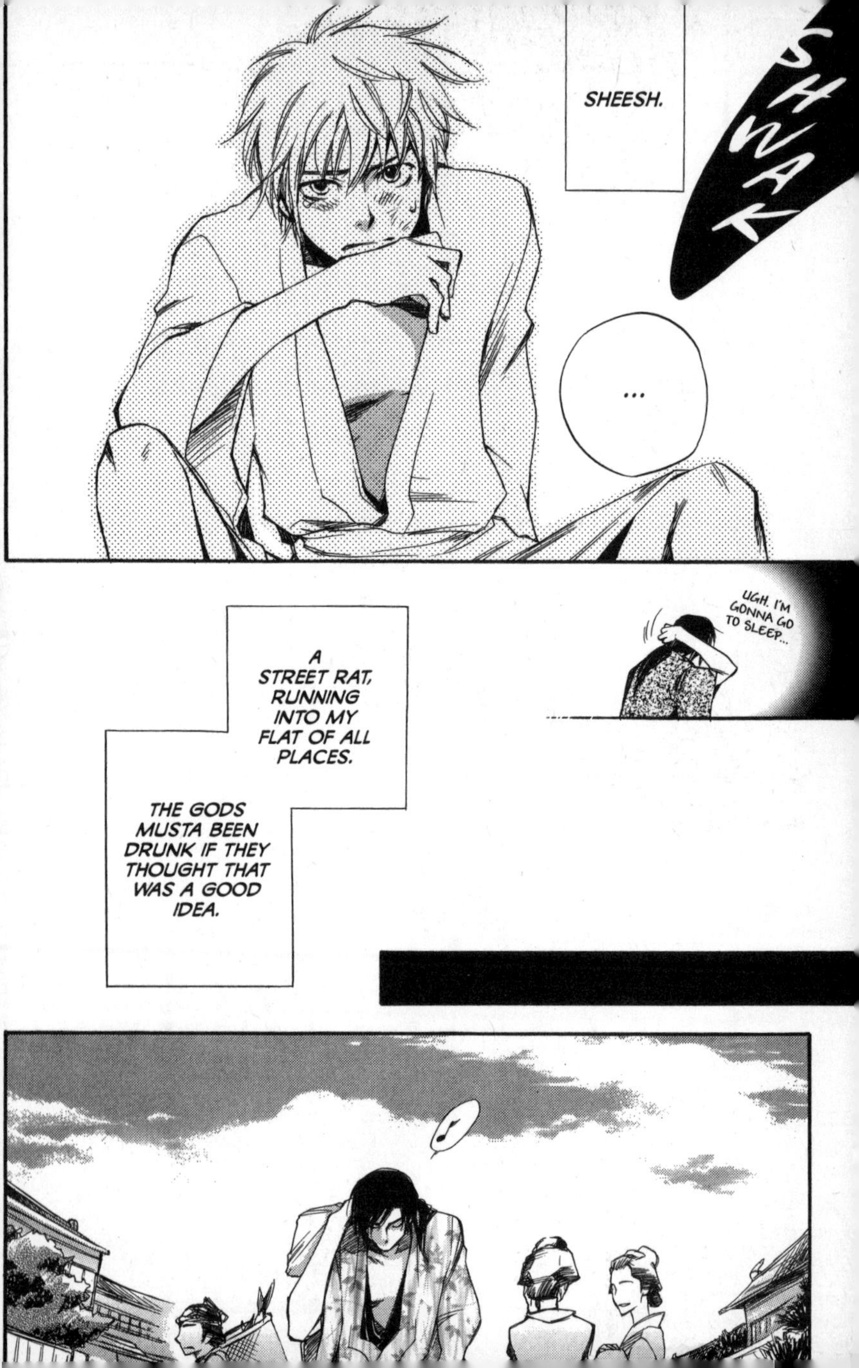
SHWAK
SHEESH.
...
UGH. I'M GONNA GO TO SLEEP...
A STREET RAT, RUNNING INTO MY FLAT OF ALL PLACES.
THE GODS MUSTA BEEN DRUNK IF THEY THOUGHT THAT WAS A GOOD IDEA.

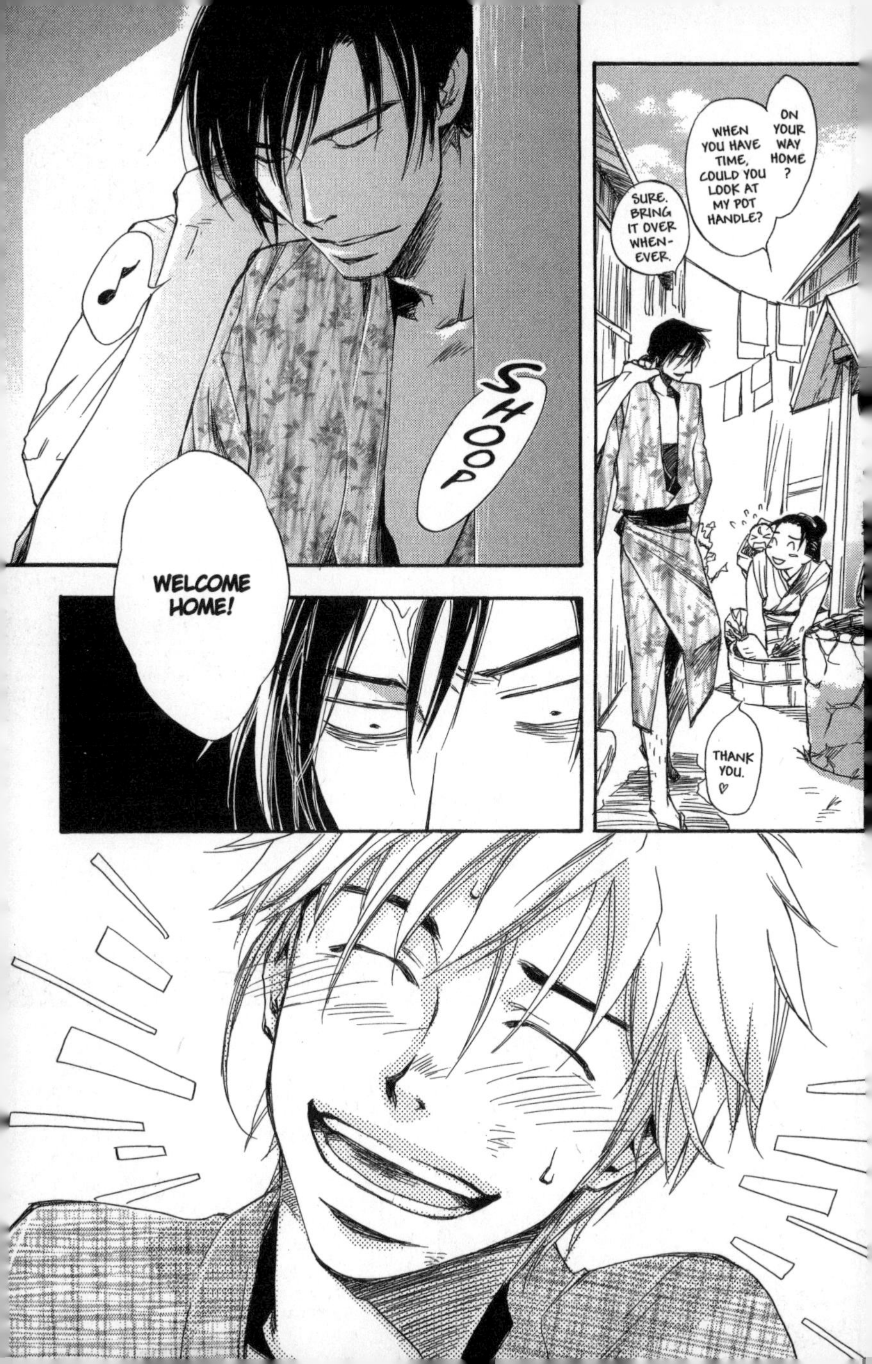
ON YOUR WAY HOME?
WHEN YOU HAVE TIME, COULD YOU LOOK AT MY POT HANDLE?
SURE. BRING IT OVER WHEN-EVER.
THANK YOU. ♡
SHOOP
WELCOME HOME!

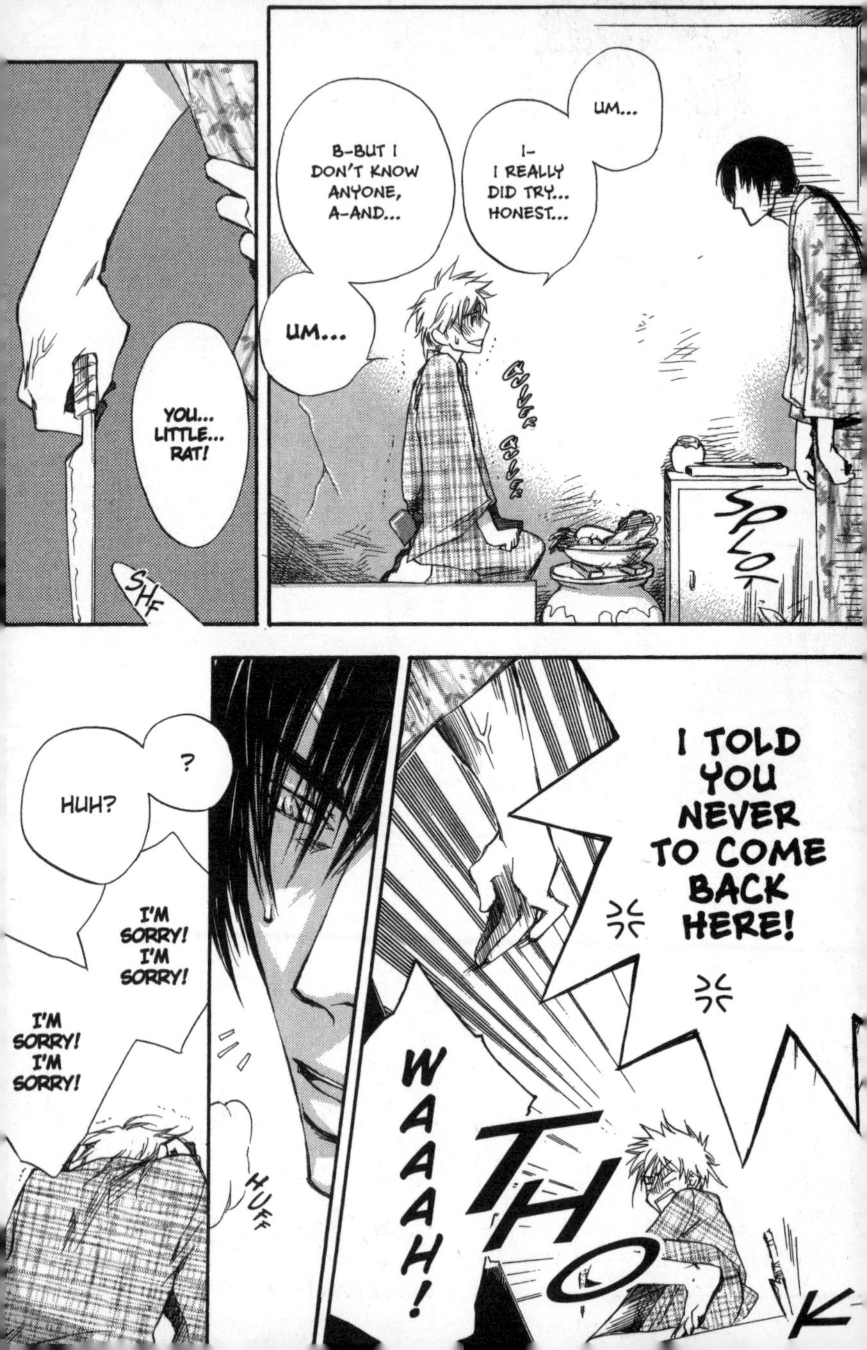
UM...
I- I REALLY DID TRY... HONEST...
B-BUT I DON'T KNOW ANYONE, A-AND...
UM...
QUIVER QUIVER
SPLOT
YOU... LITTLE... RAT!
SHF
I TOLD YOU NEVER TO COME BACK HERE!
WAAAAH!
THOK
HUFF
? HUH?
I'M SORRY! I'M SORRY!
I'M SORRY! I'M SORRY!

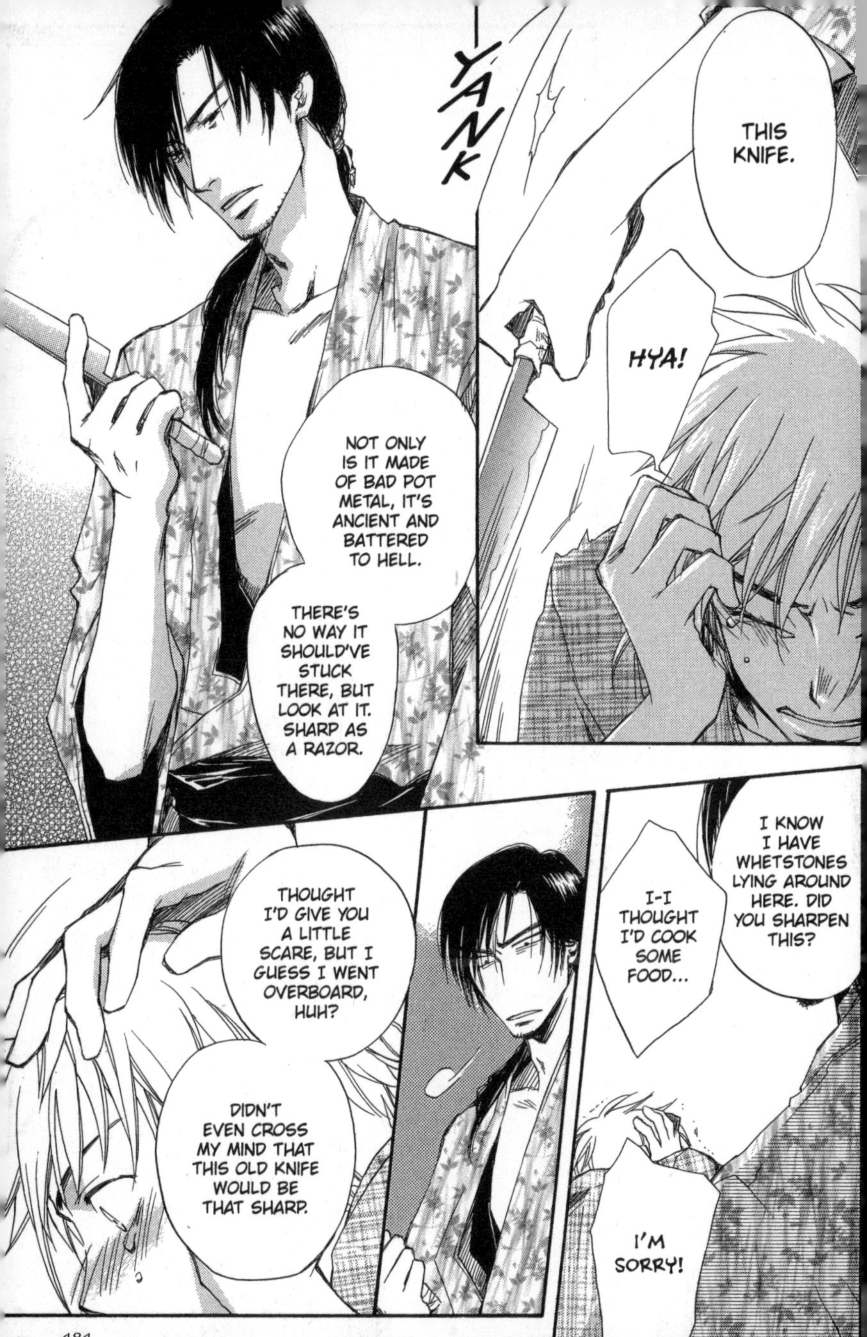
THIS KNIFE.
HYA!
YANK
NOT ONLY IS IT MADE OF BAD POT METAL, IT'S ANCIENT AND BATTERED TO HELL.
THERE'S NO WAY IT SHOULD'VE STUCK THERE, BUT LOOK AT IT. SHARP AS A RAZOR.
I KNOW I HAVE WHETSTONES LYING AROUND HERE. DID YOU SHARPEN THIS?
I-I THOUGHT I'D COOK SOME FOOD...
I'M SORRY!
THOUGHT I'D GIVE YOU A LITTLE SCARE, BUT I GUESS I WENT OVERBOARD, HUH?
DIDN'T EVEN CROSS MY MIND THAT THIS OLD KNIFE WOULD BE THAT SHARP.

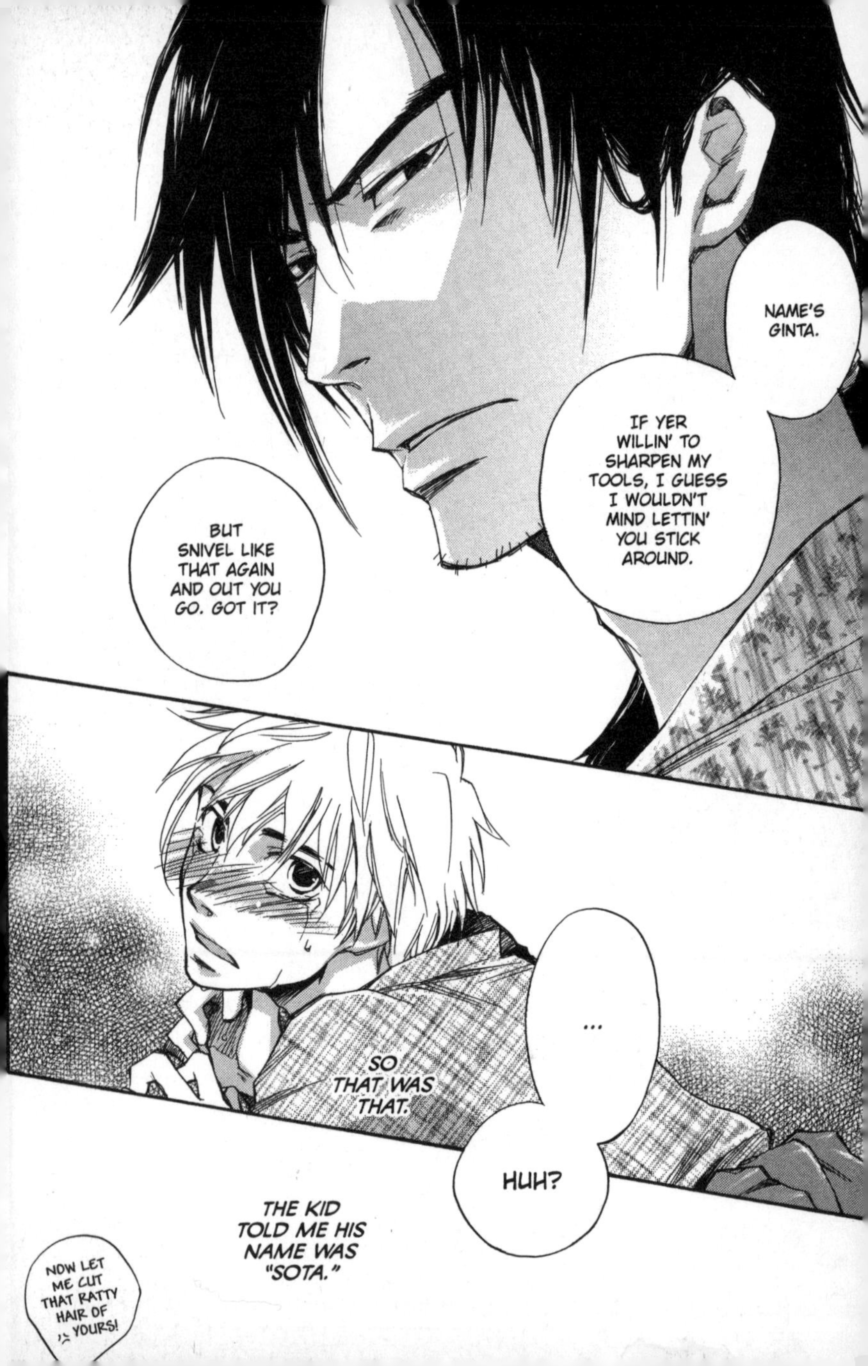
NAME'S GINTA.
IF YER WILLIN' TO SHARPEN MY TOOLS, I GUESS I WOULDN'T MIND LETTIN' YOU STICK AROUND.
BUT SNIVEL LIKE THAT AGAIN AND OUT YOU GO. GOT IT?
...
SO THAT WAS THAT.
HUH?
THE KID TOLD ME HIS NAME WAS "SOTA."
NOW LET ME CUT THAT RATTY HAIR OF YOURS!

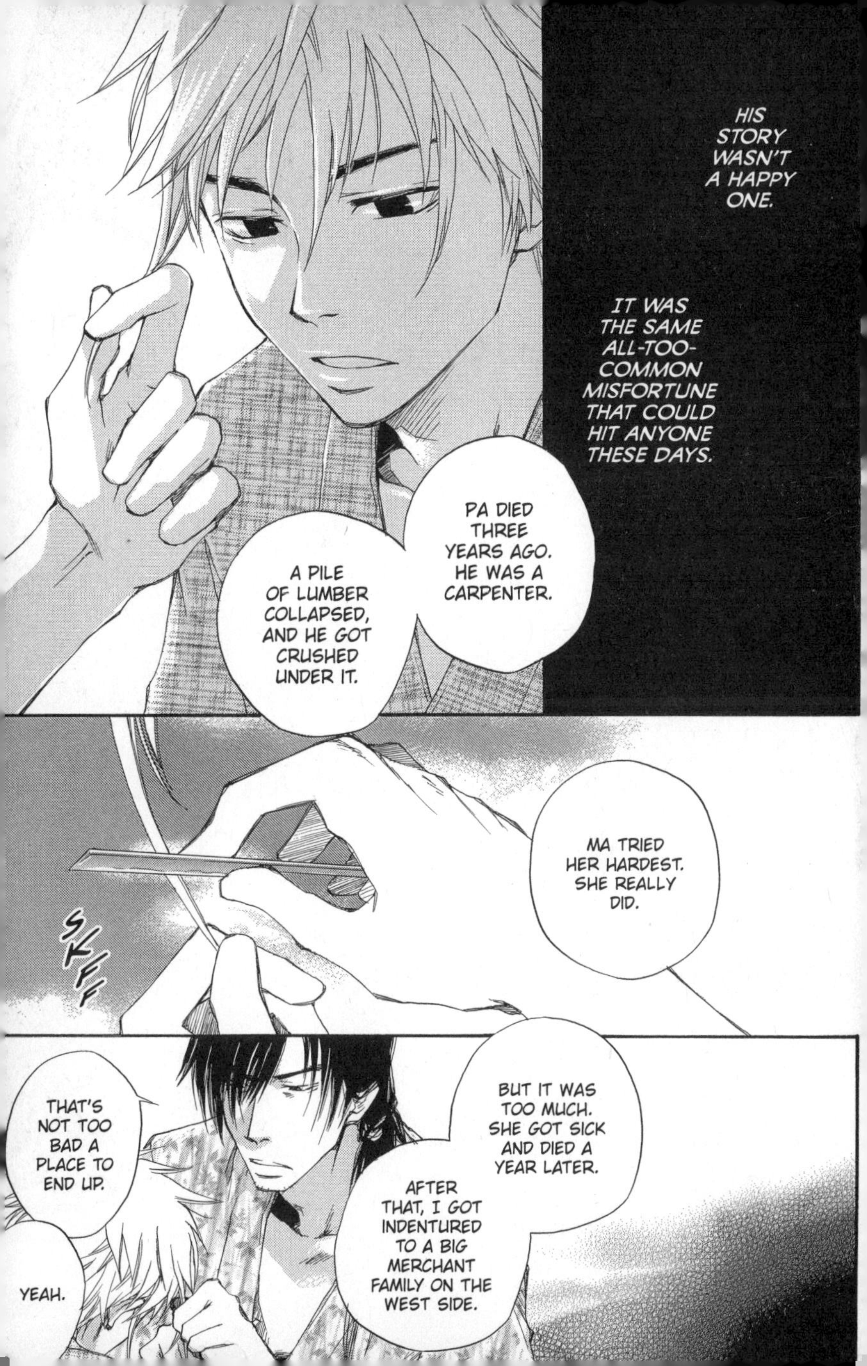
HIS STORY WASN'T A HAPPY ONE.
IT WAS THE SAME ALL-TOO-COMMON MISFORTUNE THAT COULD HIT ANYONE THESE DAYS.
PA DIED THREE YEARS AGO. HE WAS A CARPENTER.
A PILE OF LUMBER COLLAPSED, AND HE GOT CRUSHED UNDER IT.
MA TRIED HER HARDEST. SHE REALLY DID.
SKFF
BUT IT WAS TOO MUCH. SHE GOT SICK AND DIED A YEAR LATER.
AFTER THAT, I GOT INDENTURED TO A BIG MERCHANT FAMILY ON THE WEST SIDE.
THAT'S NOT TOO BAD A PLACE TO END UP.
YEAH.

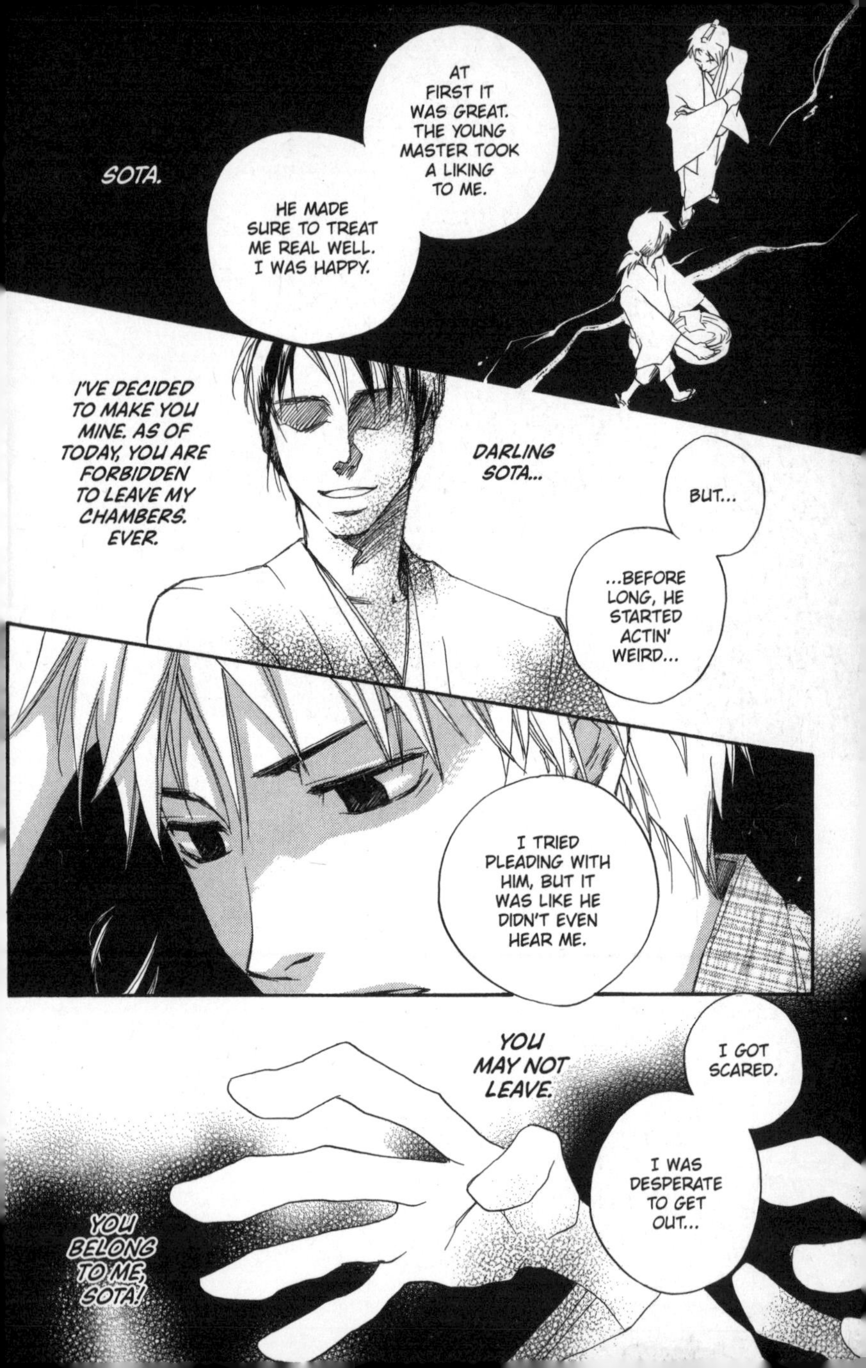
AT FIRST IT WAS GREAT. THE YOUNG MASTER TOOK A LIKING TO ME.
HE MADE SURE TO TREAT ME REAL WELL. I WAS HAPPY.
SOTA.
BUT...
...BEFORE LONG, HE STARTED ACTIN' WEIRD...
DARLING SOTA...
I'VE DECIDED TO MAKE YOU MINE. AS OF TODAY, YOU ARE FORBIDDEN TO LEAVE MY CHAMBERS. EVER.
I TRIED PLEADING WITH HIM, BUT IT WAS LIKE HE DIDN'T EVEN HEAR ME.
I GOT SCARED.
I WAS DESPERATE TO GET OUT...
YOU MAY NOT LEAVE.
YOU BELONG TO ME, SOTA!

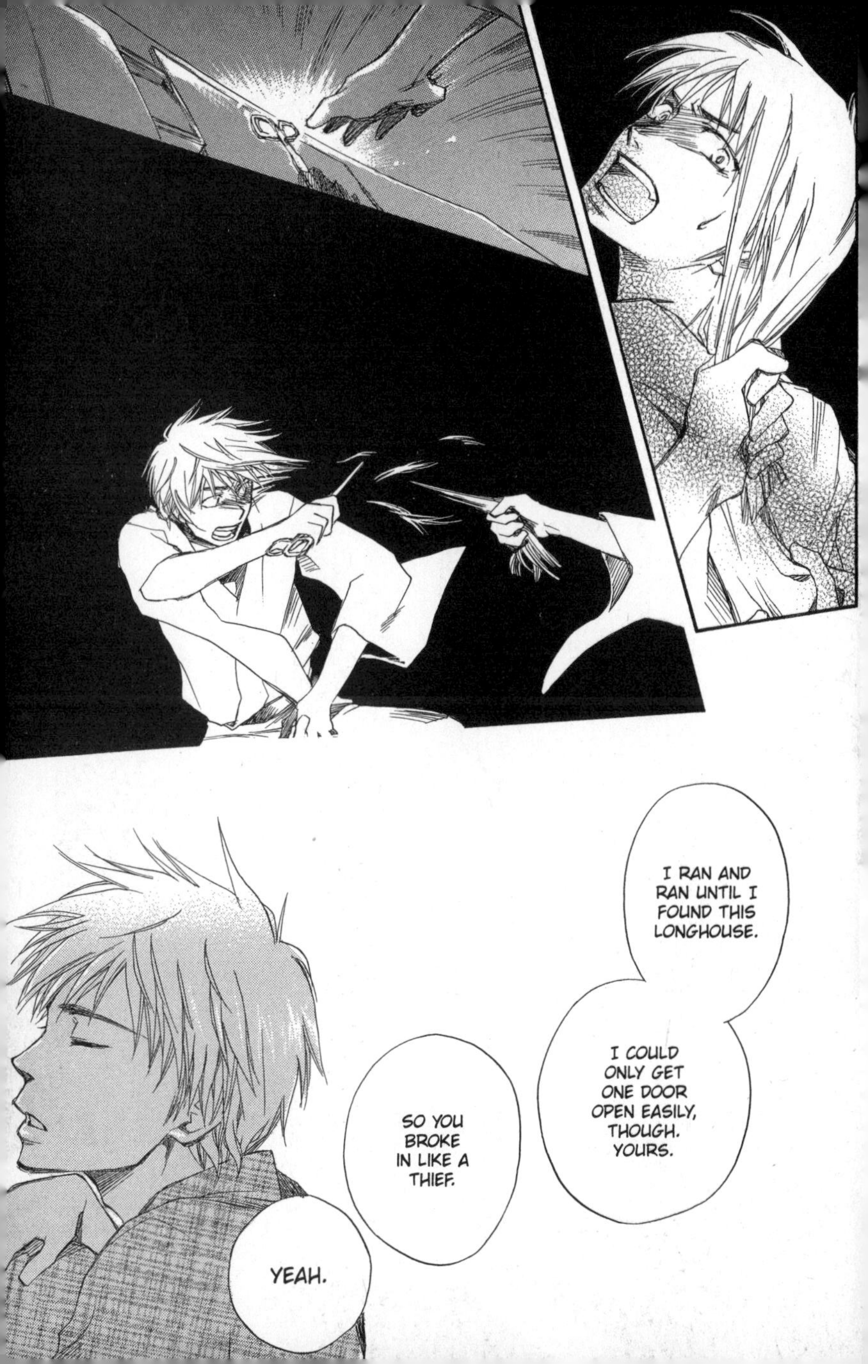
I RAN AND RAN UNTIL I FOUND THIS LONGHOUSE.
I COULD ONLY GET ONE DOOR OPEN EASILY, THOUGH. YOURS.
SO YOU BROKE IN LIKE A THIEF.
YEAH.

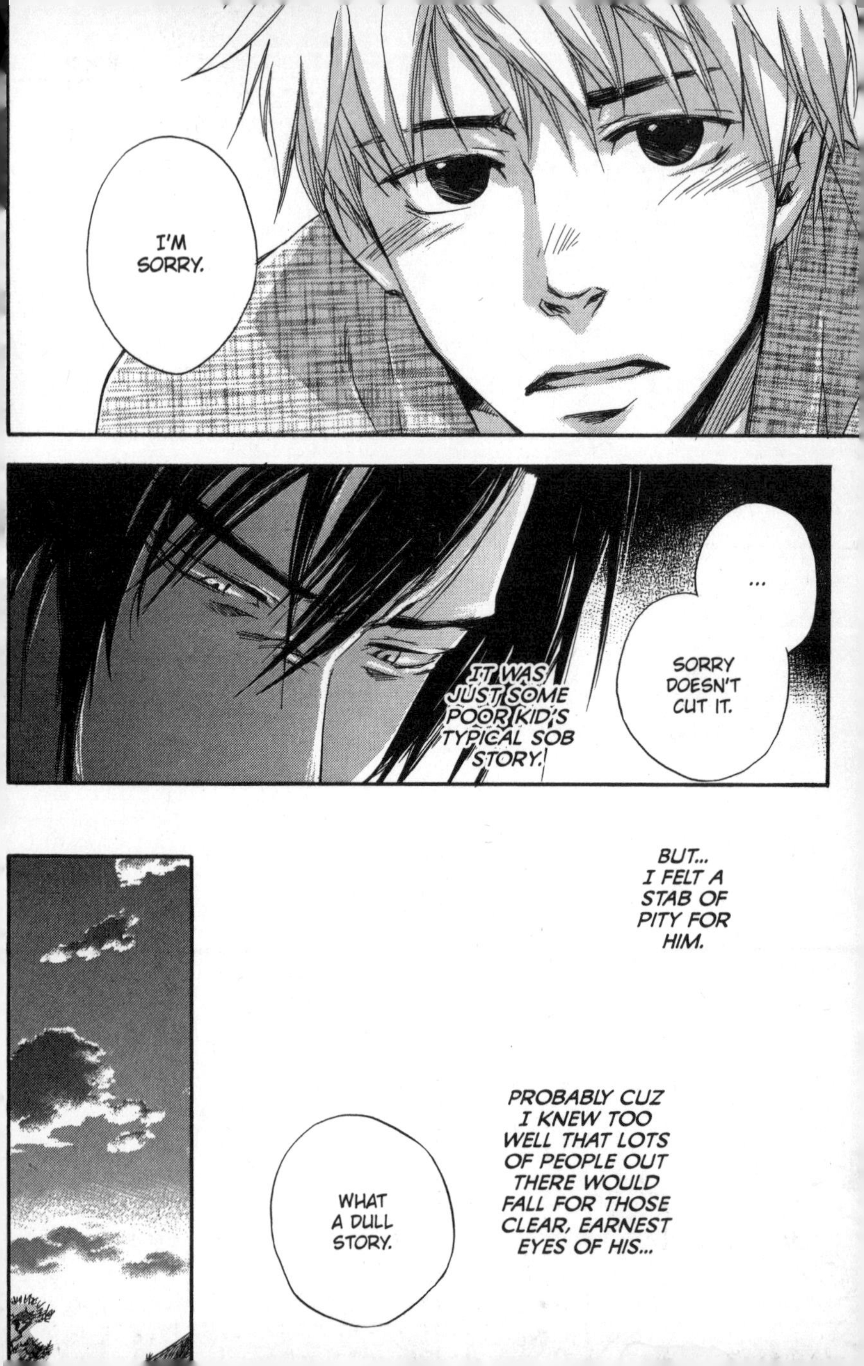
I'M SORRY.
...
SORRY DOESN'T CUT IT.
IT WAS JUST SOME POOR KID'S TYPICAL SOB STORY.
BUT... I FELT A STAB OF PITY FOR HIM.
PROBABLY CUZ I KNEW TOO WELL THAT LOTS OF PEOPLE OUT THERE WOULD FALL FOR THOSE CLEAR, EARNEST EYES OF HIS...
WHAT A DULL STORY.

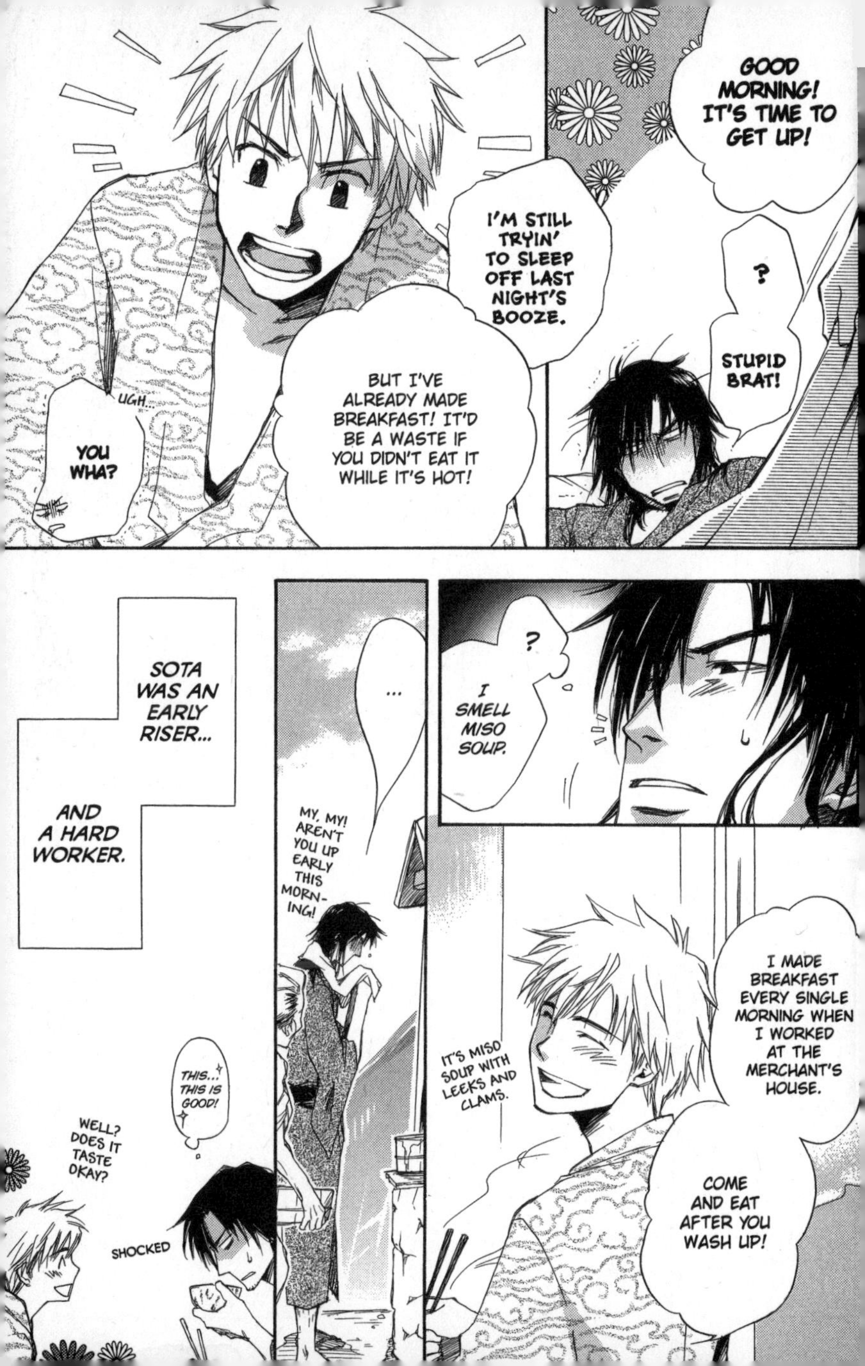
GOOD MORNING! IT'S TIME TO GET UP!
?
STUPID BRAT!
I'M STILL TRYIN' TO SLEEP OFF LAST NIGHT'S BOOZE.
BUT I'VE ALREADY MADE BREAKFAST! IT'D BE A WASTE IF YOU DIDN'T EAT IT WHILE IT'S HOT!
UGH...
YOU WHA?
?
I SMELL MISO SOUP.
...
MY, MY! AREN'T YOU UP EARLY THIS MORN-ING!
I MADE BREAKFAST EVERY SINGLE MORNING WHEN I WORKED AT THE MERCHANT'S HOUSE.
COME AND EAT AFTER YOU WASH UP!
IT'S MISO SOUP WITH LEEKS AND CLAMS.
SOTA WAS AN EARLY RISER...
AND A HARD WORKER.
THIS... THIS IS GOOD!
WELL? DOES IT TASTE OKAY?
SHOCKED

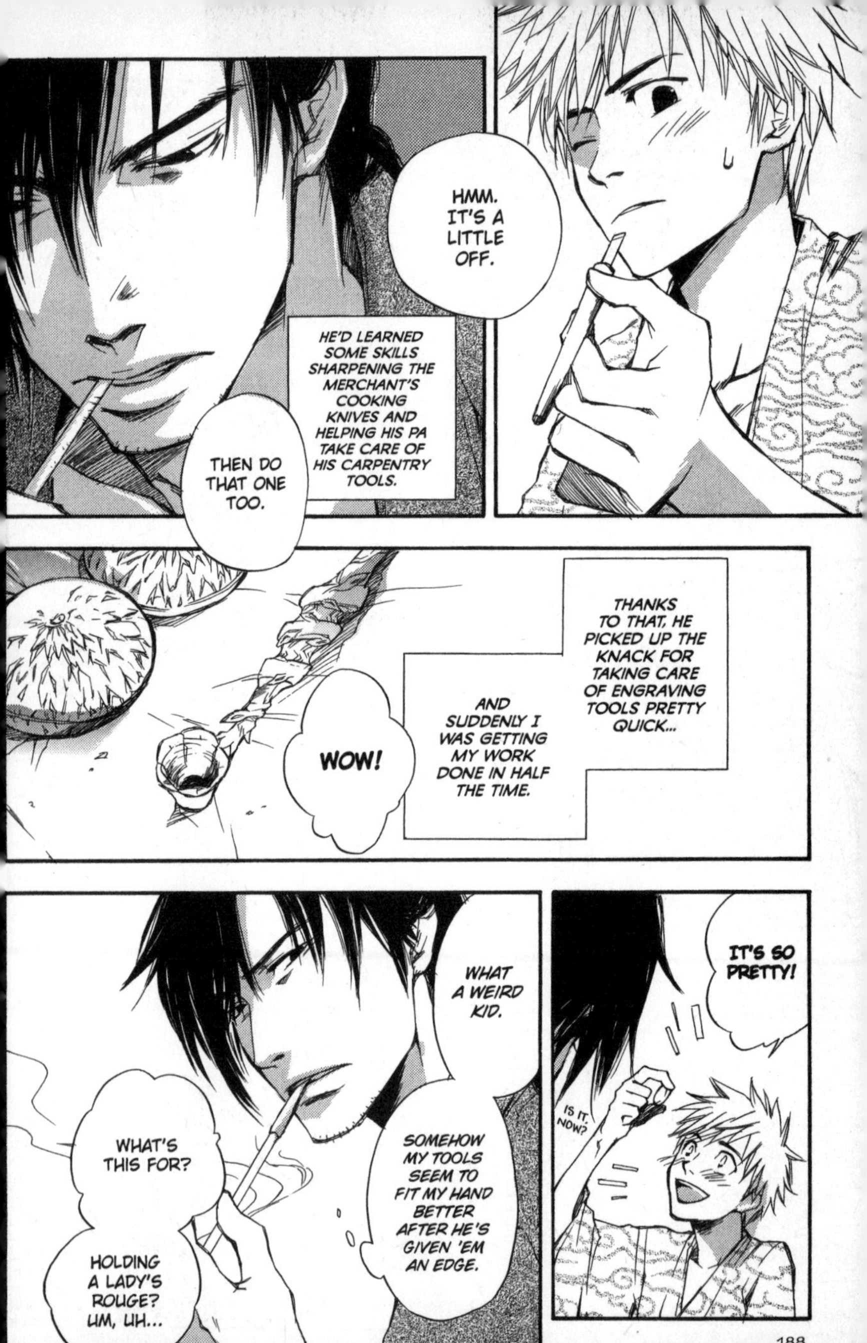
HMM. IT'S A LITTLE OFF.
HE'D LEARNED SOME SKILLS SHARPENING THE MERCHANT'S COOKING KNIVES AND HELPING HIS PA TAKE CARE OF HIS CARPENTRY TOOLS.
THEN DO THAT ONE TOO.
THANKS TO THAT, HE PICKED UP THE KNACK FOR TAKING CARE OF ENGRAVING TOOLS PRETTY QUICK...
AND SUDDENLY I WAS GETTING MY WORK DONE IN HALF THE TIME.
WOW!
IT'S SO PRETTY!
IS IT, NOW?
WHAT A WEIRD KID.
SOMEHOW MY TOOLS SEEM TO FIT MY HAND BETTER AFTER HE'S GIVEN 'EM AN EDGE.
WHAT'S THIS FOR?
HOLDING A LADY'S ROUGE? UM, UH...

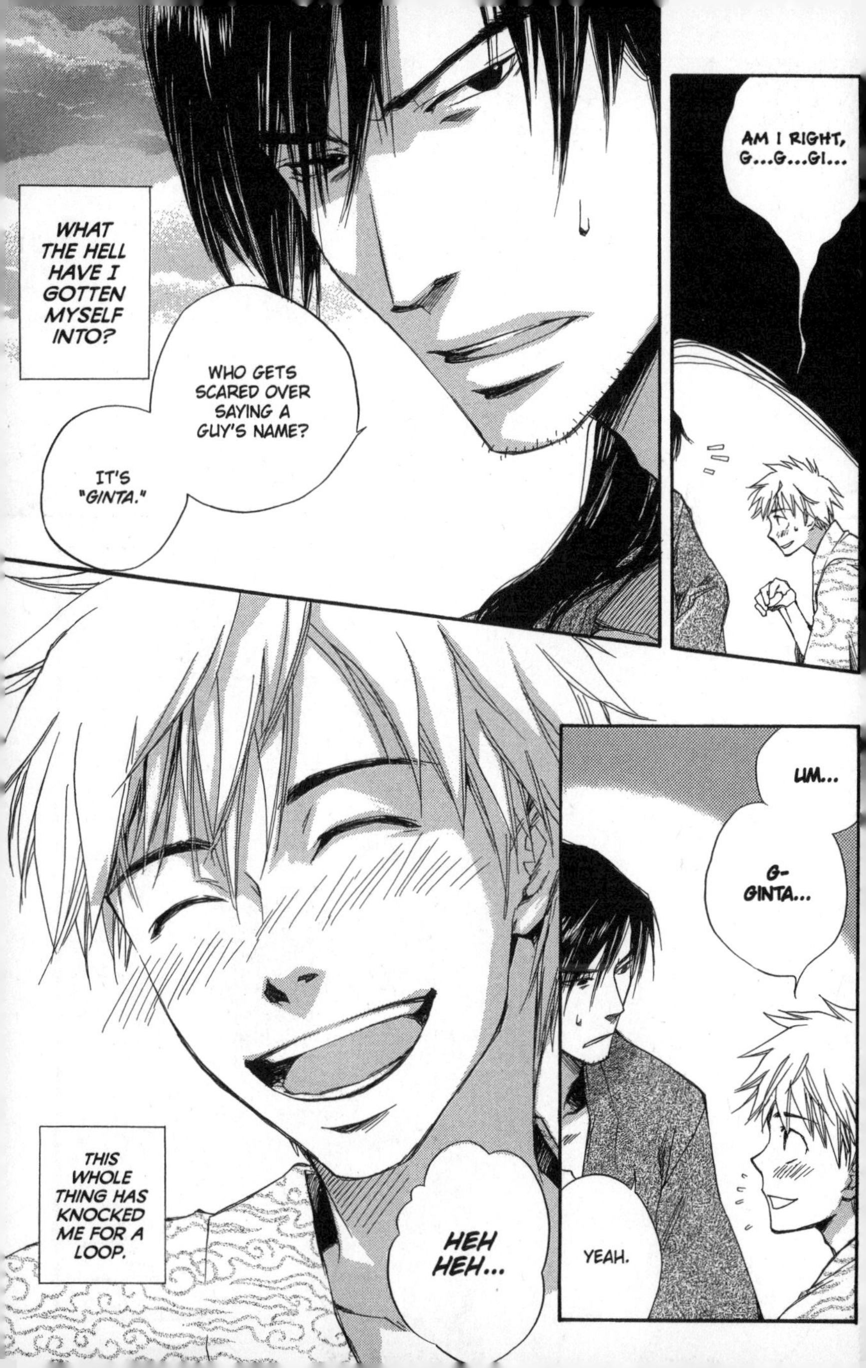
AM I RIGHT, G...G...GI...
WHO GETS SCARED OVER SAYING A GUY'S NAME?
IT'S "GINTA."
WHAT THE HELL HAVE I GOTTEN MYSELF INTO?
UM...
G-GINTA...
YEAH.
HEH HEH...
THIS WHOLE THING HAS KNOCKED ME FOR A LOOP.

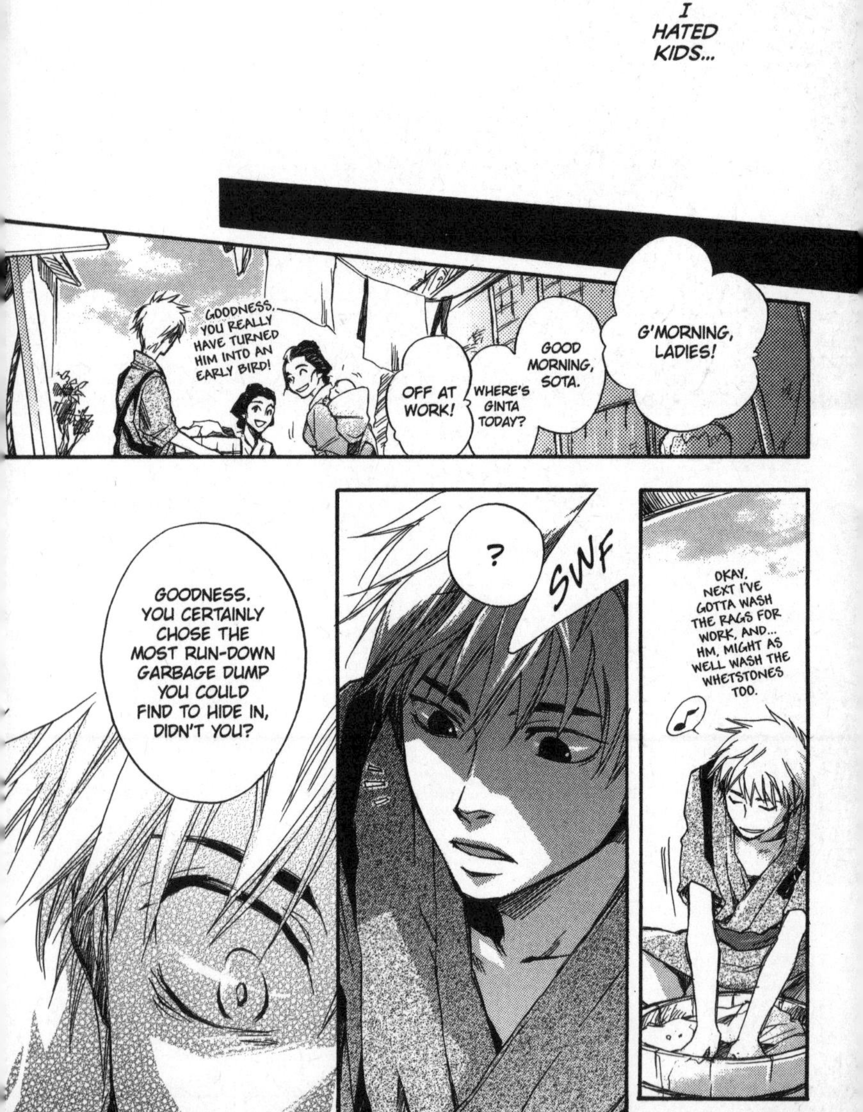
I HATED KIDS...
G'MORNING, LADIES!
GOOD MORNING, SOTA.
WHERE'S GINTA TODAY?
OFF AT WORK!
GOODNESS, YOU REALLY HAVE TURNED HIM INTO AN EARLY BIRD!
OKAY, NEXT I'VE GOTTA WASH THE RAGS FOR WORK, AND... HM, MIGHT AS WELL WASH THE WHETSTONES TOO.
♪
SWF
?
GOODNESS. YOU CERTAINLY CHOSE THE MOST RUN-DOWN GARBAGE DUMP YOU COULD FIND TO HIDE IN, DIDN'T YOU?

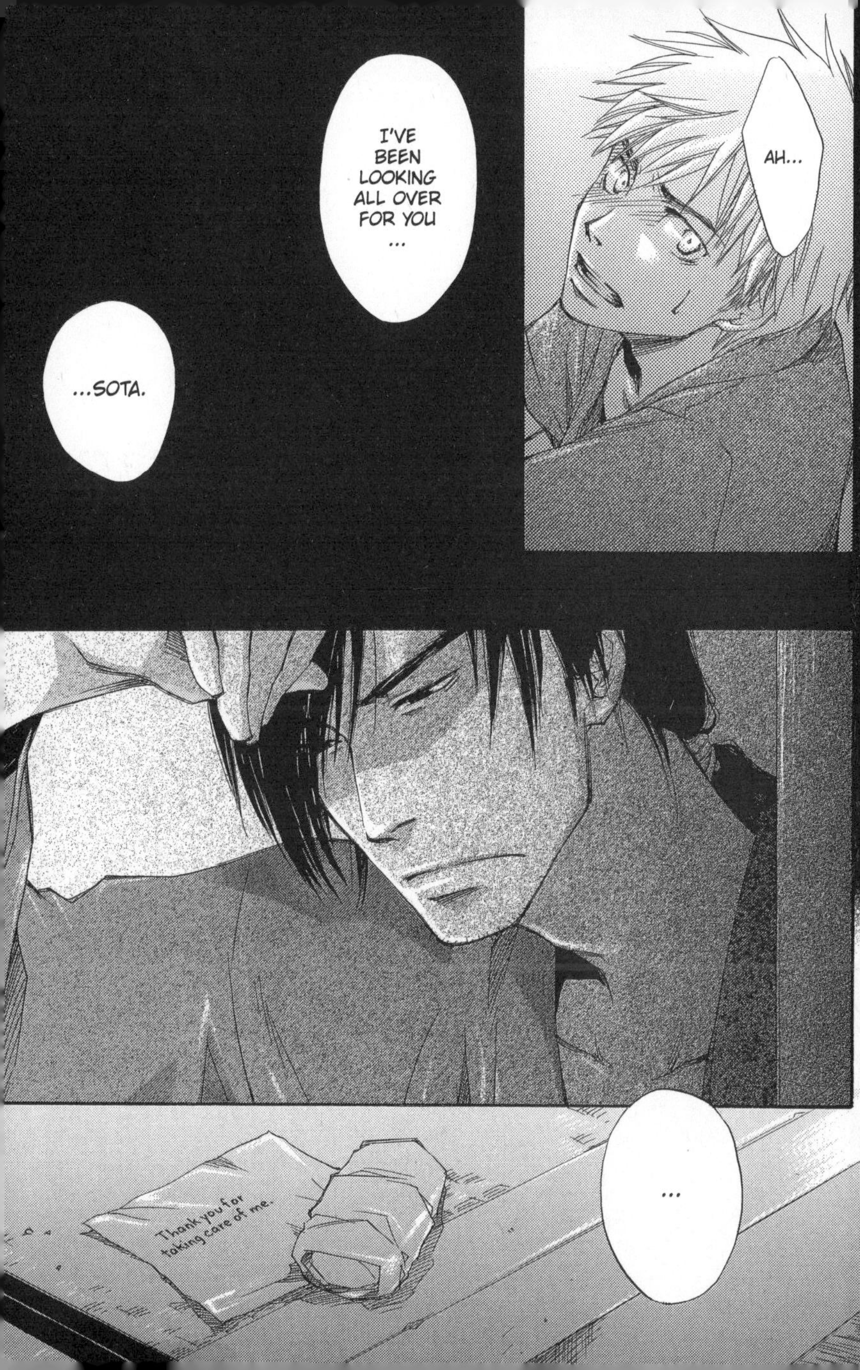
AH...
I'VE BEEN LOOKING ALL OVER FOR YOU ...
...SOTA.
...
Thank you for taking care of me.

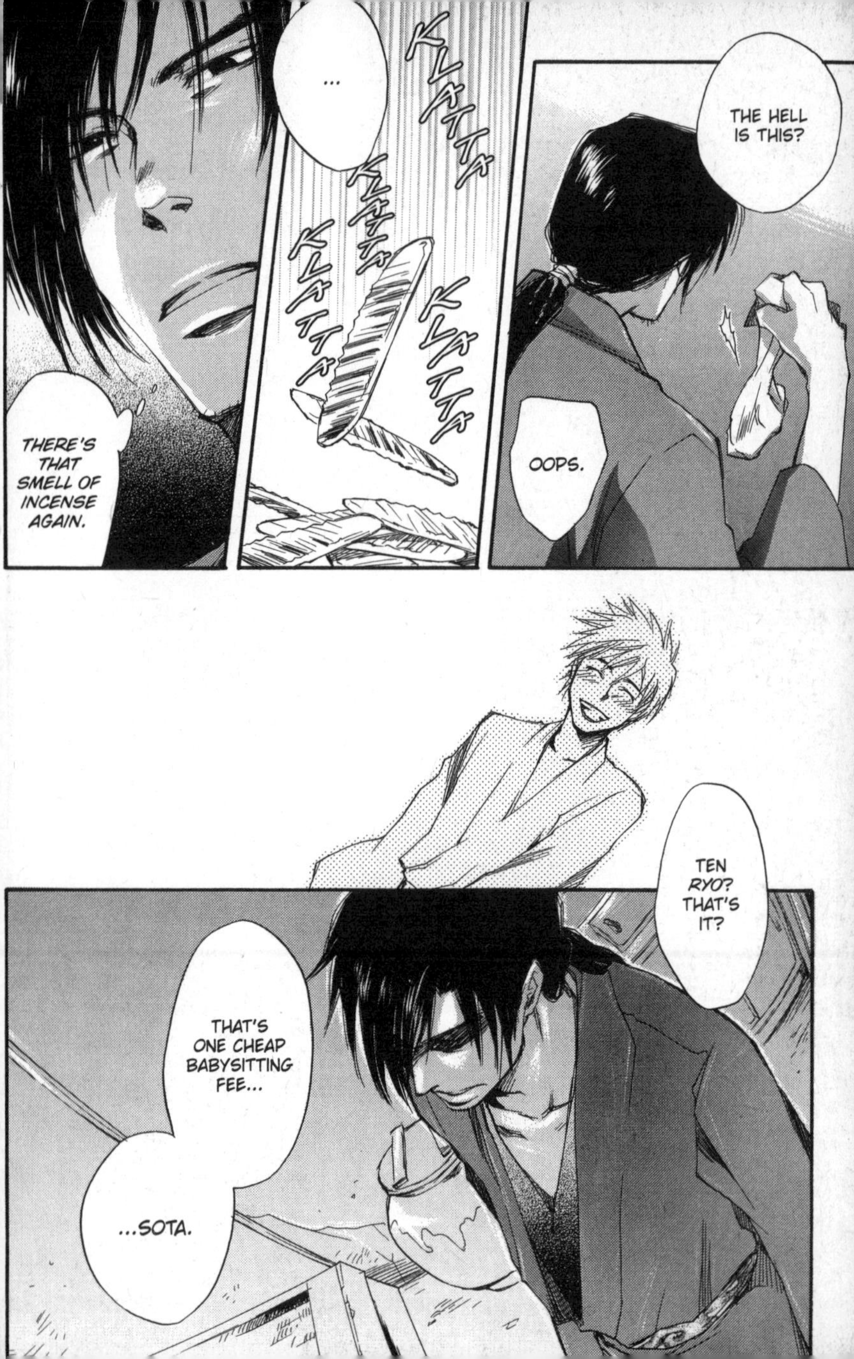
THE HELL IS THIS?
OOPS.
...
THERE'S THAT SMELL OF INCENSE AGAIN.
TEN *RYO*? THAT'S IT?
THAT'S ONE CHEAP BABYSITTING FEE...
...SOTA.

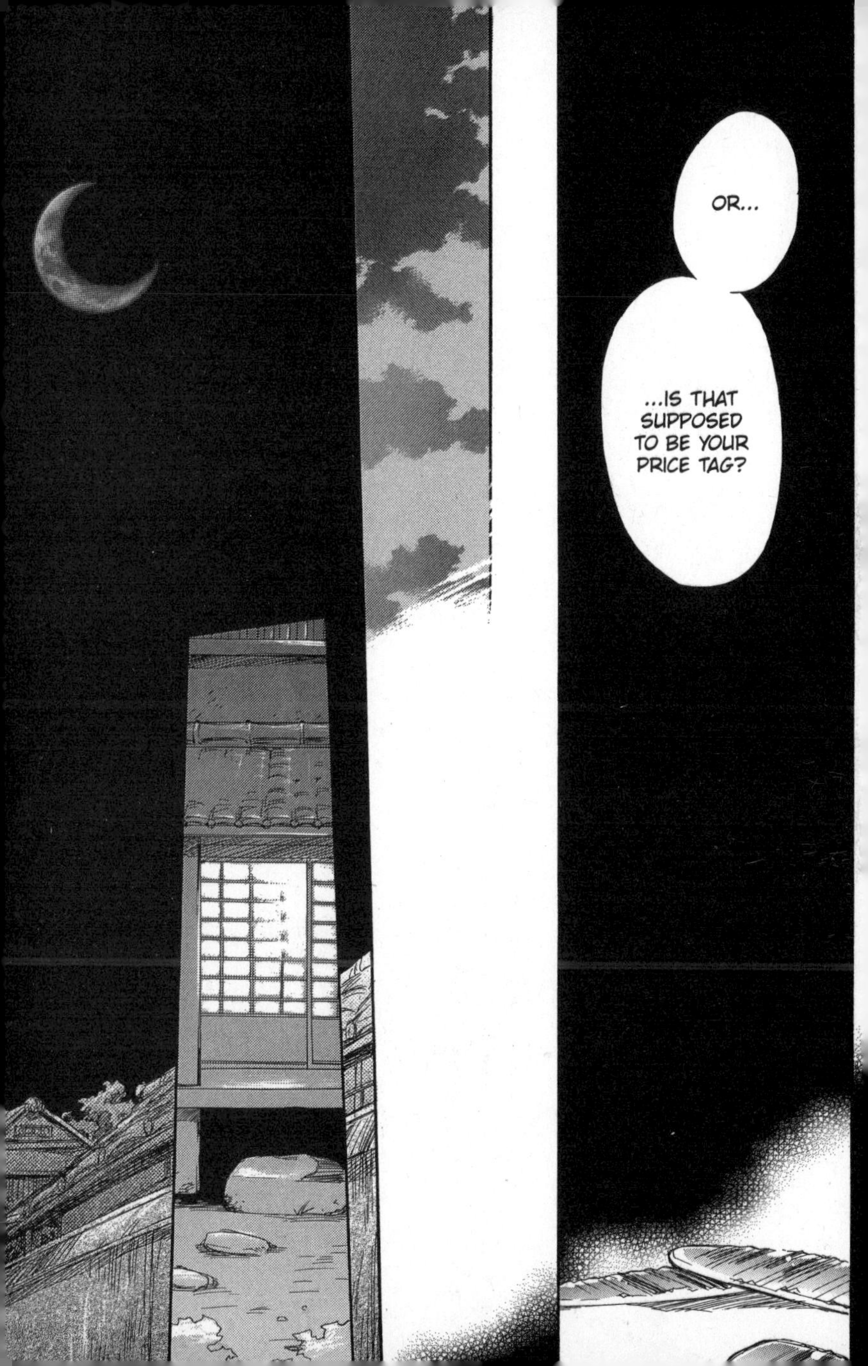
OR...
...IS THAT SUPPOSED TO BE YOUR PRICE TAG?

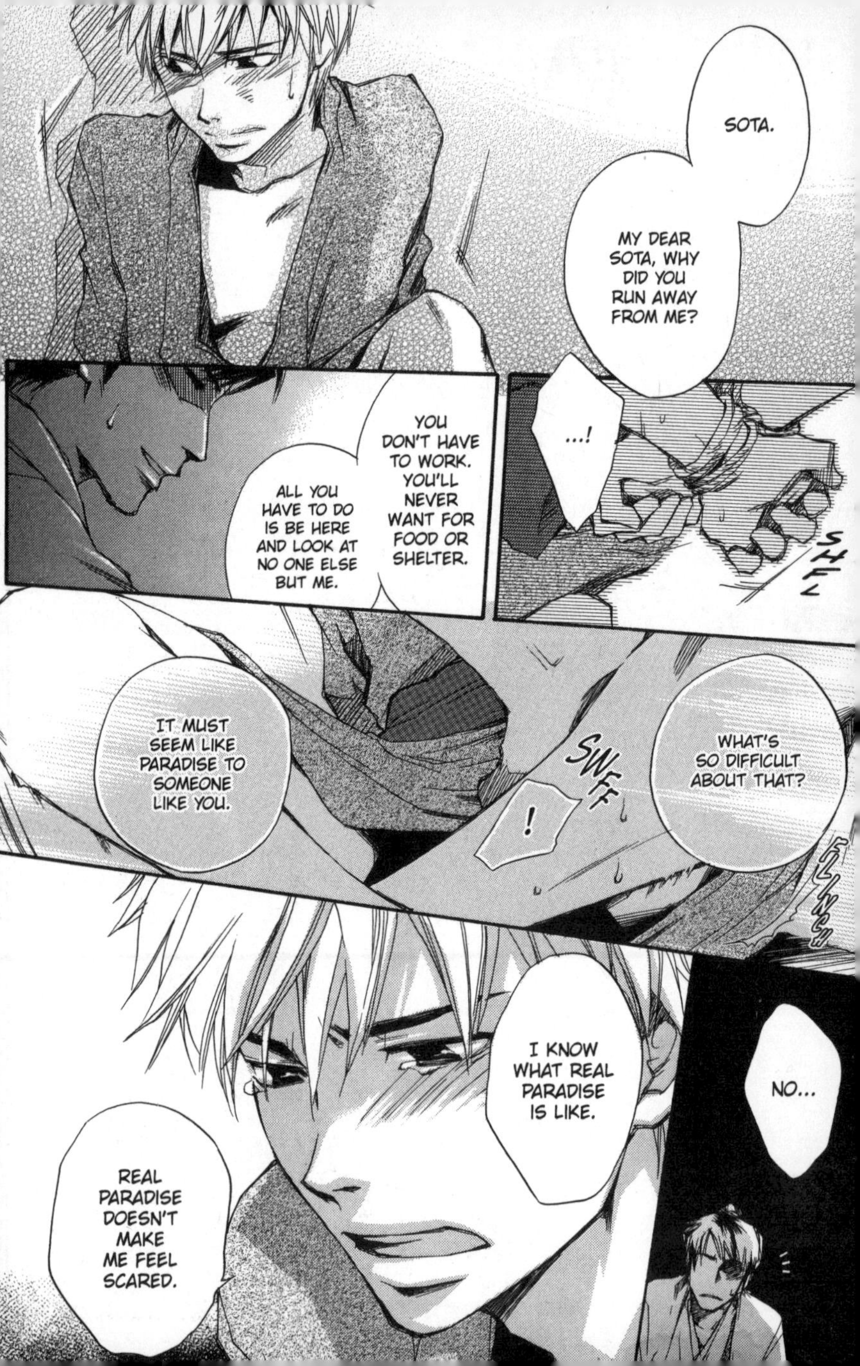
SOTA.
MY DEAR SOTA, WHY DID YOU RUN AWAY FROM ME?
...!
SHFL
YOU DON'T HAVE TO WORK. YOU'LL NEVER WANT FOR FOOD OR SHELTER.
ALL YOU HAVE TO DO IS BE HERE AND LOOK AT NO ONE ELSE BUT ME.
FLINCH
WHAT'S SO DIFFICULT ABOUT THAT?
SWFF
!
IT MUST SEEM LIKE PARADISE TO SOMEONE LIKE YOU.
NO...
I KNOW WHAT REAL PARADISE IS LIKE.
REAL PARADISE DOESN'T MAKE ME FEEL SCARED.

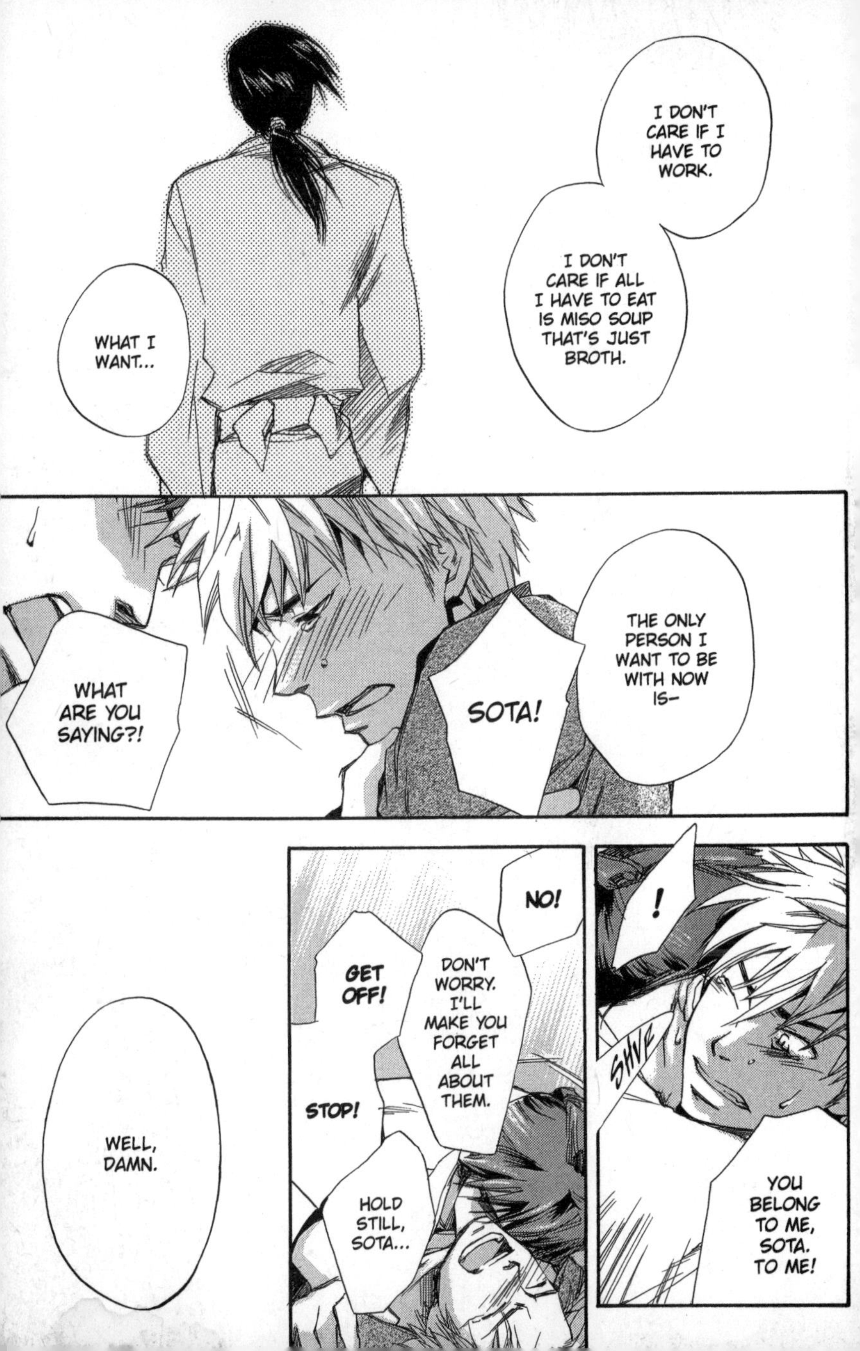
I DON'T CARE IF I HAVE TO WORK.
I DON'T CARE IF ALL I HAVE TO EAT IS MISO SOUP THAT'S JUST BROTH.
WHAT I WANT...
THE ONLY PERSON I WANT TO BE WITH NOW IS–
SOTA!
WHAT ARE YOU SAYING?!
!
SHVF
YOU BELONG TO ME, SOTA. TO ME!
NO!
DON'T WORRY. I'LL MAKE YOU FORGET ALL ABOUT THEM.
GET OFF!
STOP!
HOLD STILL, SOTA...
WELL, DAMN.

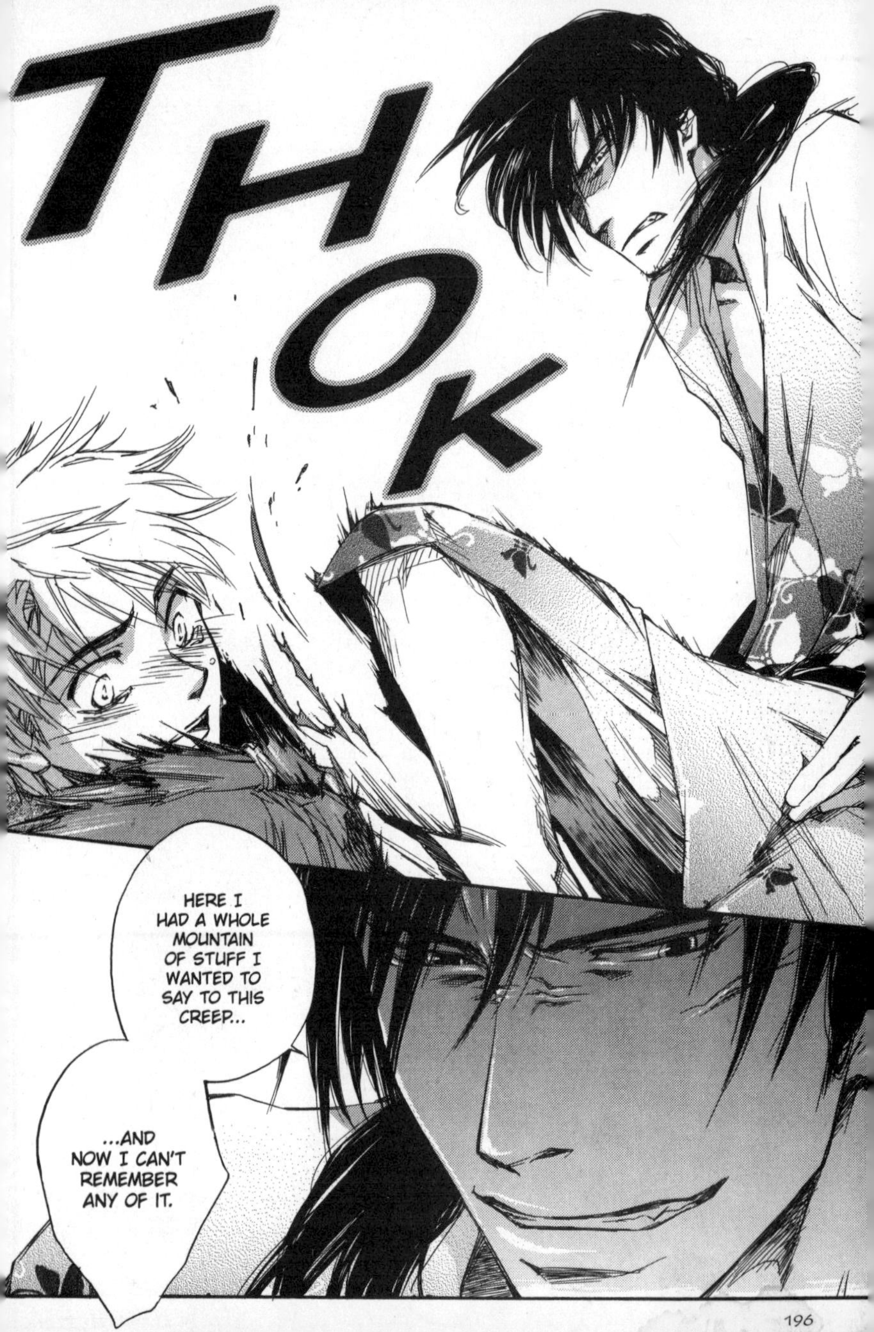
THOK
HERE I HAD A WHOLE MOUNTAIN OF STUFF I WANTED TO SAY TO THIS CREEP...
...AND NOW I CAN'T REMEMBER ANY OF IT.

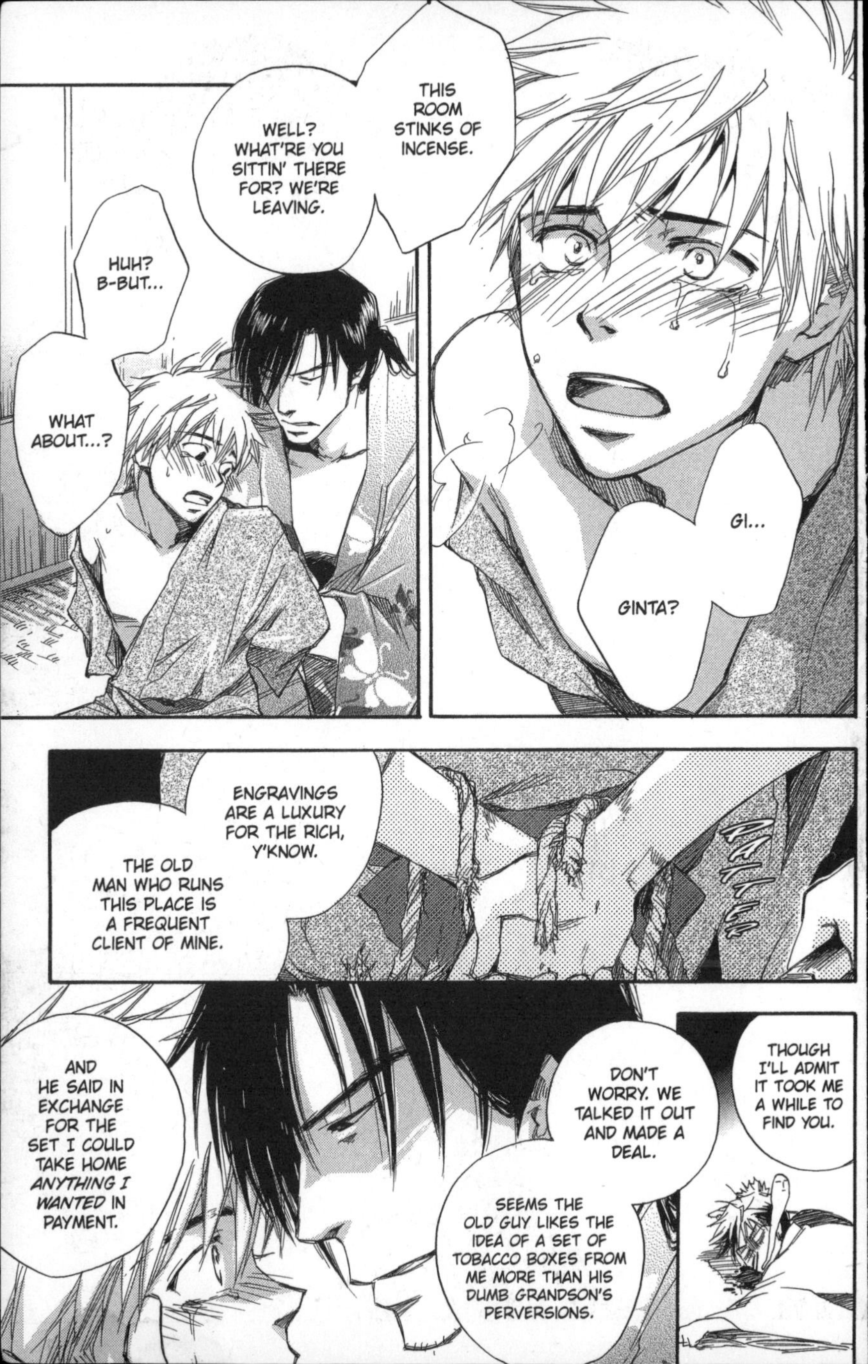
GI...
GINTA?
THIS ROOM STINKS OF INCENSE.
WELL? WHAT'RE YOU SITTIN' THERE FOR? WE'RE LEAVING.
HUH? B-BUT...
WHAT ABOUT...?
ENGRAVINGS ARE A LUXURY FOR THE RICH, Y'KNOW.
THE OLD MAN WHO RUNS THIS PLACE IS A FREQUENT CLIENT OF MINE.
THOUGH I'LL ADMIT IT TOOK ME A WHILE TO FIND YOU.
DON'T WORRY. WE TALKED IT OUT AND MADE A DEAL.
AND HE SAID IN EXCHANGE FOR THE SET I COULD TAKE HOME *ANYTHING I WANTED* IN PAYMENT.
SEEMS THE OLD GUY LIKES THE IDEA OF A SET OF TOBACCO BOXES FROM ME MORE THAN HIS DUMB GRANDSON'S PERVERSIONS.

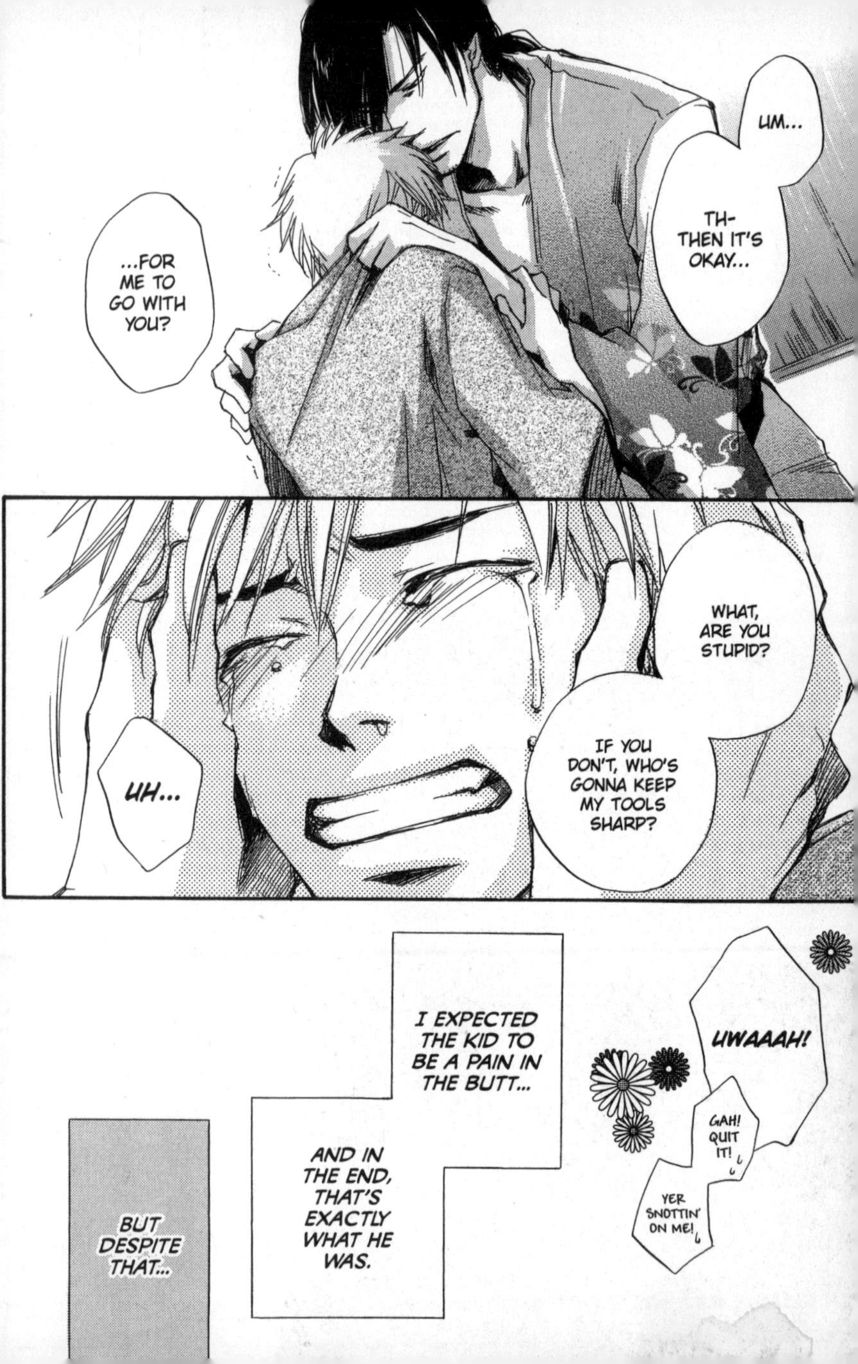
UM...
TH- THEN IT'S OKAY...
...FOR ME TO GO WITH YOU?
WHAT, ARE YOU STUPID?
IF YOU DON'T, WHO'S GONNA KEEP MY TOOLS SHARP?
UH...
UWAAAH!
GAH! QUIT IT!
YER SNOTTIN' ON ME!
I EXPECTED THE KID TO BE A PAIN IN THE BUTT...
AND IN THE END, THAT'S EXACTLY WHAT HE WAS.
BUT DESPITE THAT...

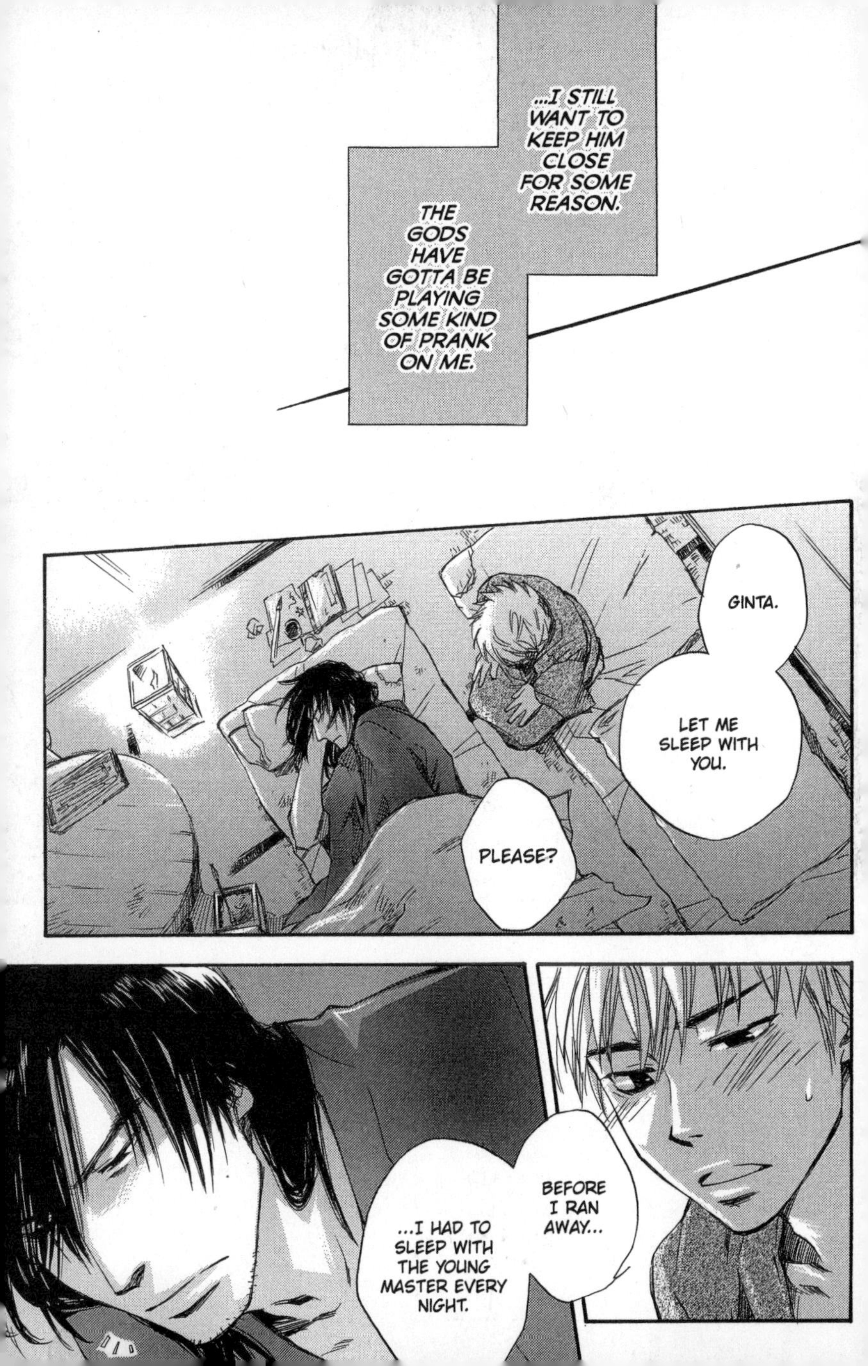
...I STILL WANT TO KEEP HIM CLOSE FOR SOME REASON.
THE GODS HAVE GOTTA BE PLAYING SOME KIND OF PRANK ON ME.
GINTA.
LET ME SLEEP WITH YOU.
PLEASE?
BEFORE I RAN AWAY...
...I HAD TO SLEEP WITH THE YOUNG MASTER EVERY NIGHT.

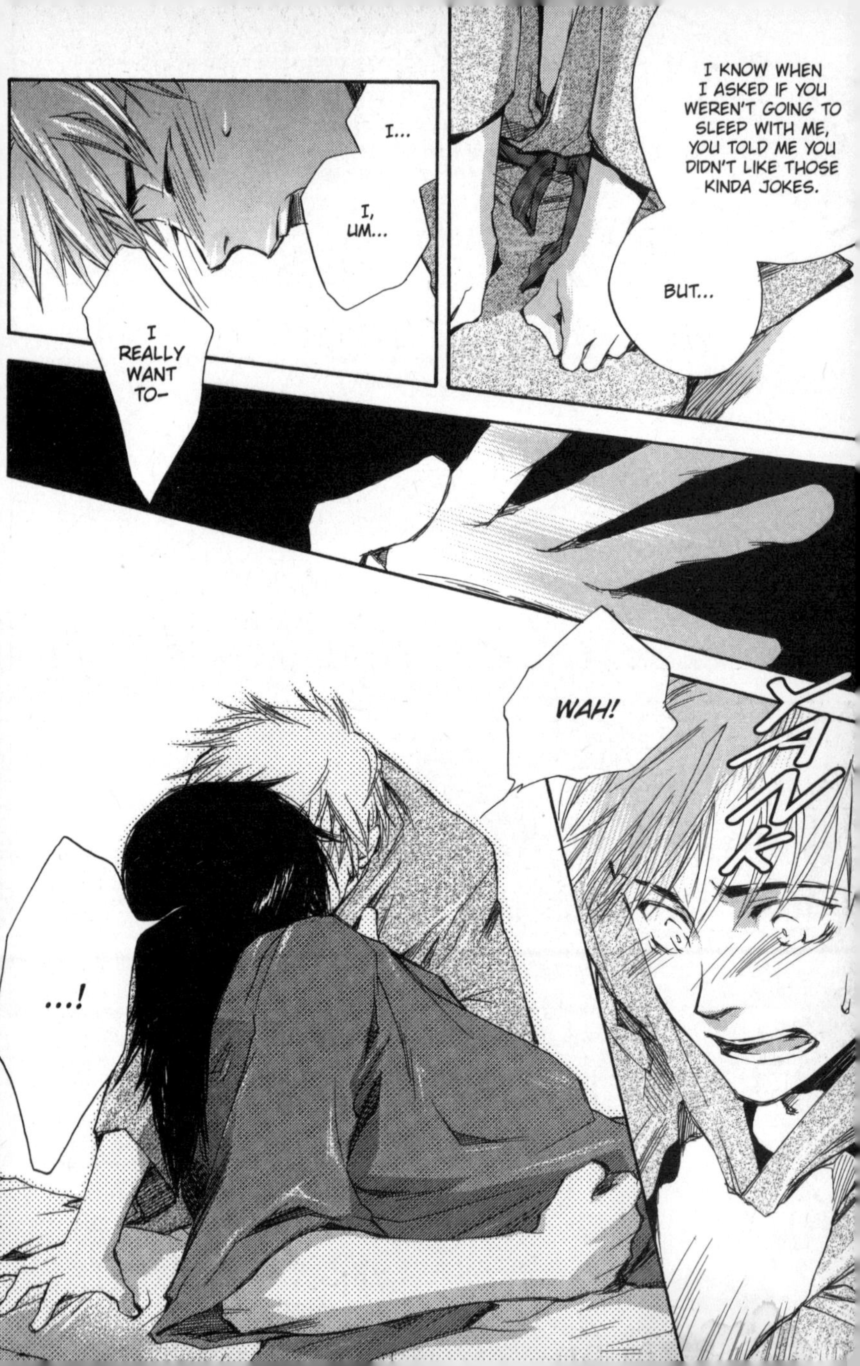
I KNOW WHEN I ASKED IF YOU WEREN'T GOING TO SLEEP WITH ME, YOU TOLD ME YOU DIDN'T LIKE THOSE KINDA JOKES.
BUT...
I...
I, UM...
I REALLY WANT TO-
YANK
WAH!
...!

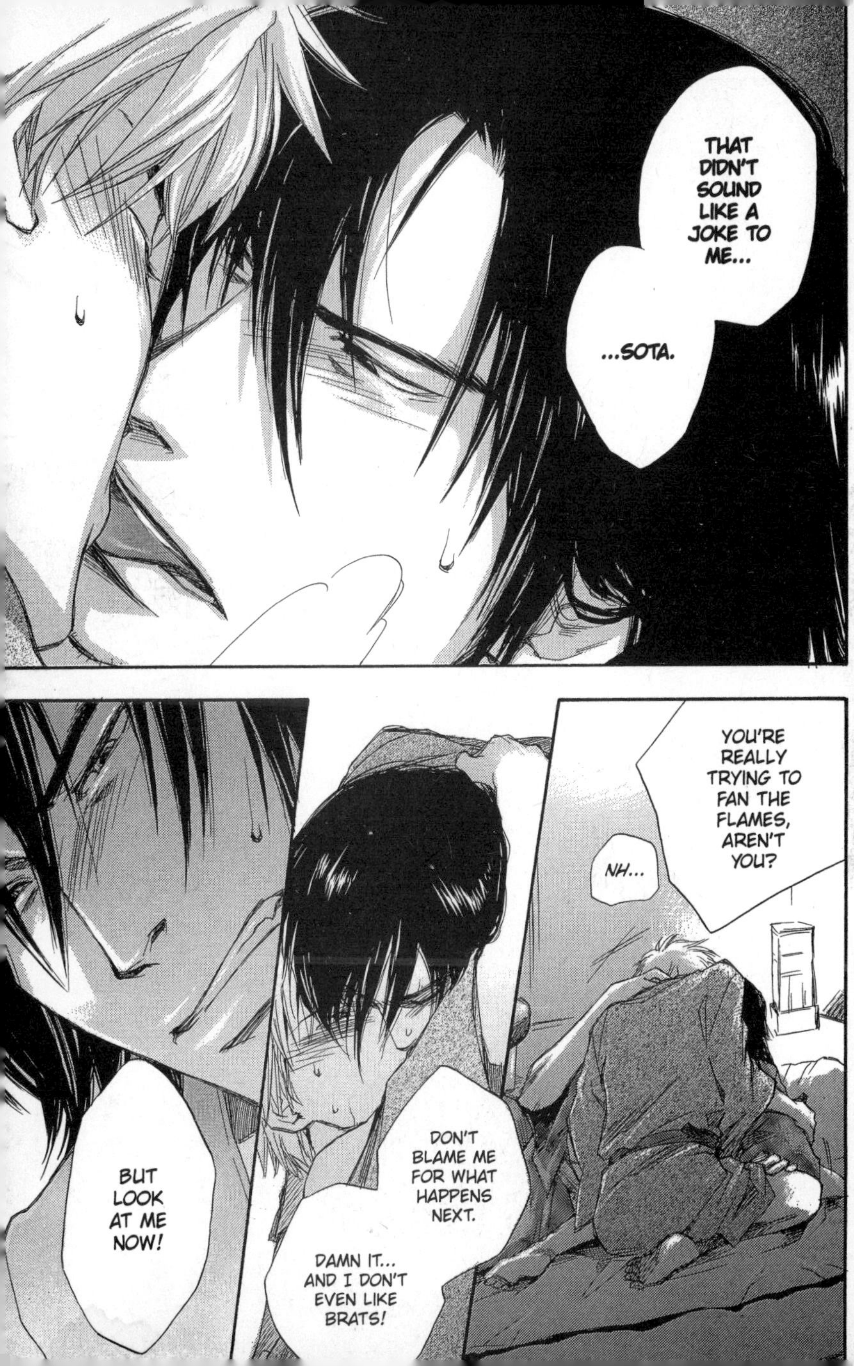
THAT DIDN'T SOUND LIKE A JOKE TO ME...
...SOTA.
YOU'RE REALLY TRYING TO FAN THE FLAMES, AREN'T YOU?
NH...
DON'T BLAME ME FOR WHAT HAPPENS NEXT.
DAMN IT... AND I DON'T EVEN LIKE BRATS!
BUT LOOK AT ME NOW!

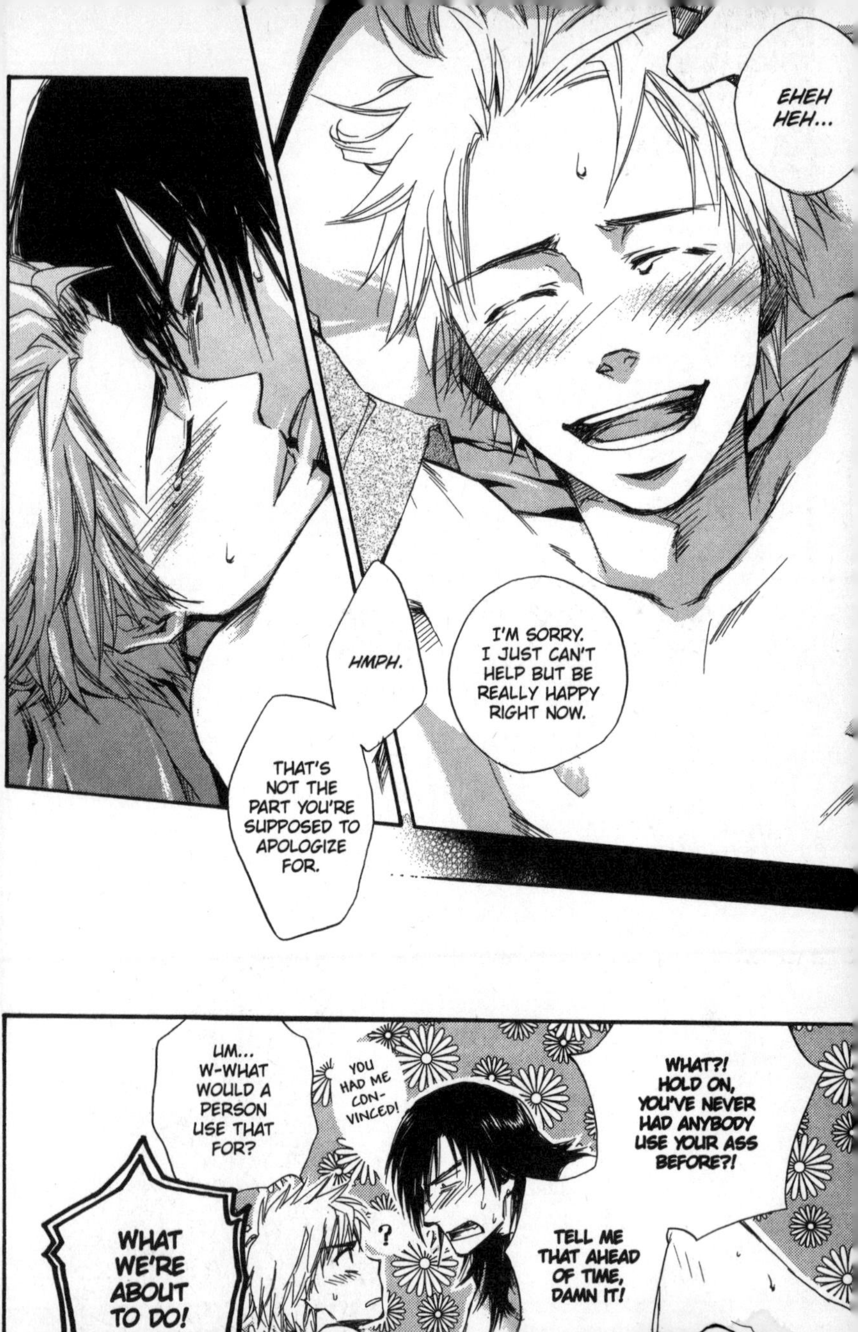
EHEH HEH...
I'M SORRY. I JUST CAN'T HELP BUT BE REALLY HAPPY RIGHT NOW.
HMPH.
THAT'S NOT THE PART YOU'RE SUPPOSED TO APOLOGIZE FOR.
WHAT?! HOLD ON, YOU'VE NEVER HAD ANYBODY USE YOUR ASS BEFORE?!
YOU HAD ME CON-VINCED!
UM... W-WHAT WOULD A PERSON USE THAT FOR?
?
TELL ME THAT AHEAD OF TIME, DAMN IT!
WHAT WE'RE ABOUT TO DO!

The Gods Don't Exist / END

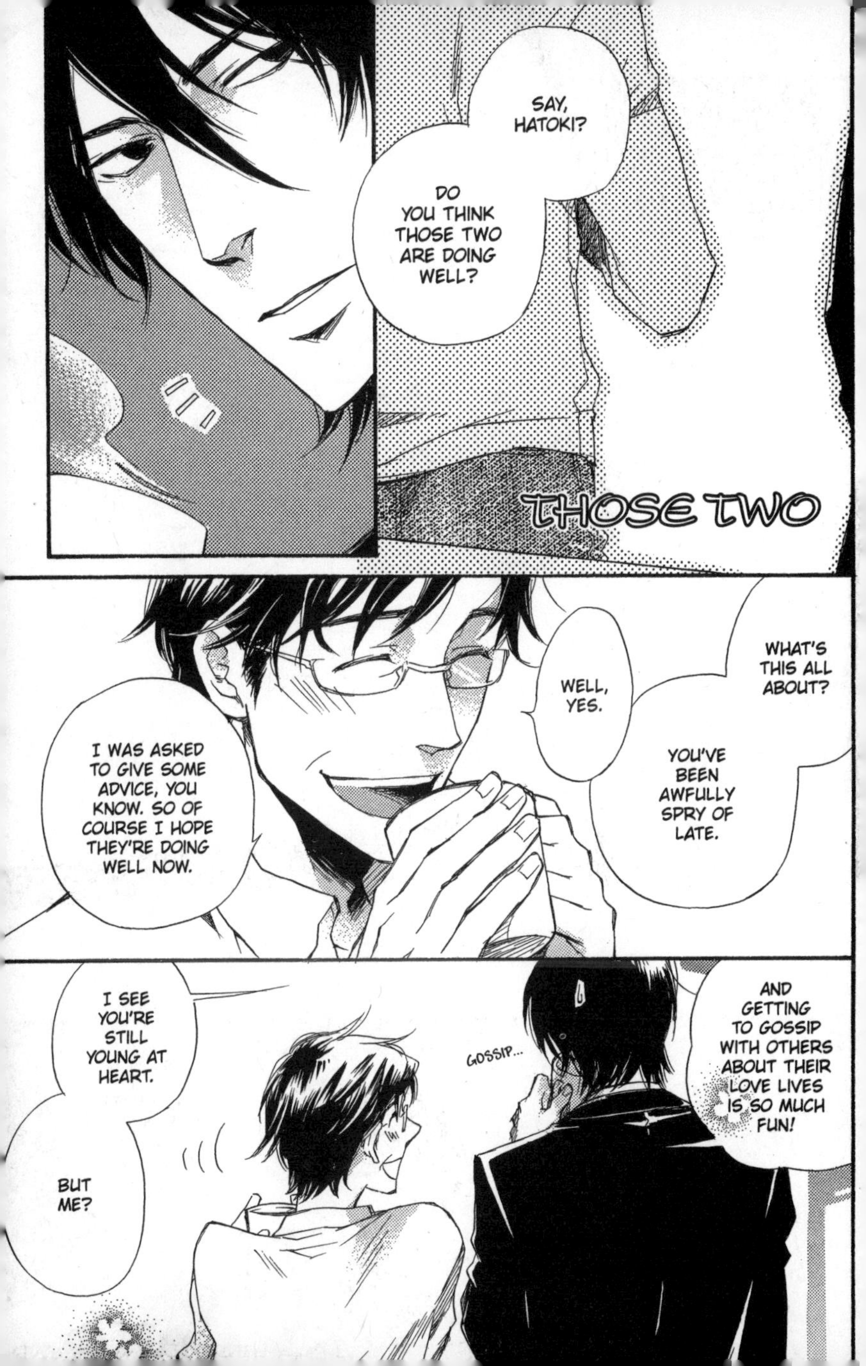
SAY, HATOKI?
DO YOU THINK THOSE TWO ARE DOING WELL?
THOSE TWO
WHAT'S THIS ALL ABOUT?
YOU'VE BEEN AWFULLY SPRY OF LATE.
WELL, YES.
I WAS ASKED TO GIVE SOME ADVICE, YOU KNOW. SO OF COURSE I HOPE THEY'RE DOING WELL NOW.
AND GETTING TO GOSSIP WITH OTHERS ABOUT THEIR LOVE LIVES IS SO MUCH FUN!
GOSSIP...
I SEE YOU'RE STILL YOUNG AT HEART.
BUT ME?

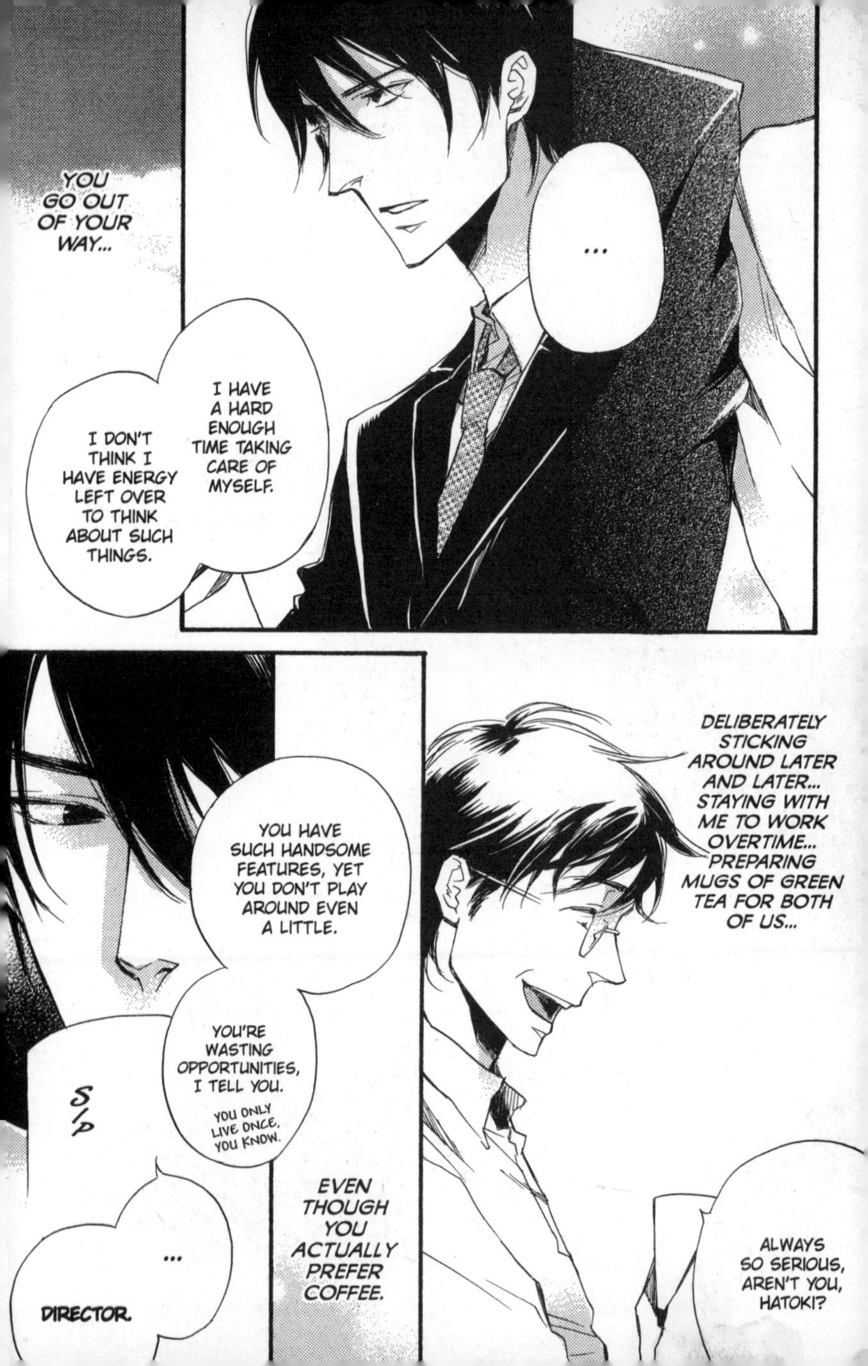
...
I HAVE A HARD ENOUGH TIME TAKING CARE OF MYSELF.
I DON'T THINK I HAVE ENERGY LEFT OVER TO THINK ABOUT SUCH THINGS.
YOU GO OUT OF YOUR WAY...
DELIBERATELY STICKING AROUND LATER AND LATER... STAYING WITH ME TO WORK OVERTIME... PREPARING MUGS OF GREEN TEA FOR BOTH OF US...
YOU HAVE SUCH HANDSOME FEATURES, YET YOU DON'T PLAY AROUND EVEN A LITTLE.
YOU'RE WASTING OPPORTUNITIES, I TELL YOU.
YOU ONLY LIVE ONCE, YOU KNOW.
ALWAYS SO SERIOUS, AREN'T YOU, HATOKI?
EVEN THOUGH YOU ACTUALLY PREFER COFFEE.
SIP
...
DIRECTOR.

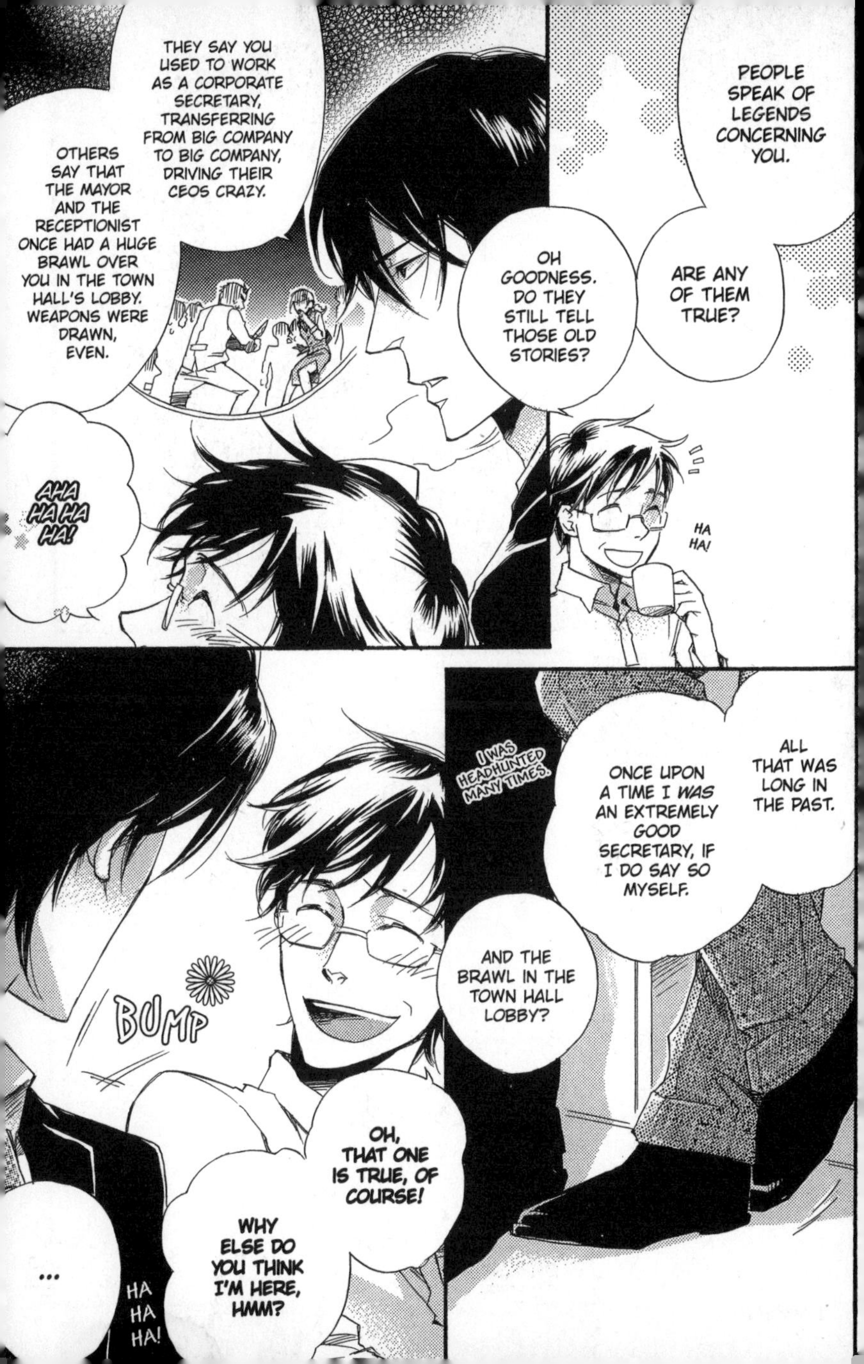
PEOPLE SPEAK OF LEGENDS CONCERNING YOU.
ARE ANY OF THEM TRUE?
OH GOODNESS. DO THEY STILL TELL THOSE OLD STORIES?
HA HA!
THEY SAY YOU USED TO WORK AS A CORPORATE SECRETARY, TRANSFERRING FROM BIG COMPANY TO BIG COMPANY, DRIVING THEIR CEOS CRAZY.
OTHERS SAY THAT THE MAYOR AND THE RECEPTIONIST ONCE HAD A HUGE BRAWL OVER YOU IN THE TOWN HALL'S LOBBY. WEAPONS WERE DRAWN, EVEN.
AHA HA HA HA!
ALL THAT WAS LONG IN THE PAST.
ONCE UPON A TIME I *WAS* AN EXTREMELY GOOD SECRETARY, IF I DO SAY SO MYSELF.
I WAS HEADHUNTED MANY TIMES.
AND THE BRAWL IN THE TOWN HALL LOBBY?
OH, THAT ONE IS TRUE, OF COURSE!
WHY ELSE DO YOU THINK I'M HERE, HMM?
BUMP
...
HA HA HA!

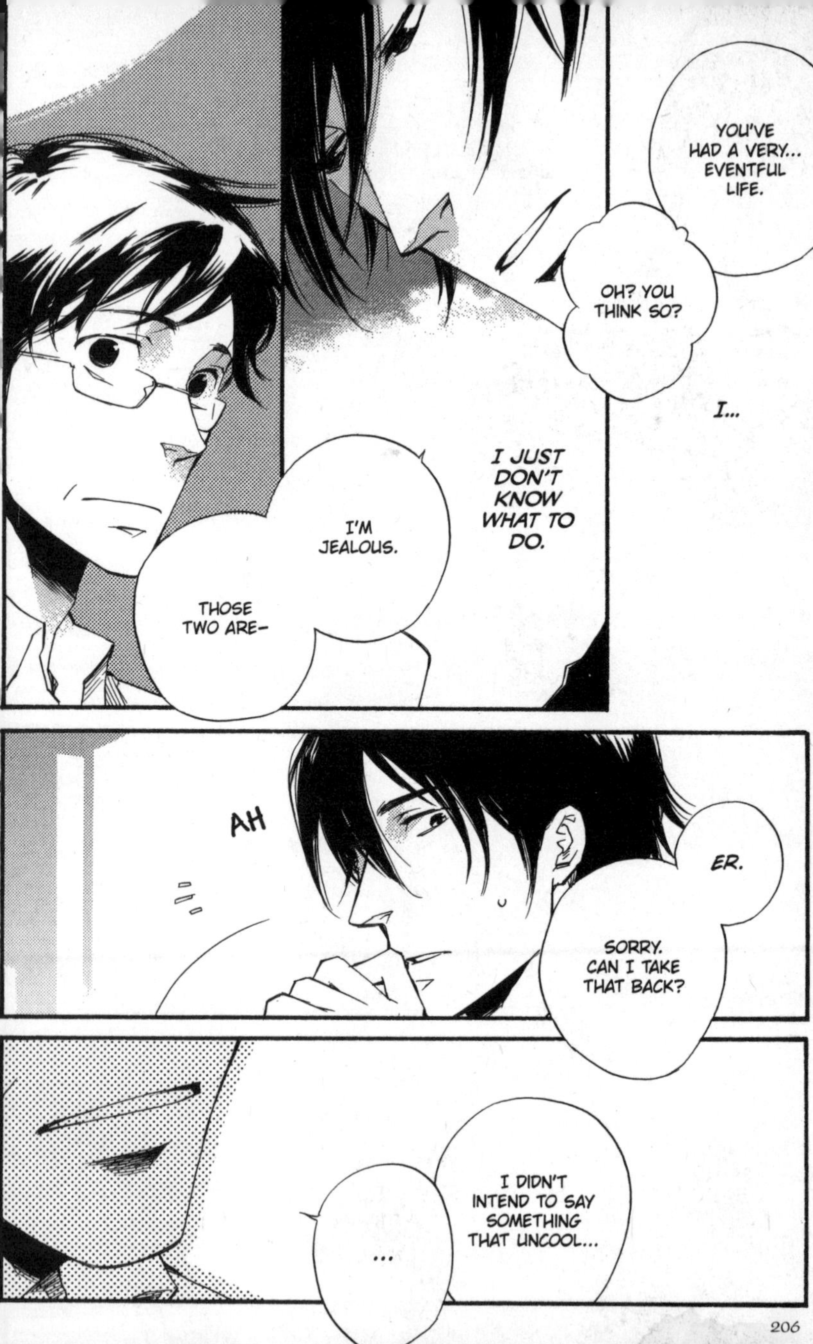
YOU'VE HAD A VERY... EVENTFUL LIFE.
OH? YOU THINK SO?
I...
I JUST DON'T KNOW WHAT TO DO.
I'M JEALOUS.
THOSE TWO ARE-
ER.
SORRY. CAN I TAKE THAT BACK?
AH
I DIDN'T INTEND TO SAY SOMETHING THAT UNCOOL...
...

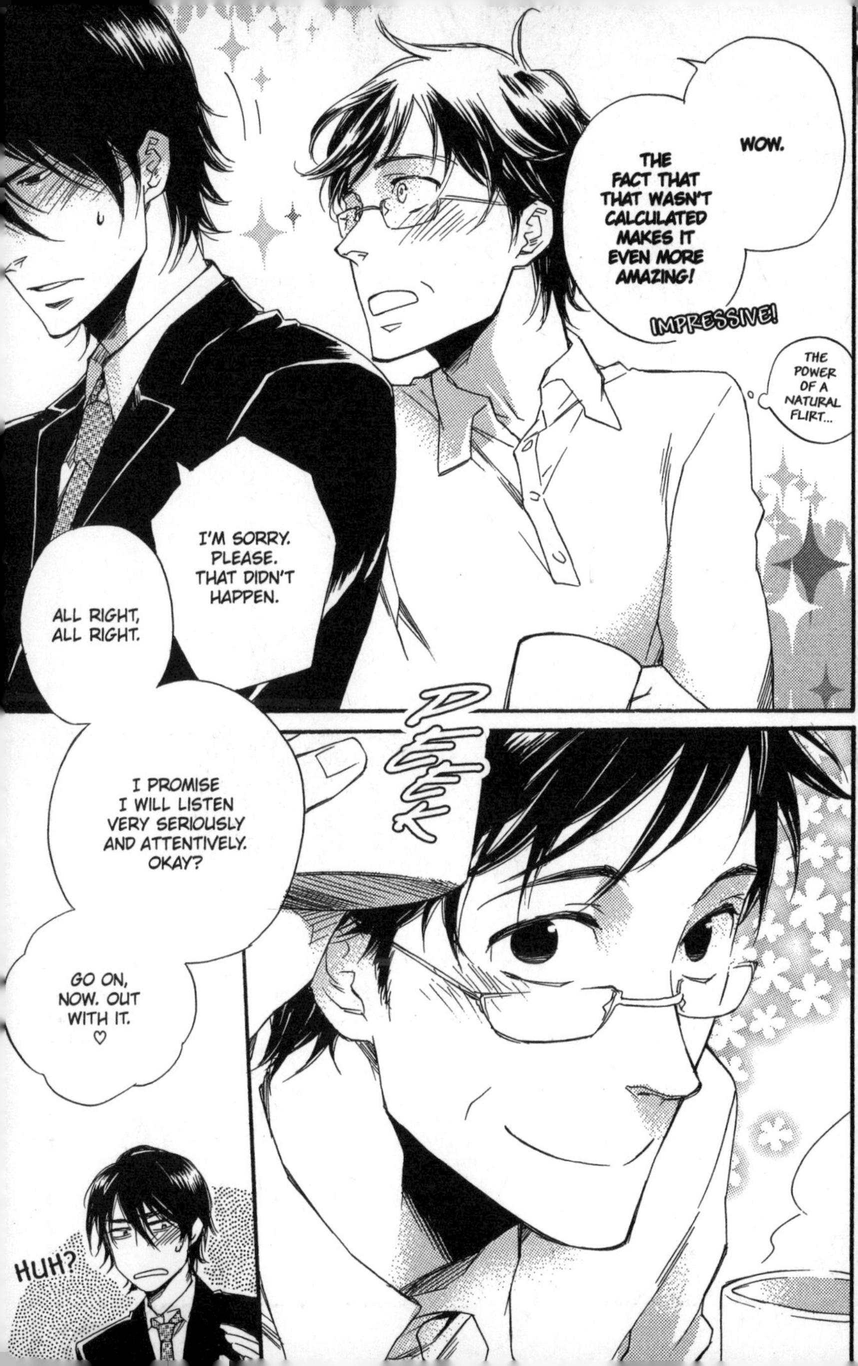
WOW. THE FACT THAT THAT WASN'T CALCULATED MAKES IT EVEN MORE AMAZING!
IMPRESSIVE!
THE POWER OF A NATURAL FLIRT...
I'M SORRY. PLEASE. THAT DIDN'T HAPPEN.
ALL RIGHT, ALL RIGHT.
PEEK
I PROMISE I WILL LISTEN VERY SERIOUSLY AND ATTENTIVELY. OKAY?
GO ON, NOW. OUT WITH IT. ♡
HUH?

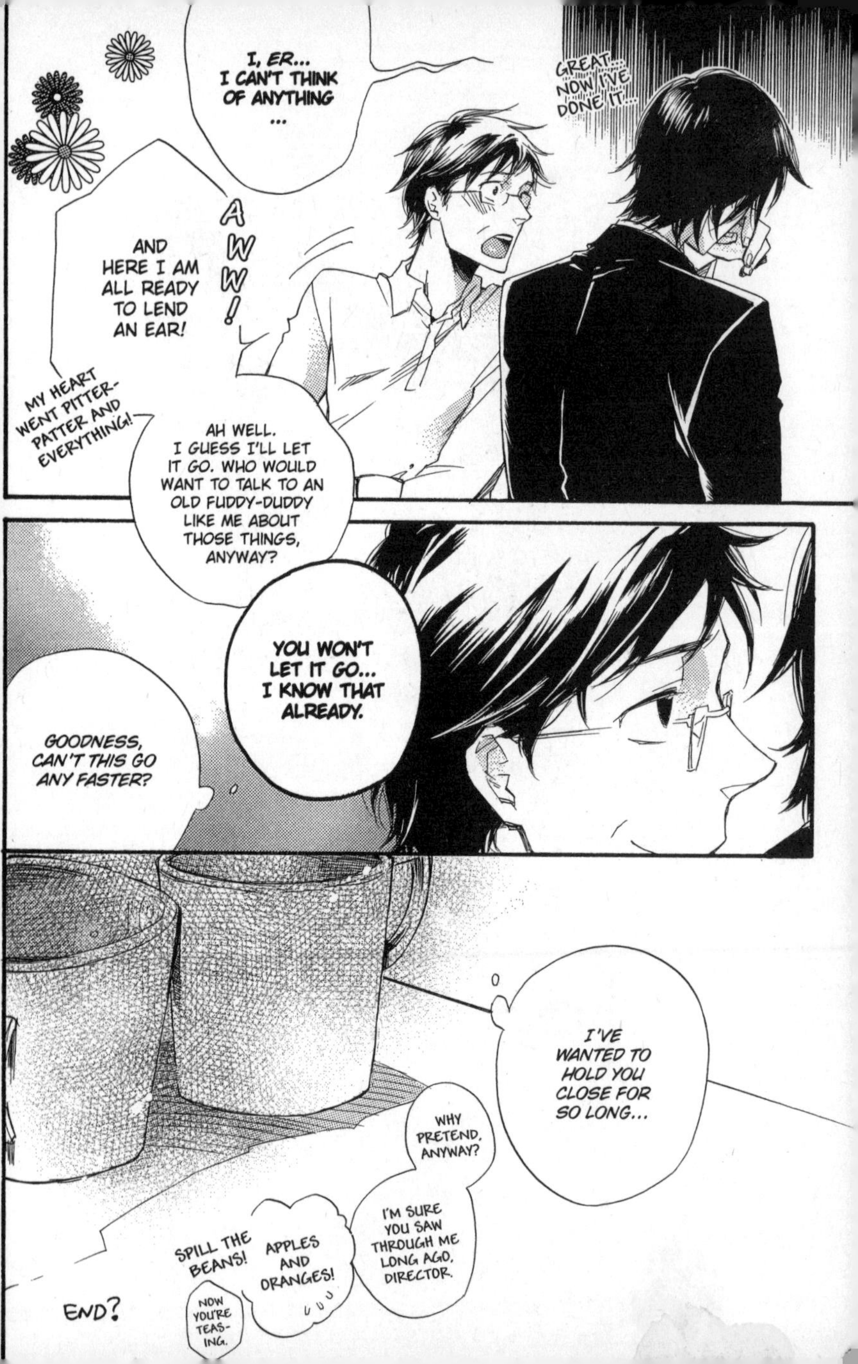
GREAT... NOW I'VE DONE IT...
I, ER... I CAN'T THINK OF ANYTHING ...
AWW!
AND HERE I AM ALL READY TO LEND AN EAR!
MY HEART WENT PITTER-PATTER AND EVERYTHING!
AH WELL. I GUESS I'LL LET IT GO. WHO WOULD WANT TO TALK TO AN OLD FUDDY-DUDDY LIKE ME ABOUT THOSE THINGS, ANYWAY?
YOU WON'T LET IT GO... I KNOW THAT ALREADY.
GOODNESS, CAN'T THIS GO ANY FASTER?
I'VE WANTED TO HOLD YOU CLOSE FOR SO LONG...
WHY PRETEND, ANYWAY?
I'M SURE YOU SAW THROUGH ME LONG AGO, DIRECTOR.
APPLES AND ORANGES!
SPILL THE BEANS!
NOW YOU'RE TEAS-ING.
END?

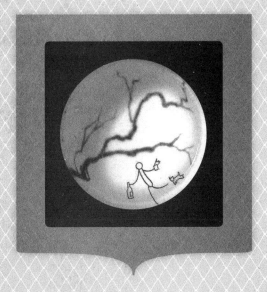

About the Author

This is **Tsuta Suzuki's** second English-language release, with her first being *Your Story I've Known*. Formerly working under the name "Yogore," she has also published *doujinshi* (independent comics) under the circle name "Muddy Pool." Born a Sagittarius in Shikoku, Japan on December 3rd, she has an A blood type and currently resides in Kyoto.

A Strange & Mystifying Story

Volume 1

SuBLime Manga Edition

Story and Art by **Tsuta Suzuki**

Translation—**Adrienne Beck**
Touch-Up Art and Lettering—**Bianca Pistillo**
Cover and Graphic Design—**Julian [JR] Robinson**
Editor—**Jennifer LeBlanc**

Originally published in Japan in 2006 by Libre Publishing Co., Ltd.
English translation rights arranged with Libre Inc.

libre

Printed in the U.S.A.

Published by SuBLime Manga
P.O. Box 77010
San Francisco, CA 94107

10 9 8 7 6 5 4 3 2 1
First printing, November 2017

M
MATURE

PARENTAL ADVISORY
A STRANGE & MYSTIFYING STORY is rated M for Mature and is recommended for mature readers. This volume contains graphic imagery and mature themes.

SUBLIME
www.SuBLimeManga.com